Sports Matters

Race, Recreation, and Culture

EDITED BY

John Bloom and Michael Nevin Willard

New York University Press

NEW YORK AND LONDON

NEW YORK UNIVERSITY PRESS
New York and London

Library of Congress Cataloguing-in Publication Data
Sports matters : race, recreation, and culture / edited by John Bloom
and Michael Williard
p. cm.
Includes bibliographical references and index.
ISBN 0–8147–9882–9 (pbk. : alk. paper) —
ISBN 0–8147–9881–0 (cloth : alk. paper)
1. Discrimination in sports—United States—History.   2. Sports—Social
aspects—United States.   3. Racism in popular culture—United States.
I. Bloom, John, 1962–   II. Willard, Michael Nevin.
GV706.32   .S75   20002
306.4'83—dc21   2002004918

New York University Press books are printed on acid-free paper,
and their binding materials are chosen for strength and durability.

Manufactured in the United States of America
10 9 8 7 6 5 4 3 2 1

Contents

Acknowledgments

The authors included in this collection of essays contributed not only their fine scholarship but also their enthusiasm and patience during the years it took to complete it. This book benefited from the timely comments of Matt Garcia and Daniel Widener. John Bloom would like to thank Amy Erdman Farrell. Michael Willard would like to thank Mary Kay Van Sistine, Sophia Rose Willard-Van Sistine; the students in the American Spectator Sports classes he taught in the Department of American Studies at California State University, Fullerton, Matthew Bokovoy, Joane Nagel; and the members of the American Seminar at the University of Kansas, David Anthony, Tyeeme Clark, Michael Ezra, Julia Goodfox, Cornelius Minor, Ray Pence, Cheryl Ragar, Sherrie Tucker, and Norm Yetman. Niko Pfund's editorial comments helped shape this book during its formative stages. As we worked with Eric Zinner, Emily Park, and Despina Papazoglou Gimbel of NYU Press, they continually established a productive balance between exacting and easygoing editorial input.

Introduction

Out of Bounds and between the Lines: Race in Twentieth-Century American Sport

John Bloom and Michael Nevin Willard

During the late 1880s and early 1890s, in the last years of his life, the great abolitionist writer and orator Frederick Douglass often pointed out a picture of the boxer Peter Jackson that hung on the wall of his study. Looking at the picture of the West Indian boxer, who was the first black heavyweight of note to fight white opponents in the United States, Douglass liked to say, "Peter is doing a great deal with his fists to solve the Negro question."[1] Douglass's comment reflects the possibilities for social transformation that he and many others saw in the modern sports culture that emerged during his time—possibilities for engaging in the struggle for human rights that the peoples of the African diaspora faced. As the twentieth century has developed, sports have indeed become a critically important cultural terrain on which most racialized groups have contested, defined, and represented their racial, national, and ethnic identities.

The success and presence that people of color have achieved in sports have been a major aspect of the history of twentieth-century popular culture, yet one that has not received the attention it deserves from those who study commercial leisure and entertainment. This book is dedicated to addressing this gap in scholarship. Each essay in this book acknowledges that sports have been a complex and critical part of twentieth-century social and cultural history, playing a vital role in the creation of nation, community, and racial/ethnic identity. Each essay addresses and acknowledges the social construction of race in the United States over this time period.

There is a need for fresh and original approaches to the relationship between race and sports. In the culture that has developed around sports, race is the proverbial elephant in the middle of the road, which everybody sees but few dare to acknowledge. In the 1980s and 1990s, the sports media have devoted extensive coverage to race only after prominent sports figures such as Jimmy "the Greek" Snyder, Al Campanis, and John Rocker made widely circulated racist comments.

The default position on race taken by sports broadcasting and publishing agents, driven by the market demand to sell a product to audiences, is one in which they portray sports institutions as benign agents that promote a "color-blind" social vision. ESPN sports broadcaster Chris Berman, for example, wrote recently that American sports exhibit the best of what he calls the country's "melting pot." Noting that Jackie Robinson broke into major league baseball eight years before the start of the Montgomery, Alabama, bus boycott and sixteen years ahead of Martin Luther King's "I Have a Dream" speech (but not remembering that Robinson's breakthrough came eighty-two years after the end of the Civil War, nor that prior to the 1890s baseball, though not an egalitarian utopia, was not segregated), he writes, "Sports in this century have often been way ahead of society." He continues, "You could argue that when it came to civil rights, sports helped spur on social change, and certainly heightened public awareness."[2]

Berman expresses important ideals in his essay, ones that many associate with the sports they watch or play in the United States. His prose projects a democratically utopian, if not naïve, vision of sports as an even field of fair play, one that rewards merit in an unbiased fashion and, in doing so, serves to break down social divisions and boundaries. Berman's essay is one that many sports fans might find extremely gratifying.

Yet any honest evaluation of U.S. sports history reveals that sports have served to shore up social distinctions and identities as often as they have served to break them down. After all, Jackie Robinson would never have had the chance to break the color line if, in the late nineteenth century, the organizers, managers, and players of major league baseball had not decided to discriminate against African Americans in the first place. What is particularly important about Berman's essay is the centrality of race in it. In these passages, as through sports, people of color serve an important ideological purpose in North American sports: their own history of subjugation and oppression can function effectively to "prove" the fairness of the American system.

On the other end of the spectrum from Berman's optimism is the gloomy analysis of John Hoberman, who argues that the success of African American athletes in sports has been a self-destructive trap. He writes that "ideas about the 'natural' physical talents of dark-skinned peoples, and the media-generated images that sustain them, probably do more than anything else in our public life to encourage the idea that blacks and whites are biologically different in a meaningful way. . . . Centuries of racial classification have made exceptional athletes into ethnic specimens."[3]

In his controversial book *Darwin's Athletes*, Hoberman writes that athletic success has historically provided an illusion of acceptance and equality for African Americans seeking respect in a society that denies them opportunities and power on the basis of their racial identities. He argues that the outcome of this illusion in African American communities has been a focus on athleticism that directs young people away from advancement in education and academic achievement and has helped propagate stereotypes about racial differences in physical and mental ability. Hoberman does not even see much that is positive in the expression of Black cultural style within sport, arguing that it only rearticulates racial difference, provokes white resentment, and contributes to continuing racial segregation.[4]

Hoberman makes some important arguments about the limitations of sports for people of African descent around the world, arguments that provide a strong check against the more popular and optimistic claims Berman puts forward. Yet he also provides conclusions that are just as overly general as, and far more dangerously reductive than, those made by the ESPN sportscaster. As sports historian Jeffery Sammons writes, Hoberman takes on a superior and condescending tone in which he lectures to people of color about the sinful pleasures they gain from sports, but he does not bother to listen to the reasons they might find athletics meaningful. Sammons writes, "Hoberman does very little to consider the Hobson's Choices that blacks have faced. They have tried to work the system, like other oppressed groups, 'to their minimum disadvantage.' A more sober mind would ask how blacks constructively reconcile the attraction of sport with the structural inequity that surrounds it."[5]

As different as Berman and Hoberman are in approach, tone, and sentiment, they share an orientation that characterizes a great deal of popular writing about race and sports: both make extremely broad generalizations. In doing so, each misses the opportunity truly to learn something new about race in the United States and in the world at large by looking more carefully at sports. As Sammons argues in his response to Hoberman, "The most interesting, revealing, and sensitive discussions of race take place around the arena of sport. It is in that arena that notions of difference, often carrying qualitative judgments on alleged racial superiority and inferiority, are inscribed, reinforced, internalized, and contested."[6]

The authors who have written essays for this collection all learn something about race by examining sports from specific locations and concrete circumstances. In doing so, they build on the fine work of sports historians before them who have provided some of the most insightful scholarship on race as a core ingredient in the social functions that sports serve: Susan Cahn, Rob Ruck, Jeffrey Sammons, Jules Tygiel, David Wiggins, and David Zang.[7]

Similar to their predecessors, the essays herein focus on sports and race as they are played out in both gendered and multiracial—Afro-American, Asian American, and Latino—contexts, beyond the habitual Black/white and masculine frame of racial mobility through sport. The authors in *Sports Matters: Race, Recreation, and Culture* understand sports as a complex cultural form that operates on many levels simultaneously, gaining new meanings as they are experienced and read within different historical, political, and social contexts.

Over the course of the twentieth century, numerous writers have commented on the ways in which sports have developed into an important form of cultural expression and a political tool in the historical project to dismantle systems of racial apartheid. C. L. R. James argued in *Beyond a Boundary* for the importance of cricket to West Indians' postcolonial struggles against the British Empire. Richard Wright documented the emergence of a new form of Black identity and Black consciousness in his essay "Joe Louis Uncovers Dynamite." Maya Angelou documented similar inspiration in the passages about Joe Louis in her novel *I Know Why the Caged Bird Sings*, as did Malcolm X in passages about Louis and Muhammad Ali in his *Autobiography*.[8]

In their celebration of such sports heroes, these writers explore the power of sports as an affective experience. For example, Frederick Douglass could recognize the larger political importance of Peter Jackson's achievements in the ring only because he was also speaking as a fan, as someone engaged in his own, as well as a collective African American, process of creating meaning, of defining the social significance of race. When approached this way, Douglass's statement shows that sport comprises polysemic cultural practices, ones that do not convey but instead engage multiple voices in critical dialogues over matters of social significance. As the most perceptive writers have noted, the most adept athletes have demonstrated, and the essays in *Sports Matters* implicitly argue, there are ways of winning other than crossing the finish line first. How an athlete scores, moves, and performs is often more important than the score itself.

We have organized the book into three chronological sections that conform loosely to three periods in the history of race in the United States: (1) segregation, (2) color-blind integration, and (3) race-conscious identity and difference. These eras correspond with some of the iconic moments in the history of race and sports: the segregation of baseball and the rise of Joe Louis; the breaking of the color barrier in baseball in 1947; and the rise of racialized superathletes who are global industries unto themselves, such as Michael Jordan and Tiger Woods. However, they also provide useful markers for historical contexts that have been just as important to the ways in which people have defined, resisted, or rearticulated racial categories within sports: the Jim Crow era; civil rights after World War II and the sociopolitical climate of the Cold War; and the neoconservative racial politics that have come to define the Reagan and post–Cold War eras.

The first section explores sports and race during the first half of the twentieth century. By the early part of the century, organized sports had become institutionalized, a part of the social fabric of daily life, education, and entertainment in North America. At the same time that sports were part of a national culture, however, they also were local, characterized by more regional and community diversity than would exist after World War II. The essays in this section explore the politics of race in the sports culture of this era, one that encompasses the "golden years" of American sports during the 1920s, the Great Depression, the era leading up to the integration of baseball, and the era before the introduction of television to widespread markets. The discrimination against nonwhite athletes during the era mirrored the larger system of segregation that characterized the nation at large. Yet sports in marginalized ghettos or ethnic enclaves also became an important vehicle by which disenfranchised communities defined their identities and created alternative ways of representing their bodies and their understandings of selfhood.

Michael Willard contrasts the cultural significance of surfing in Hawaii to the reception that Duke Kahanamoku received when he became a symbol of American national unity through his participation and success in

Olympic swimming in 1912 and 1920. Kahanamoku's reception in the mainland media was striking for its acceptance, yet Kahanamoku still had to negotiate the racialized difference between the social meaning of surfing in Hawaii and his participation in swimming on the mainland.

Gena Caponi-Tabery explores issues of discrimination and resistance in her chapter on the evolution of Black style in both basketball and jazz in Harlem of the 1930s. Caponi-Tabery not only recognizes the importance of sports as a vehicle for cultural expression but also links these expressions to the social construction of race during the Great Depression.

Samuel Regalado explores the social function of baseball for rural Nisei living in towns along the Columbia River in Oregon during the late 1930s. Regalado examines how small Japanese immigrant communities, defined by race as "outsiders" and greatly outnumbered in rural areas, developed empowering social ties to urban Nisei through baseball.

José Alamillo explores Mexican American baseball in Los Angeles during the 1930s and 1940s. While dark-skinned Mexican Americans were barred from playing in major and minor league baseball, they often played in industrial leagues designed to inculcate "American" values of individualism and national patriotism. Yet, as Alamillo discovers, Mexican Americans created community ties within their baseball clubs that trained them to confront struggles that they faced as nonwhites and as workers.

The essays in the second section examine sports in the post–World War II era between the late 1940s and the early 1970s. During this period, North American sports became increasingly wedded to televised entertainment, corporate marketing practices, and metropolitan economic formations. In addition, the era represented a paradigm shift in racial politics after the integration of baseball. Although sports commentators such as Chris Berman often present the entrance of Jackie Robinson into major league baseball as signaling the end of racial apartheid in American sports, the authors in this section argue that integration was never smooth, nor did it necessarily end any relationship between sports and ideologies surrounding race.

Montye Fuse and Keith Miller look directly at Jackie Robinson's style of play, arguing that he offered a sharp on-field critique of white professional sports even while he was attempting to achieve success within that world. Like Caponi-Tabery in the first section, Fuse and Miller develop an argument that illustrates the power of Black cultural style in sports as political critique.

Annie Gilbert Coleman critically examines whiteness in her essay on the development and promotion of the tourist industry surrounding skiing in the 1950s and 1960s. Coleman argues that the ski tourism industry has helped construct an image of the American west, one that erases or fetishizes its indigenous history while foregrounding images of northern European culture.

Like Fuse and Miller, Sharon O'Brien looks at the integration of baseball from the point of view of a lifelong Irish American Red Sox fan. She writes that the greatest curse on the team was not that of the "Bambino" but that of racism. O'Brien writes of how Boston was the last team to accept racial integration, costing them the opportunity to sign both Willie Mays and Jackie Robinson. She connects this history to identity politics of whiteness that were central to the local history of the team's Irish American fan base.

Amy Bass explores the politics of race embodied in patriotic rituals associated with sports. Her chapter examines the "Black Power" salute protest by John Carlos and Tommy Smith in their award ceremony at the 1968 Olympics in Mexico City. This protest signaled a critical new phase for people of color in U.S. sports. In contrast to movements that sought inclusion in sporting arenas that had been exclusively white, the 1968 protest understood Black athletes as both exploited and alienated from dominant understandings of the American nation. Bass interprets the Carlos and Smith protest as a direct and empowering act of contestation.

Like Bass, Julio Rodriguez examines a sports icon commonly associated with civil rights protest: Muhammad Ali. Rodriguez focuses on the film *When We Were Kings*, a documentary about the 1974 "Rumble in the Jungle" bout, in which Ali knocked out George Foreman to reclaim the world heavyweight title for the first time since he was stripped of it in the 1960s for his objection to being drafted into the Vietnam War. Rodriguez sees the film not only as a celebration of Ali's victory but also as a particular framing of the event in terms of social Darwinism, where the main actors are not Ali and Foreman but are, instead, East coast white male intelligentsia struggling to maintain their intellectual and masculine authority.

The final section examines sports in contemporary contexts, defined by a "post–Civil rights" atmosphere, globalization, the increasingly fluid nature of media imagery, and multiple paradigms of racial identity. Sports have become a central component of a vast, globally commercialized media apparatus. In addition, the American sports franchises have become important social institutions in cities, transforming urban landscapes and serving the interests of elites seeking to protect and increase their wealth. All the articles in the final section explore racial formations created through the media images and social institutions that have been created around sports.

George Lipsitz's article focuses on the continuity of narratives of civic pride and economic development that business interests in Houston, St. Louis, and Los Angeles employed to justify the removal of people of color for the sake of building major league baseball stadiums. Stadium construction has become a critical issue in contemporary urban politics over the past twenty years, as cities and states have spent billions of dollars of public money to construct state-of-the-art sports palaces with luxury boxes. Lipsitz illustrates how new stadiums redistribute wealth disproportionately, from poor communities and people of color to wealthy white corporate leaders and urban officials.

John Bloom and Randy Hanson explore the media images that dominate writing about Native Americans in sports, focusing on the motif of the warrior. The authors examine a divergent pair of texts: one on popular writing about Native American basketball, the other basketball coach Phil Jackson's appropriation of Native American warrior rituals to motivate professional athletes. Both seem to portray Native Americans in a sympathetic manner, yet both draw similarly on a one-dimensional, nostalgic portrayal of Native Americans that highlights particular images of the warrior.

In their respective articles, Connie Razza, Gregory Rodríguez, and Henry Yu, consider the popular images and meanings of highly successful people of color. Connie Razza examines Oprah Winfrey. Although Winfrey did not reach fame and fortune as an athlete, Razza discusses the importance of the exercise videos and products sold in her name. She argues that these products are important to understanding how Winfrey has propelled her fame, speaking particularly to middle-class African American women through narratives about weight loss and her body.

Gregory Rodríguez considers the career of Oscar de la Hoya, a contemporary media "golden boy" of Mexican American boxing. Rodríguez argues that de la Hoya has served as a potent symbol of assimilation and accommodation for the dominant media, someone who celebrates individual success and upward mobility. Yet Rodríguez also explores de la Hoya's complex relationship to the ethnic Mexican communities in the 1990s, and his refusal to accept any single interpretation of his identity.

Henry Yu in a similar vein examines the imagery and iconography surrounding Tiger Woods. Yu covers a vast body of popular literature about Woods and connects narratives of the star golfer's success to contemporary debates about identity politics that surround race.

Michiko Hase's essay broadens the consideration of race beyond the boundaries of the United States. She explores forces of globalization that have reframed issues of sports and race at the end of the twentieth century and the beginning of the twenty-first. Her essay on neocolonialism and race in World Cup soccer provides a vantage point from which to reconsider the nationalist narratives that framed sports in previous eras of segregation and color-blind integration.

This book provides a unique collection of essays. Not only do they address racism within sports, but they also explore the relationships of popular athletics to racial formations and politics in society at large, outside the lines drawn on the playing field. Each section provides a variety of perspectives. In many cases, meanings played out inside the lines of the playing field are narrated in other genres and venues, especially the mass media. Many articles in this collection read the construction of race between the lines of text and framings of photographs that make up the cultural narratives of sport. In some articles, authors explore the social and historical construction of race and racism through sports. Others focus on racial discourses circulated through popular media. Some articles focus on the ways in which sports provide a context for creative performance within a culture defined by racial hierarchies, while still others look at how sports have provided contexts for people to engage actively in processes of racial (and gender) identity formation through fan communities. Together, the chapters of this anthology provide a collection of scholarship that will open up new ways of thinking about race, sports, and popular culture in the United States.

NOTES

1. See Jeffrey Sammons, *Beyond the Ring: The Role of Boxing in American Society* (Urbana: University of Illinois Press, 1988); and Gerald Early, *The Culture of Bruising: Essays on Prizefighting, Literature, and Modern Culture* (Hopewell, NJ: Ecco Press, 1994), for accounts of Peter Jackson's career, and Frederick Douglass's interest in Peter Jackson.

2. Chris Berman, "Forward," in Michael MacCambridge, ed., *ESPN SportsCentury* (New York: Hyperion, 1999).

3. John Hoberman, *Darwin's Athletes: How Sport Has Damaged Black America and Preserved the Myth of Race* (New York: Houghton Mifflin, 1997), xxiii.

4. Ibid. See Richard Majors, "Cool Pose: Black Masculinity and Sports," in Michael A. Messner and Donald F. Sabo, eds., *Sport, Men and the Gender Order: Critical Feminist Perspectives* (Champaign, IL: Human Kinetics Books 1990); and Robin D. G. Kelley, "Looking for the 'Real' Nigga: Social Scientists Construct the Ghetto" and "Looking to Get Paid: How Some Black Youth Put Culture to Work," in *Yo' Mama's Dysfunktional! Fighting the Culture Wars in Urban America* (Boston: Beacon Press, 1997), for different explanations of Black cultural style. Kelley calls attention to the continuities of Black cultural style by showing its collective history. See also Kelley's chapter on gangster rap in his *Race Rebels: Culture, Politics, and the Black Working Class* (New York: Free Press, 1994).

5. Jeffrey Sammons, "A Proportionate and Measured Response to the Provocation That Is *Darwin's Athletes*," *Journal of Sport History* 24, 2 (Fall 1997): 378–388.

6. Ibid.

7. Susan Cahn, *Coming on Strong: Gender and Sexuality in Twentieth Century Women's Sport* (Cambridge, MA: Harvard University Press, 1994); Rob Ruck, *Sandlot Seasons: Sport in Black Pittsburgh* (Urbana: University of Illinois Press, 1987); Sammons, *Beyond the Ring*; David K. Wiggins, *Glory Bound: Black Athletes in White America* (Syracuse: Syracuse University Press, 1997); George Eisen and David K. Wiggins, *Ethnicity and Sport in North American History and Culture* (Westport, CT: Greenwood Press, 1994); Jules Tygiel, *Baseball's Great Experiment: Jackie Robinson and His Legacy* (New York: Vintage, 1983); David Zang, *Fleet Walker's Divided Heart: The Life of Baseball's First Black Major Leaguer* (Lincoln: University of Nebraska Press, 1995).

8. Richard Wright, "Joe Louis Uncovers Dynamite," *New Masses*, 8 October 1935; Maya Angelou, *I Know Why the Caged Bird Sings* (1969; reprint, New York: Bantam Books, 1980); Malcolm X, *The Autobiography of Malcolm X* (1965; reprint, New York: Ballantine Books, 1992).

Part I

Sports in the Era of Segregation

Chapter One

Duke Kahanamoku's Body
Biography of Hawai'i

Michael Nevin Willard

Duke Paoa Kahanamoku was born in downtown Honolulu in 1890, only three years before American business interests in the islands engineered the overthrow of the Hawaiian monarchy in 1893.[1] In 1898, Hawai'i was annexed as a United States territory, the result of which, as Elizabeth Buck points out, "was the total appropriation of the Hawaiian Islands by American economic and political interests."[2] By 1900, when the Organic Act made him a United States citizen, Kahanamoku could be found at Honolulu harbor "playing Hawaiian" with other boys—diving for coins thrown by tourists from passing steamships and exploiting the paternalistic blind spots in the Anglo-Americans' preconceptions about island "natives."[3] Along with American tourists, those steamships imported the American racial ideologies that were used to redefine Hawai'i as a destination for the blossoming tourist industry.[4] Beginning with those early days when steamship passengers leaned on the guardrails to watch him dive for coins, Kahanamoku never left the public eye or the racial gaze of tourism.

Today, when people know of him at all, Duke Kahanamoku is perhaps most often remembered as one of the founders of modern surfing. During the first four decades of his life, with which this chapter is primarily concerned, he was perhaps more well known for a twenty-year-plus competitive and exhibition swimming career in which he toured the globe; broke numerous world records in the sprint distances; and won gold and silver medals at the 1912 Stockholm Olympics, double gold at the 1920 Antwerp Olympics, silver at the 1924 Paris Olympics, and, at the age of forty-one, a bronze medal as an alternate on the U.S. water polo team at the 1932 Los

Angeles Olympics.[5] As a public figure and "representative" of Hawai'i, Kahanamoku's success as a swimmer and surfer was always framed by early-twentieth-century American racial ideologies that focused explicitly on his body. In Hawai'i, Kahanamoku's athletic successes were always part of the Hawaiian tourist industry publicity machine. Even those elements of Kahanamoku's identity that fell outside his success in the mainstream of early-twentieth-century American sporting culture—namely, his numerous commitments to preserving the collective, place-based meanings of local Native Hawaiian history and culture—were all lived through his body, a body shaped by racial conditions not of his choosing.[6] To borrow a phrase from Henry Yu, his entire life was a performance "on a stage built by others."[7]

To make sense of the racial conditions that framed Duke Kahanamoku as an icon of the Hawaiian tourist industry, I focus on three moments that occurred in 1911 as windows onto the strands of American and Hawaiian cultures that intersected on the surface of his body to become the fabric of his life and identity.[8] Each moment reveals a specific racial pattern or discourse that shaped Kahanamoku's body throughout his life. The first moment, the 1911 publication of Jack London's book *The Cruise of the Snark*, reveals the racial discourse of civilization that shaped Kahanamoku's body into an icon of the Hawaiian tourist industry.[9] The second moment, the controversy over three world records that Kahanamoku set in his very first international swim meet, an Amateur Athletic Union (AAU) swimming competition on 12 August 1911 at Honolulu Harbor, reveals the racial discourse of sport that shaped Kahanamoku's body into a symbol of American national belonging.[10] The third moment, the January 1911 publication of Kahanamoku's essay "Riding the Surf," reveals one instance of his lifelong labors to "maintain control over the future of Hawaii and its communities." By placing himself within a collective history that opposed the colonial and postcolonial relations of tourism, Kahanamoku expressed the principles of a counterracial discourse in Hawai'i that would later become known as "local identity."[11]

Inverted Arrival, Taking Place: Jack London's "Hawaiian Aloha," Civilization, and Waikiki as Anglo-American Playground

A standard trope of anthropological writing is to assert ownership over a landscape by describing the moment of arrival.[12] In one story in *The Cruise of the Snark*, his amateur ethnological account of his and his wife

Charmian's 1907 travels in Hawai'i and other "exotic" Pacific islands, Jack London inverts this trope in order to make his eventual claim to Waikiki all the more forceful through a reassertion of racial hierarchy. Throughout his travels, London was compelled to make sense of the racial difference he encountered. He devoted four chapters of *Cruise of the Snark* to Hawai'i, and in them the figure of the surfer is central to his explanations of race in Hawai'i. In "A Royal Sport: Surfing at Waikiki," London begins his first-person description of Hawaiian surfing with himself sitting on the beach fully clothed, feeling less than a man, feeling "tiny and fragile before the tremendous force" of the raw, uncontrolled, and unmediated nature he observes in the "fury, foam and sound" of the waves. "Suddenly," as his "shrinking ego" concludes that "a man" has "no chance at all" against such "bull-mouthed," "thousand ton" waves, London sees, far out to sea, "the dark head of a man," and he discovers a model physique from which he can sculpt civilized manliness—the Darwinist solution to his own feelings of ineffectual manliness.[13]

London recovers his manhood by asserting a racially superior definition of white civilization over nature. At the same time, he racializes nature as nonwhite. He does so by creating a racial hierarchy on the surface of the Native Hawaiian surfer's body. In so doing, he asserts an evolutionary narrative of civilized white progress by figuratively *taking the place* of the Native Hawaiian surfer whom he watches from his seat at the water's edge on Waikiki Beach. London's replacement of the dark-skinned Native Hawaiian surfer's body with his own white body is more than figurative, however. London's text was part of a concerted effort to reproduce a racial ideology that enabled the literal replacement of Native Hawaiians and their water traditions with the Anglo-American tradition of sport, as well as Native Hawaiians' physical displacement from the land. The racial ideology that London's essay reproduced was the racial logic that became necessary to carry out the transformation of Hawai'i from a plantation landscape and economy to a landscape and economy of tourism.[14]

As London watches the dark surfer move closer to shore, he locates him in an in-between, brown, and inferior position on a hierarchical racial continuum. His description of the surfer's manly prowess follows the surfer's "progress" toward shore and smelts his body from black to brown to golden brown:[15]

> Swiftly he rises through the rushing white. His black shoulders, his chest, his loins, his limbs—all is abruptly projected on one's vision. Where but

another moment before was only the wide desolation and invincible roar, is now a man, erect, full-statured, . . . standing above them all, calm and superb, . . . and he is flying through the air, . . . flying fast as the surge on which he stands. He is a Mercury—a brown Mercury. His heels are winged, and in them is the swiftness of the sea. . . . He is impassive, motionless as a statue carved suddenly by some miracle out of the sea's depth from which he rose. And straight on toward shore he flies on his winged heels and the white crest of the breaker. There is a wild burst of foam, a long tumultuous rushing sound as the breaker falls futile and spent on the beach at your feet; and there, at your feet, steps calmly ashore a Kanaka, burnt golden and brown by the tropic sun. . . . he glances for a moment carelessly at you. . . . He is a Kanaka—and more, he is a man, a member of the kingly species that has mastered matter and the brutes and lorded it over creation.[16]

London defuses the initial racial threat posed by the surfer's muscled black shoulders, chest, and loins by sculpting them into the motionless calm of classical statuary and the transcendent Mercury—winged flier of brown Roman gods. Significantly, the surfer's black body is placed in the distance and quickly becomes the past as the surfer moves toward the shore, all the while morphing ever lighter (if not whiter) under London's scribal chisel. Posing the example of the Hawaiian surfer as his model for an ideal of transcendent, manly omnipotence, London completes his racial hierarchy of civilized manliness by writing himself over the now "golden" brown surfer. He places himself in the highest (implicitly white) position on the ladder of racial evolution. London sheds his clothes, enters the water, and surfs himself:

What that Kanaka can do, you can do yourself. Go to. Strip off your clothes that are a nuisance in this mellow clime. Get in and wrestle with the sea; wing your heels with the skill and power that reside in you; bit the sea's breakers, master them, and ride upon their backs as a king should.[17]

Before London's essay was published in *The Cruise of the Snark*, it had appeared in the widely circulated middle-class magazine *A Woman's Home Companion* in October 1907. As representations of Hawaii were exported to the U.S. mainland, both publications helped reinforce the racial ideologies that Americans had imported to Hawai'i, and which in turn allowed Americans to promote the Hawaiian surfer as the visual image that enabled white American men, as tourists, to recreate London's formula of achieving manly civilization by taking the place of primitive, brown-bodied Hawaiian surfers. The place white American men took was not only the space occupied by the body of the surfer but also Hawai'i itself, which became a landscape stripped of the specific historical meanings given to it by collective Native Hawaiian traditions and refurbished with meanings clustered around tourism. In his essay, London can carry out this replacement of male Hawaiian bodies and the Hawaiian landscape because he invokes an established visual convention specific to images of Pacific Island men that defined their "masculinity as fundamentally a thing of the sea."[18]

Anthropologists Catherine Lutz and Jane Collins explain that "the addition of a woman to a photographed scene often succeeds . . . in changing the scene from a still life or object of contemplation to a purchasable commodity. This is because women have traditionally been seen as objects to be possessed."[19] Images of "alluring, entertaining, sensual, graceful, and natural" female Hawaiian bodies were used to transform the islands into a tourist destination commodity. By the 1920s, such images would become dominant in the visual economy of Hawaiian tourism, most prominently on postcards.[20] If images of women relied on their implied—and explicit, when bare-breasted—sensuality, images of Hawaiian men relied on a similar sensuality of bare-chested muscularity to render the Hawaiian landscape a purchasable tourist destination. (See Figure 1.1.)

In early-twentieth-century educational and scientific discourses, Hawai'i and Hawaiians were "placed at the top of the nonwhite hierarchy, above the Chinese, Japanese, and Filipinos and the North American Indian, as well."[21] Such positioning was intended to call attention to Hawaiians' greater potential for becoming civilized and their greater similarities to whites. Within the visual economy of tourism, such racial hierarchies had the effect of making Hawai'i a more acceptable and desirable place to visit. These discourses located their evidence for their mapping of racial hierarchy on the surface of Native Hawaiian bodies, and thus, to reinforce such hierarchies and their accompanying typologies of bodily appearance, it was important to insist that Hawaiians were neither black nor red but brown.[22]

Just as London focused on the muscular shoulders, chest, and loins of the surfer in his story and changed them from black to brown to golden brown, the promotion of manly Hawaiian tourism through images of male Hawaiian bodies meant ensuring that those bodies were clearly understood to be brown and not black. Photographed against the background of the sea and the distinct profile of Diamond Head mountain, the Hawaiian surfer's body established the ocean at Waikiki Beach as the specific tourist destination in Hawai'i where American (and European) men

1.1 This photo from the 1899 book *Our Islands and Their People* portrays a Native Hawaiian man in the conventional pose, bare-chested with surfboard, though wearing western work pants. The man behind him also wears western clothes. Photographic evidence suggests that Native Hawaiian men often fished and surfed bare-chested, but this picture shows that they also wore western clothes including shirts when they worked. Just as often they also wore one-piece swimsuits when they swam or surfed. Thus, the photographic convention of the bare-chested pose of the Native Hawaiian man with surfboard became the object of desire for white men who sought to step outside the bounds of civilization and the conventions of western dress.

could fulfill their evolutionary destiny of civilized manliness. The images of bare-chested Hawaiian surfers, the sea, and the iconic profile of the familiar and nameable landscape of Diamond Head and Waikiki worked in mutually supportive fashion to establish the overall image as specifically Hawaiian, and hence, by association, the body in the image as acceptably brown and not black. Furthermore, surfing and Native Hawaiians were rendered primitive and archaic by consistently showing them bare-chested in photos, whereas white men as surfers conformed to civilized propriety, wearing one-piece tank suits. The visual convention of depicting muscular bare-chested Hawaiian men emphasizes primitive physicality, as opposed to the physical and muscular but covered and thus civilized rationality of white men.

A significant actor in the project of creating Waikiki as the location of white manly civilization was Alexander Hume Ford, one of London's fellow white surfers, whom he mentions later in his essay. Ford and London were instrumental in the 1908 founding of the Outrigger Canoe Club on Waikiki Beach. Wording in the club's founding charter reveals that Ford, London, and others sought to redefine Hawaiian surfing in terms of tourism: "We wish to have a place where surfboard riding may be revived and those who live away from the water front may keep their surfboards. The main object of this club being to give an added and permanent attraction to Hawaii and make the Waikiki beach the home of the surfrider."[23] Thomas Hitch provides further insight into Ford's motivations.

> Ford had been active with the original Hawaii Promotional Committee in the early years of the twentieth century. In 1907 he tried to persuade the Australian government to join with Hawaii in forming a Pan-Pacific Tourist and Information Bureau. He was also instrumental in organizing the Outrigger Canoe Club in 1908 to revive the sport of surfing, and in 1911 formed an international organization called Hands-Around-The-Pacific Club, which in 1917 adopted the name Pan-Pacific Union.[24]

Thus white men replaced brown men, took over Waikiki Beach, and positioned themselves as the saviors of surfing, a dying and archaic sport, by redefining it and freezing it as a preservable object under the civilizing influence of tourism. In so doing, they elevated themselves and their civilizing mission while subordinating Native Hawaiians and their culture, a dying culture because primitive. Although the club was purportedly open to all, photos of the membership show only a token few nonwhite Hawaiians.[25]

Another version of the club's history has it that at its founding it was "conceived as an organization to revitalize the 'royal sport' of surfing on boards and in outrigger canoes, by providing 'the small boy of limited means' access to the beach." Photos of these boys from the first years of the club show only white children.[26] (See Figure 1.2.) Apparently, Native Hawaiian boys and girls of limited means were not considered. The club's seemingly noble purpose was an attempt to deal with the privatization of the beach that tourism was creating, but the club could not overcome its founders' racial discourse of white civilization, which organized the club squarely amid the privatizing forces of the tourist industry. As time

1.2 This photo (ca. 1910–1915) of young boys posing with surfboards and surf canoes at Waikiki Beach appears to be located at the site of the Outrigger Canoe Club. Although some whites who lived in Hawai'i were from Anglo and Native Hawaiian families, there are no clearly Native Hawaiian boys or Asian boys in this photo. Photo courtesy of the Hawaiian Historical Society.

passed, the prestige status that had been inherent to the club from the beginnings of its civilizing mission won out. The club's "social aspect" grew, so that by the 1930s "the club had become one of the more prestigious and exclusive organizations in the territory."[27] One can speculate that members of the club accrued prestige from the primitive and authentic connotations of surfing and outrigger canoes.

Finally, the architectural history of the club buildings recapitulates a civilizing history of "taking place." The original buildings of the club were "'authentic Hawaiian grass houses' purchased from a defunct zoo in Kaimuki."[28] These buildings were replaced by a "more modern structure" in 1939 when the clubhouse was "moved *mauka* [toward the mountains, usually toward the center of the island][29] to accommodate the Royal Hawaiian Hotel. That building was supplanted by the present Outrigger Hotel in 1964."[30]

The civilizing process of replacement is quite clear. From the grass huts, taken out of their specific Hawaiian history and collective cultural meaning and relocated as static consumer objects of authenticity, the geographical meaning of Waikiki as defined by the Outrigger Canoe Club becomes embodied in the built tourist environment itself, when the club becomes a hotel. Hotels are the physical landscape, a background of high-rise buildings that form the backbone of civilized Waikiki as a tourist destination.

Having practically grown up on the beach at Waikiki, Duke Kahanamoku was central to its visual redevelopment, which positioned brown bodies in the landscape so that white men could take the place of Native Hawaiian men and turn Waikiki into a tourist destination for the recovery of their manliness and white racial superiority. Kahanamoku had grown up surfing, but it was only after he achieved acclaim as a world-class swimmer in 1911 that images of him surfing began to appear with any regularity. Almost invariably, in every decade of his life, he was shown standing bare-chested on Waikiki Beach, in front of a surfboard, with Diamond Head in the background.

The first images of Kahanamoku as a surfer appeared in Alexander Hume Ford's *Mid-Pacific Magazine* in January 1911, seven months before Kahanamoku would break world records and become a famous swimmer. Significantly, the photos show him actually surfing, but far more often images portrayed him standing bare-chested in front of a surfboard. In these most common poses, Kahanamoku's identifiable name reinforced the visual conventions of surfing and civilization to establish him as Hawaiian and brown—as primitive. His intermediary and subordinate brownness within the racial hierarchy of Waikiki tourism was further emphasized by his positioning: on the beach, a man of the sea, but standing on land, not on the water atop a wave. His skill as a waterman was thus deemphasized and rendered more achievable for white male viewers.

Kahanamoku participated willingly in this visual economy and used it profitably to his advantage (though he never became rich), but he was also confined by and sometimes challenged it. (See Figure 1.3.) When he accommodated crowds of tourists who wanted their picture taken with him, the press of bodies and cameras often became so intense that people would begin to order him around and speak to him as an object: "Hey you. Get up there! Want your picture." He would calmly refuse and say, "I'm sorry. I'm not in the mood for a picture today."[31] His biographer cites this as an example of Kahanamoku's natural grace, his courtesy and kindness. I argue that it may also have been an effort to manage and negotiate (if not resist) the confining racial discourse of primitivism versus civilization that trapped his body in the tourist industry.

Swimming and American National Belonging

Images of Kahanamoku as a surfer in Hawai'i shaped the surface of his body as brown, bare-chested, and primitive, less than civilized, thus reproducing a racial discourse intended, in part, to turn Hawai'i into a tourist

1.3 This 1914 poster depicts a bare-chested Kahanamoku riding a surfboard, rather than the more common pose of him standing on the beach. However, as a promotional image for the Mid-Pacific Carnival, it places him and surfing in an event that must have been intended to promote tourism as much as it may have celebrated Native Hawaiian water traditions. Photo courtesy of the Bishop Museum.

destination for the revitalization of white manliness. When he performed as an athlete and swimming champion, images shaped the surface of his body as brown but already civilized—part of a representational effort to include Hawai'i in the imagined white fiction of a racially unified American nation.

On 12 August 1911, in his first international swim meet, Duke Kahanamoku broke three world records in an AAU swimming competition at Alakea Slip in Honolulu Harbor. The records were later disallowed because the course distance was found to be irregular—one account has it seventeen inches too long and another has it a few inches too short.[32] This competition brought Kahanamoku before the eyes of the nation, to the attention of more Americans than those wealthy elites who could afford to visit the islands as tourists. Kahanamoku's record was ultimately disallowed because of the cultural and racial distance between Hawai'i and America. The course would not have been remeasured, but for AAU officials' skepticism about the ability of a Hawaiian swimmer to break a world record. One such official sent a telegram from the mainland, asking whether the timers in Hawai'i had been using alarm clocks for stopwatches.[33] Such a response reveals a conception of Hawaiians as "out of time," as primitive—the same conception created through images of Kahanamoku as a surfer within the Hawaiian tourist economy.

Although scientific-educational and tourist discourses ranked Hawaiians high in their hierarchical racial typologies, when it came to the racial discourse of national belonging and the understanding of Hawai'i on the U.S. mainland, Kahanamoku's world records show that Hawaiians still presented a dilemma to carefully ordered hierarchies of early-twentieth-century white superiority. In Kahanamoku's case, however, this confusion changed within a year.

After his success at Alakea in 1911, Kahanamoku became a tourist himself and traveled to the mainland to compete for a place on the 1912 Olympic swimming team. In the competition, he again broke world records. Having easily made the team, at the 1912 Olympics in Stockholm, Sweden, Kahanamoku won a gold medal in the 100–freestyle in world record time and received a silver medal as part of the 4-by-200–meter freestyle relay.

Media coverage of the 1912 American Olympic delegation set the pattern for all subsequent images of Kahanamoku as a swimmer. The group of U.S. Olympic competitors included the Native American runners Jim Thorpe, Alfred Sockalexis, and Lewis Tewanima; African American runner Howard P. Drew; and Kahanamoku and other Hawaiian swimmers. Coverage of this multiracial American team emphasized that "class, race, and ethnic distinctions disappeared on the athletic common ground" of sport.[34] Whereas only a year before Kahanamoku had been assumed to be primitive and backward, now his body was a symbol of a racially unified American nation.

Philip Deloria explains that "sports were instrumental in transforming and reshaping modern American culture at the turn of the century."[35] One of the ways they did so, he points out, was to define the dimensions of the American racial state. Whereas, in his first success as a swimmer Kahanamoku met with the same racial assumptions of primitivism that had marked his body as a surfer in Hawai'i, his success in the 1912 Olympics brought his body into a different set of racial assumptions that sought to defuse the threat his dark-skinned physicality posed not to white manhood but to American national unity.

In this racial discourse, the visual conventions that played out across the surface of Kahanamoku's body clothed him in the universalist ideals of sport. In photos of him as a surfer, Kahanamoku was generally portrayed bare-chested in order to emphasize his primitiveness: in photos of him as a swimmer, he was almost always shown demonstrating the necessary propriety and wearing a one-piece tank suit. Kahanamoku would not have been allowed to compete bare-chested in trunks. There are few photos of him posing bare-chested as a swimmer. That so few photos of Kahanamoku as a bare-chested swimmer exist, and the fact that most photos are posed rather than shots of him swimming in competition, suggests that photos of him wearing a suit were not merely following the rules of the sport (themselves already a part of middle-class Victorian ideologies of civilized propriety) but were necessary to reinforce the ideology of sport itself as a civilizing force. Thus, photos of Kahanamoku as a modern athlete and swimmer civilized him in order to include him in an imaginary of American national belonging. To portray him bare-chested would have violated the morality of middle-class Victorian ideals that sport was meant to uphold. Such photos of Kahanamoku posed in his swim suit individualize him, showing him out of the water rather than competing. They emphasize the individual success to be gained from competition.

The consistent pattern of the visual representations of Kahanamoku as a swimmer contrasts with the multiple racial meanings that circulated around his swimmer's body in other media. Philip Deloria points out that Native American men were permitted to participate in college and professional sports in the early twentieth century when Black athletes were not, precisely because Indians had "long been enmeshed in the discourse of American assimilation."[36] Deloria concludes, however, that this assimilationist discourse was suspended in favor of primitivist imaginings that made Native American men the premodern source of masculinity, which was in crisis in the early twentieth-century due to the anonymity of mass consumption in an industrializing society. Audiences who watched Kahanamoku swim may have interpreted his brown body in the same manner—and thus in the same terms in which his body had been represented in his other persona as a Native Hawaiian surfer. Accounts of Kahanamoku's swimming exploits in mainland newspapers reveal as much. He was often portrayed and described as safely brown and not black. But at other times he was described as "ebony" and "black" for the purposes of celebrating white swimmers. To many fans, he was racially ambiguous. People often thought he was Black, American Indian, and even East Indian. In print accounts of his swimming accomplishments, Kahanamoku's racial identity was multiple and contradictory.

However, despite the multiple racial meanings that audiences and the written media made of his body, the visual conventions that shaped the surface of Kahanamoku's body emphasized not his primitivism or any racial ambiguity that stemmed from his Hawaiianness but instead his assimilability. Given his status as an "athlete" and swimmer, any threat still accruing to his muscled physique was rendered safe by the civilized parameters of sport and the propriety of the suit that covered his body. While there are some photos of Kahanamoku competing in swimming events, more often he was portrayed outside the pool. In such promotional photos, the only rules dictating the appearance of his body in a one-piece suit were social and aesthetic (realism), not athletic.

These seemingly contradictory explanations are not at odds. Racial discourses of primitivist exoticism and of assimilationist national belonging have existed side by side in sport. They reinforced each other. The exotic primitive proved the civilized status and rank of white civilization, and the assimilation of the nonwhite athlete proved sport's civilizing and elevating influence. These racial discourses could also exist side by side because both functioned to render dark-skinned bodies safe within acceptable racial definitions of blackness, American Indianness, and Hawaiianness, which removed those bodies from specific historical contexts and collective cultural traditions that were understood to be antithetical and threatening to the individualist, acquisitive ethic of Anglo-American capitalism.[37] The possibility of national racial unification that was played out upon Kahanamoku's body individualized his physical success as the result of athletic competition itself and not as the result of any collective values coming from Native Hawaiian traditions of swimming that placed high importance on and created cultural meaning from skill in the water.[38]

The flux between primitivism and assimilationism also characterizes relationship between sports and modernization in the colonial context of Hawai'i, as compared to the already urban context of the U.S. mainland.

In many ways, primitivist rhetoric was the racial discourse of choice in Hawai'i because it functioned to encourage a process of modernization and urbanization (privatized hotel development, for example) that had only just begun, and in which white domination was always challenged and always in doubt. Significantly, organizations of Anglo elites such as the Outrigger Canoe Club, sought to turn surfing and canoeing into sports by redefining them within the individualist rhetoric of the Protestant work ethic. In Hawaiian societies, canoes were instruments of travel and labor (fishing) in addition to their use in sporting competition and physical recreation (wave riding). As usable relics preserved by the Outrigger Canoe Club, they were only objects of sport and recreation. Surfing and canoeing thus became leisure items, the rewards for disciplined work rather than tools in its practice.

On the already modernized, urbanized, and white-dominated U.S. mainland, the assimilationist rhetoric and racial discourse of sport was more suitable than the primitivist rhetoric of colonial Hawai'i. The assimilationist ideal in sport served the functions of policing, dehistoricizing, and delegitimating forms of collectivity (e.g., unions and labor organization, the histories of nonwhite collective cultural traditions in America) that threatened the individualist ethos of industrial and monopoly capitalism. Racial differences were thus defused of any threat, as achievement was safely attributed to the unique individual rather than to any collective group.

Hawaiians may have been subjected to a double racial discourse, of both primitivist exoticism and assimilability into civilization, precisely because they were placed so close to whites in nineteenth-century hierarchical racial typologies. Hawaiian bodies could be distinctly classified as brown, thus keeping the racial order intact while providing acceptable models for white ideologies of gender and acceptable examples of non-white "progress" toward a never-reachable white ideal. At the same time, any threat they posed to that racial order could be defused by rendering them subordinate because they were brown and not white.

Aloha A'ina, Becoming Local

At the beginning of 1911, Kahanamoku, with the assistance of his friends from the surfing club Hui Nalu (literally, "surf together" or surf organization), wrote "Riding the Surf," an explanation of surfing at Waikiki. In January 1911 the essay was published, along with photos of surfing on the front and back covers, as the lead article in the premier issue of the *Mid-Pacific Magazine*, a monthly magazine intended, in the words of its founder Alexander Hume Ford, to promote "the wonderful lands and islands of the Pacific Ocean."[39] However, the essay contrasts with Ford's promotional emphasis in ways that prefigure a counterracial discourse of local identity.

Images on the covers of the first two issues of *Mid-Pacific Magazine* show yet another example of the visual conventions of race and civilization. These photos of Kahanamoku create a subordinate and primitive brown body in a tourist landscape, as is evident in the drawing that frames the cover photos. The drawing depicts a palm-lined shore with a grass hut. In the first issue, the drawing focuses on the silhouette of a surfer riding a wave and is paralleled in the cover photo of a surfer that it frames. In the second issue, however, the cover photo of a modern ocean liner contrasts with the same surrounding drawing of palm-lined shore and surfer, thus emphasizing Ford's and the magazine's tourist-promotional mission. The ideal technological progress embodied in the ocean liner renders the surfer in the drawing primitive and part of a landscape to be consumed by the civilizing logic and technological superiority of tourism, a consumption made possible by the steamship.

Although the photos accompanying Kahanamoku and Hui Nalu's essay, like the photos of surfers on the front and back covers, bring Kahanamoku's body within familiar visual conventions of civilized tourism, showing surfers in all their bare-chested manly splendor, the text contrasts with and challenges the racial discourse embodied in those visual conventions. The Kahanamoku/Hui Nalu essay also provides a point of contrast to Jack London's essay "A Royal Sport: Surfing at Waikiki," published in the same year. The beginning of Kahanamoku's essay shows many similarities to London's. Perhaps London's essay influenced it or even served as a model, for Kahanamoku admits in "Riding the Surf" that he has borrowed liberally from already published sources:

> I have never seen snow and do not know what winter means. I have never coasted down a hill of frozen rain, but every day of the year, where the water is 76, day and night, and the waves roll high, I take my sled, without runners, and coast down the face of the big waves that roll in at Waikiki.
>
> How would you like to stand like a god before the crest of a monster billow, always rushing to the bottom of a hill and never reaching its base, and to come rushing in for a half a mile at express speed, in graceful attitude, of

course until you reach the beach and step easily from the wave to the strand?

Find the locality, as we Hawaiians did, where the rollers are long in forming, slow to break, and then run for a great distance over a flat, level bottom, and the rest is possible.

Perhaps the ideal surfing stretch in all the world is at Waikiki beach, near Honolulu, Hawaii. Here centuries ago was born the sport of running foot races upon the crests of the billows, and here bronze skinned men and women vie today with the white man for honors in aquatic sports once exclusively Hawaiian, but in which the white man now rivals the native.[40]

Like London, Kahanamoku elevates the surfer to a godlike status in his ability to stand on a wave. But whereas London displaced surfing into the context of classical antiquity and western civilization, Kahanamoku places surfing in a specific and local history of centuries of Hawaiians surfing at Waikiki. In this essay, Kahanamoku works within the codes of surfing, civilization, and Hawaiian tourism that London's essay reproduced in order to weave his own pattern of race, place, and history into a different set of codes, which constitute an alternative racial discourse of "local identity."

Also of significance, Kahanamoku does not write the surfer's godlike status on the surface of his own or any other body. While the construction of masculine prowess over nature is similar to London's, there is in Kahanamoku's description no transformation of the surfer's body for the purposes creating of a racial hierarchy. Kahanamoku acknowledges racial differences and even says that "the white man now rivals the native" in surfing, but he makes no effort to create a sense of superiority and does not focus on the body in particular.

In the passage quoted above, Kahanamoku's identification of racial difference is ambiguous. He may be acknowledging the rivalry between whites and natives as friendly competition and offering praise for whites' surfing skill. Or the rivalry may refer to the tense racial relations created by the kind of discourses exhibited in London's essay and, more immediately for Kahanamoku, in the Americanization of Hawaiian society that those racial discourses carried out around him, most significantly in the urban development of Waikiki for the tourist industry.

If Kahanamoku's identification of racial difference is ambiguous in this passage, it becomes clear in the rest of his essay. Kahanamoku wrote the essay with the assistance of his friends from Hui Nalu, the surf club he cofounded with Knute Cottrell in 1909. The first-person passage that begins the essay reads as if written by Kahanamoku—though he acknowledges assistance from other member of Hui Nalu. The rest of the essay, however, is a series of excerpts and quotations about surfing from other written sources. Although Kahanamoku and the members of Hui Nalu did not themselves write the essay, the excerpts they used constitute a process of selection and thus become a representation. The racial pattern or discourse that becomes evident in this process of selection is one that reclaims Waikiki for local surfers and emphasizes an equality between whites and Native Hawaiians.

Although the sources of these excerpts are not cited in the essay, one gets the sense that their original authors wrote them according to the racial discourse of primitivism versus civilization that London employs in his essay. However, Kahanamoku/Hui Nalu managed to find excerpts that cut against the grain of such hierarchical racial ideologies. Although one could read the excerpts as an idealization of Hawai'i as a multiracial place, and that was probably the intent of their original authors, one can read the intent of the Kahanamoku/Hui Nalu selection process as an attempt to emphasize an ethic of collectivity.[41] These excerpts also express a brief critique of the privatization of Waikiki Beach. The racial discourse that the members of Hui Nalu expressed in their "representation" of surfing is what scholars of Hawaiian history such as Jonathan Okamura and John Rosa call "local identity."[42]

Jonathan Okamura explains that local identity emerged from the transformation of Hawaiian society as it began to incorporate American values and traditions. What distinguishes local identity, however, is the effort to "maintain control over the future of Hawaii and its communities."[43] This effort to control the future of Hawai'i is defined by a commitment to the many peoples of Hawai'i and the significance of place. Okamura explains that the word *local* did not gain widespread use until 1931, when a group of nonwhite boys were unfairly tried for the rape of a white woman. John Rosa explains that this trial gave Native Hawaiians a broader sense of collective identity.[44]

Although Kahanamoku and the members of Hui Nalu predate the emergence of local identity, which Okamura and Rosa place in the 1930s, their essay on Hawaiian surfing contains the elements that would become local identity. They consciously employ a concept of local culture that acknowledges diversity and develops a shared sense of Waikiki and surfing as a place for Native Hawaiians and whites. This is evident in photos of the club, in which one sees white, Native Hawaiian, Asian, and women members. (See Figure 1.4.) This contrasts with the token few Native Hawaiian

1.4 This photo of Hui Nalu (ca. 1920) shows the club's diverse Native Hawaiian, Asian, white, male, and female membership. Kahanamoku sits in the front row, fourth from the right. In contrast to the bare-chested conventions of tourist imagery, here the young men and women all wear one-piece suits, just as Kahanamoku did when he worked as a Waikiki beach boy for the hotel industry. Photo courtesy of the Bishop Museum.

members of the Outrigger Canoe Club. Similarly, Hui Nalu opposed the private development of Waikiki, whereas the Outrigger Canoe Club (OCC) abetted it. Finally, the Kahanamoku/Hui Nalu essay, as an example of an alternative racial ideology of mutuality and collectivity, is created from pieces of American texts that in their original contexts were efforts to modify Native Hawaiian culture. This parallels the process that Okamura identifies as the formation of local identity that occurred through the recuperation and reinvention of Hawaiian traditions that had been modified by the imperialist forces of the Anglo-American tourist industry.

Evidence of Kahanamoku's "local" sensibility is scattered throughout his life story. With regard to Hui Nalu and the Outrigger Canoe Club, for nine years Kahanamoku refused invitations to join the OCC.[45] Although the OCC had buildings and Hui Nalu had none, conducting their informal gatherings under a hau tree, he seems to have preferred the tree and the sessions of "talk story"—a form of local oral tradition—he knew he could always find there.[46] When considered in relation to the taking of place such as London carried out in his essay or the OCC carried out in fact, both of which were the result of representations of surfing created according to the racialized conventions of civilization, Kahanamoku's emphasis on a tree as a meeting place takes on larger significance as an example of commitment to place, given value and meaning by Native Hawaiian cultural traditions such as "talk story." It can be said to embody one of the elements of local identity that Okamura identifies as *aloha 'aina*, or commitment to place.[47]

Kahanamoku retained a commitment to controlling the future of Hawai'i and its communities by working behind the scenes. As Hawai'i approached statehood, he wrote:

> We are crossing our fingers in high hopes that one of our boys, the Hon. Samuel Wilder King, be appointed Governor of Hawai'i. Should this materialize it would signal for every Hawaiian to rejoice, because it would be the very first time since 1898, when a Native Hawaiian is selected for the high post.
>
> To us, we feel that this is "full recognition" of our citizenship in this Great Country. Up to this point it has been a case of "you Hawaiians can go so far and then stop" while everybody else has been given consideration.[48]

When Kahanamoku achieved international acclaim with his first world record in the 100–meter freestyle in 1911, he did so with a swimming stroke that affirmed the history of Pacific Island culture. Using a modified flutter kick that he had seen Australians use, Kahanamoku was able to generate world-record-breaking speed and advantage over other swimmers. At the time, there was much debate over the origins of the flutter kick. Many attributed the development of the flutter kick to Anglo-Australians. However, there is some historical evidence that suggests the crawl stroke used by Kahanamoku was originally used by native peoples of the Solomon Islands. Similarly the flutter kick was in used in Samoa. In both cases, Europeans travelling in the South Pacific seem to have adopted these swimming strokes. His biographer quotes Kahanamoku as saying, "I've always used the flutter and crawl. I think Hawaiians have always used it—with slight changes . . . I call it the 'Hawaiian Crawl.'"[49] Just as local identity reinvents Hawaiian traditions already altered by American colonial influence, Kahanamoku could quickly adapt a swimming stroke that started in the Solomon Islands and was subsequently claimed by Australians, who altered it by placing it in a Victorian tradition of sport, because he had spent so much of his life in the water living out and continuing a Native Hawaiian relationship to the ocean. Thus, whether he was aware of it or not, Kahanamoku had found a form of swimming that corresponded to his life spent in Native Hawaiian water traditions, and that embodied his commitment to the values of those traditions.

In 1990, at the end of the twentieth century, a seventeen-and-a-half-foot "bronze" statue of Duke Kahanamoku's body was dedicated at Waikiki's Kuhio Beach. Kahanamoku stands bare-chested, on the beach, as he did in so many tourist photographs, with arms open wide in a gesture of welcome. Kahanamoku's body embodies aloha, but a tourist aloha that is only possible by freezing Kahanamoku in place, in the same way that so many elements of Hawaiian culture have been "preserved," "revived," and "promoted." In this rendering of Kahanamoku's body, the familiar surfboard is standing behind him in the sand.

The placement of the statue continues the racial discourse of adding Kahanamoku's body to the Hawaiian landscape to turn both landscape and body into a commodity. The statue faces away from the beach so that tourists can "have" the sand and ocean as a backdrop when they have their picture "taken" in front of him. It would seem that the brownness and bronze tones that Jack London worked to hard to write onto the surface of Native Hawaiian surfers' bodies in 1907 solidified by the end of the twentieth century. But just as Kahanamoku refused to have his picture taken with people who treated him as an object within the tourist landscape, the beach boys who work on Waikiki for the hotels—as Kahanamoku did in his youth—insist that "Duke would 'Nevvah, nevvah turn his back on the ocean.'"[50] Speaking in Hawaiian Creole English, or pidgin, the vernacular of local identity, and expressing a clear sense of local identity through local meanings of Waikiki Beach, these beach boys have rewritten the placement of Kahanamoku's statue by recalling his commitment to the future of local Hawaiian culture and community. Even today, over a century after he was born, the meaning of surfing and of Hawai'i, located as it is in the struggle between postcolonial and local racial ideologies, is still written on the surface of Duke Kahanamoku's body.

Alternate Ending

In 1990, exactly one month to the day after Duke Kahanamoku's tenth birthday, in a speech titled "To the Nations of the World," delivered at the first Pan-African Congress in London at the Westminster Town Hall, W. E. B. DuBois issued his famous prophecy for the coming century: "The problem of the twentieth century is the problem of the colour line."[51] It is significant that he was speaking in an international context, at a Pan-African Congress that he defined as "assembled . . . to deliberate . . . upon the . . . outlook of the darker races of mankind," for it gives global and multiracial meaning to his proclamation.[52] When he gave name to the problem that would define the coming century, DuBois recognized all people of color. Speaking, only two years after the annexation of Hawai'i in 1898, DuBois expressed a mutual recognition of all people of color in opposition to hierarchical white racial ideologies. His expression of multiracial solidarity was very similar to the ethic of mutual recognition that informed local identity in Hawai'i. Significantly, DuBois's magazines—*The Crisis*, which he founded to "show the danger of race prejudice . . . as manifested towards colored people,"[53] and *Phylon*, "a journal of the darker races"—were sensitive to the plight of Native Hawaiians and published articles about racial problems in Hawai'i.[54] In 1932 DuBois wrote in his straight-to-the-point *Crisis* column "As the Crow Flies": "Learn the logic of Hawaii: missions, debt, slavery, rape, sugar, pineapples. Net result: millionaires, moonlight music, rape, bad government, battleships."[55] And in 1953, in a letter responding to a young graduate student who doubted DuBois's claims about American imperialism and the colonization of the world by big business, he recapitulated the global context he had referenced in his London speech in 1900:

> I feel very strongly that American Imperialism financed by Big Business is the cause of our being today the chief world advocate of war. This imperialism started, of course, with the annexation of Hawaii, the Spanish War, and Central and South American investments.[56]

Throughout the twentieth century, from the days of his youth in the early 1900s, when he dove for coins thrown by tourists from passing steamships, to the dedication of his statue at Waikiki Beach in 1990, on the one hundredth anniversary of his birth, the meaning of surfing and Native Hawaiian water traditions, the meaning of Hawai'i as a place, and the meaning of the color line in Hawai'i—located as these are in the struggle among colonial, postcolonial, and local racial projects and ideologies—have been written on the surface of Duke Kahanamoku's body.

NOTES

1. I would like to thank Mary Kay Van Sistine, Sophia Rose Willard-Van Sistine, John Bloom, Jeffrey Rangel, Krista Comer, and Henry Yu for their help with this essay. Any mistakes are, of course, my own.

On the economics of overthrow and annexation, see Noel J. Kent, *Hawaii: Islands under the Influence* (Honolulu: University of Hawaii Press, 1993); Thomas Kemper Hitch, *Islands in Transition: The Past, Present, and Future of Hawaii's Economy* (Honolulu: First Hawaiian Bank, 1992). Kent explains that the overthrow of the monarchy came at a time when "influential sectors of the oligarchy" were "proprietors of *four-fifths* of the arable land in the Islands, holding $23 million of the $33 million invested in sugar plantations." The idea of annexation was "accelerated by the McKinley Tariff of 1891 which allowed *all* sugar into the United States duty free (but provided for subsidies for U.S. domestic producers)" (59).

2. Elizabeth Buck, *Paradise Remade: The Politics of Culture and History in Hawai'i* (Philadelphia: Temple University Press, 1993), 76.

3. Joseph Brennan, *Duke: The Life History of Hawai'i's Duke Kahanamoku* (Honolulu: Ku Pa'a Publishing, 1994), 17–20; Charmian London's *Our Hawaii: Islands and Islanders* (1917; rev. ed., New York: Macmillan, 1922) contains a representative example of the paternalism tourists invested in their generosity when they threw coins from steamships. She describes the ceremonial held for the departure of a steamship that would take a group of U.S. congressmen who had been visiting the islands back to the mainland. After noting the multiracial scene of faces "from white through all the browns to yellow skins, mingling in good fellowship and oneness of spirit in this our farewell to the lawmakers of their common cause," in which the benevolence of the politicians is given emphasis, London describes the departure of the ship:

> As the huge black transport cleared, suddenly her surface seemed to be flying to pieces. A perfect fusilade of small dark objects in human form sprang from her sides, rails, rigging, from every height of ringbolt and sill, and disappeared in almost unrippling dives through the swirling blossomy [flower-strewn] carpet of the harbor.
>
> "Look—look at them!" Jack cried, incoherent with the excitement of his joy in the kanaka imps who entered the water so perfectly and came up shaking petals from their curly heads, white teeth flashing, their child faces eloquent with expectation of a lucrative shower from the passengers. A bountiful hour it was for them, and little their bright eyes and brown hands lost of the copper and silver disks that slowly angled through the bubbling flood. We wished we were down there with them, for it is great fun to pick a coin from the deep as it filters down with a short, tipping motion. (90–92)

In an excerpt from "The Autobiography of a Winnebago Indian," originally published by ethnologist Paul Radin in 1920, in Ronald Takaki, ed., *A Larger Memory: A History of Our Diversity, with Voices* (Boston: Little Brown, 1998), 74, is a similar account by a Winnebago man of time spent in his boyhood when his family went to town. He and his brother would take their bows and arrows and shoot five-cent pieces that whites placed as targets. Or he would let his brother shoot twenty-five-cent pieces held between his fingers. In this retelling the man explicitly ties the activity to the economic support of his family: "We would often make as much as five dollars in this manner and we always gave this money to our parents" (74). For a bibliography on Native Hawaiians and citizenship, see John Rosa, "Local Story: The Massie Case and the Politics of Local Identity in Hawai'i" (Ph.D. diss., University of California Irvine, 1999).

4. Virginia Domínguez, "Exporting U.S. Concepts of Race: Are There Limits to the U.S. Model?" *Social Research* 65,2 (Summer 1998): 369–399; Jane Desmond, *Staging Tourism: Bodies on Display from Waikiki to Sea World* (Chicago: University of Chicago Press, 1999).

5. Sandra Kimberly Hall and Greg Ambrose, *Memories of Duke: The Legend Comes to Life: Duke Kahanamoku, 1890–1968* (Honolulu: Bess Press, 1995), x and *passim.*

6. My analysis of the centrality of Kahanamoku's body to the construction of the gendered and racial ideologies of white civilization and national belonging owes a great debt to the scholarship of Philip Deloria and Hazel Carby. See Philip Deloria's essay "'I Am of the Body': Thoughts on My Grandfather, Culture and Sports," *South Atlantic Quarterly* 95,2 (Spring 1996): 321–338; Hazel Carby, *Race Men* (Cambridge, MA: Harvard University Press, 1998), esp. chap. 2 on Paul Robeson.

7. Henry Yu, "On a Stage Built by Others: Creating an Intellectual History of Asian America," *Amerasia Journal* 26,1 (2000): 141–161.

8. My understanding of the ways in which the complex interplay between American and Hawaiian traditions and values shaped "the Hawaiian social system" and led to the emergence of "local identity" comes from Jonathan Y. Okamura, "Aloha Kanaka Me Ke Aloha 'Aina: Local Culture and Society in Hawaii," *Amerasia Journal* 7,2 (1980): 119–137. Rosa, "Local Story," picks up on and further elaborates the history of local identity where Okamura leaves off. Rosa's study directed me to Okamura.

9. For a more extensive analysis of the relationship between concepts of race, gender, and civilization, see Gail Bederman, *Manliness and Civilization: A Cultural History of Gender and Race in the United States, 1880–1917* (Chicago: University of Chicago Press, 1995).

10. Carby, *Race Men*, provides a more extensive analysis of race and national belonging as they intersect with ideologies of masculinity.

11. Okamura, "Aloha Kanaka Me Ke Aloha ʻAina," 120.

12. James Clifford, *Routes: Travel and Translation in the Late Twentieth Century* (Cambridge, MA: Harvard University Press, 1997), provides a broader discussion of the arrival trope.

13. Jack London, *The Cruise of the Snark* (New York: Macmillan, 1911), 75–76.

14. One of London's contemporaries inadvertently called attention to the importance of London's Hawaiʻi writings to the promotion of tourism when he declared three articles that had been published in 1916 in the *Cosmopolitan Magazine* "as of a worth not to be estimated in gold and silver." See Charmian London, *Our Hawaii*, vii.

15. In his article "My Hawaiian Aloha: Three Articles by Jack London," in Charmian London, Our Hawaii, London refers to Hawaiʻi as a "smelting pot" (23).

16. London, Cruise of the Snark, 76–78.

17. Ibid., 78.

18. Catherine Lutz and Jane Collins, *Reading National Geographic* (Chicago: University of Chicago Press, 1993), 136; Desmond, *Staging Tourism*.

19. Lutz and Collins, *Reading National Geographic*, 177.

20. Desmond, *Staging Tourism*, 48.

21. Ibid. 58.

22. Ibid. 54.

23. Tom Blake, *Hawaiian Surfriders 135* (Redondo Beach, CA: Mountain and Sea Publishing, 1983); see also http://www.legendarysurfers.com/surf/legends/l504.html

24. Hitch, *Islands in Transition*, 301.

25. It is possible that some of these men are Native Hawaiian Portuguese.

26. Don Hibbard and David Franzen, *The View from Diamond Head: Royal Residence to Urban Resort* (Honolulu: Editions Unlimited, 1986).

27. Ibid., 75–76.

28. The irony of buildings coming from a zoo is that they had already been established as tourist icons, taken out of their Native Hawaiian context and "placed" in another set of institutional relations that produced a tourist rhetoric of civilization through contrast to savage, threatening, and thus inferior animal bodies. Zoo animals were also racialized, and their bodies were used to racialize human bodies by linking their beastly "natures" to the geographies of their original habitats in a racial hierarchy of places and nations.

29. Rosa, "Local Story," 84.

30. Hibbard and Franzen, *View from Diamond Head*, 76–77.

31. Hall and Ambrose, *Memories of Duke*, 81.

32. Ibid., x, 3. For another account, which includes reprints of newspaper articles written in 1911, see Brennan, *Duke*, 5–14.

33. Brennan, *Duke*.

34. Mark Dyreson, *Making the American Team: Sport, Culture and the Olympic Experience* (Urbana: University of Illinois Press, 1998), 157–158.

35. Deloria, "'I am of the Body,'" 327.

36. Ibid.

37. My understanding of the creation of acceptable de-historicized racial definitions of "Blackness" comes from Carby, *Race Men*.

38. For an extensive explanation of the high value placed on water throughout the history of Hawaiian culture, see George Hu'eu Sanford Kanahele, *Ku Kanaka, Stand Tall: A Search for Hawaiian Values* (Honolulu: University of Hawaii Press, 1986).

39. Alexander Hume Ford, "Announcement," *Mid-Pacific Magazine* 1,1 (January 1911); inside front cover.

40. Duke Paoa [Kahanamoku], "Riding the Surf," *Mid-Pacific Magazine* 1,1 (January 1911): 2.

41. Okamura, "Aloha Kanaka Me Ke Aloha 'Aina," 122, cautions against a "sanguine notion of Hawai'i as a 'laboratory of race relations' where peoples of sharply differing traditions are able to live together in harmony with one another."

42. Ibid.; Rosa, "Local Story."

43. Okamura, "Aloha Kanaka Me Ke Aloha 'Aina," 120.

44. Ibid.; Rosa, "Local Story."

45. Brennan, *Duke*, 22.

46. Brennan, 20–23; see Hibbard and Franzen, *The View from Diamond Head* for a photo of the hau tree.

47. Okamura, "Aloha Kanaka Me Ke Aloha 'Aina."

48. Hall and Ambrose, *Memories of Duke*, 124.

49. Brennan, *Duke*, 22,30.

50. As quoted in Hall and Ambrose, *Memories of Duke*, 138.

51. W. E. B. DuBois, "To the Nations of the World," *Report of the Pan-African Conference*, in Herbert Aptheker, ed., *Writings by W.E.B. DuBois in Non-Periodical Literature Edited by Others* (Millwood, NY: Kraus-Thomson, 1982), 11–12, cited in David Levering Lewis, *W. E. B. DuBois: Biography of a Race* (New York: Henry Holt, 1993), 249–251.

52. Ibid., 250.

53. W. E. B. DuBois, "The Crisis," *Crisis* 1 (November 1910): 10, quoted in Michael Fultz, "'The Morning Cometh': African-American Periodicals, Education, and the Black Middle Class, 1900–1930," in James P. Danky and Wayne A. Wiegand, eds., *Print Culture in a Diverse America* (Urbana: University of Illinois Press, 1998), 132.

54. John Rosa, "Local Story," cites articles from *The Crisis* that covered developments in the Massie trial in the 1930s. Rosa also cites articles from the *Chicago Defender* that drew attention to similarities between the Massie trial and the Scottsboro trial.

55. Henry Lee Moon, ed., *The Emerging Thought of W. E. B. DuBois: Essays and*

Editorials from The Crisis *with an Introduction, Commentaries and a Personal Memoir* (New York: Simon and Schuster, 1972), 389.

56. Herbert Aptheker, ed., *The Correspondence of W. E. B. DuBois,* vol. 3 (Amherst: University of Massachusetts Press, 1978), 340–341.

Chapter Two

Jump for Joy
Jump Blues, Dance, and Basketball in 1930s African America[1]

Gena Caponi-Tabery

Former Boston Celtics player and coach Bill Russell wrote,

> People in all kinds of cultures are known to "jump for joy" in moments of supreme happiness. Jumping is an internationally recognized expression of joy, and basketball is a sport organized around jumping. . . . It's possible for a player to jump because he's happy, but it's more likely that he's happy because he's jumping. I have heard players complain about almost every detail of the game—the rules, the size or color of the ball, the shape or temperature of the dressing room—but I've never heard anybody complain about the fact that the game requires jumping.[2]

Yet the game didn't always require jumping. Russell remembers playing ball in high school in the 1950s, at a time when jump shots were exclusively associated with African American players and traditionalists benched players for taking jump shots. The jump shot was part of a distinctively black style of play and began to appear about 1937, when the National Basketball Committee introduced a rule change that indirectly made the shot possible. That same year, Count Basie recorded "One O'-Clock Jump," and soon the words *stomp* and *shuffle* disappeared from the titles of jazz recordings, replaced by the word *jump*. Only a year before, the Lindy Hop, also called the jitterbug, had begun to include jumping "air steps." Jump tunes, the jumping jitterbug, and jump shots all burst out of the same arenas, at a time when dance bands traveled with basketball teams and clubs across the country hosted predance basketball games.

These forms of expressive culture are connected through site, impulse, cultural meaning, and a common gesture: the jump. Coinciding with late 1930s America's lust for the airborne and for speed, the jump for African Americans embodied rising confidence, assertiveness, and enthusiasm. Reflecting "the accelerated tempo of black life during and after the urban migration as well as an upbeat sense of expanded possibility," nothing better captured the feeling of spiritual uplift and hopes for upward mobility than this intersection of dance, music, and sport.[3] The jump symbolized and expressed joy in the present and optimism for the future.

Jump blues, dance, and basketball embodied blackness in America and then diffused into American popular culture. An exclusively African American dance during the late 1920s, during and after World War II the Lindy Hop came to symbolize American culture all over the world. In 1959, looking back on a career that began before the Lindy Hop, veteran dancer George Wendler sadly acknowledged that the Lindy had changed American dance forever. "I don't recall any conservative style of dancing making a hit since the Lindy revolution."[4] In the mid-1940s, jump tunes evolved into jump blues, a stubbornly rhythmic and identifiably black offshoot of swing music. In the 1940s, the word *jump* superseded *race* as a designation for African American blues.[5] By the late 1940s, "jump" was used interchangeably with "rhythm and blues," the African American predecessor of what became rock and roll, which has dominated American popular music for nearly half a century. Basketball's jump shot and the fast-break style signified blackness up to the 1960s, when they began to dominate the game.

Jump tunes, the jitterbug, and fast-break basketball were interconnected elements of an African American cultural life to which bodily expression was central. The music, dance, and basketball of that time amounted to self-conscious assertions of ethnicity in social rituals of affirmation, celebration, and play.[6] But because they evolved and diffused so thoroughly throughout contemporary American popular culture, it is easy to forget that original message.

The Ones with Slow Feet Are the First You Cut

In late 1930s African America, music, dance, and sport converged in a single expressive gesture, captured by the word *jump*. Yet juncture of these three different disciplines is easy to overlook: while some scholars have noted the interdependence of music and dance, few have thought to include sports.[7] An exception might be historian David Stowe, who, in *Swing Changes*, cites parallels between music and baseball—the constant touring and pressures of performing—and notes that swing bands on tour often played pickup games. But virtually all historians have ignored the obvious connections between basketball and jazz in the 1930s. And while this element may be invisible to contemporary historians, it was very much a part of 1930s social life.

Both basketball and dancing were indoor forms of physical entertainment, relying on expert bodies and active crowds; and combining the two made the best use of all resources, not the least of which was hardwood flooring. By the 1930s, basketball had replaced track and baseball as the second most popular sport on college campuses, but professional basketball struggled for places to play. For a brief period in the 1930s, the professional game moved to theater stages, but most teams played on a makeshift circuit of armories, high school and college gyms, and dance halls.[8]

Ballrooms regularly booked basketball games before dances or when no dance was scheduled. Chicago's Savoy Ballroom had its own team, the Savoy Big Five (who became the Harlem Globetrotters), as did New York's Renaissance Casino. Many other cities also held combination basketball and dance events. Philadelphia, Pittsburgh, Kansas City, and Brooklyn regularly hosted professional teams and top-notch bands—the Bennie Moten Orchestra played after games in Kansas City.[9] At the college level, basketball games often ended with dances. At least one team—the all-black Alabama State Hornets—traveled with their own dance band: Erskine Hawkins's 'Bama State Collegians, a favorite on campuses across the country.

Black youth often played basketball at community centers because few black high schools and relatively few colleges could afford gymnasiums, and black youth who attended integrated schools often were not allowed to participate in school activities.[10] Former professional player and columnist Cumberland "Cum" Posey wrote that during his early years of playing in Pittsburgh, black youth were allowed in only one gym for two hours a week, when "every colored boy in Allegheny county who owned a pair of rubber soled shoes" would crowd the floor. Then, in 1915, a group of basketball enthusiasts saw potential in the Labor Temple and rented it for basketball and dances.[11] Posey complained that, even then, the few large halls available to black players in Pittsburgh were "not really suitable to develop exceptional talent."[12]

The nation's premier black professional team, the New York Renaissance, or Rens, traveled almost constantly and played their home games in the Renaissance Casino over Thanksgiving and Christmas holidays. With the addition of baskets and markers for the foul lines, the high-ceilinged ballroom became a basketball court. A musicians' bandstand flanked one side of the court, and spectators sat at tables arranged in three tiers behind a wooden barrier. Rens star William (Pop) Gates remembered players "flying over that barrier into people's laps" while playing on the "very slippery floor."[13]

For African Americans across the country, the Rens belonged to the pantheon of African American public achievers, with celebrity status equivalent to the bandleaders and musicians of the day.[14] The high-profile Rens and Harlem Globetrotters represented success in one of the few areas of American life where competition between the races was permitted. The first time that the organizers of basketball's World Tournament invited both black teams was 1939, and the Rens won the championship, defeating the Oshkosh All-Stars in the final game. The Rens finished that year with 122 wins in 129 games, and the New York *Evening Telegram* declared, "They are the champions of professional basketball in the whole world. It is time we dropped the 'colored' champions title."[15]

Combining basketball and dancing was a shrewd marketing move, designed to promote the young sport. New York Rens' star Eyre Saitch recalled, "We had to have a dance afterwards, or else nobody would come to the damn thing."[16] John J. O'Brien Jr., who played at the casino with the Brooklyn Visitations, remembered, "The fans were the wealthiest black people in Harlem, dressed, believe it or not, in tuxedos. A good-looking crowd—handsome women, good-looking guys—and they loved the basketball game, but they loved to get the game over for dancing afterward."[17]

In the Renaissance Casino and many other places, basketball players were among those dancing after games, which raises the question of who inspired whom to jump. Whether the cultural exchange flowed from musicians to dancers to basketball players or from basketball players to dancers to musicians, all were connected to one another. College coach Clarence "Big House" Gaines said of his players in the 1940s, "Those kids were all excellent dancers. To be a good basketball player you have to have an excellent sense of rhythm and good feet. The ones with slow feet were the first you cut."[18] The different forms of jump marked the brightest points in these social constellations that writer Albert Murray christened "ceremonies of affirmation."[19] Linking these expressions was a common tradition based on an aesthetic and philosophy more African than European.[20]

Jumping swing tunes, dances, and high-jumping basketball games were festive events of "black cultural unity," social rituals whose underlying purpose was "confrontation, improvisation, affirmation, celebration."[21] Pioneering play theorist Johan Huizinga wrote that sport and play provide "the stylizing of the very feeling of youth, strength, and life, a spiritual value of enormous weight. Play is culture."[22] Play occurs in a playground—a "closed space . . . hedged off from ordinary life," in Huizinga's words, "forbidden spots, isolated, hedged round, hallowed, within which special rules obtain. All are temporary worlds within the ordinary world dedicated to the performance of an act apart."[23]

With regard to black-white relations in the 1930s, African American nightclubs and dance halls functioned as democratic islands—or playgrounds—of neutrality, where ordinary social restrictions, such as segregation, were laid aside. As the 1930s drew to a close, more venues than ever began to draw mixed audiences, and white Americans caught an eyeful and earful of what people of color could do in music, dance, and sport on these very narrow but level playing fields.

Music, dance, and sport flowed into, out of, and within community gatherings, connecting participants to the community and to one another. Sociologist Ray Oldenburg says that communities create and sustain themselves in informal public gathering places, which he calls the "third place," a "generic designation for a great variety of public places that host the regular, voluntary, informal, and happily anticipated gatherings of individuals beyond the realms of home and work."[24] Oldenburg found third places to be "levelers" where status distinctions were laid aside. Within third places, Oldenburg discovered, "the charm and flavor of one's personality, irrespective of his or her station in life, is what counts." Where third places exist, even the poorest member of society has access to a richly "engaging and sustaining public life."[25] In beauty shops, barber shops, pool halls, dance halls, gymnasiums, and playgrounds, community life flourishes and individual personalities stylize conversation, dance, and play.

The celebration of African American cultural life in a racist society is by definition subversive, and African American third places were places of contestation of racism as much as celebration of race. In such marginal and oppositional sites, black and white youth drew together to flout the conventions and restrictions of middle-class society, in a harmony of the underclasses that scholars such as W. T. Lhamon and Dale Cockrell argue has existed since at least the eighteenth century.[26]

Ceremonies of Affirmation

Through the decade culminating in World War II, swing music, of which jump was a particular variety, exemplified the American melting pot. Duke Ellington's 1932 "It Don't Mean a Thing (If It Ain't Got That Swing)" gave the music and the era its name, and if audiences hadn't heard the black swing bands firsthand, they had heard Ellington's Cotton Club broadcasts on the CBS and NBC radio networks. In February 1937, when Ellington played for President Franklin Roosevelt's Birthday Ball, that, too, was broadcast on radio. In 1938, Ellington melodies provided themes for thirty-seven different radio programs.[27] Of the 50 million records of all types sold in 1939, an estimated 17 million—over one-third—were swing, a style that African American musicians pioneered. Stowe wrote, "Not since the heyday of blackface minstrelsy in the decades before the Civil War had America been forced to confront so directly its indebtedness to African-American culture, to acknowledge that its culture was unmistakably formed by a racial group systematically excluded from its society."[28]

Although audiences were often integrated, bands seldom were, and in 1938 news of an integrated concert at Carnegie Hall swept the country. At the highly publicized January 16 event, Benny Goodman and trumpeter Harry James performed with members of the Count Basie band, while pianist Teddy Wilson and vibraharpist Lionel Hampton joined Goodman and drummer Gene Krupa on stage. Attendance that night was thirty-nine hundred, larger than that for the New York Philharmonic, and thousands more read about it afterward.

Few Americans knew that after the 1938 Carnegie Hall concert, Goodman and his musicians, along with Ellington and many others, rushed to Harlem's Savoy Ballroom to witness the battle between the Chick Webb and Count Basie orchestras, both African American. Drummer Chick Webb's band, the local favorite, let loose a "sensational, whirl-wind barrage," while Basie's blues-oriented band "devoted its attack to the body, to the heart." At Carnegie Hall, when dancers crowded the aisles, ushers urged them to return to their seats; but the Savoy was not for bystanders. Four thousand dancers packed the hall that night, and another five thousand were turned away. Although a splendid array of musical luminaries witnessed the competition, it was the dancers who, at one o'clock in the morning, delivered the verdict: Basie bested Webb. Unlike the Carnegie Hall concert, the Savoy battle of the bands emphasized physical participation over spectatorship, "dissolving the barriers between performers and audience, by making the 'spectators' co-creators of cultural meaning through their dancing, cheers, and partisanship."[29] Invisible to the majority of white Americans, the contest at the Savoy stood in opposition to the Carnegie Hall concert, participatory and body-oriented, simultaneously the vanguard and hinterland of American popular culture.

Historian John Hope Franklin attributes the surge of artistic activity in Harlem during the 1920s and 1930s to the newly formed sense of community and self-confidence emanating from the masses who had migrated from the south to the urban north.[30] Such a "massive concentration of Black experiential energy," to quote poet Stephen Henderson, nurtured and boosted community consciousness and expression.[31] Swing music and dance offered "an urban model of freedom . . . in the big band form."[32] Examples of upward economic and geographic mobility, the big bands fused African American idioms with modern sensibilities, improvisation with structure and tradition.

Basketball also flourished in the city, where immigrants from Europe and the south settled. Most schoolyards and playgrounds had a hoop, and if they didn't, players could make their own. Some teams were organized along ethnic lines: the Original Celtics, Olson's Terrible Swedes, and the Buffalo Germans were among the great white teams of the 1920s and 1930s. But there were also Chinese (the Hong Wah Q'ues), and African American teams, and an all-women's team called the Red Heads. Jews dominated the sport: some estimates suggest that half of all players in the American Basketball League in the 1930s were Jewish.[33] Industries sponsored teams: players on these teams were company employees, paid to work but hired for their basketball skills. Some businesses would sponsor a team but cede all its operations to a basketball expert, while others ran their own teams.[34] There were also independents, such as the Buffalo Bisons and the Pittsburgh Young Men's Hebrew Association. Few of these teams paid well and work was seasonal, so professional athletes in the 1930s often played for more than one team.

Basketball is called "the city game," but people played basketball in rural areas and small towns too, sometimes nailing a tire rim to a tree. Barnstorming teams traveled throughout the country, concentrating on games in the midwest and west, where attendance was often ten times that of games on the East Coast. Particular styles of play were associated with particular regions of the country, and coaches recruited from regions or towns known for the style or skill they needed. Smaller cities and towns held games and dances in every location imaginable: barns, auditoriums, armories, skating rinks, warehouses, roadhouses, and open fields.[35]

The newest styles in basketball, dance, and jazz spread across the country through transportation and communication networks connecting African Americans nationwide. One such network was the Brotherhood of Sleeping Car Porters. Operating as a reverse underground railroad, porters smuggled African American newspapers into the south by transporting papers to local ministers, who then delivered them to parishioners.[36] In 1937 the Brotherhood of Sleeping Car Porters pulled off a highly publicized and successful strike, winning their first contract with the Pullman Company, and one that reduced working hours, increased wages, and gave them job security and union representation. Since the Pullman Company provided one of the few middle-class jobs available to African American men, the porters' union contract resonated throughout African America and raised hopes for future advances.

Another event with real and symbolic aftereffects also occurred in 1937, when Joe Louis defeated James J. Braddock to become the second—and youngest ever—Negro heavyweight champion of the world and the most recognized black man in history. Louis's win ignited celebrations in black communities across the country—thousands stayed up all night in Chicago, Harlem, Detroit, and Pittsburgh, in celebration and affirmation of Louis's victory. Louis remembered, "Black people were calling out saying, 'We got another chance' . . . We're depending on you."[37] One headline in the *Pittsburgh Courier* captured the sentiment: "Fight of the Century—Joe Louis vs Jim-Crow."[38]

Fighting to become a champion in a world that refused him social equality, Louis defeated opponents more powerful than those he met in the ring. When Louis fought Germany's Max Schmeling in 1938, he told fans he was fighting "for America against the challenge of a foreign invader." The event marked boxing's first million-dollar gate, and while seventy thousand fans cheered at Yankee Stadium, millions more listened on radio. Louis leveled Schmeling in the first round, cracking his spine in two places, and his victory was a national triumph.[39] During World War II, the laconic Louis became America's unofficial spokesman with the famous unifying phrase "We will win, because we are on God's side." Never before had white Americans embraced a black man as their representative to the world.

No athlete of the day, and no other African American, was more greatly respected and revered than Joe Louis, who became, in the words of Gerald Early, "the greatest, the most expansive and mythical blues hero in twentieth-century America, nothing less." While some black intellectuals of the day may have believed a mere boxer an unworthy model to emulate, Louis was getting an average of three hundred letters a day from fans, hundreds of whom wrote to tell him that they were naming their sons after him.[40] Historian Thomas Sowell remembers of Louis, "How he fared in the ring mattered more to black Americans than the fate of any other athlete in any other sport, before or since. He was all we had."[41] Novelist Richard Wright stated it as clearly as one could: "Joe was the concentrated essence of black triumph over white."[42] Trumpeter Dizzy Gillespie wrote that he identified with Joe Louis: "Black people appreciate my playing in the same way I looked up to Paul Robeson or to Joe Louis. When Joe would knock out someone, I'd say, 'Hey . . . ! and felt like I'd scored a knockout. Just because of his prowess in the field and because he's black like me."[43]

The same black bourgeoisie who repudiated Louis rejected jazz, swing, and the dances of the Savoy as unworthy representations of black genius. Yet Louis and other outstanding athletes and entertainers of the day were conspicuous black achievers in a racist society that discouraged black achievement. They symbolized—and demonstrated—the possibility of fulfillment in a world that otherwise offered little. Perhaps the elite deplored mere physical accomplishments, but it was these very acts that gave the prospect of any improvement at all to the lives of hundreds of thousands of African Americans. To demean or to ignore such deeds because they happened in the gymnasium or dance hall instead of in the laboratory or halls of academe is to discount the value of symbolic action in the lives of ordinary people.

Up, Up, and Away

The year 1938 marked the debut of a new superhero in *Action Comics*: Superman.[44] Exclaiming, "Up, up, and away!" Superman was more powerful than a locomotive and able to leap tall buildings at a single bound. This fantastic jumping seemed somehow a muscular interpretation of American technological progress. Mobility, speed, and flight were the bywords of the era, and in swing music and dance, these values became human. Music critic Stanley Dance compared a swing band to "an airplane taking off after roaring down a runway."[45] And jumping swing dancers found they could almost fly. At the same time, basketball and football took to the air: both the forward pass and the jump shot appeared in the 1930s.[46] Nearly every part of American culture seemed poised to leap into the future.

For African Americans, the jump that would take the country forward had deep roots in the past. It was a lively dance, a bouncy kind of tune, a way of partying, a basketball move, a children's game, a synonym for "joyful." To "jump in" meant to become involved; to "jump salty" meant to become suddenly angry; the word also held sexual connotations.[47] "Jumping" described a state of mind and a way of behaving: nervous, excited, playful, energetic, joyful, angry, or simply having fun.

African American secular music is full of words that mean different things on different levels and in different arenas that are somehow all connected. "Ragtime" may refer to a genre of music, to the "ragged time" (syncopation) characteristic of the music, to African American clog dancing, to the headrags dancers often wore, to the rags that were hoisted outside a barn or meeting hall to signal a dance, or to rags stuffed in the cracks of cabin walls to block out Sunday morning's light.[48] So, too, "boogie-woogie," "swing," "blues," "jazz," "scat," "rock and roll," and "rap" carry different levels of meaning, bridging these levels at the same time.

Widespread use of the term *jump*, historically connected to children's play, athleticism, dance, and joy itself, does not appear with frequency in popular recordings until after 1937, when Count Basie recorded "One O'Clock Jump," one of many late 1930s swing tunes that "jumped" or that were called "jumps." Brian Rust's *Jazz Records 1897–1942* lists 114 titles in which the word *jump* appears: 105 of these tunes were recorded between 1937 and 1942.[49] By the late 1930s, jump tunes were the specialty of small rhythm bands that "made the customers want to jump and dance."[50]

Before 1937, other words described vernacular dance. The 1921 hit musical *Shuffle Along* probably established the word *shuffle* as a generic term for African American dance.[51] "Stomp" is another term that appeared on many dance recordings of the 1920s and early 1930s.[52] The change from the sideways shuffle and the downward stomp to the upward jump reflects not simply a new style of music but a public naming and claiming of an increasingly upbeat attitude. As Albert Murray notes, the most distinctive characteristic of jump tunes was their "upbeat" nature.

Both musicians and dancers "jumped," and musicians freely acknowledge the inspiration they got from dancers. Dickie Wells, who played at the Savoy during the 1940s, said, "The Lindy Hoppers there made you watch your P's and Q's. The dancers would come and tell you if you didn't play. They made the guys play, and they'd stand in front patting their hands until you got the right tempo."[53]

The dance that cemented relations among musicians and dancers between the wars was the Lindy.

Although it had been around Harlem since the 1920s and began to be called the Lindbergh Hop in 1927, the lindy evolved at the Savoy Ballroom during the mid-1930s. Once described as "choreographed swing music," the Lindy "flowed horizontally and smoothly," with a syncopated two-step or box step accenting the offbeat.[54] The Lindy—or jitterbug—became a truly national sensation in the late 1930s. Its emphasis on couples dancing apart changed American social dance forever, and its breakaway persists in contemporary hip-hop. The Lindy Hop has been called the only true American folk dance; it revolutionized American dance, and that of the rest of the world as well.

The crucial point in the evolution of the Lindy, according to jazz and dance historian Marshall Stearns, was the splitting of Lindy dancers into two groups: those who used floor steps and those who used air steps. Air steps, or aerials, an innovation in which one partner lifted, flipped, tossed, or threw the other in the air, began to appear in New York in 1936.[55] Young dancers Frankie Manning and Frieda Washington introduced air steps to the Lindy during a competition at the Savoy Ballroom. For months, Manning and Washington—who were Harlem neighbors—practiced the step where she flipped over his back. The trick, Manning said, wasn't getting up but coming down: what they had to get right was the landing. It had to be on the beat. "We worked on it every single day till we got it down to a point where I could bring her over every single time in time with the music." The night of the competition, Manning says, the Chick Webb band was playing. "I was having a good time," Manning said, "and Frieda said, 'Yeah, let's go for it.' I flipped her over, she landed—bam." Webb, who had never before seen this move but was watching, crashed down on his drums just as Washington hit the floor. "The Savoy Ballroom just exploded," Manning says, and the contest was called, then and there.[56]

Manning and Washington danced for Whitey's Lindy Hoppers, amateur dancers handpicked from the Savoy Ballroom dance floor and trained by former prizefighter Herbert White. Whitey's Lindy Hoppers specialized in exactly the kind of athletic abandon that dismayed some African American leaders and dominated showbusiness dance jobs for nearly a half-dozen years. Their innovations spread throughout the country via feature-length films, newsreels, short "soundies," and Broadway appearances.[57]

Many sophisticated white New York clubs had no room for dancing. But African American swing audiences expected to dance, and dancers and musicians inspired each other to greater heights. "The bands seemed to be swinging faster every night," said one Savoy dancer, "and all the best dancers could follow them, in new and different ways."[58] White dancers who wanted to learn the latest steps traveled to the Savoy in New York or to black clubs in other cities. John Martin, dance critic for the *New York Times*, visited the Savoy and wrote, "Of all the ballroom dancing these prying eyes have seen, this is unquestionably the finest."[59]

Perhaps the climax in the Lindy's stage presence occurred during the late 1930s, in a show-stopping scene at Radio City Music Hall when a group of Whitey's Lindy Hoppers, performing in the stage show titled *The World of Tomorrow*, rebelled and took over the show. Marshall and Jean Stearns describe the moment when the Lindy Hoppers began "ignoring the accompaniment and clapping their hands and stomping their feet to give themselves some kind of beat. They even screamed and hollered encouragement to each other. In fact, they forgot where they were, and their dancing improved astonishingly. Whereupon the huge audience forgot where it was, too, and began to clap, stomp, scream, and holler, but more loudly." While the show's star literally hung in the wings, suspended from wires and waiting to swoop onto stage, the audience cheered the Lindy Hoppers for five curtain calls. The next day they received their checks and were told not to perform at the music hall again.[60]

It was the newly improvised air steps that propelled the Lindy to nationwide fame.[61] When the Lindy went airborne, it projected the energy not only of the young African American jitterbuggers but of the future itself. The beauty of the Lindy was the way it allowed dancers to stylize, authorizing each version with innovation and personality, retaining individuality in the midst of a group exercise. By endowing their dancing with personal style, Lindy dancers managed to keep from being simply faces in the crowd.

Yet the faces of the style's originators faded into invisibility. When the Lindy made it to the cover of *Life* magazine in 1943, all the dancers pictured were white. White jitterbuggers began to appear in movies, while the dance's inventors were forgotten. Whitey's Lindy Hoppers disbanded when many of their members were drafted, including Frankie Manning, who joined Betty Grable onstage in the Philippines for one memorable USO (United Service Organizations) performance. By that time the Lindy was no longer considered black vernacular dance but rather a symbol of America itself.[62]

"That's Not Basketball": Barring Black Basketball

In the 1990s, the symbol of American culture across the globe was not Joe Louis or a Lindy-Hopping serviceman but Michael Jordan, whose fan club is called simply "Jump, Inc." Michael Jordan, whom novelist John Edgar Wideman called the "truest prophet of what might be possible," made a career of jumping, "whittling and expanding simultaneously the territory in which the game is enacted . . . soaring and swooping, extending, refining the combat zone of basketball into a fourth, outer, other dimension, the dreamy ozone of flight without wings."[63] Michael Eric Dyson writes that Jordan's body is "the symbolic carrier of racial and cultural desires to fly beyond limits and obstacles, a fluid metaphor or mobility and ascent to heights of excellence secured by genius and industry."[64] Jordan was the 1990s equivalent of the Greek hero-figure, the "visible emblem of the human spirit victorious in its perpetual combat to overcome the world."[65] Most significant, Jordan institutionalized a style of basketball historically associated with and introduced to the game by black players.

Basketball has changed since its invention by a white man in 1891. In the 1930s, it was still a young sport and bore little resemblance to today's more spectacular fast-breaking, slam-dunking, and jumping game. Games were considerably slower than today's, and final scores often did not exceed the twenties.[66] After each basket, players returned to centercourt for a tip-off, which made for a slow, half-court game. As early as 1928, several college conferences began to experiment with eliminating the center jump, but it was not until 1937 that the National Basketball Committee rejected the center tip-off after every score. Faster, running-style teams immediately began using what was then called the "racehorse" maneuver, today known as the "fast break."[67]

Clarence "Big House" Gaines, basketball coach for forty-six years at Winston-Salem State, remembers fast-break style in the 1940s. "In fast-break basketball, players would run, jump, and throw at the same time," he

says. Gaines says the one-handed shot and the jump evolved along with
the fast break. "You don't throw a ball with two hands in any other sport.
Shooting with one hand is a natural reaction. If a player's got good hands
and good skills and he's running, he's not going to stop and use two
hands. The jump just came along with it."[68]

Coach Calvin "Cal" Irvin of North Carolina A&T also attributes the rise
of fast-break basketball to the innovations and improvisations of African
American players. "What we were playing [in the 1940s] in the Afro-
American colleges, that's the kind of basketball they're playing now. . . . It
was a fast-paced basketball. We didn't have the slowdown, holding the ball.
We didn't need the thirty-five-second clock; we never held onto it that
long. It was not exactly run-and-gun, but it had a lot of run-and-gun in it.
. . . What we called 'Our Basketball' is the basketball you are playing
today."[69]

Like bandleaders, basketball coaches who encouraged an African American style required their players both to improvise as soloists and to col-
laborate as part of an ensemble. "Basketball is a situation game; a reaction
game," says Gaines. "You can't call 'play number one.' You have to learn to
adjust and adapt to the defense. Most of the kids didn't have the movements, the rhythm, to innovate."[70] The fast break depended on improvisation, as in swing music or the Lindy Hop when musicians took off on solo
flights or couples briefly broke away from each other to improvise solo
steps. And while it is true that other sports allow players to improvise, to
perform virtuosically, or to create a personal style of play, basketball depends on fluid interaction among a group of players whose roles are inter-
changeable, any one of whom may score at any moment, and any one of
whom may showcase a personal style or "trademark" in the process of
scoring. No other sport so closely resembles the flow and flair of jazz and
jazz dance.

Basketball styles varied from region to region, but African American
teams played a style different from that of most of the white teams. When
former Howard University player "Showboat" Ware joined Pittsburgh's
Iron City Elks, a sportswriter described him "flashing the form that made
him so well known all along the Eastern coast" while "hooking [shots] in
with one hand under the hoop or calmly dropping them in from the side
court."[71] When the Virginia Union Panthers and Kentucky State College
beat the undefeated (and Eastern College Tournament champion) Long
Island University Blackbirds in early April 1939, the Negro press was ecsta-

tic in praising a style of ballplaying that could win over opponents from better-funded white universities.[72]

Fast-break basketball was part of an African American aesthetic, and white coaches often denounced it as such. In addition to the fast break and the jump shot, the African American style included fancy passing, at which the New York Rens excelled. "The Rens' specialty was blinding speed and passing," writes Frank Davis. "So swiftly did they whip the ball from one player to another that often competing athletes quit and, placing hands on hips, watched as if they were spectators."[73] An African American team who beat a white team in those days could not afford to resort to the "roughness and holding that was the trademark of the American League."[74] Instead, they relied on "flashy work," passing described as "dazzling," shooting that was "uncanny," and a "magic pattern of speed and deception."[75]

The fast break, jump shot, and fancy ball handling were branded "Negro basketball" for several decades.[76] Yet, in the official history of sports, white players are routinely given credit for introducing or developing these key innovations.[77] Stephen Fox's *Big League*, the most recent book to trace the history of the jump shot, fails to mention a single African American player who contributed to its development. The most often mentioned jump shooter of the 1930s was Stanford's white all-American Angelo "Hank" Luisetti, who was taking unorthodox one-handed shots as early as 1936. Luisetti was revolutionary because he shot on the run and occasionally from a soft jump, rising all of two inches off the floor. Robert Peterson, a sports historian with perspective, objects to calling this a jump shot, saying that in a true jump shot "the player springs high and releases the ball at the apex of his jump."[78] Still, Luisetti's one-handed shots shocked and enthralled spectators when Stanford defeated Long Island University at Madison Square Garden in December 1936, by a score of forty-five to thirty-one. Luisetti scored fifteen points. The next morning the *New York Times* proclaimed, "It seemed Luisetti could do nothing wrong. . . . Some of his shots would have been deemed foolhardy if attempted by anybody else, but with Luisetti shooting, these were accepted by the enchanted crowd."[79] Nat Holman, coach at City College of New York, was not among the spellbound. "That's not basketball," he complained. "If my boys ever shot one-handed, I'd quit coaching."[80]

Other white players are singled out in the history of the one-handed jump shot. Fox mentions John Cooper from western Kentucky, who in three years of varsity ball at the University of Missouri in the early 1930s never saw anybody else shoot a jumper. Neither did Glenn Roberts from western Virginia, who used the jump shot at Emory and Henry College and on the Dayton and Akron Firestone teams in the late 1930s (But were they playing African Americans? We are not told.) "Jumping" Jim Pollard led Stanford to an NCAA (National Collegiate Athletic Association) championship in 1942.[81] Wyoming's Kenny Sailors "dazzled" Garden audiences in the 1943 NIT (National Invitational Tournament) championship.[82] Sportswriters said Sailors's jump shot was an innovation from the west that East Coast teams had to copy if they wanted to stay competitive. "Jumping" Joe Fulks, a six-foot five-inch "self-described hillbilly" who played for Murray State Teachers College in western Kentucky, captivated crowds in 1946 with his "turnaround jumpers" for the Washington Capitols. Sports historians say he was the "first to exploit the shot to the fullest," while Bud Palmer is said to have "pioneered" the jump shot in the east, playing for Princeton in the late 1940s.[83] Historians hail Paul Arizin as a trailblazer as late as the 1950s, when he took Villanova to the nation's lead in scoring with a "spectacular low-trajectory jump shot."[84] The point is, these players stand out among white players because everyone knew the jump shot was part of Negro ball.

The jump shot's history among African American players has not been explored, but evidence of it crops up from time to time and increases after 1937. Pittsburgh's Loendi Five center Cum Posey wrote about a 1918 game against the Jewish Original Coffey Club in which he scored the winning basket with "a one hand shot through the nets."[85] When this "Negro" play was adopted by white players, opponents, fans, sportswriters, and historians took note. In March 1937, three months after Long Island watched its team lose to Luisetti's, the Long Island University Blackbirds hailed the play of their first African American athlete, freshman William "Dolly" King, a three-sport letterman from Brooklyn's Alexander Hamilton High.[86] That year King became the first black player in the National AAU (Amateur Athletic Union) tournament. In his history of African American basketball, Arthur Ashe names "Dolly" King as one of the leading contributors to a developing and distinctive black style.[87]

In a history of college basketball, Neil D. Isaacs calls King "the first black star to shine in the all-white college game."[88] Pronouncements like these perpetuate themselves; yet King's visibility ought to signal the invisibility of other black players. Basketball at the college level was hardly all white: there were countless black players in all-black college games across the country, and several black players shone on mainly white college teams. Arthur Ashe's roster of African American *stars* (his term) on white college basketball teams begins in 1904, including eight before 1918, the most notable of whom was Paul Robeson, playing for Rutgers from 1915 to 1918. The list of black players at white colleges from 1920 to 1946 numbers twenty-four, including Jackie Robinson at UCLA from 1939 to 1941.

Frank "Doc" Kelker, another black player in white college games, played for Western Reserve beginning in 1937. Like Robinson, Kelker was a star athlete, in football and basketball. Writers in the *Pittsburgh Courier* said Kelker shot baskets the same way he bagged passes on the football field, "leaping high above his opponents and throwing the ball far from danger."[89] The description is vague, but it could be a jump shot. Photos of Kelker in the black press show him several feet off the floor, and headlines proclaim "Kelker Outjumps Opponent," although most of these jumps seem to have been to tap the ball in the basket rather than execute true jump shots.[90] Kelker was also fast and delighted fans by tipping the ball to a teammate from the center line, dashing under the basket, taking a pass and "bagging" a basket, a half-court version of the full-court fast break.[91] After college, Kelker formed a professional team, dubbed Kelker's Log Cabin Big Five, playing out of Cleveland.[92]

Kelker and King were not called "Jumping" Kelker or "Jumping" King, probably because jumping was not unusual for African American players. In a land where red hair abounds, no one is called Red. The jump was part of the developing and culturally distinct Negro style of play, and reports of African American teams after 1937 who defeated their opponents by out-jumping them are not unusual.[93] Although the professional teams played "a more deliberate and set style of game," reports of professional games occasionally mention the heights achieved by their players.[94]

Some white players who were exposed to the jump immediately saw its potential. Bob Davies, who played for Seton Hall from 1941 on, recalled his early exposure to basketball in his hometown, Harrisburg, Pennsylvania, during the 1930s: "When I was a kid I couldn't afford to pay to see the high school team, so we would look through a crack in the door. The only thing I could see was the foul-lane area and the basket at the other end of the court. I'd see these great black players *jump in the air*, throw the ball, hit somebody with a pass, or *shoot the ball*, and I guess that stuck in my mind. I think that's what helped me to become a playmaker" (my emphasis).[95] Bob Davies became one of the best ball handlers of the game; his name and deeds are recorded in every basketball chronicle, where, more often than not, he is called the "father of the behind-the-back dribble," the "original showtime guard," and the player who "brought a sense of style" to the game.[96] The great black players he saw as a kid are lost to history. They created the style that transformed the game, but they remain nameless.

It is time to open wide that crack through which Davies and others saw their first black basketball. "Pistol" Pete Maravich learned his style from watching black players, at the urging of his father, Clemson coach Press Maravich. Players from Magic Johnson to Isiah Thomas still call Maravich the game's "greatest showman." Yet he was so far ahead of his time, critics claim, "Maravich was turned into a freak by his father," playing more black than white.[97] Innovative white players such as Maravich, Davies, Bob Cousy, and the jumpers already cited did not steal this style from the black players they observed. But like the dancers and musicians we have been discussing, and the minstrel performers of the nineteenth century, white basketball players noticed the difference, practiced it, transported it to their own arenas, and transmitted it to white audiences. Players and audiences appreciated this new form of play's emphasis on style, speed, and height long before white coaches were willing to relinquish the slow, deliberate, ground-bound game they hoped to continue to control. It was precisely the speed, showiness, and innovation of the African American style that simultaneously thrilled audiences and disturbed traditionalists.

It is difficult today to appreciate how late the jump shot became standard in basketball. When Bill Russell was playing high school ball, from 1948 to 1952, jumping was still new to the game. As Russell describes it, the standard offensive strategy was to "dribble, fake and move past the man guarding you so that you had a clear path to the basket for a moment. Then you would try to drive in for a lay-up. If your path was blocked you would shoot a set shot if you had time; if not, you would pass." Traditional white players left their feet only on rebounds or blocks. White coaches considered the jump shot a "hot-dog" move that should be "confined to the playgrounds where it originated." Russell claims strict disciplinarians threw players off their teams for such an offense. Jumping was part of Negro basketball, and white coaches feared it would ruin the game. The jump was awkward, it threw players off-balance, and white coaches said it would be the downfall of anyone who used it.[98]

The term *Negro basketball* is no longer used, but phrases like "playground ball," "street ball," or "hotdogging" serve the same purpose. Clarence Gaines likes to remind people of Earl "the Pearl" Monroe, the

New York Knicks star who played for Gaines at Winston-Salem in 1967, when Gaines became the first black coach to win an NCAA Division II title. The 1968 Olympic team refused Monroe because of the same ball-handling tactics that won the title for Winston-Salem: they said he was "showboating," a racially loaded term if ever there was one.[99] In 1967, the NCAA had instituted what was called the "Alcindor Rule," a ban against the slam dunk, designed specifically to eliminate the spectacular dunks Kareem Abdul-Jabbar (then Lew Alcindor) was making for UCLA. The most extreme example of personal style, slam dunking is a jamming of the ball into the basket that has no parallel in any other sport. A football player may spike the ball and dance in the end zone after making a touchdown; a baseball player may make a victory run around the bases; but no other sport allows the athlete to celebrate his individuality at the moment of triumph, to "personaliz(e) the act of scoring."[100] Of its banning Jabbar wrote, "The dunk is one of basketball's great crowd pleasers, and there was no good reason to give it up except that this and other n[egroes] were running away with the sport."[101] Former college coach Robert Bownes said, "Look, if a guy is seven feet tall, he is going to score from in close whether he stuffs or just lays the ball in. That rule wasn't put in to stop seven-footers. It was put in to stop the six-foot-two brothers who could dazzle the crowd and embarrass much bigger white kids by dunking. . . . Everyone knows that dunking is a trademark of great playground black athletes. And so they took it away. It's as simple as that."[102]

The slam dunk, an in-your-face form of, in Nelson George's words, "intimidation through improvisation," is only one example of several moves now common to basketball but that were initially dismissed as schoolyard or playground ball.[103] John Edgar Wideman played ball for the University of Pennsylvania in the 1960s, but he missed the "spontaneity, the free-form improvisation and electricity of the playground game. . . . 'Playground move' was synonymous with bad move. Not *bad* move, but something undisciplined, selfish, possibly immoral." Wideman echoes Cal Irvin: "Twenty years later, coaches are attempting to systematize and teach the essence of the game invented on the playgrounds."[104]

Part of the essence of that game is something composer Olly Wilson calls the "soul focal moment," a point of unity between audience and player that occurs when a player—whether musician or athlete—performs what is necessary with exceptional ease, grace, and flair, taking a risk while maintaining control.[105] The soul focal moment is not gratuitous showmanship—its artistry is functional and accomplishes what the moment requires, but with a degree and twist of virtuosity that is unnecessary and unexpected. The audience gasps in surprise, exclaims with pleasure, bursts into applause, and audience and player are united in appreciation for the endless inventiveness of human expression. The soul focal moment is showy, to be sure, but this is not a one-person show, for the soul focal moment elevates a community, and its master is the ultimate team player.

Jump Jim Crow or Jump Legba?

The fast-break style, the jump shot, and the athleticism of African American dancing reclaimed the jump, which at one time had been integral to public displays of African American expressive culture. Africans carried a rich culture of sports all over the Diaspora, gaining a reputation for extraordinary athletic prowess, particularly in footracing, jumping, and dancing. Along with wrestling, stick fighting, hunting, and fishing, jumping was and remains an important part of African athletic competitions. And jumping had its place in many different slave festivals and celebrations. According to Mura Dehn, the winner of nineteenth-century cakewalk contests was "whoever jumped the highest."[106]

The single most prevalent American art of the nineteenth century was minstrelsy, drawing on the actions, humor, song, and dance of African Americans. Minstrelsy traveled as far south as Santiago de Chile, as far west as California mining camps during the gold rush, and as far abroad as South Africa.[107] Although there were black blackface performers in minstrelsy's early years, it was after the Civil War that groups of African American performers began to "black up." Minstrelsy provided training and employment and was instrumental in the development of ragtime, vaudeville, and black musical theater.[108]

"Jump Jim Crow" was perhaps the first popular portrayal of African Americans as jumpers, the first great international American song hit, and one of the most popular pieces of the nineteenth century. Tradition says that a minor actor named Thomas Dartmouth Rice saw a disabled African American man working in a stable near the Louisville Theater where Rice was performing in 1830.[109] According to the official story, as the man worked he sang to himself, and on the chorus of his song, he turned and gave a little jump. Yet W. T. Lhamon insists that far from being the creation of a single performer (Rice) or stable hand, Jump Jim Crow was part of a black folk pattern, a "widespread African-American folk dance imperson-ating—delineating—crows."[110]

White minstrel performers had plenty of contact with African Ameri-can singers and dancers and often drew ideas from African American en-tertainers, such as Juba or the legendary Jim Crow, but Rice's assemblage "Jump Jim Crow" was the best-known dance in all minstrelsy. Although later performers invented hundreds of verses, the words of the chorus nearly always remained the same:

> Weel about and turn about and do jis so,
> Eb'ry time I weel about I jump Jim Crow.[111]

The lyrics closely resemble the following recollection of a sacred Haitian possession dance invoking the African god Legba, guardian of the cross-roads:

> One of the things he may do is to go about limping, since Legba is thought of as an old man with one lamed leg. . . . Sometimes a person mounted by this deity may dance or spin around with a kind of cane-crutch called a Legba-stick, around which he twines his leg. Under conditions of posses-sion, the spinning and twirling often become a true acrobatic feat.[112]

At the time Thomas Dartmouth Rice observed the Jim Crow dance, lit-tle more than thirty years had passed since the revolution in Santo Domingo, when thousands of Haitians migrated to the United States. Even discounting the possibility of firsthand transmission, one could fairly state that here is an American dance with identifiable African-derived traits that are found in other parts of the Diaspora. One of those traits was the jump.[113]

As a song, "Jim Crow" functioned as political satire, entertaining its male fans with endless raucous verses, up to forty-four in one version.[114] But it was the dance, not the tune, that made Jump Jim Crow an interna-tional craze.[115] The *New York Tribune* carried an article in 1855 that noted:

> Never was there such an excitement in the musical or dramatic world; noth-ing was talked of, nothing written of, and nothing dreamed of, but "Jim Crow." The most sober citizens began to "wheel about, and turn about, and jump Jim Crow." It seemed as though the entire population had been bitten by the tarantula; in the parlor, in the kitchen, in the shop and in the street, Jim Crow monopolized public attention.[116]

Jim Crow was popular among white and black Americans alike. On one occasion, several African American children were charged with creating a public nuisance by dancing Jim Crow in front of a paint shop. Their attorney argued that no one could "withstand the temptation of listening to 'Jim Crow.'"[117] Dale Cockrell, who unearthed this account, wonders whether "'Jim Crow' and kindred songs functioned for black people much as they did for common white people, as songs of subversion, songs about movement, the body, and laughter, about how the performance of joy and pleasure could remake a cruel world."[118]

Originally, the phrase "jump Jim Crow" might have been a reflexive statement, a command for the dancer to jump in the middle of what was otherwise a flat-footed performance.[119] But as minstrelsy evolved throughout the nineteenth century, Jump Jim Crow lost the powerful connections it originally had with African American culture. The Jim Crow stereotype devolved on the minstrel stage and solidified in popular imagination, and its chief physical feature was not an athletic or powerful jump, a true expression of jubilation, but rather the shuffle, with all its connotations of slavery. The original Jim Crow dance persisted in early-twentieth-century-dances and, according to Lhamon, is performed to this day across the south, from Florida to Indiana.[120] Jumpin' Crow, Trucking, Jump Dem Bars, the Buzzard Lope, the Funky Chicken, the Eagle Rock, and Knock Jim Crow are among its successors. Few readers will have witnessed Knock Jim Crow, but many have seen Chuck Berry perform a variant in his famous duckwalk.[121]

Jim Crow became synonymous with civil and political segregation and oppression and acquired a life of its own as a vivid symbol for the same. A 1936 poster for the National Negro Congress, an umbrella organization for black rights groups headed by A. Philip Randolph, displayed a powerful black fist enclosing and crushing a struggling blackbird.[122] In a cultural and etymological turnabout, African Americans had to kill Jim Crow before they were free to jump without prejudice or restraint. In the late 1930s, Lindy Hop dancers and basketball players replaced the shuffle with athletic jumping. And in the summer of 1941, Duke Ellington, writer Sid Kuller, and lyricist Paul Francis Webster officially put Jim Crow to rest in a musical called *Jump for Joy.*

Jump for Joy!

Hollywood writer Sid Kuller arrived home one Sunday morning in early February 1941 to find Duke Ellington, Ben Webster, Sonny Greer, and others jamming in his living room. "Hey, this joint sure is jumping!" Kuller exclaimed, and Ellington responded, "Jumping for joy!" thus beginning the free-associative process that led to the musical revue five months later.[123] Ellington said the show was part of an attempt "to correct the race situation in the U.S.A. through a form of theatrical propaganda." A series of discussions led to the creation of *Jump for Joy*, in Ellington's words, "a show that would take Uncle Tom out of the theater, eliminate the stereotyped image that had been exploited by Hollywood and Broadway, and say things that would make the audience think."[124] The show included a deathbed scene in which Uncle Tom's children danced around him as he lay dying.

Ellington called *Jump for Joy* "the first social significance show" and said that of all his achievements, the one thing outside music he was most proud of was his part in producing it.[125] In the 1960s, when San Francisco demonstrators challenged Ellington to make a statement on civil rights, he answered, "I made my statement in 1941 in *Jump for Joy* and I stand by it."[126]

The musical *Jump for Joy* marked a cultural watershed, a moment when African American artists determined to turn their backs publicly on theatrical stereotypes. The first song, eventually eliminated from the show because of death threats, was "I've Got a Passport from Georgia." Actor Paul White, waving goodbye to friends on board a steamship, began with these words:

> Farewell, Charlie, so long Joe,
> Good-bye, *Jim*, and I do mean *crow*.[127]

Tickets for *Jump for Joy* went on sale at the Mayan Theater box office on 2 July 1941, and the show opened eight days later. The black press raved about the show. The *Herald-Express* reported, "No question about the Mayan these nights. The joint really jumps."[128] Along with the jump blues and dance, *Jump for Joy* popularized zoot-suit fashion and may even have introduced the term *zoot suit* to America in a sketch performed by Potts, Pan, and Skillet.[129] Teenagers in the balcony began showing up with "unbelievably loud zoot suits, trying to compete with Potts," Kuller remembers.[130] The zoot suits were a "form of visual protest," says Frank Davis, a silent complement to the show's blatant anti-racist position.[131]

In *Stomping the Blues*, Albert Murray wrote:

> The most fundamental prerequisite for mediating between the work of art
> and the audience, spectators, or readers . . . is . . . an understanding of what

is being stylized plus an accurate insight into how it is being stylized. Each masterwork of art . . . is always first of all a comprehensive synthesis of all the aspects of its idiom.[132]

The jump was an important stylizing element for prewar African American culture, and *Jump for Joy* was a "comprehensive synthesis" of the jump style and its cultural meaning.

In 1937, the year of "One O'Clock Jump," air steps, and the speeding up of basketball, Richard Wright published an autobiographical sketch called "The Ethics of Living Jim Crow" in the Federal Writers' Project *American Stuff*. Wright described several lessons in his "Jim Crow education," all of which were, he said, dedicated to the single purpose of learning to "stay in your place."[133] African men, women, and children who jumped refused to stay in their place, and the presence of the jump throughout African American culture should be read as a transcript of that refusal. While many ordinary African Americans were challenging Jim Crow segregation, others publicly defied the enfeebled Jim Crow stereotype on stage, in dance halls, in clubs, in gymnasiums, and at YMCAs.[134] As remarkable an achievement as it was, *Jump for Joy* should not be considered singular. Rather, it was part of a broader cultural movement, one of many examples in which African American musicians, dancers, artists, athletes, men, women, and children refused to maintain the Jim Crow shuffle. *Jump for Joy* was a formal celebration and public embrace of the informal jump style, a hidden strength suddenly made visible.

In the lives and culture of oppressed groups is a hidden transcript of "daily conversations, folklore, jokes, songs, and other cultural practices" that challenges those in power and often arises in disguised form "on stage," in public spaces controlled by the powerful.[135] Jazz music, dance, and basketball were three such cultural practices through which African Americans challenged those in power, and the jump was a key part of that challenge. Through the powerful, assertive, and identifiably black jump, African American men, women, and adolescents reappropriated a central gesture of African American culture, defying the Jim Crow stereotype by reclaiming Jim Crow's African jump. Jump tunes, the athletic jitterbug, and the jump shot admitted a positive identification with a traditional African American culture, and through them emerged a new black image: not self-deprecating or shuffling but self-assertive and literally uplifted.

Many African American leaders did not see such forms of culture as uplifting. To them, vernacular dance and jazz music were degrading and debasing, the very thing to avoid for the sake of political and social advances.[136] While athletic prowess in dance and sport may have confirmed certain stereotypes for white (and black intellectual) Americans, such exhibitions resisted stereotypes through the public display of powerful, graceful, and sensual black bodies.

The double irony of the position of African American intellectuals is that the very music and dance they deplored became for millions an everyday solution to the intellectual dilemma of the decade: how to form a social group without sacrificing individuality and personal creativity.[137] While intellectuals focused on a thinking few, the multitude was acting out solutions to social issues, theorizing through behavior.[138]

Built into the structure of jazz, jazz dance, and basketball were complex rhythms, improvisation and stylization, call-and-response patterns, and competitive interaction that required individuals to coordinate and synchronize their efforts. The music, dance, and sport allowed individuals to assert their excellence as soloists while remaining part of the group. Further, they offered a working model of balanced group and individual expression. As soloists stood to perform alone and then relinquished the spotlight to blend with the group, big bands showed the rest of the country how it was possible to work in precision with others without losing a sense of individuality.[139] The dancers who followed and inspired them did the same, offering 1930s Americans, in Warren Susman's words, a "pattern of large-scale participation and close cooperation."[140] Basketball players, too, modeled a way of group interaction that has become more important as large-scale industrial models of management have given way to postindustrial theories focusing on small groups and encouraging individual contributions.

The 1937 Brotherhood of Sleeping Car Porters contract, the 1941 March on Washington, the "Double-V" movement of the World War II era—a *Pittsburgh Courier* campaign for victory at home and victory abroad—are the recognized emblems of a "new consciousness" in civil rights history. Yet a history of opposition is also present in the hidden transcript of jazz, dance, and basketball. James Scott has written, "Only in rare moments of historical crisis are these transcripts and the actions they imply brought into a direct confrontation. When they are, it is often assumed that there has come into being a new consciousness, a new anger, or a new ideology that has transformed class relations. It is far more likely, however, that this new 'consciousness' was already there in the unedited transcript and it is the situation that has changed in a way that allows or requires one or both parties to act on that basis."[141]

Although the jump began as African American music and the jitterbug as African American dance, both spread rapidly through American culture. By 1941, when *Jump for Joy* had its run on stage, smaller-scale, punchier jump blues were already replacing big-band swing. With a lead vocalist, rhythm section, and one or two horns, jump-blues bands such as Louis Jordan and his Tympany Five scored several million copy hits in the 1940s, at a time when record production was limited and larger swing bands were pining for bookings. Jordan and countless jump-blues imitators pointed the way and laid the paving for *their* successors: rhythm and blues and rock and roll.[142]

Jump was a more pervasive cultural statement than bebop because it remained the consistently danceable offspring of the swing era, the missing link between swing music and rock and roll. With the jump, African American athletes, entertainers, and their African American mass audiences achieved true racial uplift, on a scale few but religious leaders could match, using the performance of joy and pleasure "to remake a cruel world." The jump was health and vigor in your face, a central component of a shared African American culture. As a cultural gesture, the jump offers a focal point for studying cultural diffusion that transcends disciplinary boundaries and reverses the usual trend: the culture of an excluded minority has transformed that of the majority. Jump blues, the Lindy Hop, and the fast-break style are the identifiably black foundation of post–World War II popular music, dance, and basketball.[143]

NOTES

1. For an in-depth exploration of the topics in this chapter, particularly those sections dealing with music, please see Gena Caponi "Jump for Joy: The Jump Trope in African America, 1937–1941," in *Prospects: An Annual of American Cultural Studies* 24 (1999): 521–74. This topic is the subject of a forthcoming volume titled *Jump for Joy*. I thank Clarence Gaines, Clarence Gaines Jr., Cal Irvin, and Charley Rosen for kindly sharing their knowledge of basketball history. Albert Murray and Stanley Crouch both talked with me about a range of topics, and those conversations are reflected in this essay. Joel Dinerstein has been generous with research suggestions and ideas generated from his dissertation, "Swingin' the

Machine: White Technology and Black Culture between the World Wars" (University of Texas at Austin, 2000). David Brackett, Richard Crawford, John Gennari, and Guthrie Ramsey Jr. read earlier versions of this essay and made many valuable suggestions, as did Charles Keil and the late William D. Piersen, both of whom encouraged me to explore this topic.

2. Bill Russell, *Second Wind: The Memoirs of an Opinionated Man* (New York: Random House, 1979), 73.

3. Barry Pearson, "Jump Steady: The Roots of R&B," in Lawrence Cohn, ed., *Nothing but the Blues: The Music and the Musicians* (New York: Abbeville Press, 1993), 316–17.

4. Marshall Stearns and Jean Stearns, *Jazz Dance: The Story of American Vernacular Dance* (New York: Macmillan, 1968), 329.

5. David Stowe, *Swing Changes: Big-Band Jazz in New Deal America* (Cambridge: Harvard University Press, 1994), 193.

6. Scholars Eric Lott and Scott DeVeaux have made compelling arguments for bebop as an assertion of ethnicity. See Eric Lott, "Double V, Double-Time: Bebop's Politics of Style," *Callaloo* 36 (1988): 597–605; and Scott DeVeaux, "Constructing the Jazz Tradition: Jazz Historiography," *Black American Literature Forum* 25 (1991): 525–60.

7. In his 1945 essay "The Dance-Basis of Jazz," jazz critic, dancer, and choreographer Roger Pryor Dodge reminded readers that "jazz is dance music" and that it ia not "mere coincidence that we find it enjoyable to dance to." Dodge also reviewed eighteenth-century European music and dance as interconnected activities. Robert Farris Thompson's "The Aesthetic of the Cool" and John Miller Chernoff's *African Rhythm and Sensibility* discuss African music and dance as inseparable, interconnected expressions with overlapping formal aesthetic patterns. In *Jazz Dance*, for many years the authoritative text on the subject, Marshall and Jean Stearns traced the African roots of American social dances and reiterated the inseparability of music from movement. More recently, Jacqui Malone has explored these connections in *Steppin' on the Blues*, an updated history of African American vernacular dance. For Malone, dance is "visible rhythm," and dancers are drummers who use their feet instead of sticks. In *Swing Changes*, David Stowe calls for a consideration of music as "social practice" and suggests we broaden our "conception of 'the music' to include social elements: audience, performance context, ideology, and mass media." Similarly, Albert Murray insists one has to understand the "idiomatic roots" of African American artistic expression, or one is in danger of missing "the essential nature of its statement." See Roger Pryor Dodge, *Hot Jazz and Jazz Dance: Collected Writings 1929–1964* (New York: Oxford University Press, 1995), 143; Robert Farris Thompson, "An Aesthetic of the Cool: West African Dance," in Gena Dagel Caponi, ed., *Signifyin(g), Sanctifyin', and Slam Dunking: A Reader in African American Expressive Culture* (Amherst: University of Massachusetts Press, 1999), 72–86; John Miller Chernoff, *African Rhythm and African Sensi-*

bility: Aesthetics and Social Action in African Musical Idioms (Chicago: University of Chicago Press, 1979); Stearns and Stearns, *Jazz Dance*; Jacqui Malone, *Steppin' on the Blues: The Visible Rhythms of African American Dance* (Urbana: University of Illinois Press, 1996); Stowe, *Swing Changes*, 9; Albert Murray, *Stomping the Blues* (New York: DaCapo Press, 1976), 196.

8. Steven A. Riess, *City Games: The Evolution of American Urban Society and the Rise of Sports* (Urbana: University of Illinois Press, 1989), 108; Robert W. Peterson, *Cages to Jump Shots* (New York: Oxford University Press, 1990), 122.

9. The all-Jewish Sphas (sponsored by the South Philadelphia Hebrew Association) held Saturday-night "basketball-and-dance" parties at their home court, a hotel ballroom in Philadelphia, where the Sphas' Gil Fitch sometimes changed into a tuxedo after games to lead his band for the dance; Pittsburgh's Iron City Elks hosted game-and-dance combinations at the Pythian Temple; in Kansas City, basketball dances were held at the Labor Temple. See *Pittsburgh Courier*, 14 December 1935; *Kansas City Call*, 12 January 1923.

10. Journalist and poet Frank Marshall Davis remembers the Arkansas City, Kansas, YMCA secretary forming a basketball team for black youth, who were allowed to practice in the high school gym only at night. See Frank Marshall Davis, *Livin' the Blues: Memoirs of a Black Journalist and Poet*, ed. John Edgar Tidwell (Madison: University of Wisconsin Press, 1991), 52.

11. *Pittsburgh Courier*, 28 January 1939.

12. *Pittsburgh Courier*, 18 January 1936.

13. Peterson, *Cages to Jump Shots*, 97–98.

14. Trumpeter Rex Stewart of the Duke Ellington Orchestra and his fellow musicians Ben Webster and Sid Catlett often worked out with the Rens at the casino in the afternoons and once formed a musicians' team to play against the Rens for a benefit game. See Rex Stewart, *Jazz Masters of the 30s* (New York, 1972; reprint, New York: Da Capo Press, 1985), 164. Bandleader Cab Calloway was another basketball fan, and for a while the Cab Calloway Jitter-Bugs, a team composed entirely of Calloway band members, played local basketball teams when the Calloway Cotton Club Orchestra was touring. One newspaper article declared that Calloway himself was one of "Harlem's speediest basketball hurlers" ("Cab Calloway's Basketball Team to Play Miles Brothers, Local Champs, for Charity," unidentified newspaper clipping [ca. January 1935] from the Cab Calloway scrapbooks, Cab Calloway archives, Boston University). Once, in 1936, the Calloway team challenged and defeated a Jimmy Lunceford–led team in a game refereed by Jesse Owens (*New York Amsterdam News*, 21 November 1936).

15. Cited in Nelson George, *Elevating the Game: Black Men and Basketball* (New York: HarperCollins, 1992), 40.

16. Arthur R. Ashe Jr., *A Hard Road to Glory: The African-American Athlete in Basketball* (New York: Amistad Press, 1988), 10.

17. Peterson, *Cages to Jump Shots*, 98.

18. Clarence Gaines, telephone interview with author, 5 March 1996.

19. Murray, *Stomping the Blues*, 230.

20. For an extended discussion of this aesthetic and its African roots, including a detailed historiography, see my introduction to *Signifyin(g), Sanctifying, and Slam Dunking: A Reader in African American Expressive Culture.*

21. Lewis A. Erenberg, "News from the Great Wide World: Duke Ellington, Count Basie, and Black Popular Music, 1927–1943," *Prospects* 18 (1993): 487; Murray, *Stomping the Blues*, 42, 12. See also Lewis Erenberg, *Swingin' the Dream: Big Band Jazz and the Rebirth of American Culture* (Chicago: University of Chicago Press, 1999), particularly chap. 4.

22. Cited in Warren Susman, *Culture as History: The Transformation of American Society in the Twentieth Century* (New York: Pantheon Books, 1984), 148.

23. Johan Huizinga, *Homo Ludens: A Study of the Play Element in Culture* (1950; reprint, Boston: Beacon Press, 1960), 10.

24. Ray Oldenburg, *The Great Good Place: Cafés, Coffee Shops, Community Centers, Beauty Parlors, General Stores, Bars, Hangouts, and How They Get You through the Day* (New York: Paragon House, 1989), 16.

25. Ibid., 11. See also Elijah Anderson, *A Place on the Corner* (Chicago: University of Chicago Press, 1976).

26. See W. T. Lhamon Jr., *Raising Cain: Blackface Performance from Jim Crow to Hip Hop*; (Cambridge: Harvard University Press, 1998) and Dale Cockrell, *Demons of Disorder: Early Blackface Minstrels and Their World* (New York: Cambridge University Press, 1997).

27. "Duke Sets the Pace in Themes," *Afro-American*, 2 July 1938, 10; cited in John Hasse, *Beyond Category: The Life and Genius of Duke Ellington* (New York: 1993; reprint, New York: Da Capo Press, 1995), 217.

28. Stowe, *Swing Changes*, 14.

29. Ibid., 21.

30. John Hope Franklin, *From Slavery to Freedom: A History of Negro Americans*, 3rd edition (New York: Vintage Books, 1969), 498ff.

31. Stephen Henderson, *Understanding the New Black Poetry: Black Speech and Black Music as Poetic References* (New York: William Morrow and Company, 1973), 44.

32. Erenberg, "News from the Great Wide World," 483–84.

33. Peterson, *Cages to Jump Shots*, 116.

34. Among industry teams were the Akron Firestones (later the Akron Firestone Non-Skids), Akron Goodyear Wingfoots, Fort Wayne General Electrics, and Indianapolis U.S. Tires. Frank Kautsky, owner of two grocery stores in Indianapolis, owned and managed the Indianapolis Kautsky's, whom he paid in cash after each game—an unusually high $25 per game, more if he were "particularly pleased." See Peterson, *Cages to Jump Shots*, 114.

35. Stowe, *Swing Changes*, 255 n.47.

36. Frank Bolden, remarks addressed to American Studies Association Conference, Pittsburgh, 10 November 1995.

37. Joe Louis, with Edna Rust and Art Rust Jr., *Joe Louis: My Life* (New York: Harcourt Brace Jovanovich, 1978), 118–19.

38. "Fight of the Century—Joe Louis vs Jim-Crow," *Pittsburgh Courier*, 29 February 1936, sec. 2, 4.

39. Chris Mead, *Champion: Joe Louis, Black Hero in White America* (New York: Viking Penguin, 1986), 145.

40. Chester L. Washington, "Ches' Sez," *Pittsburgh Courier*, 29 February 1936, sec. 2, 5.

41. Cited in Jom Entine, *Taboo: Why Black Athletes Dominate Sports and Why We're Afraid to Talk about It* (New York: Public Affairs, 2000), 195.

42. Richard Wright, "Joe Louis Uncovers Dynamite," *New Masses*, 8 October 1935, 163.

43. Dizzy Gillespie, with Al Fraser, *To Be or Not . . . to Bop* (New York: Da Capo, 1979), 499.

44. For a discussion of Superman in 1930s America, see Lawrence W. Levine, *The Unpredictable Past: Explorations in American Cultural History* (New York: Oxford University Press, 1993), 227.

45. Cited in Erenberg, "News from the Great Wide World," 494.

46. Stephen R. Fox, *Big Leagues: Professional Baseball, Football, and Basketball in National Memory* (New York: William Morrow and Company, 1994), 15.

47. Clarence Major, *Dictionary of Afro-American Slang* (New York: International Publishers: 1970), 72. Edward Kennedy Ellington, *Music Is My Mistress* (Garden City, N.Y.: Doubleday, 1973), 179. In his introduction to the anthology *Understanding the New Black Poetry*, Henderson coined the term *mascon* to describe words such as *jump*—words with "a *massive concentration of Black experiential energy* which powerfully affects the meaning of Black speech, Black song, and Black poetry" (Henderson, *Understanding the New Black Poetry*, 44).

48. See Samuel A. Floyd Jr., *The Power of Black Music: Interpreting Its History from Africa to the United States* (New York: Oxford University Press, 1995), 70.

49. Seven of the 114 tunes were recorded before 1930 and use the word in ways that differ from post-1937 usage. The two 1930s recordings made before 1937 seem to use the word *jump* only incidentally ("Jump on the Wagon," and "Hop, Skip, and Jump"). See Brian Rust, *Jazz Records 1897–1942* (Chigwell, Essex: Storeyville Publishers, 1969).

50. John Chilton, *Let the Good Times Roll: The Story of Louis Jordan and His Music* (London: Quartet Books, 1992), 63. According to Chilton, Louis Jordan's Tympany Four, his first jump band, made its debut at the Elks Rendezvous, close to the Savoy Ballroom, on 4 August 1938. An announcement in the *New York Amsterdam News* on 15 October of that year identified the band in print as a "Jump Band." See Chilton, *Let the Good Times Roll*, 61, 63.

51. Interestingly, Louis Jordan, a jump blues bandleader, made a career of jump tunes and pieces that relied on a "shuffle" beat, which his drummer achieved by subdividing each beat into three and emphasizing the first and third segments of the beat. Even though the terminology had disappeared from titles by the 1940s, the shuffle beat remained in tunes called "jump" tunes.

52. "A lot of tunes were called stomps, and a lot of bands were called stomp bands," Count Basie said. See Albert Murray, *Good Morning Blues: An Autobiography of Count Basie* (New York: Random House, 1985), 6.

53. Dicky Wells and Stanley Dance, *The Night People: Reminiscences of a Jazzman* (Boston: Crescendo Press, 1971), 77. Cited in Malone, *Steppin' on the Blues*, 102.

54. Stearns and Stearns, *Jazz Dance*, 325. According to Stearns, the Lindy owes its origins to the Texas Tommy, introduced in 1913, consisting of a kick and hop three times on each foot.

55. Robert P. Crease, "The Lindy Hop, 1937–1942," in Krin Gabbard, ed., *Representing Jazz* (Durham: Duke University Press, 1995), 213–19; Malone, *Steppin' on the Blues*, 103.

56. Frank Manning in *Swinging at the Savoy: Frankie Manning's Story*, prod. Rosemary Hemp (Seattle: Living Traditions, 1995).

57. Feature-length films included MGM's *A Day at the Races* (1937), RKO's *Radio City Revels* (1938), MGM's *Everybody Sing* (1938), and Universal's *Hellzapoppin* (1941); soundies included *Hot Chocolate* (1941), *Outline of Jitterbug History* (1942), and *Sugar Hill Masquerade* (1942); Broadway appearances included *Knickerbocker Holiday* (1938), *Hellzapoppin* (1938), *The Hot Mikado* (1939), and *Swinging the Dream* (1939).

58. Stearns and Stearns, *Jazz Dance*, 323.

59. *New York Times*, 10 January 1933; cited in Stearns and Stearns, *Jazz Dance*, 331.

60. Stearns and Stearns, *Jazz Dance*, 333.

61. See ibid., 327; Malone, *Steppin' on the Blues*, 103–4.

62. Crease, "Lindy Hop," 224.

63. John Edgar Wideman, "Michael Jordan's Great Leap Forward," in Caponi, *Signifyin(g), Sanctifyin' and Slam Dunking*, 389.

64. Michael Eric Dyson, "Be like Mike? Michael Jordan and the Pedagogy of Desire," in Caponi, *Signifyin(g), Sanctifyin' and Slam Dunking*, 415–16.

65. Kenneth R. Dutton, *The Perfectible Body: The Western Ideal of Male Physical Development* (New York: Continuum Books, 1995), 63.

66. Peterson, *Cages to Jump Shots*, 110.

67. Ashe, *Hard Road to Glory*, 12.

68. Gaines, telephone interview with author, 5 March 1996.

69. Calvin Irvin, telephone interview with author, 11 March 1996.

70. Gaines, telephone interview with author, 5 March 1996.

71. *Pittsburgh Courier*, 12 December 1935.

72. "The defeats suffered at the hands of Ky. State and Union is proof that Negro college basketball is on par with white" (*Pittsburgh Courier*, 8 April 1939). "The brand of basketball played in sepia rah! rah! seats is on a keel with the paleface product," wrote Randy Dixon in the *Pittsburgh Courier*, 1 April 1939.

73. Davis, *Livin' the Blues*, 232.

74. *Pittsburgh Courier*, 11 January 1940.

75. *Pittsburgh Courier*, 14 December 1935; 7 January 1939. Fifty years later, the same words applied to Michael Jordan, as Michael Eric Dyson tried to explain what links his style to an African American tradition: spontaneity, stylization, and "edifying deception" (Dyson, "Be like Mike?" 411).

76. Bill Russell played on a post–high school all-star team in the early spring of 1952, coached by a maverick named Brick Swegle, who let his players play "Negro basketball" even though there were only two black players on the team. The white players had the time of their lives. Opposing coaches either complained the tactics were "not cricket" (an interesting Eurocentric metaphor) or vowed the team that lived by the jump shot would die by the jump shot. One coach considered the move so repugnant that he refused to let his players defend against it. Russell's team won that game 144 to 41, and Russell himself pioneered a defensive jump for shot-blocking when he entered the NBA in 1956. See Russell, *Second Wind*, 64–65.

77. Coaches Piggy Lambert at Purdue and Frank Keaney at Rhode Island are sometimes said to have developed fast-break basketball in the 1920s and 1930s, but it is difficult to imagine the fast break prior to 1937, when basketball was essentially a half-court game. See Neil D. Isaacs, *All the Moves: A History of College Basketball* (New York: J. B. Lippincott Company, 1975), 57–60.

78. Peterson, *Cages to Jump Shots*, 109.

79. Cited in ibid.

80. Ibid., 109.

81. Isaacs, *All the Moves*, 123.

82. Ibid., 115.

83. Ibid., 262.

84. Ibid., 262, 222.

85. *Pittsburgh Courier*, 28 January 1939.

86. *Pittsburgh Courier*, 6 March 1937.

87. Ashe, *Hard Road to Glory*, 24.

88. Isaacs, *All the Moves*, 83.

89. *Pittsburgh Courier*, 13 March 1937.

90. *Pittsburgh Courier*, 27 February 1937; 13 March 1937.

91. *Pittsburgh Courier*, 26 December 1926.

92. *Pittsburgh Courier*, 28 January 1939.

93. For instance, a story about a 1937 Virginia State College win reads: "The

second half was a repetition of the first, with the lanky Trojans out-reaching and out-jumping the shorter Shaw team to make all sorts of hair-raising baskets" (*Pittsburgh Courier*, 30 January 1937).

94. Photos accompanying a *Pittsburgh Courier* article published in April 1939 show "Pop" Gates as he "soars skyward over the outstretched hands of Oshkosh guards" to score. See *Pittsburgh Courier*, 8 April 1939.

95. Charles Salzberg, *From Set Shot to Slam Dunk: The Glory Days of Basketball in the Words of Those Who Played It* (New York: Dell Publishing, 1987), 51.

96. Alex Sachare, *The Naismith Memorial Basketball Hall of Fame's 100 Greatest Basketball Players of All Time* (New York: Byron Preiss Multimedia Company, 1997), 64.

97. Bob Ryan, quoted in Ken Shouler, *The Experts Pick Basketball's Best 50 Players in the Last 50 Years* (Lenexa, Kans.: Addax Publishing Group, 1998), 60

98. Russell, *Second Wind*, 63–64.

99. Gaines, telephone interview with author, 5 March 1996.

100. George, *Elevating the Game*, xv.

101. Kareem Abdul-Jabbar and Peter Knobler, *Giant Steps* (New York: Bantam: 1983), 160.

102. Pete Axthelm, *The City Game* (New York: Penguin, 1970), 127.

103. George, *Elevating the Game*, xix.

104. John Edgar Wideman, *Brothers and Keepers* (1984; reprint, New York: Vintage Books, 1995), 226.

105. Olly Wilson's remarks on the "soul focal moment" were made at a conference of the Center for the Study of Black Music, New Orleans, 1994. See Olly Wilson, "Black Music as an Art Form," *Black Music Research Journal* 3 (1983): 1–22; "The Association of Movement and Music as a Manifestation of a Black Conceptual Approach to Music-Making," in Irene V. Jackson, ed., *More than Dancing: Essays on Afro-American Music and Musicians* (Westport, Conn.: Greenwood Press, 1985).

106. Mura Dehn, "The Spirit Moves: Jazz Dance from the Turn of the Century to 1950," manuscript in Dance Collection, New York Public Library.

107. Stearns and Stearns, *Jazz Dance*, 39; Gilbert Chase, *America's Music: From the Pilgrims to the Present* (New York: McGraw-Hill Book Company, 1966), 260; see also Dale Cockrell, "Of Gospel Hymns, Minstrel Shows, and Jubilee Singers: Toward Some Black South African Musics," *American Music* 5 (Winter 1987): 418.

108. See Robert C. Toll, *Blacking Up: The Minstrel Show in Nineteenth-Century America* (New York: Oxford University Press, 1974); Thomas L. Riis, *Just before Jazz: Black Musical Theater in New York, 1890 to 1915* (Washington, D.C.: Smithsonian Institution, 1989); Eric Lott, *Love and Theft: Blackface Minstrelsy and the American Working Class* (New York: Oxford University Press, 1993).

109. Dale Cockrell, "Jim Crow, Demon of Disorder," *American Music* 14 (Summer 1996): 161.

110. Lhamon, *Raising Cain*, 180, 181.

111. Chase, *America's Music*, 265.

112. Harold Courlander, "Dance and Dance Drama in Haiti," in Franziska Boas, ed., *The Function of Dance in Human Society* (New York: Boas School, 1944), 42; cited in Lynne Fauley Emery, *Black Dance in the United States from 1619 to 1970* (Palo Alto: National Press Books, 1972), 56.

113. W. T. Lhamon Jr. notes the limp as another persistent Legba/Jim Crow characteristic, reappearing in Little Richard's limp and Chuck Berry's duckwalk. See Lhamon, *Raising Cain*, 255 n.30.

114. Cockrell, "Jim Crow, Demon of Disorder," 169.

115. Stearns and Stearns, *Jazz Dance*, 42.

116. *New York Tribune*, 1855; cited in Lott, *Love and Theft*, 3.

117. *Barbadoes v. Bolcolm*, *Boston Post*, 30 March 1840, as cited in Cockrell, "Jim Crow, Demon of Disorder," 175.

118. Cockrell, "Jim Crow, Demon of Disorder," 176.

119. Contemporary descriptions of the dance Rice incorporated into his stage career call it a "jig and shuffle." Stearns says even the jig of Jump Jim Crow was a "syncopated hop in the flat-footed Shuffle manner rather than a jump 'high up,'" and the chief feature of the dance was the "rhythmic circling *before the jump*" (Stearns and Stearns, *Jazz Dance*, 41). Joseph Ireland, writing in 1867, noted Rice's "shambling negro gait." See Joseph Ireland, *Records of the New York Stage from 1750 to 1860* (New York: B. Bloom, 1867), 55–56; cited in Molly N. Ramshaw, "Jump, Jim Crow!" 36. *A Biographical Sketch of Thomas D. Rice (1808–1860) Theater Annual 1960* 17 (1961).

120. Lhamon, *Raising Cain*, 152, 181.

121. Bessie Jones and Bess Lomax Hawes, *Step It Down: Games, Plays, Songs and Stories from the Afro-American Heritage* (Athens: University of Georgia Press, 1972), 55–56; Lhamon, *Raising Cain*, 255 n.30.

122. Poster on display in National Civil Rights Museum, Memphis, Tennessee. For more on the National Negro Congress, see Paula F. Pfeffer, *A. Philip Randolph, Pioneer of the Civil Rights Movement* (Baton Rouge: Louisiana State University Press, 1990), 32.

123. Patricia Willard, program notes to *Jump for Joy* (Washington, D.C.: Smithsonian Institution, 1988), 1.

124. Ellington, *Music Is My Mistress*, 175. *Jump for Joy* has its roots in the Hollywood Theatre Alliance's "Negro Revue." See Arnold Rampersad, *The Life of Langston Hughes*, vol. 2: *1941–1967* (New York: Oxford University Press, 1988), 26.

125. Ellington, *Music Is My Mistress*, 460. Out of *Jump for Joy* came what Ellington described as a "feeling of responsibility" that culminated in his long masterwork *Black, Brown, and Beige* (1943).

126. Willard, program notes to *Jump for Joy*, 31.

127. Paul Webster, Ray Golden, Hal Borne, "I've Got a Passport from Georgia,"

manuscript in Smithsonian American Archives, Duke Ellington Collection. I thank Ann Kuebler and Deborah Richardson at the Smithsonian Institution for their assistance.

128. W. E. Oliver, in the *Herald-Express*, 8 August 1941; cited in Willard, program notes to *Jump for Joy*, 22.

129. Willard, program notes to *Jump for Joy*, 31.

130. Ibid., 21.

131. Davis, *Livin' the Blues*, 49.

132. Murray, *Stomping the Blues*, 196.

133. Richard Wright, "The Ethics of Living Jim Crow," in *American Stuff: An Anthology of Prose and Verse by Members of the Federal Writers' Project* (New York: Viking Press, 1937), 44.

134. For discussion and examples of early resistance, see Robin D. G. Kelley, "'We Are Not What We Seem': Rethinking Black Working-Class Opposition in the Jim Crow South," and Kenneth W. Goings and Gerald L. Smith, "'Unhidden' Transcripts: Memphis and African American Agency, 1862–1920," both in Kenneth W. Goings and Raymond A. Mohl, eds., *New African American Urban History* (Thousand Oaks, Calif.: Sage Publications, 1996).

135. See James C. Scott, *Domination and the Arts of Resistance: Hidden Transcripts* (New Haven: Yale University Press, 1990); also James C. Scott, *Weapons of the Weak: Everyday Forms of Peasant Resistance* (New Haven: Yale University Press, 1985); cited in Kelley, "'We Are Not What We Seem,'" 189.

136. Ralph Matthews, theatrical editor of the *Afro-American*, wrote that the ability to "dance with feverish abandon" the "dances reminiscent of the levee and the plantation" simply confirmed stereotypes white audiences held of African Americans. See Ralph Matthews, "The Negro Theatre—A Dodo Bird," in Nancy Cunard, ed., *Negro: An Anthology* (New York, 1933; reprint, New York: Frederick Ungar Publishing Company, 1970), 195.

137. For a survey of intellectual positions on this issue in the 1930s, see Richard Pells, *Radical Visions and American Dreams: Culture and Social Thought in the Depression Years* (New York: Harper and Row, 1973), 96–150.

138. For criticism of the masses, see Alain LeRoy Locke, *The New Negro* (1925; reprint, New York: Atheneum, 1970), 4. For an opposing approach, see Lawrence W. Levine, who writes, "Failure to understand the reaction of the Negro masses has stemmed directly from failure to look seriously at their lives and their culture" (*Unpredictable Past*, 92).

139. Joel Dinerstein has presented a fuller discussion of these ideas in his dissertation "Swingin' the Machine."

140. Susman, *Culture as History*, 162.

141. Scott, *Weapons of the Weak*, 288; cited in Goings and Smith, "'Unhidden' Transcripts," 147.

142. The jump is long lived. Chuck Berry's 1956 "Around and Around" con-

tains the line "The joint was jumpin' goin' round and 'round." Hadda Brooks recorded "Jump Back Honey" in 1952 (Blackhawk Music Co.). In 1968, Mick Jagger and Keith Richard's "Jumpin' Jack Flash" (Mirage) recalled the jump-blues craze, and Curtis Mayfield's "Jump" became a best-selling record for Aretha Franklin (Atlantic) in 1976. Carolyn Rodgers's poem "Jump Bad" carries some of the political overtones of jumping, when she says that "us Black Folk is gonna have to sho'nuf JUMP BAD to git ourselves liberated from this honkie" (in Gwendolyn Brooks, *Jump Bad: A New Chicago Anthology* [Detroit: Broadside Press, 1971], 109). Blues singer Koko Taylor brought back "Jump for Joy" on her 1990 album (Alligator). A women-oriented sports magazine for teen girls, called *Jump*, appeared in 1997.

143. As Morroe Berger noted in 1947, the diffusion of jazz has differed from the models predicted in anthropology and sociology—in jazz, the "superordinate culture has borrowed from the subordinate." See Morroe Berger, "Jazz: Resistance to the Diffusion of a Culture Pattern," in Charles Nanry, ed., *American Music: From Storyville to Woodstock* (New Brunswick, N.J.: Transaction, 1972), 40. Marshall and Jean Stearns noted the same: "The over-all trend was one way—Afro-American dance exerted an increasingly strong influence on the dance as a whole. This trend reverses the usual pattern described by anthropologists in which the culture of an early majority swallows up the culture of later minorities" (*Jazz Dance*, 24).

Chapter Three

Baseball along the Columbia

The Nisei, Their Community, Their Sport
in Northern Oregon

Samuel O. Regalado

Jerry Inouye walked piously into his church in Japantown. Dressed not in formal attire but wearing knickers and a flannel jersey with his small cap politely by his side, his appearance did not catch the Reverend Bunijiro Hirayama by surprise. Familiar with his parishioners, he knew well that Inouye's presence was a matter of great importance. The now-retired ballplayer recalled that his visit to the church "pertained to the championship baseball game between the Portland Midgets and the Gresham-Troutdale Fujis. I was a teenage pitcher for the Portland Midgets."[1] Opting not to choose sides, the wise minister simply counseled his young friend to "never pray to win, but pray to perform your best for a good, clean ball game regardless of the outcome."[2]

During the period of the late 1930s, in many of the northern Oregon Nisei (second-generation Japanese) communities, baseball was an important recreational and social pastime. Along the Columbia River, clubs from Portland proper, Gresham-Troutdale, and Hood River competed against one another during the summer months for regional honors. Additionally, they ventured south into Salem and to Wapato, Washington, in search of recreational opponents and prospective friendships. The games not only represented the competitive nature of these Japanese Americans but also helped better to link the urban and rural Nisei of northern Oregon. And this was not unimportant, as the Beaver State's Japanese enclave represented one of the smallest in the American west. As of 1930, Oregon's Japanese population was a mere 3.5 percent of the total number of

Japanese living in the United States.[3] Their roots, however, had been planted in Oregonian soil for nearly a hundred years.

In 1834, Japanese sailors shipwrecked off the coast of Cape Flattery were the first of their kind to land in the region. But it was Miyo Iwakoshi who, in 1880, arrived to marry an Australian Scot then living in Gresham. Thus, Iwakoshi was the first Japanese to settle down in the region. During the next few years other Issei (first-generation Japanese) arrived, including two labor contractors named Shintaro Takaki and Shinzaburo Ban. Takaki and Ban were instrumental in the recruitment of fellow Issei to the region. By the turn of the century, Japanese workers made up a good percentage of those toiling in Oregon's railroad, sugar-beet, and cattle-ranching industries.[4] Japanese farmers also came into northern Oregon and fanned into areas that today outline the periphery of greater Portland. In the Gresham-Troutdale community, for instance, sixty-five Issei farmers formed a settlement in 1902. By 1920 their numbers had increased to three hundred. Further east and slightly past the Columbia River gorge, Issei agrarians in Hood River valley region cultivated some twelve hundred acres of land as they produced apples, pears, and other marketable agricultural products.[5]

The first decades of the twentieth century also characterized a change in the goals of Oregon's Japanese. Until then, many Issei migrants did not intend to make Oregon their permanent home. But as the fortunes of many appeared brighter in their adopted land, leaders emerged to set a new course. Masuo Yasui, who had arrived in Portland in 1907, was struck with the potential of the region and prodded his neighbors to remain. "People always talk about 'going back to Japan as soon as possible,'" he wrote to his brother, who lived in another part of the northwest. "[But] should it really be the ultimate goal to live an idle life [in Japan] with American dollars? I hope that you summon your wife and make a peaceful home in this great land of freedom," he concluded.[6] In an attempt to make his dream a reality, Yasui opened a grocery store in Hood River that sold "Japanese goods from the flowery kingdom," and he helped advance a farming settlement in the valley south of that town.[7]

Between 1910 and 1920, the Issei female population also grew in Oregon when "picture brides" came to join their husbands. During these years the number of Issei women went from 294 to 1,349. By 1920, Oregon's small community of Japanese residents were largely settled. In recognition of their current circumstances, they routinely sought to network with one another through their businesses. "Commercial and agricultural alliances

were the best resource available to Issei on their way to social and economic advancement in Oregon," said historian Eiichiro Azuma.[8]

But not all Oregonians appreciated the Issei presence. In an era of anti-
immigrant hysteria, xenophobic episodes haunted the state's Issei residents. A series of events designed to curb Japanese growth, including the
infamous *Tadeo Ozawa v. United States* (1922) decision that barred the
Issei from securing citizenship, Oregon's Alien Land Law of 1923, a man-
date to prohibit business licenses to Issei, and the 1924 Immigration Act,
sent chilling signals to Japanese residents and raised grave doubts about
their future in the United States. Violence against the Issei also broke out.
In 1925, for instance, a mob of white settlers drove several Japanese
sawmill workers out of Lincoln County, a region along the Pacific coast.
Indeed, the racist atmosphere made its mark: between 1924 and 1928,
Oregon's Japanese population dropped from 2,374 to 1,568, a decrease of
nearly 30 percent.[9]

Those who remained tenaciously overcame the social and legal barriers
cast in front of them and proceeded to strengthen their communities. The
Japanese Association provided one important tool for cohesion. From
1900 to 1910, a number of such associations sprang up and served as both
a liaison between Japanese and Caucasian groups and centers for Japanese
social enrichment. Churches, language schools, and cultural activities were
other means by which the Japanese communities closed ranks. Sports programs, however, ranked among the most important means for this purpose.[10]

Organized athletic activities emerged from a number of sources. At
times the Japanese Association put together programs for the area's youth.
The growing Japanese American Citizens League (JACL) also sponsored
basketball tournaments. But churches, too, played a role. The Buddhist
church, in particular, not only boasted the largest contingent of followers
but was critical in its capacity as a social nucleus for the Nisei, the offspring of the Issei. "[The church] served not only a religious function, but
was also a body for discussing vocational and civic problems. In addition,
it gave the Nisei a chance to get to know each other socially and to have a
good time," writer Barbara Yasui pointed out.[11] And baseball was a part of
that socialization.

Baseball had found a home in northern Oregon long before the Nisei
matured. As early as 1903, Portland had an entry in the famed Pacific
Coast League. Farther north, in Seattle, Japanese athletic clubs had fielded
strong baseball teams by the 1920s. In fact, as early as 1904, Issei baseball

teams competed for community honors. Signs of baseball activity among the Japanese were seen as far east at the central Washington community of Wapato. There, Nisei boys in 1926 converted their literature organization into an athletic club and began participating in the national pastime.[12] It was Frank Fukada, however, the Pacific Northwest's heralded "father of Japanese baseball," who stimulated the interests of baseball proponents in Oregon's northern periphery. Fukada, who spearheaded organized baseball among the Japanese in Seattle, also took teams to compete in Japan on three different occasions. In 1927, he moved to Portland. There, while working as principal of a language school, he came in direct contact with many of the area's Nisei, and, as he had done in Seattle, the popular coach helped organize a number of baseball programs. Fukada continued to work with local baseball enthusiasts until he moved on to Wapato in 1931.[13]

Baseball activity in northern Oregon, however, was sparse. Though there was much enthusiasm among the Nisei, their small population hindered development of a large-scale league akin to the popular thirty-team Courier League in Seattle. Hence, to compete against other Nisei clubs, teams along the Columbia River had to branch out in search of opponents. In this manner, the seeds for further regional networking were planted. Though some of their elders had, in earlier times, developed economic alliances, the national pastime took these contacts to a different level. These baseball connections brought metropolitan and rural residents together. On Sundays, Portland clubs inevitably planted their spikes into the turf of Gresham-Troutdale, Hood River, Salem, and even Wapato, Washington.

But not all Nisei clubs competed against one another. The most powerful of the Portland teams was the Nippon Giants. Formed in 1933, this organization took in the best Nisei talent the region had to offer. Moreover, the Giants competed in Portland's municipal city leagues, where they routinely finished high in the standings throughout the 1930s. Kats Nakayama was among the team's founders. Born in Seattle in 1906, Nakayama grew up in a region where baseball took center stage in recreation among the Nisei. Seattle's heralded Courier League, as well as smaller athletic clubs, provided the fertile ground in which Nakayama developed his baseball skills. Because work was scarce in the Puget Sound, however, Nakayama migrated to Portland in 1933, where he secured employment at a grocery store. But Nakayama had baseball in his blood, and he used contacts he made at the local Buddhist church to bring some of the top Japanese baseball talent to a single club. Within a year, Nakayama and his cohorts had their team, and for the remainder of the decade the Nippon Giants held their own against many of the strong Caucasian teams in Portland. Considered to be among the older of the Nisei athletes, the team featured a standout player named Ralph Takami, who had starred as an all-city pitcher for Lincoln High School. Takami eventually played at Oregon State College.[14]

In addition to their athletic talent, the Giants utilized their bilingual skills to their advantage. As bat boy to the club, Jerry Inouye recalled, "When they played Caucasian teams, the Giants would speak in Japanese to each other to send signals. They always caught the white players off guard; sometimes going over strategy right in front of the Caucasian players' face."[15] "We didn't lose too many games too often," remembered Nakayama.[16] The club also competed in the fabled Japanese American Pacific Northwest Baseball Tournament, held annually on July 4 in Seattle and sponsored by the *Japanese American Courier* newspaper. In 1936, they took the tournament championship without a defeat.

By the mid-1930s other Nisei clubs in northern Oregon had formed. Eventually, five teams spanned the region from Salem to Hood River. While not as talented as the Giants, the newer teams were no less competitive. Moreover, they spawned from different sources. In Portland, for instance, the Portland Midgets were not only a baseball club. They began as a social organization. To be courted for membership was a matter of honor. "I was excited to be asked to join the club. I wanted very much to meet new people," remembered Jerry Inouye.[17] Athletes were among the organization's founding members and, eventually, came to form a baseball club. "Sundays became exciting during the summer. Baseball was not only fun, but it was a way of bonding with the other Nisei," said Inouye.[18]

The leader of the Midgets was John Murakami. Born in Sherwood in 1919, Murakami came to Portland with his family when he was seven years old. His Issei father, involved in agriculture, never took to sports, but not so the son. "There used to be ball games in the local park in Lake Oswego. And when my father and I went to sell produce, I used to look forward to driving past that park so I could see them playing. I just knew that when I got old enough that that is what I wanted to do," Murakami recalled.[19]

Murakami even maintained hopes of playing at the professional ranks until his dreams were shattered in his sixteenth year. Playing on a largely Caucasian team, he learned that big-league scouts were in attendance at one of their games and planned to meet the players after the contest. "I played real hard that day and then, after the game, they made us all stand in a single line as they spoke to each player," he said. With his heart pounding, the possibility of someday wearing a big league uniform crossed the young man's mind. The scout, however, took but a second to determine Murakami's fate. "He said, 'You might as well forget it kid, you'll never play professional ball,'" he remembered. Crushed, the young Nisei faced additional frustration when not allowed to play high school baseball. He said, "I wanted to play high school ball real badly, but my parents thought that was just out of the question."[20]

Murakami found solace in the Buddhist church, where, coincidentally, he met others who shared his love for the national pastime. By the time he turned eighteen, he had expanded his baseball interests, and he eventually joined two of the area's most popular teams, the Oseis and the Mikados. Murakami and his brother Jumbo became blue-chip players and spurred others to compete. "Sundays was a day we looked forward to. We could participate in athletics and then socialize afterwards," said Murakami.[21] Baseball, some Nisei sheepishly admitted later, took priority over church services during those occasions when teams traveled to such spots as Hood River and Wapato, Washington. "Well, the ministers didn't like it, but it wasn't an every-week occurrence either. Only once or twice in a season. I think they were willing to forgive us."[22]

Indeed, the golden age for Nisei baseball had begun. "The thirties was the beginning of a fun time for us. We were old enough to drive and some of us started to date," Murakami said.[23] For baseball games, Murakami gladly got behind the wheel. Using a grocery-store pickup truck as their mode of transportation, the Midgets, dressed in their flannel uniforms, weekly piled into the back of the truck for what could be up to three-hour drives. "Johnny [Murakami] was our chauffeur," claimed Jerry Inouye.[24]

Among their opponents was another Nisei club in the Gresham-Troutdale area. As in the case of the Portland Midgets, baseball in Gresham-Troutdale was the outgrowth of a social organization that Issei parents had manufactured for their offspring. Known as the Fujis, the club's rural setting on the outskirts of Portland allowed them the space to build their own baseball diamond. "We were proud of that home field," recalled former player Hiro Takeuchi. "We had a real home-field advantage because our ground was rougher than the other parks."[25] Baseball, indeed, was revered by these young players. "We worked real hard during the week so we could play ball on Sundays. My dad even said that baseball took priority over the farm. He loved it."[26] Like the Giants, the Fujis traveled to Seattle to participate in the Pacific Northwest Baseball Tournament. "It was exciting for us to go there. We were just country kids and it was a great thrill. And we never got blown out up there," Takeuchi proudly stated.[27]

Salem also provided Oregon's northern periphery with a competitive team. Like Gresham-Troutdale, Salem's Japanese constituency was largely rural. "It was really the only thing we had going," said Tats Yada.[28] Indeed, so small was the community that players who eventually joined the Yamatos were generally recruited from as far away as Independence some twenty miles to the south. Competition was also sparse—so sparse that they even turned to playing the inmates at the state prison nearby. "That was interesting. The inmates often cheered for us. We needed opponents and ended up playing there because, of course, they couldn't go on the road and play us at our field," Yada stated.[29]

Like their counterparts at Greshman-Troutdale, the Yamatos put together their own makeshift field. "There were no stands or anything else except a backstop and a lot of space," Yada explained.[30] The Yamatos, however, got their biggest enjoyment from playing other Nisei teams to the north of them. Because the team members felt isolated, the trips became an important means of networking. Yada claimed that without those baseball trips "we'[d']ve been stuck in Salem. Instead, we were able to meet other Nisei and share time with them." But Yada also made it clear that, socializing aside, the Salem crew "wanted to win." And in 1937 the Yamatos returned to their home in the Willamette Valley with the Portland Japanese Association Baseball League Tournament first-place trophy. Throughout the second half of the 1930s, the Nisei teams crisscrossed the Columbia River region during the summer months, sometimes passing each other, sometimes playing each other; but all eventually encountered the Hood River team and Kay "Schoolboy" Kiyokawa.

Though a substantial number of Japanese lived in the Hood River valley by 1930, they were nonetheless isolated from one another living in separate communities. However, in an effort to bridge their gaps, they formed farming associations and developed language schools for the Nisei. But sport also tied the broader community together. To that end, in 1935 several Nisei met to form the Nisei Athletic Club. Soon thereafter, Ray "Chop" Yasui took the lead in forming a Nisei baseball club. "Everybody enjoyed our teams because of him. He chattered, kept everybody loose, and joked with the fans," recalled Kay Kiyokawa.[31] "Our district would have been more isolated had it not been for baseball." Homer Yasui remembered, "Baseball was the biggest draw. A lot of families came together during those games."[32] Indeed, players from all regions of the Hood River valley came together each Sunday to compete and share friendships. "Chop" Yasui also kept the club busy by scheduling games against most local clubs and others, including Native Americans on the Warm Springs Reservation, sixty miles to the south, and in Ontario, which lay six hours to the east on the Oregon-Idaho border.

Hood River also featured some interesting baseball facilities. At one point, the club played in a redesigned rodeo arena in nearby Parkdale. Kiyokawa remembered, "I guess the rodeo didn't go over so good, so we played baseball there instead."[33] Another time they used the bottom of an old gravel pit as their diamond. "The city excavated a hole," claimed Kiyokawa. "The field was large enough, but the infield still had gravel in it. There was no turf." Homer Yasui added, "It was a terrible field. But it was all that we had."[34] Kiyokawa and his teammates just took everything in stride. "You erect a backstop, place the bases and play."[35]

By the late 1930s, Kiyokawa was clearly the star of the Hood River squad. Small in stature, the southpaw nonetheless stymied opponents with an assortment of pitches that became legendary throughout the Columbia region. John Murakami recalled of his Hood River rival, "He threw a ball that barely came across the plate. But you could not hit that pitch. If you hit it you just flied out. He was the hardest guy to hit."[36] Jerry Inouye added, "Oh ya, 'schoolboy' Kiyokawa was tough. In fact, Hood River always had good talent. They were farm boys. I think they were stronger than us."[37] Even the Salem players remembered, "That Kiyokawa fellow was good. We never did hit him very well."[38] One Gresham player, according to Kiyokawa, struck out seven straight times to the lefty, "and I still remind him of that at our golf tournaments today."[39] Kiyokawa later went on to play at Oregon State College and, during World War II, threw for the University of Connecticut.

Young women were not immune to baseball's magnetism. Many had played competitive softball and understood and attended the baseball games. Indeed, as John Murakami found out, they were difficult to fool. Attempting to "make [him]self sound good" to the woman who later became his wife, Murakami one afternoon proudly announced that he had made three hits that day. "No you didn't," she responded, having watched the contest. "You only got two hits and a fielder's choice," she clarified.[40] The women also were supportive of their local teams. Murakami recalled the adventures of a young woman who would "drive herself and her parents all the way to Wapato to see the ball games. I thought that was really something that a young woman would drive that distance."[41] (The woman in question also had a favorite player in George Azumano, whom she later married.)

"Meeting the gals was another reason the guys liked to play on Sundays," said Murakami. "It was that way with me."[42] Kay Kiyokawa agreed: "Some of the Wapato guys married some of the Hood River girls. And some of the Hood River guys married some of the Ontario girls that they met at and after the games."[43] Indeed, the postgame socials proved to be as enjoyable as the games themselves. Jerry Inouye remembered that "those guys in Hood River were good hosts. They always had sandwiches for us after the game."[44] Sometimes, however, the socials proved awkward. "When our [Gresham-Troutdale] club visited Wapato, they put on a dance for us after the game. What they didn't count on was that none of us knew how to dance," said Hiro Takeuchi.[45]

Baseball's value to the Japanese of northern Oregon clearly went well beyond competition. In a region where their communities often lay distant from one another, the games brought people together for the first time. "Meeting others was the most important aspect of the game to me. For instance, without the team, we in Salem would have never gone to Hood River," said Tats Yada.[46] Kay Kiyokawa claimed, "We were close to the Gresham players. And those association[s] which began with baseball have remained through life."[47] "We [in Hood River] were country bumpkins. Coming to Portland was a wonderful and thrilling experience for me because they had taxis, buses, trolley cars, and elevators. To young men like us, this was big time," said Homer Yasui.[48] Hiro Takeuchi added, "We just loved our sports. [And] the fellowship that came from [our baseball] was really important."[49]

While baseball was not the sole means of bridging the geographical distances among the Japanese in northern Oregon, it was one of the most effective. Indeed, from the fields of the Willamette Valley to the pear and apple orchards beneath the shadow of majestic Mount Hood, no other activity brought the Nisei together as often as did the Sunday games during the summer months. Nisei players competed and shook hands at Peninsula playground and Benson High School in Portland, while others shared their stories and hoped to impress the young women of Wapato, Washington. Indeed, the baseball contests prompted social, romantic, and sometimes business relationships that lasted lifelong. Though few in numbers, Nisei baseball teams held a position of prominence in the hearts of the players and their respective communities in the region of the mighty Columbia. As such, the Reverend Hirayama was probably not too surprised to see young Jerry Inouye return to his chapel later in the day to thank the supportive minister for his time and fatherly counsel—and to proudly inform the preacher that he had just pitched his Portland Midgets past the Gresham-Troutdale Fujis for the regional championship of 1939.

Notes

1. Jerry Inouye, "Reverend Hirayama," *Konko Review* 19, 3 (May/June 1993): 18–19.

2. Ibid., 19.

3. Linda Tamura, *The Hood River Issei: An Oral History of the Japanese Settlers in Oregon's Hood River Valley* (Urbana: University of Illinois Press, 1993), 284.

4. Eiichiro Azuma, "A History of Oregon's Issei, 1880–1952," *Oregon Historical Quarterly* 94, 4 (Winter 1993–94): 317–319.

5. Ibid., 328.

6. Ibid., 329.

7. Tamura, *Hood River Issei*, 76.

8. Azuma "History of Oregon's Issei," 333.

9. Ibid., 335.

10. Barbara Yasui, "The Nikkei in Oregon, 1834–1940," *Oregon Historical Quarterly* 76, 3 (September 1975): 251.

11. Ibid.

12. Gail Nomura, "Beyond the Playing Field: The Significance of Pre–World War II Japanese American Baseball in the Yakima Valley," in *Bearing Dreams, Shaping Visions: Asian Pacific American Perspectives*, ed. Linda A. Revilla (Pullman, WA: Washington State University Press 1993), 17.

13. Ryoichi Shibazaki, "Seattle and the Japanese-United States Baseball Connection, 1905–1926" (M.S. thesis, University of Washington, 1981), 67.

14. Deena K. Nakata, *The Gift: The Oregon Nikkei Story . . . Retold* (Portland: Deena K. Takata, 1995), 49.

15. Interview with Jerry Inouye, Portland, Oregon, June 7, 1997.

16. Interview with Kats Nakayama, Portland, Oregon, July 31, 1996.

17. Inouye interview.

18. Ibid.

19. Interview with John Murakami, Portland, Oregon, July 31, 1996.

20. Ibid.

21. Ibid.

22. Ibid.

23. Ibid.
24. Inouye interview.
25. Interview with Hiro Takeuchi, Portland, Oregon, August 20, 1996.
26. Ibid.
27. Ibid.
28. Interview with Tats Yada, Salem, Oregon, June 7, 1997.
29. Ibid.
30. Ibid.
31. Interview with Kay Kiyokawa, Dee, Oregon, August 1, 1996.
32. Interview with Dr. Homer Yasui, Portland, Oregon, August 2, 1996.
33. Kiyokawa interview.
34. Yasui interview.
35. Kiyokawa interview.
36. Murakami interview.
37. Inouye interview.
38. Yada interview.
39. Kiyokawa interview.
40. Murakami interview.
41. Ibid.
42. Ibid.
43. Kiyokawa interview.
44. Inouye interview.
45. Takeuchi interview.
46. Yada interview.
47. Kiyokawa interview.
48. Yasui interview.
49. Takeuchi interview.

Chapter Four

Mexican American Baseball
Masculinity, Racial Struggle, and Labor Politics in Southern California, 1930–1950

José M. Alamillo

"We were the best team around. We played all over Southern California and everyone wanted to beat us. Other teams would recruit the best players around so they could come to our town [Corona] and try to beat us," explained Tito Cortez with a proud look on his face as he pointed to a large framed picture of the Corona Athletics baseball team adorning his living room wall. "Everyone used to come out on Sundays after church to watch the Athletics games and when someone hit a homerun they would honk the car horns."[1] Cortez remembered the all–Mexican American Corona Athletics as one of the most fiercely competitive semi-professional baseball teams in Southern California. First organized in 1933, this independent baseball club boasted a lineup of all-star players, claimed several tournament championships, and earned a reputation among baseball scouts for producing players with major league potential.

Because of U.S. baseball's deeply entrenched "color line," Tito Cortez and other dark-skinned Latinos and blacks were barred from the major leagues until Jackie Robinson joined the Brooklyn Dodgers in 1947. Major league teams, however, did recruit mostly light-skinned Latino baseball players prior to World War II. Baseball historian Samuel Regalado notes in *Viva Baseball!*, that over forty-nine Latinos played in the major leagues, mostly originating from Cuba and a few from Mexico.[2] However, a majority of Latinos never reached the big leagues, but remained playing community-based baseball also known as sandlot ball.

In Southern California, semi-pro baseball attracted minority players and audiences largely because of the racial and class dynamics of professional sports and the region's ethnically mixed working class neighborhoods. Sandlot baseball teams sprung up during the 1920s and the 1930s in *barrios* and *colonias* introducing this national pastime to immigrant children at a time where Mexican heroes were few and far between. During the 1920s and 1930s the Mexican-origin population faced limited economic opportunities and a racially restricted environment. Within this context, community baseball clubs provided a counterpoint to grim material realities encountered at work and community, and team members could potentially attain social status, respect, dignity and realize their own "field of dreams."

While baseball brought the Mexican community together on Sunday afternoons, it did so at a time when agricultural companies and city government sought to organize and control the community's sporting life. In the early decades of the twentieth century, Southwestern growers organized baseball clubs to potentially increase discipline, obedience, and productivity of its immigrant workforce. Private industry and reformers viewed baseball as a mechanism to insure submission to authority and provide an antidote to labor organizing and disruptive recreational pursuits. Baseball also promoted a particular kind of white middle-class masculinity—self-sacrifice, discipline, obedience, and competitive drive—that reproduced existing gender, racial, and class hierarchies.

While some accepted baseball's accommodation to industrial capitalism and brand of middle-class masculinity, other Mexican American players resisted and imposed their own meanings on this "national pastime" that differed from the intentions of reformers and employers. Mexican Americans defined and used sandlot baseball as a means for cultural expression, racial and masculine pride, and community empowerment. Within the context of economic marginalization and pervasive racial discrimination affecting the Mexican community, baseball matches took on real and symbolic political meanings. As C. L. R. James noted long ago about the wider social significance of cricket contests: "The cricket field was a stage on which selected individuals played representative roles which were charged with social significance."[3] Like black cricket players, Mexican Americans viewed competitive baseball matches against all-white teams as real and symbolic of larger racial and class struggles that transcended the playing field. Using baseball clubs as a forum to discuss, establish networks, and hone their organizing and leadership skills, Mexican American players entered the realm of labor politics. Members of the Corona Athletics traded their baseball gloves for picket signs and waged a two-month strike in the spring months of 1941, with the assistance of the United Cannery and Packinghouse and Agricultural Workers of America (UCA-PAWA), an affiliate of the Congress of Industrial Organizations (CIO).

This chapter examines the meanings and uses of baseball matches and clubs among Mexican Americans in Southern California between 1930 and 1950. First I will trace agricultural employers' efforts to implement recreational programs and baseball clubs in order to assimilate Mexican workers and increase their productivity. Then I will look at how and why Mexican Americans formed baseball clubs, such as the Corona Athletics Club to express racial and masculine pride, and community empowerment. Finally, I will examine the ways in which baseball games were an arena for real and symbolic political assertion, and launching pad for wider collective actions. While the Athletics club became an important source of organization and leadership, I argue that baseball collectivities contributed to the formation of unions, and that baseball players-turned-labor organizers and participants recreated in turn a masculine culture that extended into the union, thus reproducing unequal gender relations that severely limited the politics of opposition.

Scholars in the field of Chicano/a history still have yet to examine fully the racialized, gendered, working class, and transnational dimensions of sport and leisure among Mexican American working classes.[4] Within sports scholarship baseball histories far outnumber those of any other sport, but a large number are still limited to white and black players and their respective communities.[5] More recently with the increasing number of Latinos in major league baseball the long-neglected history of Latino baseball history has begun to emerge; however, the scholarship tends to focus on professional players at the national major league level.[6] Unlike previous works, this study examines community-based semi-pro Mexican American baseball and their cultural, social and political role in ethnic Mexican community and the Southern California region.[7]

Industrial Recreation, Immigrant Labor, and the "Baseball Solution"

Before arriving in the United States, Mexicans had already been introduced to America's "national pastime" by U.S. railroad, agricultural, and mining companies during the Porfiriato, the thirty-four year period (1976–1910) of Porfiro Díaz's presidencies characterized by modernization such as the construction of the railroads. During leisure hours, the Mexican National and Mexican Central Railroad Companies organized baseball matches between Anglo supervisors and Mexican track laborers. By the late 1880s, baseball had gained popularity and spread to the border towns and Mexico City, where some of the first matches drew large crowds, convincing Porfirian liberals of the sport's potential to teach modern industrial values to the masses. In his *Mexican Mind*, travel writer Wallace Thompson stated, "A magnificent beginning has thus been made in the training of Mexican boys in the development of teamwork and sportsmanship and in the encouragement of participation instead of observation. It seems that these features are being developed by baseball." American employers hoped that skills and "good sportsmanlike" habits learned on the playing field among Mexican employees would be channeled into higher productivity in the workplace and increased company loyalty. Ironically, this transnational "good sportsman" ideology flowed back into the United States through industrial recreational programs applied to Mexican immigrant workers, many of whom labored for the same agricultural, railroad, and mining interests.[8]

American companies launched a series of welfare capitalist measures in the early twentieth century, to combat labor problems such as job turnover and rising worker militancy and in the hopes of building a more efficient, stable, and contented workforce. In the 1920s, East Coast and Midwest industrial giants opened branches, plants, and factories in Southern California to take advantage of "open shop" conditions, with the backing of anti-union allies such as the Los Angeles Chamber of Commerce. A decade later, when labor unions began making inroads and economic conditions were improving, some companies renewed efforts to offer social welfare programs to win over workers' loyalty.[9] More than any other welfare activity, industrial recreation received widespread support among manufacturing and agricultural interests. One of these agricultural giants was the California Fruit Growers Exchange (CFGE). Although CFGE was organized as marketing cooperative, it functioned more like a large-scale corporation, with bureaucratic personnel, a board of directors, scientific managers, and labor relations advisers.[10] The CFGE encouraged citrus growers to organize baseball teams among their largely Mexican-origin workforce, purportedly to improve workers' physical health and to prepare them mentally for ten-hour workdays, six days a week, and arduous, back-breaking field and packinghouse work.

In the aftermath of labor disturbances during World War I, the CFGE formed the Industrial Relations Department (IRD) to organize a corporate welfare system that included a recreational component. According to IRD director G. B. Hodgkin, "There is something, even in a Mexican, that cannot be satisfied merely by a good place to sleep and plenty to eat. That something must have an outlet. Rightly directed it would express itself in the ordinary forms of social relaxation, [and] recreation." In order "to produce the desired [Mexican] workers," Hodgkin added, "the [Mexican] had to become a member of a local society or baseball team or band . . . to increase their physical and mental capacity [and] for doing more work." Citrus industry officials believed that this "national pastime" leisure activity would instill self-discipline on and off the job, create goodwill between company management and Mexican workers, and, most of all, offer an antidote to labor organizing.[11]

Hodgkin's proposed "baseball solution" to improve industrial labor relations gained support among citrus growers, chief among whom was Keith Spalding, son and heir of A. J. Spalding Sporting Goods Corporation. Spalding owned and operated the Ventura County citrus ranch Rancho Sespe. This old California *rancho* was transformed into a "model scientific farm," with modern packinghouses, office buildings, housing accommodations, and a baseball diamond. Like his father, Spalding viewed baseball as an Americanizing agent for the promotion of white Protestant American values and a capitalist work ethic, to ensure a "spirit of loyalty and co-operation" between company and employees and between nation and citizens.[12] On observing a successful grower-sponsored baseball program, one investigator wrote, "The entire [Mexican] colony has become baseball conscious in a short time and the interest exhibited in this great American sport has seemingly supplanted the former Sunday diversion of cock-fighting, which is common to many Mexican colonies in Southern California."[13]

Underlying these actions were racialized and gendered constructions and political needs to reform workers' cultural lives and notions of manhood. Apart from strict economic motives, company sport offered an alternative to "immoral" and "subversive" leisure activities, such as gambling, drinking, and cockfighting. Popular among ethnic Mexican communities throughout the Southern California citrus belt, cockfighting was typically conducted undercover, inside citrus orchards and in remote locations. Despite being declared an "illegal sport" under county ordinances, cockfighting would sometimes draw up to two hundred people at a time. One reason for the political elite's strong opposition to this largely ethnic, working-class, and highly masculine sport was the possibility that this leisure space could be transformed into a politicized space of opposition. The editor of *Corona Independent* revealed this understanding of the subversive potential to this gambling sport when he wrote, "A Corona Mexican and others were taken into custody after a cock fight raid and one of the persons was found carrying communist literature." Workers used cockfighting as an important social space to (re)assert their cultural identity and to resist company surveillance and a white gaze that aimed to control, oversee and regulate their everyday behavior.[14]

To combat labor militancy and culturally "deviant" behavior, citrus companies throughout Southern California organized baseball teams for their employees. In Corona, California, known as the "lemon capital of the world" because of its large lemon by-products plant, eleven packinghouses, and several ranch operations, the largest citrus companies— Corona Foothill Lemon Company, Jameson Company, Verity and Sons Company, and American Fruit Growers—organized a citywide company baseball league. In 1928 the Corona Foothill Lemon Company cleared several rows of fruit orchards on its nine hundred-acre ranch property to build a baseball diamond for its newly formed team, the Foothill Lemoneers. (See Figure 4.1.)[15]

The Lemoneers comprised five white ranch supervisors and four Mexican workers. Ranch supervisor Carl Herklerath served as team captain for several years, in charge of scheduling games against other company teams, providing the necessary equipment, and recruiting players.[16] Former player Santos Garcia recalled that when he served as the team's bat boy, "I had to pick up all the equipment at the ranch store and carried it to the baseball diamond where everyone would get together and play ball all day on Sundays, but I never got a chance to play like my older brother Blas [Garcia]."[17] Because the Mexican players worked eight- to ten-hour days, six days a week, picking fruit, they could practice only occasionally in the evenings and played only on Sunday afternoons. Despite the sport's popularity among community residents, the company team was limited to older adults. Teenagers and young adults were relegated to spectators, bat boys, and substitute players. When Tito Cortez was asked how he learned to play baseball as a teenager at the Foothill Ranch, he responded, "The younger kids around my age used to play pickup games in the ranch, with

4.1 Playing baseball at the Foothill Ranch (ca. 1920s). *Used by permission of the Corona Public Library.*

rocks and sticks . . . some of us also learned from watching the older players like Blas Garcia, Salvador Rios, and Manuel Muñoz who played for the [Foothill Lemoneers] ranch team." Cortez and his peers continued to play ball despite being sidelined to spectator status, even if doing so interfered with their job responsibilities. Cortez remarked, "We used to get together and sometimes we played all night . . . lots of folks used to sleep until the next morning and be late for work, but the foremen did not really say anything."[18]

Several years later, a group of second-generation Mexican American youth demanded that the company provide equipment and uniforms for their newly formed baseball team, the Foothill Aces. The company responded by providing bats, balls, and access to the baseball diamond. But for some players, limited company support was not good enough, so after only two seasons (1931–1933) the Foothill Aces disbanded. Also, work schedules limited players' mobility, and the company diamond's remoteness from town reduced spectator numbers. Former Aces ballplayer Zeke Mejia explained, "Teams popped up at the local citrus picking ranches where many Hispanics lived but they did not last long . . . the games did not attract much attention because they were too far away from the town."[19] The ability to attract a larger audience limited Mexican American ballplayers' hopes of acquiring social status and public visibility for major league scouts who appeared unannounced among the spectators. Cortez explained how, after two seasons, the company failed to deliver on its promise to keep up the maintenance on the diamond: "The team ended around 1933 because they [Aces players] were too tired of the baseball field . . . it was not as good as the one in town where the Athletics played. You see many of these players picked fruit and did other kind of ranch work so they could not find the time to keep it up."[20]

While the company hoped this sporting activity would encourage Mexican males to identify closer with management, its failure to deliver a more comprehensive recreational program served instead to widen the gap between company management and second-generation workers. The Great Depression forced some companies reduce their welfare offerings, but with the large strikes that rocked the California countryside, a majority of companies continued their welfare offerings through the 1930s. Unlike the Lemoneers, the Aces made repeated demands on the company to fulfill its promises to maintain a manicured baseball field and supply the team with equipment and transportation. When the company failed to meet these demands and scaled down its welfare offerings, workers decided look elsewhere for sporting opportunities. With the demise of the Foothill Aces, several ballplayers (Natividad "Tito" Cortez, Silvestre "Silve" Balderas, Alfredo Uribe, Sammy Lopez, and Ray Zaragosa) opted to play for the independent all–Mexican American baseball club, the Corona Athletics Baseball Club.[21]

From the perspective of employers, sports were meant to serve as a diversionary tactic for workers who would succumb to the thrills of cheap amusements that were potentially subversive and threatening to industrial work ethics and values. Such activities as gambling, drinking, cockfighting, union organizing, and other anti-social behavior could be remedied by making workers "baseball conscious" and could inculcate white American middle-class values of sobriety, thrift, and discipline both on and off the playing field. But, far from molding workers in the company's image, baseball became a vehicle that second-generation Mexican Americans could skillfully exploit for their own ends. Neither cockfighting nor baseball could distract Mexican American youth from the necessity to resist company control, assert their own cultural values, and forge a "culture of opposition."[22] By negotiating their loyalty to the Foothill Lemon Company, Mexican American workers created a social space for themselves and the larger ethnic Mexican community, but when the company failed to live

up to its side of the bargain, the workers decided to look elsewhere, to negotiate a new set of leisure possibilities.

Louis Perez has suggested that Cubans became "conscious of new
meanings and mindful of new possibilities" of baseball and, on return to
the island, "started to reinvent themselves self-consciously as agents of
change."[23] As I will show, Mexican Americans, on being introduced to
company-sponsored baseball, turned to independent baseball clubs not
only for cultural cohesion and community-building purposes but to forge
a politics of opposition that helped build an interethnic labor movement.

Baseball Clubs, Ethnic Identity, and "Imagined Community"

One of the first all–Mexican American baseball clubs formed in Southern
California was the Athletics Baseball Club. (See Figure 4.2.) First organized in 1933, this baseball club held a central position in the local ethnic
Mexican community of Corona, California.[24] The club offered more than
a Sunday leisure-time activity, and more than visible male heroes for
young boys; it served as vehicle for Mexican community cultural expression, welding organizational ties and strengthening social networks across
the region. Held immediately after Sunday church services, Athletics ball
games constituted the main leisure-time activity among Mexican families.
The backbone of this organization was Corona's Mexican community,
who originated from both neighborhood *colonias* and outlying ranch
communities.[25] They rallied around the Athletics team as a marker of cultural pride and community cohesion against a backdrop of racial discrimination and segregation in the workplace and public spaces.

Baseball introduced Mexican immigrants, like other ethnic immigrants,
to "American" culture, through dialogue and confrontation with white,
Japanese American, and African American players on and off the diamond.[26] For example, on the one hand, Athletics games encouraged Mexican patriotic, religious, and mutual-aid organizations to stage cultural celebrations, sell Mexican cuisine, and entertain audiences with Mariachi
music, before and after matches. On the other hand, Athletics players had
to negotiate their way into the American mainstream by gaining Anglo allies in city council, seeking business sponsors, winning over major league
scouts, and even recruiting a few Anglo players in the post–World War II
years. Like other forces of Americanization, baseball influenced Mexican
immigrant children in ways that differed from how it had influenced their

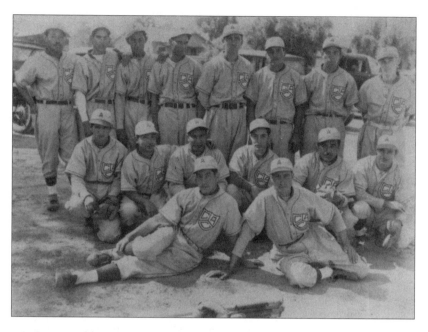

4.2 Corona Athletics baseball team, 1937. *Used by permission of the Corona Public Library.*

parents, and these new converts in turn transformed baseball at the local and semi-pro levels. (Like African Americans, dark-skinned Mexicans who could not "pass" as white players were barred from the major leagues until 1947.)[27] As a result, second-generation Mexicans in Corona forged a new cultural identity as Mexican Americans.

Two Mexican American leaders, Marcelino "Chileno" Barba and Gilbert Enriquez, founded the ball club and subsequently became manager and captain, respectively. Barba arrived in Corona in 1923, attended Corona's public schools, and was one of very few high-school graduates of Mexican descent during this period. On graduation, he was hired at the Exchange Lemon Products Plant (later renamed Sunkist). He worked for the Exchange for over twenty-five years and, during his off-hours, spent many hours scheduling ball games, soliciting sponsors, and maintaining the Athletics playing field.[28] Unlike Barba, Gilbert Enriquez avoided working for the citrus industry by working for a local department shoe store. Because of his extensive recreational work with youth, he was hired as the first Mexican American coach at Washington School.[29] Corona resident

Adelina Enriquez remembered how her father first got interested in organizing baseball clubs: "My father realized that these Mexican kids had nothing to do after school so he got a bunch of them together and formed a baseball team."[30] Apart from his duties as team captain, for several years Enriquez was involved labor and civil rights organizations and founded the city's first Spanish language newspaper, El Imparcial.[31]

Approximately twelve of the fifteen ballplayers that formed the Corona Athletics worked as citrus pickers, with half living in town and the rest in outlying citrus ranches. Although they resided in separate communities, they attended Washington School also known as a "Mexican school." Throughout the Southwest, Mexican children were segregated into Mexican schools with inferior classroom facilities, mediocre Anglo teachers, and an emphasis on vocational education.[32] On graduation, few Mexican children continued on to junior high or high school because they were forced to follow in the footsteps of their fathers who labored in the lemon orchards. Facing a bleak future picking lemons at low wages, Mexican Americans turned to baseball as an outlet for self-expression and because it offered some degree of autonomy from parental and company authority, especially for ranch worker-residents. While some parents encouraged sports activities among their children, others were suspicious of this "national pastime" because it took away valuable leisure hours that should be spent with family. Former Detroit Tigers ballplayer Hank Aguirre disclosed to his biographer that his father viewed baseball as "a big waste of time," and that it became a major source of tension between them until he was recruited into the major leagues.[33]

The possibility of social mobility loomed large in the minds of ballplayers. Former Athletics pitcher Zeke Mejia, for example, decided early in life that he did not want to pick lemons like his father, so he dedicated himself to school and sports. "Since I knew I did not want to pick lemons like my father I needed an incentive to stay in school, so I started playing sports, especially baseball. . . . It taught me something about myself. I hated to lose then and still hate to lose now [as a businessman]. I never took things lightly."[34] These comments echoed the company's ideology of middle-class respectability and social mobility, suggesting that sporting activities taught workers important lessons about discipline, loyalty, and responsibility.

Writing in the Corona Independent, a citrus grower cited the benefits of this recreational activity for worker discipline: "Mexican boys who throng the Washington school playground for baseball are having more fun this summer than they have ever had here before—and what is more, they are learning cooperation and the lasting discipline that comes with athletic competition among men."[35] Company officials promoted a middle-class form of masculinity that prescribed workers to become responsible "breadwinners" and "heads of households." A competing form was the rebellious and "insubordinate" worker who gambled away his earnings in cockfights and drank away the alienation experienced on the job. Corona baseball players, as I will show later, exhibited both forms of masculine behavior and during labor struggles attempted to fight against the most insidious form—class-based patriarchal domination—but unwittingly ended up reinforcing some form of patriarchy within the movement.

Given the grim material realities of their lives, citrus workers looked forward to their only day off to attend baseball matches on Sunday afternoons. On this day they could reclaim their dignity and pride by playing ball. Belonging to the most fierce and competitive baseball clubs in town, with the best-looking uniforms, was reason enough to show off and wear their pride on their sleeves. (See Figure 4.3.) Sunday baseball games also offered families an opportunity to reunite with family relatives and friends. Because of the lack of discretionary family income, free baseball games were particularly appealing. This weekend ritual fostered a community spirit in the Mexican community that blurred differences according to class, generation, place of residence, and citizenship status. "After picking all week we all looked forward to Sundays," remembered Jess "Chuy" Uribe, who, along with three older brothers, played for the Foothill Aces and, later, the Corona Athletics. "We use to pack the benches, there on the Railroad and Sheridan field, and cars would be parked all over. We used to have a really big crowd and things would get pretty excited."[36]

While many complained about the "back-breaking" work of picking lemons, some individuals commented on how this type of work actually prepared them for better baseball performance. As former minor league player Tito Cortez explained, "Everyone used to comment how [you] would work like a dog all week picking lemons and then went and got drunk on Saturday nights and played baseball all day on Sunday and again the following week. But you see that was the only thing to do since there was no television. We would practice on Thursday after work for a couple hours, catching flies and batting practice. In a way, working on the groves, carrying a heavy sack, climbing up and down the ladder, and using a quick eye to pick lemons helped with my [baseball] training."[37] Workers also tended to support their fellow crew buddies and often competed against

4.3 Athletics ballplayer Ralph Rodriguez in front of the Santa Fe Railroad Depot. *Used by permission of the Corona Public Library.*

other *caudrillas* (work crews) for higher productivity: thus loyalty to the work crew often translated to loyalty to a particular baseball team.[38]

In the beginning, the Athletics played on the Washington School playground for several years. Because of large crowds and school playground regulations, the team decided to relocate to an empty railroad lot owned by the Santa Fe Railroad. Another reason they preferred to play on Santa Fe's private grounds was to avoid city regulations on alcohol consumption and food sales. Also, local community groups sold Mexican food, ice cream, and drinks during the games to raise money and publicize their activities. Examples of such organizations include mutual-aid societies, patriotic-celebration committees, fraternal lodges, and social clubs. These organizations supported one another, since many Athletics ballplayers belonged to different groups.[39] Baseball offered a means by which players and spectators constructed an "imagined community" through a shared sense of nationality in the Mexican patriotic celebrations, Mexican musical performances, and Mexican food stands that predominated during and after Athletics matches.[40]

Drinking alcohol was another pastime among spectators and ballplayers. After each victory, the manager would purchase food and beer for the team. As former Athletics pitcher Tito Cortez points out, "After the game the managers would buy us *cerveza* and *tacos*. Sometimes we had a barbeque out there, roasted goat and made tacos de *chivo* [goat tacos]."[41] These postgame celebrations, however, were contingent on how much money the team collected after each game. Although they passed a hat in the audiences at every game, it rarely paid for equipment, uniforms, and transportation costs. Marcos Uribe, nicknamed "El Mocho" because of his amputated arm, became team manager during the early 1940s and introduced a small ice cream cart to sell *raspados* (shaved ice), but this venture did not pay for all the equipment costs.[42]

To offset expenses, team managers sought financial support from local Mexican businesses. As explained by Jess "Chuy" Uribe, Athletics manager during the late 1940s and early 1950s, "From all the people that came to watch us we would pass around a basket to collect money to support the team but it was never enough. . . . Only coins you would see because people were poor. But still many people helped us cover the costs. For the fifteen uniforms we had to find support from the local businesses."[43] He added, "We used to get sponsors from the Mexican business[es] especially beer bars and restaurants. Each business would buy a baseball suit but wanted to put their business name on the back. One time they gave me a baseball suit from Jalisco's Bar and put the letters on the back; in fact this place [became] one of our biggest sponsor[s]."[44] Although Jalisco's Bar was a major baseball sponsor, it was also a popular gathering place and masculine space for many of Corona's ballplayers. Local residents jokingly referred to this place as "El Resbalador" (Slippery Place) because of the large percentage of male drunkards who frequented the bar on weekend nights.[45]

Like other sandlot teams in ethnic communities, the Corona Athletics played self-organized, independent ball, not associated with any professional league and its minor league appendages.[46] After winning approximately seventy percent of their games and claiming the Orange County championship in 1933 and the Pomona Valley Championship in 1934, in

1936 they were invited to participate in the California State Championship Semi-Pro baseball tournament.[47] However, the team declined because of limited funds, and because the tournament conflicted with the peak lemon harvest. Instead, the Athletics brought teams to town to compete against them. They hosted many semi-pro teams from Southern California communities with large ethnic Mexican populations. Some of teams originated from towns such as Placentia, Riverside, Oxnard, Santa Ana, San Bernardino, Colton, Monrovia, and Azuza. The Athletics also played against Japanese American teams (Los Angeles Nisei) and African American teams (Colored Eagles) from the Los Angeles vicinity.[48] To host these teams (twenty dollars per team) and pay for the umpire, the Athletics club sponsored dances at the American Legion Hall. These public dances were announced in *El Imparcial* and on the local Spanish-language radio station and were promoted during the games. One announcement stated, "Many people both local and from out-of-town have enjoyed this wholesome addition to the town's recreational activities . . . the purpose of the dance is to raise money to cover necessary expenses since passing the hat at each game is not enough."[49] The Athletics also took great pride in not charging admission to the ball games. Unlike other Corona baseball teams that charged a fee, the Athletics tried to keep tournament games without an admission charge, making them accessible to the entire Mexican working-class community.[50]

During the summer months, when the lemon harvest was at its lowest, the Athletics traveled to surrounding towns within a thirty-mile radius. To offset transportation expense the manager borrowed a hauling truck from the local packinghouse. Many players fondly remembered traveling to nearby towns, visiting friends, and widening their social network. As Zeke Mejia pointed out, "I liked to travel to new places because I liked meeting new friends. I remember traveling to Lake Elsinore, which was a long way in those days. But the only ride we could get was from a friend who hauled fertilizer in his truck. So all the guys crawled inside the truck and tried not to breathe during the ride. By the time we arrived to play we all smelled like fertilized fields. We did it because loved the game."[51] The social networks established through tournament games became important during times of labor conflict between Mexican citrus workers and Anglo citrus growers.

For many players, traveling to other towns also meant getting noticed by scouts. Many Mexican American players had minor and major league potential, but they were not recruited until after World War II.[52] From the

4.4 Tito Cortez (second from left) and the Cleveland Indians farm team, the Tucson Cowboys, 1947. *Used by permission of the Corona Public Library.*

Corona Athletics three players, Tito Cortez, Ray Delgadillo and Remi Chagnon, were recruited by professional teams in the late 1940s. The following decade Bobby Perez and Louis Uribe, signed contracts with the Brooklyn Dodgers but remained in its minor-league farm team for several years. Athletics pitcher and batting champion Ray Delgadillo played one season for the Mexican Baseball League until the U.S. Military enlisted him to fight abroad in 1942.[53] One of the best pitchers for the Athletics was Tito Cortez, who pitched five no-hitters during his ten-year tenure (1937–1947) with the team. (See Figure 4.4.) In 1947, Tito Cortez was recruited by the Cleveland Indians and played for its farm team in Tucson, Arizona.[54] As a starting pitcher for the Tucson Cowboys, he became known as "Tucson's No. 1 Pitcher" and helped the Cowboys reach the playoffs for the Arizona-Texas League. The *Arizona Republic* described him as "a twenty-four year old right-hander who does ranch work at his home in Corona, Calif. during the winter. He started the season with three straight victories and since then has held the No. 1 hurling spot."[55] Cortez recalls his first season in Tucson:

I received $125 a month plus $20 a month for rent. I stayed in a dormitory. When they signed me up I began as a relief pitcher, then a starter pitcher. I was the only Mexican American in the team but I got along with everyone, especially an American Indian from the reservation [Al Aguilar] and another Anglo-American from the Los Angeles area. On our day off we watched baseball games or went to bars to get away from the desert heat.[56]

Cortez's promising career, however, was cut short when he was hit in the eye during an Athletics game dedicated to their "star pitcher." During a game against the Pomona Merchants, the batter hit a line drive that smashed into Cortez's left eye; Cortez was immediately rushed to the hospital, where the doctor pronounced him partially blind.[57] After this incident, Cortez explained, he refused to return to Arizona and ended his baseball career: "When I told them [Arizona Cowboys] that I had an accident, they did not believe me. They [sent] me a contract and then another one. Finally I just tore it up. I don't know why they did not believe me. So they blacklisted me, meaning I could not sign with another team especially the Mexican League. But it did not matter, I could not play anymore."[58] Cortez was probably suspected of being among several black, Latino, and even white players who defected to the more racially diverse and prosperous Mexican League. Those who signed with the Mexican League, declared the baseball commissioner, would be blacklisted from the major leagues.[59] Whatever the Indians' actual motivations for blacklisting Cortez, one cannot help but wonder whether the same action would have been taken against a white ballplayer.

Working-Class Masculinity, Racial Struggle, and Labor Politics

Workers' claims to dignity and equality also involved symbolic and real contestations of racial and masculine pride. The Corona Athletics frequent victories against white baseball teams challenged notions of white superiority and stereotypes of Mexicans as "docile workers" and racially inferior. Winning against all-white competition took on a symbolic meaning for many Mexican players who demanded respect and economic opportunities in a racially segregated town.

Because the Corona Athletics had a predominantly Mexican American membership (including one Native American and one Anglo-American married to a Mexican woman), they played all their matches in the heart of the Mexican community and were racialized by the dominant community as "Mexican." Players understood the wider racial significance of these matches. As Mexican American baseball player Frank Ruiz observed during one match against an all-white team,

> The [white] guys always wanted to beat us. If they couldn't beat us with the runs, they would try to beat us with the umpire. Because we were a little better than they were. I guess they didn't want the Mexican kids to beat them, you know, the Anglos over there. We had a little rough time sometimes, but then we'd score more runs. There's no way they could say they won without enough runs.[60]

Clearly, for Frank Ruiz, this match was more than "just a game." Racial and class differences were quite visible on the baseball diamond, especially when the Corona Athletics played their main rivals, the Corona Cardinals, an all-white independent team. Another rival was the Exchange Lemon By-Products baseball team, which comprised all-white players—not surprising, since the plant employed only white workers until after World War II. During one of the Athletics' matches against the Exchange team, class differences were made evident. The *Corona Independent* reported, "The Exchange Lemon Products team evidently felt they could make a better showing and win more games if they altered their appearance. They appeared on the diamond Friday night with a brand new outfit consisting of flashy yellow and black jerseys, black caps and white trousers, and did they look snappy!"[61] Their flashy clothes and pretentiousness, however, did nothing to improve their game: the Corona Athletics beat them by a score of eleven to two.[62]

The competition between Mexican and white men represented a struggle over racial, class, and masculine pride. As sociologist Michael Messner has suggested, "Subordinated groups of men often used sport to resist racist, colonial, and class domination, and their resistance most often took the form of a claim to 'manhood.'"[63] In the highly masculinized arena of baseball, Mexican American men attempted to (re)assert their racial and working-class identity. In this sense, contests were emotionally charged and the Mexican teams heavily invested in winning, because it was one of the ways they could challenge racism and at same time keep their masculine pride, honor, and respectability. Furthermore, we can see in the following incident how verbal and physical threats to a ballplayer's masculinity and racial pride often led to fights on and off the playing field. Tito Cortez narrated a particular incident that occurred during a match against an all-black team from Los Angeles: "We [Athletics] had guys who got into fights against the colored teams. . . . One time the Athletics was playing a black team from Los Angeles and one of the guys playing shortstop was batting and made a 'sissy' remark to the pitcher . . . something about pitching like a girl, but the catcher heard what he said. He got up and took off his mask, chest protector and ran after him. . . .[laughs] You could only see his spikes kicking dirt behind."[64]

For Mexican American ballplayers, the Athletics club served as a gendered space in which they could (re)produce a collective masculine culture and identity. Displays of masculine behavior were built around excessive drinking, gambling away hard-earned money, abusive language, aggressive and competitive behavior, and physical shows of strength and courage. These forms of "machismo" overlapped with another model based on the male head of the household, the reliable and responsible worker—a model strongly promoted by citrus companies paternalist ideology in their desire to cultivate "loyal" and "docile" Mexican workers. Athletics players selected from both models to construct their own version of machismo that included a range of characteristics, from conquering women in the bleachers to becoming close friends with other men. The construction of machismo among the Athletics ballplayers parallels Roger Lancaster's notion of a "system of manliness," in which machismo is a means not only of "structuring power relations between men and women" but also of "structuring power between and among men."[65]

Through "disreputable" social activities such as drinking and gambling, ballplayers established strong bonds of solidarity and companionship that provided the basis for teamwork on and off the field. Tito Cortez described the Athletics' favorite hangout spot: "On Third and Main there was a beer joint that was named Jalisco. We would get together every Saturday night and Sunday we played all day. Everyone used to comment how [we] would work like a dog all week picking lemons and then went and got drunk on Saturday nights and played baseball all day on Sunday and again the following week"[66] More than any other leisure activity, drinking both unified and divided ballplayers, sometimes resulting in bitter fights within the team. A ballplayer's rebellious behavior could also create divisions within the team. For example, after missing several practices and showing up late, Frankie Uribe was benched by the manager for several games. After his father and captain, Marcus Uribe, protested with the manager to no avail, they both decided to leave the team altogether and convinced several other players to join them to form a new baseball club called the Corona Cubs.[67]

Battles over the control of public space and social life constituted a central element of everyday life in Corona. Baseball players not only carved out a social and recreational space for themselves and the entire Mexican community but also utilized the organization as a political forum from in they could discuss, debate, and take action on pressing political issues impacting on the group and the larger community. In the process, many ballplayers learned their first lessons about fundraising, organizational work, and collective action. Some team members demonstrated a capacity for leadership and became dedicated union organizers and political activists.

Because spaces for union organizing were not an option in a citrus-industry town, the Athletics baseball diamond became an important meeting site for the local citrus workers' union. In 1937, Anglo- and Mexican American organizers for the United Cannery Agricultural Packing and Allied Workers of America (UCAPAWA), an affiliate with the CIO, solicited the assistance of community groups and sports clubs to build an interracial union movement in Corona.[68] Since UCAPAWA had already formed baseball teams in other parts of Southern California, they turned to the Corona Athletics for support and to find potential leaders.[69] Not only did Athletics ballplayers assist in this effort, but they offered their field as an organizing and meeting site.[70] The location was chosen because it was a popular gathering place for Mexican baseball players, making it appear to police authorities and company officials that baseball was the only topic of conversation, not political discussions. Longtime resident Rudy Ramos cited reasons for conducting union meetings at the Athletics' playing field:

> The CIO came into Corona to organize the workers and of course the ranchers, like Jameson Company and Foothill Company, did not want us to organize. We used to meet on Sheridan and Grand Boulevard. There used to be a baseball field that is where the famous Athletics played. On this ballpark is where we used to meet because it was hidden from view and away from the police.[71]

Within months of forming the Corona Agricultural Citrus Workers Union, members decided to go on strike in the early morning of February 27, 1941, more than eight hundred workers gathered at the ballpark to

4.5 1941 Corona citrus strike. *Used by permission of the Corona Public Library.*

coordinate plans for the picket lines and plan their next moves. (See Figure 4.5.)[72] Once the picketing began around the packinghouses and citrus ranches (including Foothill Ranch), citrus growers launched a public campaign to discredit the CIO organizers, Theodore Rasmussen and Alfonso Ortiz, as "communist agitators," and growers recruited law enforcement to harass strikers and disrupt meetings. Ortiz complained to the *Corona Independent* that union meetings at the ballpark had to be relocated outside town "to prevent interference from police and stool pigeons."[73] To prevent union meetings at the ballpark, the city council passed a resolution to give more power and authority to the police chief to designate the area around the baseball field as a "no parking zone."[74] In response to these council actions, labor organizer and Athletics manager Marcus Uribe led a group of workers to the city council chambers to voice their protest during their meeting. Uribe presented a petition to the mayor that read: "We petition the council to reconsider their undemocratic action of Tuesday last in order to prevent the office of chief of police from becoming that of a virtual dictator. . . . We ask this in order to allow the citizens of Corona, as a free people the opportunity and the unabridged right of liberty."[75] Protestors emphasized the "local" nature of their struggle by proclaiming themselves "citizens of Corona." By challenging citrus growers' claims as legitimate representatives of the "local identity," the protestors sought to establish the union as a legitimate community institution that could represent workers' interests.

Labor organizer Marcos Uribe played for the Corona Athletics during the late 1930s and developed leadership skills as head coach. He also utilized his extensive network of baseball teams from surrounding towns such as Placentia, Riverside, Arlington, Casa Blanca, and Santa Paula. Baseball tournament games helped cultivate important bonds of solidarity among citrus workers and contributed to the spread of the strike into nearby towns such as Casa Blanca and Riverside. These social networks also prevented Mexican strikebreakers from undermining local labor struggles and spread the word among other union-sponsored baseball teams for support. In fact, the UCAPAWA Local 120 in Orange, California, founded in the aftermath of the 1936 Orange County strike, understood the importance of regional support for local-based labor struggles, so it sent several members of the all–Mexican American CIO baseball team to assist in organizing the Corona citrus industry.[76] Nevertheless, though established regional networks were activated during the two-month 1941 Corona strike, the action was not enough to counter the intense police repression and the local-to-statewide political power of the citrus industry.

On the afternoon of March 21, a barrage of rocks and sticks were thrown by a few unidentified men in the picket line, breaking car windows and hitting an officer from Riverside. The incident prompted an order for the release of twenty tear-gas bombs. On the sidelines, Rudy Ramos barely escaped arrest. He explained that when a rock was thrown at a police car driving by the picket line, the officers responded in the following manner: "The police threw tear gas at the strikers, but they'd pick it up and threw it back, until they [the police] decided to use their stick against them . . . then some people dispersed and others got arrested."[77] The police escorted forty-nine Mexican strikers to jail and booked them on charges of disturbing the peace, inciting a riot, unlawful assembly, and aggravated assault upon two officers with a deadly weapon. After the arrests the strike ended, and although court trials ensued, the union movement suffered a big defeat.

Although Mexican women did not occupy leadership positions within the union structure, they also participated in the labor struggle. During the strike, Mexican American women participated in the picket lines, cooked food for strikers, raised money for a strike fund for destitute families, and solicited the support of local businesses.[78] According to the

Corona Independent, "Three women representing the CIO were circulating [around] city business establishments to learn whether or not they [were] employing union labor. A beauty parlor even was asked whether or not it was giving service to 'scabs.'[79] Other women indicated that although they did not join the picket lines they supported the strike, even against their husbands' wishes. "My husband did not want me to join the [picket] line so I stayed home," explained Alice Rodriguez, "so when the foreman came to the house to convince me to go back to work I told him that I did not want to go against my friends."[80] By simply staying home, Alice Rodriguez and other women enacted a form of resistance; by withholding her labor power, she challenged company authority even as she acquiesced to her husband's wishes.

These acts of individual and collective resistance among Mexican American women indicate that they were anything but passive during the labor conflict. However, women's role was limited by their exclusion from union leadership positions. In effect, women's marginal status during the labor struggle served to deny the union other creative possibilities (i.e., women's networks) to effectively challenge the citrus industry. Although the strike's defeat can be attributed to the incredible police suppression orchestrated by citrus growers and city council officials, union organizers failed to challenge the patriarchy within their ranks and the gender division of labor in the workplace, community, and household. Part of the difficulty in mounting a sustained challenge to racial, class, and gender oppression was the company policy of separating males into agriculture-related jobs and women into the packinghouses. This gender division of labor continued in the company welfare programs: Americanization classes were set up for Mexican women to train them in child-rearing practices, health and sanitation, home economics, sewing, and gardening. For young Mexican men, the companies organized sports and recreational activities to keep them busy and to regulate their nonwork lives until they were ready to accompany their fathers in the orchards. Although baseball players contributed to labor struggle, given their previous leadership experience as captains, managers, and coaches, they unintentionally reproduced male domination within the union. On the one hand, they fought against class-based patriarchal domination; on the other they faced more difficult challenges in contesting ideological forms of patriarchal domination, for while many workers rejected companies' welfare capitalist schemes, others accepted these paternalistic offerings, while still others chose a middle ground from which they could negotiate these offerings

for their own purposes. So while some Mexican American ballplayers offered their loyalty to company, they did so with the intention of holding
the company accountable to its promises and getting something in return,
such as free baseball equipment and uniforms. Ballplayers demonstrated
how they could transform baseball clubs and matches from mere recreational activities, strip them of their sporting function, and turn them into
contested sites of racial, gender, and class struggle.

Conclusion

Frank Ruiz bluntly stated, "Being a [poor] Mexican, you might say you
had two strikes against you. [We] could have made the big leagues. We had
pretty good players . . . but [eventually] a lot of them got married, had to
work and had other responsibilities, so [sandlot] kind of fizzled out."[81] By
the 1950s many of the Athletics players stopped playing altogether, but
there were a few who remained committed to the game and continued
coaching younger players. For example, former Athletics player, Jim
"Chayo" Rodriguez, established himself as Corona's leading softball coach
and was inducted into the Inland Empire Hispanic Hall of Fame. During
the height of the Chicano Movement, Rodriguez formed "The Chicanos"
softball club to steer troubled Chicano youth away from gang and prison
life. Between 1973 and 1983, the Chicanos players lived up to its team
mascot's fighting ability, the Mexican Revolutionary leader, Pancho Villa,
(emblazoned on the team jersey) winning several championship titles in
southern California softball tournaments.[82] For Mexican American and
Chicano men, baseball represented more than mere recreational pursuits;
it served to unify and empower the Mexican community through self-or-
ganization, cultural expressions, and political assertion within the context
of limited economic opportunities and racial discrimination. Mexican
American Athletics players, like their black and Asian counterparts around
the country, understood the real and symbolic implications when playing
against all-white teams, because those competitive skills on the playing
field could be extended into the realm of politics and economics. In the
context of Corona with a powerful citrus grower elite, spaces for union organizing were circumscribed and Mexican Americans utilized recreational
spaces, including the Corona Athletics club to build a CIO union. Mexican
American women did participate in baseball and softball clubs (even as
supporters and spectators), but were excluded from my narrators' tales

and andecdotes, as well as print publications, reflecting the masculine culture of this "national pastime." As important as baseball was as a source for racial unity, leadership training, and passage into American culture, I have argued that the intensely masculine behavior of baseball players became a source of tension among men and between men and women, thus contributing to the failure of achieving class solidarity during the labor strike. Notwithstanding the severe repression by police and company officials, the Athletics baseball club and CIO labor union effectively reproduced male domination and the exclusion of women as prescribed by corporate ideology in the playing field and the union.

Notes

1. I thank Gilbert González, Vicki Ruiz, Samuel Regalado and Michael Willard for their invaluable comments on earlier versions of this essay. Oral history interview with Tito Cortez by the author, April 20, 1998, Corona, CA.

2. Samuel Regalado, *Viva Baseball: Latin Major Leaguers and their Special Hunger* (Urbana, Ill., 1998, 36.

3. C. L. R. James, *Beyond a Boundary* (1963; reprint, Durham, N.C., 1993), 66. For an excellent discussion of C. L. R. James, cricket, and national identity, see Neil Lazarus, "Cricket, Modernism, National Culture: The Case of C.L.R. James," in his *Nationalism and Cultural Practice in the Postcolonial World* (Cambridge, 1999), 144–195.

4. Recently published works in Chicano/a history briefly mention the role of leisure and sport among Mexican Americans. See Douglas Monroy, *Mexican Los Angeles from the Great Migration to the Great Depression* (Berkeley, 1999), 45–47; Vicki Ruiz, *From Out of the Shadows: Mexican Women in Twentieth-Century America* (New York, 1998), 51–71; Gilbert G. González, *Labor and Community: Mexican Citrus Worker Villages in a Southern California County*, (Urbana, Ill., 1994), 91–95; George J. Sánchez, *Becoming Mexican American: Ethnicity, Culture and Identity in Chicano Los Angeles, 1900–1945* (New York, 1993), 171–172; Zaragoza Vargas, *Proletarians of the North: A History of Mexican Industrial Workers in Detroit and the Midwest, 1917–1933* (Berkeley, 1993), 161–164.

5. For a general survey that aims to offer "an adequate treatment of race and sport to include all peoples" but primarily deals with African Americans and sport from the 1800s to the present, see Jeffrey T. Sammons, "'Race' and Sport: A Critical Historical Examination," *Journal of Sport History* 21 (1994): 203–278.

6. James Cockcroft, *Latinos in Beisbol: The Hispanic Experience in the Americas* (Danbury, Conn., 1996); Regalado, *Viva Baseball*; Michael M. Oleksak and Mary Adams Oleksak, *Béisbol: Latin Americans and the Grand Old Game* (Lanham, Md.,

1991); *El Béisbol: Travels through the Pan-American Pastime* (New York, 1989); Alan Klein, *Sugarball: The American Game, the Dominican Dream* (New Haven, 1991); Rob Ruck, *The Tropic of Baseball: Baseball in the Dominican Republic* (Westport, Conn., 1991).

7. The lone exception among earlier works is Samuel Regalado, "Baseball in the Barrios: The Scene in East Los Angeles since World War II," *Baseball History* 1 (1986): 47–59.

8. Wallace Thompson, *The Mexican Mind: A Study of National Psychology* (Boston, 1922), 97–100; William Beezley, "The Rise of Baseball in Mexico and the First Valenzuela," *Studies in Latin American Popular Culture* 4 (1985): 3–13; William Beezley, *Judas at the Jockey Club and Other Episodes of Porfirian Mexico* (Lincoln, Neb., 1987), 17–26; Gilbert M. Joseph, "Forging the Regional Pastime: Baseball and Class in Yucatan," in Joseph L. Arbena, ed., *Sport and Society in Latin America: Diffusion, Dependency, and the Rise of Mass Culture* (Westport, Conn., 1988), 29–61; Norman S. Hayner, "Mexicans at Play—A Revolution," *Sociology and Social Research* 38 (1953): 80–83.

9. United States Department of Labor, *Health and Recreation Activities in Industrial Establishments, 1926* (Washington, D.C., 1928), 31–58; Stuart Brandes, *American Welfare Capitalism, 1880–1940* (Chicago, 1976), 75–82; Gerald Zahavi, *Workers, Managers, and Welfare Capitalism: The Shoeworkers and Tanners of Endicott Johnson, 1890–1950* (Urbana, Ill., 1990), 50–52; Wilma J. Pesavento, "Sport and Recreation in the Pullman Experiment, 1880–1900," *Journal of Sport History* 9 (1982): 38–62; John Schelppi, "'It Pays': John H. Patterson and Industrial Recreation at the National Cash Register Company," *Journal of Sport History* 6 (1979): 20–28.

10. Vincent Moses, "G. Harold Powell and the Corporate Consolidation of the Modern Citrus Enterprise, 1904–1922," *Business History Review* 69 (1995): 119–142.

11. Nelson Van Valen, "The Bolsheviki and the Orange Growers," *Pacific Historical Review* 22 (1953): 39; California Citrus Institute, *Second Annual Report* (May 1921), 51; *California Citrograph* (August 1921): 75.

12. A. J. Spalding, *Baseball: America's National Game* (San Francisco, 1911), 29–63; *California Citrograph* (October 1921): 67; Robert Cleland, *The Place Called Sespe: The History of a California Ranch* (Alhambra, CA, 1940), 80–88.

13. La Habra citrus company imposed rules and regulations for Campo Colorado's baseball team, Los Juveniles. Some of these rules included: (1) A good sportsman is never late for baseball practice; (2) a good sportsman is never heard to use bad language at work or at play; (3) a good sportsman is dependable, truthful, trustworthy, and makes the most of all of his time. See Jessie Hayden, "La Habra Experiment in Mexican Social Education" (master's thesis, Claremont College, 1934), 20. See also González, *Labor and Community*, 65–74.

14. *Corona Independent*, July 13, 1936. See also Alan Dundes, *The Cockfight: A Casebook* (Madison, Wisc., 1994), 38–44.

15. *Corona Courier*, February 13, 1920; Lorne Allmon, *The Story of Samuel B. Hampton and the California Citrus Industry, 1887–1918* (Riverside, CA: 1994), 1–7; Corona Foothill Lemon Company Collection, Orange Heights Orange Association (OHOA), Heritage, Corona Public Library, Corona, California.

16. Oral history interview with Carl Herklerath by the author, September 11, 1998 Corona, CA.

17. Oral history interview with Santos Garcia by the author, July 22, 1998, Corona, CA; *Riverside Enterprise*, Corona-Norco edition, November 3, 1978.

18. Cortez interview.

19. Zeke Mejia is quoted in a special feature article on the Corona Athletics in *Riverside Press-Enterprise*, Corona edition, June 29, 1996.

20. *Corona Independent*, January 4, 1933.

21. Workers and managers displayed mutual loyalties that were continually negotiated and contested, "each one pulling and tugging at one another, both without outright coercion—each attempting to extract from the other a maximum return on its 'loyalty.'" Gerald Zahavi, "Negotiated Loyalty: Welfare Capitalism and the Shoeworkers of Endicott Johnson, 1920–1940" *Journal of American History* 69 (December 1983): 605.

22. George Lipsitz, *Time Passages: Collective Memory and American Popular Culture* (Minneapolis: University of Minnesota Press, 1990.

23. Louis Perez Jr., "Between Baseball and Bullfighting: The quest for nationality in Cuba, 1868–1898," *Journal of American History* 81 (September 1994): 499.

24. *Corona Independent*, July 28, 1936.

25. *Corona Independent*, September 1, 1946.

26. Ethnic immigrants utilized sports as a means to adapt to American culture. See, for example, Gary Ross Mormino, "The Playing Fields of St. Louis: Italian Immigrants and Sports, 1925–1941," *Journal of Sport History* 9 (1982): 5–19. See also Samuel Regalado, "Sport and Community in California's Japanese American 'Yamato Colony,' 1930–1945," *Journal of Sport History* 19 (1992): 130–143; Gail Nomura, "Beyond the Playing Field: The Significance of Pre–World War II Japanese American Baseball in the Yakima Valley," in Linda Revilla, Gail Nomura, and Shirley Hine, eds., *Bearing Dreams, Shaping Visions* (Pullman, Wash., 1993).

27. For a discussion of ethnicity and identity formation among second-generation Mexicans in Los Angeles, see Sánchez, *Becoming Mexican American*, 1–10.

28. *Corona Independent*, June 22, 1938.

29. Ibid.

30. Oral history interview with Adelina Enriquez by the author, June 28, 1998, Corona, CA.

31. *El Imparcial*, August 13, 1949.

32. For a discussion of the development of "Mexican schools" in the American West, see Gilbert G. González, "Segregation of Mexican Children in a Southern

California City: The Legacy of Expansionism and the American Southwest," *Western Historical Quarterly* 26 (1985): 55–76.

33. Robert E. Copley, *The Tall Mexican: The Life of Hank Aguirre, All Star Pitcher, Businessman, Humanitarian* (Houston, 1998), 11.

34. Oral history interview with Zeke Mejia by the author, tape recording, June 5, 1998, Corona, CA.

35. *Corona Independent*, March 13, 1946.

36. Oral history interview with Jess Uribe by the author, February 20, 1998, Corona, CA.

37. Cortez interview.

38. Baseball can also be viewed as mirroring the workplace. As Steven Gelber suggests, it projects "a set of values that include a scientific world view, an appreciation of rationality, and competitiveness between groups with cooperation within them." See Steven Gelber, "Working at Playing: The Culture of the Workplace and the Rise of Baseball," *Journal of Social History* 5 (1979): 12–15.

39. Frances A. Martinez, "Corona as I Remember," in Cynthia Alvitre, *Hispanic Centennial Review, 1886–1986* (Corona, Calif., 1986), 2–3.

40. Regalado, "Baseball in the Barrios," 47–59.

41. Cortez interview.

42. Stanley Reynolds and Fred Eldridge, eds., *Corona, California Commentaries*, (Corona, Calif., 1986), 41–43.

43. Uribe interview.

44. Ibid.

45. Oral history interview with Juanita Ramirez by the author, August 15, 1997, Corona, CA.

46. Rob Ruck, *Sandlot Seasons: Sport in Black Pittsburgh* (Urbana, Ill., 1987), 3–15.

47. *Corona Independent*, July 28, 1936.

48. Martinez, "Corona as I Remember," 5.

49. *Corona Independent*, August 17, 1949.

50. Ibid.

51. Quoted in the *Corona Centennial, Riverside Press-Enterprise*, June 29, 1996.

52. Cockcroft, *Latinos in Beisbol*, 93–100; Regalado, *Viva Baseball*, 39–64.

53. Corona Independent, June 9, 1949.

54. *Corona Independent*, October 13, 1945.

55. *Arizona Republic*, March 13, 1947.

56. Cortez interview.

57. Ibid.

58. Ibid.

59. *Corona Independent*, December 29, 1947. See also Alan Klein, "Baseball Wars: The Mexican Baseball League and Nationalism in 1946," *Studies in Latin American Popular Culture* 13 (1994): 33–56.

60. Oral history interview with Frank Ruiz by Gilbert Rivera and Patti Berry (Whittier, CA, 1979).

61. *Corona Independent*, June 22, 1938.

62. Ibid.

63. Michael Messner, *Power at Play: Sports and the Problem of Masculinity* (Boston, 1992), 19. See also Michael S. Kimmel, "Baseball and the Reconstitution of American Masculinity, 1880–1920," in Michael Messner and Donald Sabo, eds., *Sport, Men, and the Gender Order* (Champaign, Ill., 1990), 19–29.

64. Cortez interview.

65. Roger Lancaster, *Life Is Hard: Machismo, Danger, and the Intimacy of Power in Nicaragua* (Berkeley, 1992), 92, 236–237. For discussions about masculinity among ethnic American groups, see Maxine Baca Zinn, "Chicano Men and Masculinity," in Laura Kramer, ed., *The Sociology of Gender* (New York, 1979), 221–232; Pierrette Hondagneu-Sotelo and Michael Messner, "Gender Displays and Men's Power: The New Man and the Mexican Immigrant Man," in Harry Boyd and Michael Kaufman, eds., *Theorizing Masculinities* (Thousand Oaks, Calif., 1994), 200–218.

66. Cortez interview.

67. Oral history interview with Jim Rodriguez by the author, October 1, 1998, Corona, CA.

68. *United Field Worker*, April 15, 1937.

69. *UCAPAWA News*, September 17, 1939. See also Vicki Ruiz, *Cannery Women, Cannery Lives: Mexican Women, Unionization, and the California Food Processing Industry, 1930–1950* (Albuquerque, 1987); Victor B. Nelson-Cisneros, "UCAPAWA and Chicanos in California: The Farm Worker Period, 1937–1940," *Aztlan* 7 (1978): 434–477; David Oberweiser Jr., "The CIO: A Vanguard for Civil Rights in Southern California, 1940–46," in Sally M. Miller and Daniel A. Cornford, eds., *American Labor in the Era of World War II* (Westport, Conn., 1995), 200–216.

70. *Corona Independent*, July 15, 1939.

71. Oral history interview with Rudy Ramos by the author, February 5, 1998, Corona, CA.

72. *Corona Independent*, February 27, 1941.

73. *Citrus Worker News* (August 1940).

74. *Minutes*, Corona City Council, February 25, 1941, Corona City Hall, City Clerk Department, Corona, CA.

75. *La Opinion*, March 31, 1941.

76. Ibid.

77. Ramos interview.

78. *Corona Independent*, March 24, 1941.

79. *Corona Independent*, March 21, 1941.

80. Oral history interview with Alice Rodriguez by the author, January 27, 1997, Corona, CA.

81. Ruiz interview.

82. Rodriguez interview.

Part II

Sports in the Era of the Civil Rights Movement

Chapter Five

Jazzing the Basepaths
Jackie Robinson and African American Aesthetics

Montye Fuse and Keith Miller

In a memorable moment from the 1949 World Series, Jackie Robinson dashed off third base, edged back, then sprinted farther off third before once again retreating. Opposing pitcher Vic Raschi, a twenty-one game winner that year, eyed Robinson's feints warily, fearing that he might suddenly steal home, as he sometimes did. The batter, Gil Hodges, stroked Raschi's next pitch for a single, scoring Robinson with the first and only run of the game. Instead of attributing the game-winning hit to Hodges's hitting prowess, as one might expect, Raschi made a surprising admission:

> I had just never seen anything like [Robinson's feints from third base] before. . . . He did something to me that almost never happened: He broke my concentration and I paid more attention to him than to Hodges. He beat me more than Hodges [did]."[1]

Where did Robinson learn this particular baserunning technique, and how was he able to destroy Raschi's concentration? Robinson claims that his bravado was encouraged by Brooklyn Dodgers owner Branch Rickey, who introduced him into what was at that time in the late 1940s a racially homogenous sport. However, Cool Papa Bell and other Negro League veterans maintain that Robinson's baserunning skills emerged after he served a crucial yearlong apprenticeship in the Negro Leagues. But, if Robinson learned this razzle-dazzle in the Negro Leagues, why did Rickey and Robinson himself conceal that fact, allowing Robinson to be viewed as a storybook individualist instead of a product of distinctly African American–styled baseball? And why do Americans continue to enshrine Robinson not only as a solitary racial pioneer but also as a "genius" on the base paths who, in the words of a recent biographer, had "no learning time, no period of seasoning to perfect his skills" when he joined the Brooklyn Dodgers?[2]

In 1946 and 1947, bringing a single African American athlete into baseball helped Rickey emplot Robinson as an isolated hero inspired by an older, white benefactor. Robinson lost no time seizing every opportunity to reinscribe Rickey's plot, crediting him with all manner of Robinson's own baseball triumphs and effectively denying any contribution time spent in the Negro Leagues may have made to his style of play. Robinson did this in the 1950 film *The Jackie Robinson Story* and in five autobiographical statements, beginning with a 1948 essay in *Ebony* magazine and continuing through his final autobiography, *I Never Had It Made* (1972), published the year of his death.[3]

Although sportswriters, biographers, and historians have never seriously challenged the Rickey/Robinson emplotment, this chapter argues that many of Robinson's baserunning tactics, which served to distract and stymie opponents, were developed in the Negro Leagues. Indeed, informed by jazz, blues, and other African American cultural aesthetics of the time, African American baseball reached its improvisational apotheosis in the careers of Satchel Paige, Cool Papa Bell, and Robinson himself. Robinson succeeded in major league baseball because his style of play embodied African American cultural forms (as understood by African Americans and exoticized by whites) while appearing to embody the romanticized, Horatio Alger–like individualism so highly prized by whites.

This paradox is highlighted by contrasting African American and white styles of baseball through the application of theories by Kenneth Burke, Roland Barthes, Cornel West, and others. Through such analysis, this chapter reveals Robinson's on-the-field critique of white baseball, a critique that has remained largely buried for almost fifty years.[4] While it should be acknowledged that black baseball players, jazz musicians, and historians do not argue for parallels between African American baseball styles and bebop, this chapter maintains that Paige, Bell, Robinson, and other African American baseball players joined with Dizzy Gillespie, Max Roach, Ralph Ellison, Zora Neale Hurston, Richard Wright, and other artists in a "project" of exposing, interrogating, and critiquing dominant cultural forms, including America's favorite pastime.

In words and music, African American musicians, writers, and other artists offered an implicit challenge to American society, just as did Negro

League players who barnstormed against major league all-stars, and as did Robinson when he made his debut in the major leagues. Arguing that jazz represents a dramatic inversion of the European orchestral tradition, bebop drummer Max Roach describes

> a democratic process, which is opposed to most European classical music in which the two most important people are the composer and the conductor. They are like the king and the queen. . . . As a musician your job may depend on how you conform to the conductor's interpretation of the composer's wishes. However, in a jazz performance, everyone has an opportunity to create a thing of beauty collectively, based on their own personalities.[5]

Roach's bebop cohorts also interpreted their music as a partly extemporized alternative to predictable American music. Although Dizzy Gillespie sometimes combined white and black musicians in his bands, he—like Bell—identified the flowering of ensemble serendipity as more characteristic of African American culture than of American mainstream (white) culture:

> In the different black bands, you had to play differently, because every "colored" band played, or phrased, in its own unique way. . . . In the white bands I worked with . . . everything was more standardized, and a musician didn't have to change too much as he moved from one band to the other. The black bands, on a whole, were much more unique stylistically. . . . That experience playing in black bands I wouldn't trade for anything.[6]

Gillespie told and retold an anecdote about popular musician Jimmy Dorsey, who, Gillespie stated, grew "completely flabbergasted" when he heard Gillespie's group. Dorsey ventured that he would want Gillespie to join his band if Gillespie were white. Gillespie replied, "You know any trumpet players, white ones, who play like this?" Dorsey "just laughed," Gillespie reported.[7] According to Gillespie, Dorsey's band suffered from a self-imposed cultural impasse.

Bebop rebels explain that they transformed banal popular songs—from an allegedly superior culture—into harmonies richly bewildering. Gillespie recalls:

> We'd take the chord structures of various standard and pop tunes and create new chords, melodies, and songs from them. We found out what the composers were doing by analyzing these tunes, and then added substitute chords to songs like "Night and Day," "How High the Moon," "Lover," "What Is This Thing Called Love?" and "Whispering." When we borrowed from a

standard, we added and substituted so many chords that most people didn't know what song we really were playing. "How High the Moon" became "Ornithology" and "What Is This Thing Called Love?" was "Hothouse."[8]

Roach explains such change as a racial and economic maneuver as well as a musical one:

> So in playing these [standards], the black musicians recognized that the royalties were going back to these people, like ASCAP, the Jerome Kerns, the Gershwins. So one revolutionary thing that happened, [blacks] began to write parodies on the harmonic structures. Which was really revolutionary. . . . If you made a record, you could say, "This is an original."[9]

For Gillespie, Roach, Bud Powell, and others, white popular and symphonic music was "stuffy" and predictable, while bebop was innovative.

The early African American influence in baseball has not been acknowledged, as whites have failed to take the Negro Leagues seriously. Although several times each week thousands of baseball enthusiasts flocked to African American games during extended summer seasons, white newspapers and radio stations seldom acknowledged the league's existence. One Negro League veteran wrote, "Some people didn't know the Negro Leagues existed before Jackie Robinson signed with the Brooklyn Dodgers."[10] Americans' lack of awareness of African American baseball led one historian to dub blackball players "invisible men" and another, in 1995, to deem the Negro Leagues "a lost American society."[11]

Beginning in the 1970s, a handful of enthusiastic historians and former Negro League players resisted this near erasure by creating a small but invaluable bank of oral histories and autobiographies and by preserving Negro League statistics. Combined with other evidence, white and black athletes' mutually reinforcing testimony argues persuasively that Negro League baseball included a strong improvisational dimension that contrasted starkly to more predictable major league play, especially during the 1940s and early 1950s.

Distinguishing their sport from its white counterpart, Negro League veterans describe their play as "colorful," "unorthodox," "showboating," "smart baseball," "inside baseball," "unwritten baseball," and "tricky baseball."[12] Newt Allen recalls that he and others used "every trick in the book" and "any kind of play you think you can get by with."[13] Larry Brown observes, "I used to do a whole lot of trickeration." He adds, "You take the [white] major leagues, they don't pull off any trickeration. . . . We used to do everything."[14]

Players and historians agree that the Negro Leagues balanced power with bunting and speed.[15] Often called the "father" of the Negro Leagues, Rube Foster especially favored bunting, having, in Allen's words, "five or six men who didn't do anything but push and bunt, kept you moving all the time. Just kept us playing on the grass, and then they'd hit it by you."[16] In a single game his team once bunted eleven times and performed six squeeze plays.[17]

Bunt-and-run artist Ted Page regarded Foster's strategy as shrewd, arguing, "There is not much defense for a man who can hit hard and bunt, too."[18] As Page, Gene Benson, and Quincy Trouppe observe, batters would surprise opponents by bunting at unpredictable moments, sometimes with two strikes on them.[19] Benson recalls when, in an extra inning, his manager, the legendary Oscar Charleston, ordered him to squeeze a runner home when there were two strikes and two outs. Benson adds that runners would advance from first base to third on a bunt instead of stopping at second—a standard practice in major league baseball.[20]

Manager Dave Malarcher, a disciple of Foster, explains how he taught Turkey Stearnes, a spectacular power hitter, to bunt. Once, cheered by the crowd, Stearnes disobeyed Malarcher's orders by taking two strikes instead of bunting, expecting to be allowed to swing with an 0–2 count. Malarcher recalls that he then embarrassed Stearnes by removing him from the game and sending up a pitcher to bunt the next pitch. The manager concludes, "[Stearnes] developed into a really great diversified player after that. Turkey could bunt, and he could pull them down to first base—and fly—and then when his time to hit came, he could really plaster them."[21]

Skill on the base paths was a particular trait of the Negro Leagues, as acknowledged in 1922 by respected sportswriter Eddie Batchelor. Batchelor commented in a feature-length story on Negro League players' tendency "to run a little wild on the bases."[22] For example, Cool Papa Bell, whom everyone hails as the great speedster in the Negro Leagues, estimates that he once swiped 175 bases in 180 or 200 games. Bell observes, "They said, 'You're faster than these guys.' I said, 'I don't know, they're just slow in thinking.'"[23] Newt Allen reports that, for some time, Bell would reduce his distance to third base by gliding inside second without ever touching the bag.[24] Also, by guiding the next hitter to step back in the box, Bell declares, he forced the catcher to retreat and throw the ball farther when trying to nip him at second base.[25] "Trickeration," or an improvisational style of play, assumed many other forms as well. Dave Barnhill recalls turning his back on home plate while pitching.[26] Benson remembers relaxing into an "unorthodox" batting stance that would fool pitchers, as he appeared not to be ready and not to swing hard.[27] Dropping a pitcher's throw on purpose, Brown would let a ball roll eight or ten feet to lure a runner into attempting an extra base before throwing him out. He also explains tossing a decoy pickoff to a third baseman, who would then nail a runner at second.[28] Bill Drake describes the "old angle play," in which a batter would square off to bunt with a runner at second. If the third baseman came in, the hitter would take the pitch, allowing the runner to advance to a vacated third base. If the third baseman stayed put, the batter would bunt for a hit.[29] Bell declares that a batter might walk, stroll to first, and sprint to second, drawing a throw to permit a runner at third to score. He remembers darting in from center field to tag an unwary runner leaning off second or caught in a rundown. He also tells of runners on first slowing on the way to third in order to draw a throw—a maneuver that would allow a trailing runner to reach second.[30]

Pitcher Satchel Paige lists his motions on the mound—"my single windup, my double windup, my triple windup, my hesitation windup—and my no windup"—and catalogs an arsenal of fool-the-eye pitches unknown to anyone else: "I got bloopers, loopers, and droopers. I got a jump ball, a bee ball, a screw ball, a wobbly ball, a whipsy-dipsy-do, a hurry-up ball, a nothin' ball and a bat dodger."[31] Paige's legerdemain on the mound puzzled battalions of hitters, including the most formidable. Mickey Mantle recalls, "What was [Paige], forty-five or fifty at the time? Well, he still had more moves than a snake: the corkscrew windup, the submarine pitch, and that great rainbow curve of his."[32] Willie Mays adds:

> [Paige] showed me the darnedest stuff I ever saw, along with some of the screwiest motions and combinations of different speeds. Old Satchel could really drive you crazy. He had a knuckleball, a screwball, an assortment of curves—and his hesitation pitch. He'd pump his arm around like a windmill, and bring it over his head, and you expected to see the ball coming down, because that's the point at which a pitcher would throw. But nothing happened. He would be almost in his follow-through when all of a sudden the darn ball would appear and you would be swinging way in front of it.[33]

. . .

Following Ty Cobb's triumphs on the base paths early in the twentieth century, Babe Ruth's prodigious home runs transformed major league baseball toward the long ball. One historian explains, "Since the appearance of Babe Ruth, the home run has dominated [major league] baseball to the exclusion of the bunt, the stolen base, and the hit-and-run."[34] Negro Leaguers complained that the major leagues during the 1920s, 1930s, and (especially) 1940s and early 1950s followed rigid procedures that valorized power hitting and discounted speed and baserunning skill. Typifying African American criticism of the emphasis on power hitting, Troupe suggests that "baseball shouldn't put too much emphasis on one thing. . . . Have you ever been to a game where three or four home runs were hit and still the game was badly played and boring?"[35]

Some whites agreed. When maverick major league owner Bill Veeck labeled traditional white owners the "old fossils of baseball," he implied that their game, too, had ossified.[36] Describing white major league play in 1947, Brooklyn Dodgers' radio announcer Red Barber notes its rigid orthodoxy:

> People in baseball go around referring to the Book—the Book says bunt in this situation, the Book says have a right-handed batter face a left-handed pitcher, the Book says use experience in a big situation, etc. The Book, the Book, the Book. . . .[37]

"The Book" also precluded fooling batters with unorthodox pitches. Thus, when Paige was finally invited to join a major league team in 1948, the league president outlawed his famous hesitation pitch. Apparently, he too-successfully baffled hitters and umpires with it.[38]

Further, the Book stipulated that hitters should not pitch and pitchers should not hit. With the exception of Ruth, extremely few major league hurlers ever bothered to become proficient hitters, which is why the American League eventually exempted pitchers from batting altogether. But because Negro League teams saved money by carrying fewer players, many pitchers filled other positions; as a consequence, they often learned to bat as though a game might hinge on their hitting, which it sometimes did. Bullet Joe Rogan, Wilmer Fields, Hilton Smith, Leon Day, Martin Dihigo, Double Duty Radcliffe (both an all-star pitcher and all-star catcher), Troupe, and others were repeatedly trumpeted as both extraordinary pitchers and outstanding hitters.

Another standard of major league baseball was that "tough guys" like Ted Williams and Joe DiMaggio should pound the ball and never bunt.

When opponents regularly packed the right side of the diamond, deserting the entire left half of the infield, Williams tried different hitting tactics; but he did not bunt, even though a bunt would have meant a sure hit.[39] Once, in 1946, when a slumping Williams executed what he terms a "lousy little bunt," a Boston headline screamed, "WILLIAMS BUNTS."[40] DiMaggio, too, declared that he never learned bunting.[41] On the day in 1941 that his unmatched fifty-six-game hitting streak ended, he reports smashing two ground balls down the left-field line to Cleveland third baseman Ken Keltner, who, playing far behind his normal spot, twice threw DiMaggio out. DiMaggio complained about Keltner's position: "'Deep? . . . My God, he was standing in left field.'"[42] Realizing that the muscular hitter would swing hard, Keltner had positioned himself perfectly. Had DiMaggio bunted down the third-base line, he might have easily extended his streak. In contrast to Malarcher, no white manager claims to have suggested to Williams, DiMaggio, or any other major league slugger that he diversify his offensive approach by bunting.

In part, the rigidity of major league baseball stemmed from players' attempts to measure themselves against other players' statistical achievements. Much of the mystique of the major leagues revolves around numerical compilations, which supply "proof" of athletic accomplishment and enable people to speculate that a player from, say, the 1940s was better or worse than others from previous eras. As if to illustrate the prevalent reverence for numbers, Mickey Mantle records that, when he learned that his lifetime average had slipped beneath the landmark .300 mark to a mere .298, the knowledge "made" him "want to cry."[43]

By contrast, records for African American games were shoddily kept and are today still being tabulated from box scores. Despite the efforts of John Holway and others, these numbers will never be fully accurate and thus worthy of genuflection. Negro League stalwart Buck Leonard explains, "Until the late years of the league, we never kept any statistics."[44] A player would be assigned to record the box score, Leonard notes, but might fail to do so or forget to mail it in. Although some African American newspapers printed figures, Leonard states, their efforts prompted a joke:

> But [the reporter] wouldn't get to the game on time. He'd show up in the third inning and ask . . . "What happened in the first inning?" . . . Maybe the player couldn't remember. And if the guy didn't see what happened . . . he'd put down "singled to center" . . . so finally we gave him the nickname "Single to Center."[45]

Leonard comments about the cultural problem resulting from whites' adoration of statistics:

> Roy Campanella is on the committee to name old-time Negro stars to the Hall of Fame. He says the other members of the committee told him, "If only you could prove these things, if only you had the figures."[46]

When combined, the reports of Bell, Benson, Brown, Paige, Trouppe, Barber, Williams, DiMaggio, Mantle, and Leonard imply that major league baseball was characterized by conformist play and an emphasis on player statistics as a measure of greatness. Explaining what he terms the "bureaucratization of the imagination," Kenneth Burke writes:

> Every machine contains a cowpath. That is: there are embodied somewhere in its parts the variants of a process that remains simply because the originators of the machine embodied this process in their invention. It has been retained, not because it has been criticized, evaluated, and judged to be the best possible process, but simply because no one ever thought of questioning it.[47]

After the arrival of Babe Ruth, power hitting became a cowpath in major league baseball partly because whites adhered to Burke's "Neo-Malthusian principle," which, as Burke observes, "is simply another way of stating the admonition that every structure has its 'bottle neck.'"[48] Negro Leaguer Judy Johnson repeats Connie Mack's explanation of a racial bottleneck:

> I was a good friend of Connie Mack, the owner of the Philadelphia Athletics. One day I asked him why he didn't sign a black player. He told me, "There were too many of you to go in. It would have taken too many jobs away from the white boys."[49]

By excluding African Americans, Negro League veterans claim, not only did the white major leagues prevent Paige, Bell, Stearnes, and other athletes from gracing their lineups; whites also reinforced their devotion to power hitting and delayed needed variation in the style of play. The bottleneck choked off cultural variation.

Despite racial segregation, Bell and other Negro Leaguers argue that they exposed the conformist nature of major league baseball by barnstorming against white major league teams led by such luminaries as Ruth, Jimmie Foxx, Dizzy Dean, and Bob Feller. Of the recorded interracial contests, blacks won 268 while whites won only 168.[50] By repeatedly outplaying their white opponents, African Americans refuted the shibboleth of white superiority, at one point prompting commissioner Kennisaw Mouintain Landis to outlaw certain black-white contests out of sheer embarrassment for major league players.

Benson and Bell explain the lopsided barnstorming record as the result of what Burke calls a "perspective by incongruity"[51] or "atom-cracking." Such a perspective, Burke explains, violates what he terms "piety," which is "a schema of orientation" or *the sense of what properly goes with what* (emphasis added).[52] Two scholars elaborate: "By juxtaposing incongruous ideas, Burke says, we 'shatter pieties.'" When "one ideological correctness" is juxtaposed against another, they add, "the two call each other into question" and "the piety will thus be 'shattered.'"[53]

Benson evokes a "perspective by incongruity" when he asserts that white slugger Jimmie Foxx could not understand how he could succeed by hitting from a seemingly relaxed position: what Foxx thought Benson accomplished by "reflexes" was actually achieved by "striding." Unlike white players, Benson observes, Negro Leaguers "were all so unorthodox. I taught myself to hit. [Whites] went by the book."[54] Bell elaborates:

> When I came up, we didn't play baseball like they play in the major leagues. We played tricky baseball. When we played the big leaguers . . . our pitchers would curve the ball on the 3–2. They'd say, "What, are you trying to make us look bad?" We'd bunt and run and they'd say, "Why are you trying to do that in the first inning?" When we were supposed to bunt, they'd come in and we'd hit away. Oh, we played tricky baseball.
>
> That's why we beat the major league teams so many times. . . . The major leaguers would play for one big inning. They'd go by "written baseball." But there's so much "unwritten baseball."[55]

Bell explains other ways of shattering piety. He reports speeding home from second on a long sacrifice fly to center—razzle-dazzle that humiliated his white opponents. He notes that, as he slid safely underneath the catcher's tag, the umpire called him out, insisting, "'Look, you don't do that against a big-league team—score from second on an outfield fly.'"[56] As Malarcher remembers, even at age forty-five, Bell's style of play remained incongruous with major league expectations, as he shocked Bob Lemon's major league all-stars by scoring from first base on a bunt.[57] Bell argues, "I think we had a better system than the majors."[58] He and others claimed that major league baseball was inferior due to its adherence to standards of play. Negro Leaguers testify that Ruth, Cobb, and pitcher Lefty Grove unwittingly acknowledged Bell's contention. Paige maintains that Ruth rejected each of several opportunities to bat against him.[59] Bell repeats the report that, after being thrown out by a black catcher while trying to steal, Cobb refused to play any more interracial games, his racist pieties apparently shattered.[60] Crush Holloway contends that Grove stopped playing after African Americans beat him; then, claims Holloway, Grove lied by claiming that he had never pitched in interracial matches.[61]

Although Negro League and major league baseball followed the same on-the-field rules, the Negro Leagues manifested a different semiological system or code. By offering a perspective by incongruity, blacks exposed elements of major league baseball as amounting to what Roland Barthes calls "mythology." Barthes explains:

> What allows the [viewer/participant] to consume myth innocently is that he does not see it as a semiological system but as an inductive one. . . . Any semiological system is a system of values; now the myth-consumer takes the signification for a system of facts: myth is read as a factual system, whereas it is but a semiological system.[62]

According to black oral histories and other testimony, major league baseball embodied three of the elements that Barthes identifies as characteristic of bourgeois myth: the privation of history, the quantification of quality, and identification (or its failure). Barthes writes, "Myth deprives the object of which it speaks of all history."[63] In this case, whites denied the efficacy of the baserunning skills and improvisational style of Negro League players. Cobb's skill on the base paths was forgotten, allowing major league baseball to idealize the home-run hitter.

Barthes observes, "By reducing any quality to quantity, myth economizes intelligence: it understands reality more cheaply."[64] By claiming that—despite incomplete numbers and complaints from Campanella's committee—additional Negro Leaguers should be added to the Hall of Fame, Leonard, Bell, and other African Americans implicitly question the entire edifice of baseball statistics.[65] Bell explains, "I couldn't say who really was the best hitter. How can you name the best hitter? You can't name him. . . . Every team had four or five great hitters on it, and I don't know *who* was the best."[66] Unlike Mantle, who wanted to cry because his career batting average dropped below .300, Bell insists that quality does not reduce to quantity.

Further, Barthes asks, "How can one assimilate the Negro, the Russian? There is here a figure for emergencies: exoticism. The Other becomes a pure object, a spectacle, a clown."[67] African Americans complain that prejudiced whites mistakenly viewed one or two avowedly comic black teams, such as the Indianapolis Clowns, as a synecdoche for the entire Negro Leagues. Whites defined African Americans as too much unlike themselves. The racial bottleneck prompted the major leagues to treat African American players as exotic curiosities in the white-versus-black barnstorming spectacles. And, commenting on Barthes, critic Jonathan Culler declares that myth is "perhaps indomitable."[68] However, African Americans and Negro League baseball threatened to expose the in- domitability of major league baseball as a mere illusion.

Although the literature about Robinson repeatedly discusses Rickey's process of choosing him over other players, writers consistently ignore the significance of Rickey's most important decision: to tap a single black player who alone would shoulder the burden of racial abuse and receive the glory due a racial pioneer.

For Robinson, entering major league baseball meant entering a racial pressure cooker: he faced spikings; pitchers throwing at him; vicious, ever- present taunting; and death threats. Robinson's stress apparently was so great that it led friends to speculate that it played a role in his death from diabetes at age fifty-two.[69] Rickey could have reduced this stress by bring- ing other African Americans to his team simultaneously with Robinson. Plenty of gifted prospects were available, many of whom were older and far more experienced than Robinson.[70]

But isolating Robinson enabled Rickey to emplot baseball integration as a Horatio Alger–like narrative in which a lonely, ethical male of suppos- edly lower status struggled on to a higher social stratum with a boost from a well-established businessman. As Carl Bode explains, Horatio Alger's young hero typically confronts evil in the form of "a malicious young snob" and "a middle-aged rascal"—villains the protagonist easily van- quishes.[71] In his first three years as a Dodger, Robinson overcame many malicious young snobs and middle-age rascals who spewed abuse from stands and opposing dugouts. By playing well and not retaliating, this pro- tagonist secured his position in a higher social, if not moral, stratum.

For Rickey, creating this plot variation meant generating his own per- spective by incongruity: by emplotting baseball integration as an Alger- like struggle, he gave many whites the uncomfortable choice of either questioning their racial prejudice or questioning their faith in an Alger- like effort to achieve an American Dream.

In four important ways, Robinson's six autobiographical statements reinscribe Rickey's storybook plot. First, Robinson rhetorically severs his tie to the Negro Leagues by consistently heaping on them unmitigated scorn, refusing to offer a single positive word about them. Unlike the major leagues, African American teams, he explains, followed schedules that were "notoriously unreliable" and "unbelievably hectic."[72] Players faced "humiliating segregation" in the form of poor pay and hotels that were "usually of the cheapest kind" and sometimes entirely unavailable.[73] Teams suffered "long trips" on "bouncing buses," during which players "could never sit down to a relaxed hot meal."[74] Fulminating against such conditions, he blasts black teams as "Jim Crow clubs" in "Jim Crow leagues," as though African American baseball were somehow responsible for segregation.[75] He endorses Rickey's denunciation of the Negro Leagues as "a racket" and vigorously defends Rickey for refusing to pay any compensation to the Kansas City Monarchs when Rickey signed him.[76] This opprobrium is entirely unrelieved even by a description of a game that might punctuate the endless bouncing bus rides.

Second, whereas Rickey was obliged to begin his plot when Robinson was an adult, Robinson fills in the narrative by describing a childhood spent as an Alger-like waif. He relates his mother's inability to feed her children three meals per day and remembers when his sister repeatedly abandoned him in a sandbox for hours at a time.[77] He also records his troubles as a young teen. Later, despite his triumphs as an all-American football star, he dropped out of UCLA.

Third, Robinson attributes his success to Rickey. In typical Alger-like fashion, Robinson prevails through hard work and Protestant virtues. During his stint in the Negro Leagues, on what he calls an "unforgettable day," he follows Rickey's summons to New York for an unexpected three-hour meeting with the baseball mahatma.[78] Testing Robinson's suitability as a vanguard for integration, Rickey searches his interviewee for signs of wholesomeness, asking, "Do you drink?"[79] When Rickey hears "No," the answer he wants, he asks whether Robinson would like to marry. "'Yes, sir,' [Robinson] said, 'I have a girlfriend.' 'Well,' he ordered, 'you marry her right away!' He said it just like that."[80] As one of Robinson's coauthors explains, Rickey was frightened "by the image of [black boxing champion] Jack Johnson and his three white wives" and wanted "a clean-living family man whose character [and observance of certain racial boundaries] was above reproach."[81] In addition, citing Jesus' teaching, Rickey convinced

Robinson to "turn the other cheek" when confronting racial slurs, bean-balls, and spikings—all of which occurred, Robinson notes, just as Rickey predicted.[82]

Robinson reassigns Rickey the role of a typical supporting character in an Alger novel—a successful businessman who aids the street-urchin hero—and also designates Rickey as author of the narrative. Robinson de-clares, "I must tell you that it was Mr. Rickey's drama and that I was only a principal actor."[83] Robinson describes Rickey not only as "baseball's most far-sighted innovator" but as "the Einstein who provided the magic for-mula"; he and others were only "raw material."[84] After recalling that his own father deserted him when he was only six months old, Robinson de-clares that Rickey became "like the father I never knew."[85] Twenty-four years later, he recalls his bond with Rickey: "I feel I was the son [Rickey] had lost and he was the father I had lost."[86] Just as an author emplots a story, so Rickey takes "raw material"—a young man who admits to career uncertainties and an on-again, off-again long-distance engagement—and alchemizes him into a great athlete and "the most talked about and written about Negro in the world."[87]

Finally, Robinson credits Rickey for his skill on major league diamonds. Although Robinson records that he only dabbled in college baseball and "suffered" through his year in Negro League baseball, he says that Rickey's encouragement enabled him to surprise pitchers with bunts, speed, and dancing on the bases. Robinson asserts that, during his first spring train-ing, Rickey exhorted him to "be daring" "run wild," and "steal the pants" off opponents by becoming a "whirling demon."[88] Completing the (re)in-scription of Rickey-as-author, this anecdote serves as the only explanation that Robinson ever provided for the level of play that won him Rookie of the Year and Most Valuable Player awards.[89]

Although all of Robinson's biographers, including the most recent ones, reiterate the Alger-like plot, Negro Leaguers disagree. Although they often laud Robinson for his unusual courage in absorbing racial abuse without retaliating, they reject the Robinson-as-individualist plot and re-peatedly affirm his debt to Negro League baseball. Newt Allen declares, "The Monarchs developed several players who starred in the majors, espe-cially, of course, Jackie Robinson."[90] Sug Cornelius contends, "Had there not been a Kansas City Monarch ball club, Robinson wouldn't have been in organized [major league] baseball."[91]

In segregated America, there was literally no other baseball league that Robinson could join after he left the army. Not only did the Negro Leagues afford Robinson an opportunity to learn baseball, but they gave him a chance to decide that baseball would be his primary sport—something he indicated he never thought while scoring touchdowns as a running back at UCLA. Charlie Biot, however, reports that, while still living in Los Angeles, Robinson began to learn the intricacies of baseball by accepting free tickets to see the New York Black Yankees:

> He'd get there an hour before [the game] and sit there, like a doctor in an operating room, studying the batting styles. Same thing during the game. Seven games. He was studying us. He was studying us hard.[92]

Negro Leaguers unanimously agree that Robinson was less than outstanding when he arrived in Kansas City, partly because his arm was not strong enough to succeed at shortstop—the position he preferred. Claiming that he served as Robinson's mentor, Bell says that he followed the manager's instructions to expose the young player's weakness by hitting balls to his right and outrunning his throws to first. Bell then advised, "Jackie, shortstop is not your position."[93] After Rickey lured Robinson away from the Kansas City Monarchs and onto a white minor league team, he began at shortstop but soon switched to second base. Upon joining the Dodgers, he played first base for a year then settled at second—a position that does not require a strong arm.

Bell insists that by the time Robinson became a Brooklyn Dodger, his footwork exemplified that of the Negro League. Bell remembers teaching Robinson how to slide:

> I stole four bases . . . trying to confuse [Robinson]. So I would go into the bag, and put one foot for him to see. He'd reach for it, I would jerk it back, and slide, and step over his hand. These are the kinds of tricks he did in the majors, he learned them from me.[94]

Robinson fooled outfielders by turning widely at first or second, hesitating slightly to lure a throw from the outfield, then streaking safely to the next base.[95] Bell argues that Robinson also mastered that ploy in the Negro Leagues.[96] Bell's claims are plausible in part because neither Robinson nor Rickey, nor anyone else, claims to have taught Robinson *how* to perform as a "whirling demon" on the base paths—something that Bell did quite well and that was not a trademark of any of Rickey's white Dodger players.

And how Robinson whirled! Entering major league baseball, he persistently lured opponents into making fundamental mistakes. Red Barber mentions that, in the heat of Robinson's initial pennant race, he "electrified fans at Wrigley Field when he scored from first on a bunt"[97]—an act of daredevilry that, at age forty-five, Bell could apparently still work successfully against white major leaguers. Using the plodding predictability of 1940s major league baseball as an implicit backdrop, Barber records Robinson's syncopated baserunning in his first World Series:

> Jackie Robinson captured all attention when he got on base. People who hadn't seen Jackie dance off first, draw a throw, dart back . . . dance off again, worry the pitcher, draw a throw, dart back . . . dance off, and GO . . . and make it safely at second! . . . could hardly believe the testimony of their startled eyes.[98]

Moving base runners, however, did not worry or startle the Negro League pitchers observed in 1922 by sportswriter Eddie Batchelor, who noted, "Most of the [Negro League] catchers are fine throwers, as indeed they have to be to cover up for a very general tendency among the pitchers to give base runners a flying start." This practice, Batchelor explained, "seems to be one of the most conspicuous faults in the mounds men."[99] This criticism is misguided. Because Negro League pitchers assumed that stealing is part of the game, they wisely avoided distractions by concentrating on batters, not runners. However, because Raschi and other white pitchers twenty-seven years later were still unfamiliar with daring base runners, they were easily distracted by Robinson. In city after city, Robinson received a tumultuous reception from crowds of African Americans, who gleefully cheered whenever he—a single African American—would embarrass an entire team—indeed, an entire league—of whites, *each* of whom was held to be superior to all blacks. His style of play, "trickeration" if you will, asserted that major league baseball was starchy, predictable, and even inferior.

One of Robinson's white minor league teammates declared; "What he taught me specifically were things that were not in the book."[100] The book, however, would survive Robinson's stay in baseball. Even after his stunning career, major league baseball placed little value on steals and bunts, Maury Wills argues, until 1962, when Wills broke Cobb's season-high record for steals, a record considered unassailable. Along with two Hall-of-Fame pitchers, Wills, a bunter and slap hitter, led his team to a world championship. He laments the eight years that he languished in the minor leagues before joining the majors. But, he observes, the major leagues did not care about bunting: "They don't have a column in the papers to tell who's leading the league in sacrifice bunts."[101] He adds that aspiring home-run hitters told him not to steal because they "didn't want someone moving on the bases when they were hitting."[102]

Accepting Negro Leaguers' view of Robinson means interpreting the Rickey/Robinson emplotment as an example of what Burke calls "casuistic stretching," or introducing "new principles while theoretically remaining faithful to the old principles."[103] While theoretically faithful to old principles of individualism, Robinson triumphed by introducing a perspective by incongruity in the form of new principles of African American improvisation and cultural aesthetic.

Although Cornel West does not write about baseball, his comment below seems not only to represent jazz musicians' accounts of the prestidigitation of their fingers but also to crystallize Bell's argument about his—and Robinson's—sleight of foot:

> I use the term "jazz" here not so much as a term for a musical art form as for a mode of being in the world, an improvisational mode of protean, fluid, and flexible dispositions toward reality suspicious of either/or viewpoints, dogmatic pronouncements, and supremacist ideologies. . . . The interplay of individuality and unity is not one of uniformity and unanimity imposed from above but rather of conflict among diverse groupings that reach a dynamic consensus.[104]

Bell's, Paige's, and other African Americans' performances assaulted a sacred, dogmatic Book and illuminated major league baseball as a machine with a cowpath waiting for Robinson to discombobulate it. As "the Bojangles of Basepaths,"[105] Robinson mastered Bell's trickeration and through it, in Roger Kahn's words, "humiliated a legion of visiting players"[106]—each of whom was allegedly smarter and more capable than every black person on earth.

For Gillespie and Roach, white popular and symphonic music suffered from bureaucratized imagination and constituted a semiological system or mythology presenting itself as logical and immutable. To them, white popular and symphonic music appear "timeless" because its practitioners suppress the process of its invention when they present it in an ultrapolished, ultrapredictable form. Just as myth deprived major league baseball of its history, so myth deprived this music of its compositional history. The "timeless" element of music is exactly what jazz artists interrogated and shattered.

Weighing the unity of blackball reports and bebop testimony, one could infer that Satchel Paige and Dizzy Gillespie juggled equally unpredictable pitches through the same cultural legerdemain. Despite pain caused by a racial bottleneck, Negro League athletes and bebop artists alike persuasively claim that their trickeration dismantled the rigid, seemingly indomitable machinery/mythology of the dominant society and, in doing so, revealed white claims to universality as absurd, exposed white superiority as a flimsy pretension, and unmasked white culture as boredom itself—but boredom that was anything but inevitable. His casuistic stretching notwithstanding, Jackie Robinson did likewise.[107]

Notes

1. David Halberstam, *Summer of '49* (New York, 1989), 258. Raschi gave a similar account to another writer: see Jules Tygiel, *Baseball's Great Experiment: Jackie Robinson and His Legacy* (New York, 1983), 191.

2. David Falkner, *Great Time Coming: The Life of Jackie Robinson from Baseball to Birmingham* (New York, 1995), 227–228.

3. *The Jackie Robinson Story* (1950); Jackie Robinson, "What's Wrong with Negro Baseball?" *Ebony* 3, June 1948, 16–18; Jackie Robinson (as told to Wendell Smith), *Jackie Robinson: My Own Story* (New York, 1948); Jackie Robinson, *Baseball Has Done It*, ed. Charles Dexter (Philadelphia, 1964); Carl Rowan (with Jackie Robinson), *Wait Till Next Year: The Life Story of Jackie Robinson* (New York, 1960); Jackie Robinson (as told to Alfred Duckett), *I Never Had It Made* (New York, 1972: reprint, Hopewell, NJ, 1995).

4. In one of the best books written about Robinson, *Baseball's Great Experiment*, Tygiel alludes to routinized white play, briefly contrasts it to the Negro Leagues, and briefly mentions Robinson's debt to blackball. Others writing about Robinson erase this relationship almost completely.

5. Qtd. in Paul Berliner, *Thinking in Jazz* (Chicago, 1994), 417.

6. Dizzy Gillespie (with Al Fraser), *To Be or Not . . . to Bop* (New York, 1979), 158.

7. Ibid., 209–210; see also Dizzy Gillespie, "Dizzy Gillespie," in *Jazz Spoken Here*, ed. Wayne Enstice and Paul Rubin (New York, 1994), 171–184. We realize that Gillespie might be viewed as coming perilously close to essentializing racial difference. But inasmuch as Gillespie played fairly often (and congenially) with white musicians, he seems to be making a cultural distinction rather than anything else.

8. Qtd. in Gillespie, *To Be*, 207.

9. Ibid., 209.

10. Wilmer Fields, *My Life in the Negro Leagues* (Westport, CT, 1992).

11. Donn Rogosin, *Invisible Men* (New York, 1983); Mark Ribowsky, *The Complete History of the Negro Leagues* (New York, 1995), ix.

12. See Gene Benson, "Black Star of Philadelphia," in John Holway, *Black Diamonds: Life in the Negro Leagues from the Men Who Lived It* (New York, 1991), 70–88; Bill Drake, "Bill Drake," in John Holway, *Voices from the Great Black Baseball Leagues* (New York, 1992), 22–38; Newt Allen, "Newt Allen," in Holway, *Voices*, 90–105; Ted Radcliff, "Ted 'Double Duty' Radcliffe," in Holway, *Voices*, 169–187; Othello Renfroe, "Othello Renfroe," in Holway, *Voices*, 339–352; Cool Papa Bell, "Cool Papa Bell," in Holway, *Voices*, 107–139.

13. Allen, "Newt Allen," 95, 96.

14. Larry Brown, "Larry Brown," in Holway, *Voices*, 212–213.

15. For the importance of bunting, see Allen, "Newt Allen"; Benson, "Black Star"; Drake, "Bill Drake"; Willie Powell, "An American Giant," in Holway, *Black Diamonds*, 39–54; Jake Stephens, "Country Jake," in Holway, *Black Diamonds*, 1–17.

16. Allen, "Newt Allen," 94.

17. Ribowsky, *Complete History*, 115.

18. Ted Page, "Ted Page," in Holway, *Voices*, 140–166.

19. Ibid.; Benson, "Black Star"; Quincy Trouppe, *Twenty Years Too Soon* (Los Angeles, 1977), 208.

20. Benson, "Black Star," 85.

21. Dave Malarcher, "Dave Malarcher," in Holway, *Voices*, 39–58.

22. Eddie Batchelor, "Afro-American Rooters Are the Best Part of the Show at Mack Park," reprinted in Richard Bak, *Turkey Stearnes and the Detroit Stars: The Negro Leagues in Detroit, 1919–1933* (Detroit, 1994), 81–89.

23. Cool Papa Bell, "Cool Papa Bell," in Holway, *Voices*, 111, 123.

24. Allen, "Newt Allen," 96.

25. Bell, "Cool Papa Bell," 110; see also George Giles, "The Black Terry," in Holway, *Black Diamonds*, 55–69; Page, "Ted Page," 160.

26. Dave Barnhill, "The Millers' Giant Killer," in Holway, *Black Diamonds*, 131–146.

27. Benson, "Black Star," 70–71.

28. Brown, "Larry Brown," 212–213.

29. Drake, "Bill Drake," 35.

30. Bell, "Cool Papa Bell," 119–120.

31. Satchel Paige (as told to Hal Lebovitz), *Pitchin' Man: Satchel Paige's Own Story* (New York, 1948; reprint, Westport, CT, 1992), 2, 64.

32. Mickey Mantle (with Herb Gluck), *The Mick* (New York, 1985), 64.

33. Willie Mays (with Lou Sahadi), *Say Hey: The Autobiography of Willie Mays* (New York, 1988), 27.

34. Tygiel, *Baseball's Great Experiment*, 21.

35. Trouppe, *Twenty Years*, 257.

36. Bill Veeck (with Ed Linn), *Veeck as in Wreck* (New York, 1962), 171.

37. Red Barber, *1947: When All Hell Broke Loose in Baseball* (Garden City, NY, 1982), 305.

38. Mark Ribowsky, *Don't Look Back: Satchel Paige in the Shadows of Baseball* (New York, 1994), 256–258.

39. Ted Williams (with John Underwood), *My Turn at Bat: The Story of My Life* (New York, 1969), 106–110.

40. Ibid., 116.

41. Qtd. in Thomas Boswell, *The Heart of the Order* (New York, 1989), 8.

42. Qtd. in Michael Seidel, *Streak: Joe DiMaggio and the Summer of 1941* (New York, 1988), 202.

43. Mantle, *The Mick*, 240.

44. Buck Leonard, "Buck Leonard," in Holway, *Voices*, 250–279.

45. Ibid., 263.

46. Ibid.

47. Kenneth Burke, *Attitudes toward History* (New York, 1937; reprint, Berkeley, CA, 1984), 228, 229.

48. Ibid.

49. Qtd. in Art Rust Jr., *"Get That Nigger off the Field!" A Sparkling, Informal History of the Black Man in Baseball* (n.p., 1976), 38–41. See also John Holway, *Blackball Stars: Negro League Pioneers* (New York, 1988), 162–163; Robert Peterson, *Only the Ball Was White* (New York, 1970), 173; Rogosin, *Invisible Men*, 201.

50. Holway, *Blackball Stars*, xiv.

51. Burke, *Attitudes*, 308.

52. Kenneth Burke, *Permanence and Change* (New York, 1954; reprint, Berkeley, CA, 1984), 74, 76.

53. Julia Allen and Lester Faigley, "Discursive Strategies for Social Change: An Alternative Rhetoric of Argument," *Rhetoric Review* 14 (1995): 142–172.

54. Benson, "Black Star," 71.

55. Bell, "Cool Papa Bell," 119. See also Benson, "Black Star," 71.

56. Bell, "Cool Papa Bell," 124; see also Cool Papa Bell, "James 'Cool Papa' Bell," in *Baseball When the Grass Was Real*, ed. Donald Honig (Lincoln, NE, 1993), 164–177.

57. Malarcher, "Dave Malarcher," 108–109.

58. Bell, "Cool Papa Bell," 120.

59. Satchel Paige (as told to David Lipman), *Maybe I'll Pitch Forever* (New York, 1962; reprint, Lincoln, NE, 1993), 58.

60. Bell, "Cool Papa Bell," 117; see also Bak, *Turkey Stearnes*, 60–61.

61. Crush Holloway, "Crush Holloway," in Holway, *Voices*, 67.

62. Roland Barthes, *Mythologies* (New York, 1957; reprint, New York, 1993), 131.

63. Ibid., 151.

64. Ibid., 153.

65. See Leonard, "Buck Leonard," 262–263; and Buck Leonard (with James Riley), *Buck Leonard: The Black Lou Gehrig* (New York, 1995), 252–258.

66. Bell, "Cool Papa Bell," 133.

67. Barthes, *Mythologies*, 151, 152.

68. Jonathan Culler, *Roland Barthes* (New York, 1983), 40.

69. Pee Wee Reese, qtd. in Maury Allen, *Jackie Robinson: A Life Remembered* (New York, 1987), 5.

70. Given that the notoriously stingy Rickey never paid Robinson's Negro League team for Robinson's services (despite protests from Robinson's team owner), Rickey could undoubtedly have brought others up without paying for them either.

71. Carl Bode, "Introduction," in *Ragged Dick and Struggling Upward*, by Horatio Alger Jr. (New York; 1984), xi.

72. Rowan, *Wait*, 112; Robinson, *I Never*, 36.

73. Robinson, "What's Wrong?"; Robinson, *Jackie*, 11; Robinson, *Baseball*, 38.

74. Robinson, *Baseball*, 38; Robinson, *Jackie*, 11; Robinson, *I Never*, 36.

75. Robinson, *I Never*, 35, 48, 59; Rowan, *Wait*, 97.

76. Robinson, "What's Wrong?"; Robinson, *Jackie*, 52; Rowan, *Wait*, 50–55. Some Negro League owners (e.g., Gus Greenlee) ran numbers operations and other illicit activities. But their baseball operations did not constitute a racket. Had segregation not existed, Gus Greenlee would probably have been CEO of a Fortune 500 company. Once scorned, numbers operations are now run by many state governments, who call them "lotteries."

77. Rowan, *Wait*, 25; Robinson, *I Never*, 16–17.

78. Robinson, *Baseball*, 38.

79. Robinson, *Jackie*, 22.

80. Ibid., 12. In a later version, Robinson claimed that he answered Rickey's query "You got a girl?" with a more irresolute "I don't know." See Rowan, *Wait*, 113–114.

81. Rowan, *Wait*, 107–109.

82. Robinson, *I Never*, 73.

83. Robinson, *Jackie*, 12.

84. Robinson, *I Never*, 12.

85. Ibid., 40; Robinson, *Baseball*, 10.

86. Robinson, *Jackie*, 86.

87. Robinson, *I Never*, 11, 15–16, 269.

88. Rowan, *Wait*, 196.

89. Robinson confuses Rickey's *encouragement*, which inspired Robinson, with Rickey's *teaching*, which did not occur.

90. Allen, "Newt Allen," 103.

91. Sug Cornelius, "William 'Sug' Cornelius," in Holway, *Voices,* 234–249. See also Benson, "Black Star."

92. Qtd. in Bruce Chadwick, *When the Game Was Black and White: The Illustrated History of the Negro Leagues* (New York, 1992), 169.

93. Cool Papa Bell, "Cool Papa Bell" in Rust, *"Get that Nigger off the Field,"* 40–41; see also Bell, "Cool Papa Bell," in Holway, *Voices,* 128; for players who concur that Robinson was unsuited for shortstop, see Hilton Smith, "Hilton Smith," in Holway, *Voices,* 280–298; Allen, "Newt Allen," 103; Barnhill, "The Millers' Giant Killer," 142; Renfroe, "Othello Renfroe," 339–352.

94. Bell, "Cool Papa Bell," in Rust, *"Get that Nigger off the Field."* 40–41.

95. Peter Golenbock, *Bums: An Oral History of the Brooklyn Dodgers* (New York, 1984), 162.

96. Bell, "Cool Papa Bell," in Holway, *Voices,* 119.

97. Barber, *When All Hell,* 223.

98. Ibid., 304. Punctuation in the original.

99. Batchelor, "Afro-American Rooters," 84.

100. Qtd. in Falkner, *Great Time Coming,* 138.

101. Maury Wills and Mike Celizic, *On the Run: The Never Dull and Often Shocking Life of Maury Wills* (New York, 1991), 87.

102. Ibid., 207.

103. Burke, *Attitudes,* 229–234.

104. Cornel West, "Malcolm X and Black Rage," in *Malcolm X: In Our Own Image,* ed. Joe Wood (New York, 1990), 48–58.

105. Tygiel, *Baseball's Great Experiment,* 190.

106. Roger Kahn, *The Boys of Summer* (New York, 1987), xix.

107. A version of this essay was presented at Cambridge University during a conference of the British Association of American Studies. For their encouragement and criticism, the authors thank Bert Bender, Cheree Carlson, Jim Corder, Frank D'Angelo, Grant Farrad, Faith Miller, Ernest Miller, Mike Sewell, Fawzia Topan, Jennie Walker, and Brian Ward. For their great support, we especially salute Mark Harris and Aaron Baker.

Chapter Six

The Unbearable Whiteness of Skiing

Annie Gilbert Coleman

On a clear day, skiers might see blue sky above and green trees below, or flashes of brightly clad people whizzing by, but mostly they see white. Even in the American West, a region noted for its racial and ethnic diversity, ski resorts have remained as white as snow. In the 1960s, for example, only two Hispanics held skiing jobs at Vail, Colorado. George Sisneros, the son of a miner who lived in nearby Minturn, fell in love with skiing as a kid and eventually asked for a job with the Vail ski patrol. "They must have been laughing," he said. "Here was a local kid who wanted to be on the ski patrol. . . . [I got the job] but I had a hard time of it. Some people didn't think I should be there because I was just a local Mexican boy. I had to learn what the ski business was all about. . . . I was lucky I survived that first year."[1] George's wife, Eleanor, became an instructor in the ski school and the second Hispanic to ski for Vail. American Indians were even more difficult to spot at western ski resorts. Perhaps the largest group of Indians present on the Vail slopes at one time appeared on December 9, 1963: Eddie Box and the Southern Ute Ceremonial Dancers had come to perform a "snow" dance for the ski area.[2] Even at Taos Ski Valley—in the heart of New Mexico's Indian country—Peter Totemoff stood out as the only Indian who held a skiing job. Totemoff, an Aleutian who had moved from Alaska, found a niche instructing at Taos only after some difficulty: "[The ski instructor examiners] couldn't see an Indian skiing better than they did. I always had to beat them in a race to prove myself, and they didn't like that either."[3] Aside from Totemoff, the only Indians working at Taos Ski Valley in the 1950s hauled *poma* lift parts up the mountain by hand and performed other menial jobs.

Except for its manual labor and service employees, who are in many ways hidden from view, the ski industry has crafted unusually "white" settings within the American West. That is not to deny the significance of these workers; the ski industry has come to depend on them—especially in the last decade or so—but its reliance on people of color for wage work lurks deep in the shadow of the glitz, glamour, powder snow, and vacationing commonly associated with western destination ski resorts. These resorts brought equipment, fashion, restaurant, hotel, and real estate businesses into the fold of the ski industry, and they all shared the common goal of creating and selling attractive commodities to skiing tourists.

Ski tourism has been an economic force in the West since World War II. It has equally significantly, however, (re)shaped western culture, peddling "western" and "European" images in powerful advertising campaigns.[4] Ski resorts have ultimately reproduced the dual western mythic impulses articulated by Elliott West, constructing western ski sites around cultural memories of the Old World—in this case, alpine villages—or as places populated with exotic Indians or masculine cowboys.[5] These mythic impulses coincided with—and reinforced—the construction of a white ethnicity centered on an emerging destination resort ski culture. Historians have recently examined the creation of white ethnic identities in the context of American political, class, and gender relations; the case of western skiing links this dynamic to consumption, class, sport, and region.[6] As the ski industry sold winter vacations and other ski commodities, it connected dynamics of ethnicity, consumption, and class, "whitewashing" western destination ski resorts and transforming local people of color into invisible workers or exotic objects of tourism.

The whiteness of these places has clear historical roots. Scandinavian and European immigrants to the West brought knowledge of skiing and ski making with them and, in doing so, significantly altered western mountain culture. Inhabitants of nineteenth-century mountain towns quickly picked up the sport and took to huge homemade skis in order to get from place to place. "Snowshoe" Thompson—a Norwegian who came with his family to Illinois and ended up in gold rush California—acquired legendary status, skiing ninety miles across the Sierras on a regular basis to deliver the mail.[7] Mail carriers, itinerant ministers, doctors, and most mountain townspeople depended on skis for winter transportation, and they recognized their debt to the Swedes and Norwegians who taught them.[8] They used skis for more than transportation, too: mining camps and towns in the Sierras and the Rockies started their own ski clubs and sponsored downhill races and jumping contests to break up the monotony of their winters.[9] Carl Howelson, "The Flying Norseman," instituted Steamboat Springs's winter carnival in 1914, and townspeople still consider him the father of Nordic jumping in Colorado.

By the late nineteenth century, downhill skiing had also become a popular sport in the European Alps. By the 1920s, St. Moritz was attracting winter tourists from all over the world, and Hannes Schneider had opened the first ski school in St. Anton, Austria.[10] In the 1930s, wealthy Americans traveled to Europe on ski vacations and returned home anxious to practice their new sport on American hills. European skiers also came to the United States and, with their experience and skills, encouraged the growth of American recreational skiing. The town of Aspen honored Andre Roch, the Swiss mountaineer who designed their first downhill run and helped start their ski club, by declaring October 26 "Andre Roch Day."[11] Although Roch returned to Switzerland, other Europeans moved to the United States permanently. Hannes Schneider, Friedl Pfeifer, and Ernie Blake emigrated to the United States to avoid the Nazis.[12] They and many others like them took jobs as highly respected ski coaches and instructors in America's growing ski world and encouraged still more European skiers to come and work in the States. Whereas nineteenth-century Scandinavian immigrants had established the sport of Nordic skiing and jumping in the American West, this group of European skiers in the 1930s brought technical knowledge and energy that jump-started the sport of downhill skiing in America. Many of them headed west for the mountains, good snow, and jobs at burgeoning resorts like Sun Valley.

European immigrants, be they miners or mountaineers, introduced and shaped the sport of downhill skiing in the American West—skiing history and ethnic history are closely connected in that regard.[13] This historical context of the sport, however, does not explain why the growing ski industry and its clientele managed to retain such an enthusiasm for white ethnicities even after the influence of European immigration fell off. New dynamics came into play after World War II: the ski industry combined the sport of skiing with the business of tourism as never before, encouraging the growth of new ski resorts across the West and a new culture of consumption to go along with them. Aspen and the new Aspen Skiing Corporation best exemplified this trend, opening the area's first—and the world's longest—chairlift in 1946. Arapahoe Basin also created its own ski corporation and opened for business immediately after World War II, when Berthoud Pass—also in Colorado—installed the nation's first double chairlift. The year 1949 ushered in the first season at California's Squaw Valley; Taos Ski Valley opened in 1956, followed the next season by Aspen Highland's and Buttermilk in Colorado. By 1963, Crested Butte and the granddaddy of destination resorts—Vail—were attracting skiers to their slopes with new lifts and trails. Taking advantage of a growing middle and upper class ready to spend their money on tourism and recreation, the skiing and advertising industries worked together to market destination ski resorts. They did so by creating an attractive image of "European" ski culture that excluded people of color, helping create an ethnic whiteout on the ski slopes.[14]

The consumerism of the 1950s brought with it a new ethic of consumption, fueled by widespread proclamations of America's high standard of living. Middle- and upper-class Americans generally accepted this ideology and identified themselves as recipients and buyers of the commodities that would "improve" their lives in various ways.[15] Ski resorts and businesses associated with skiing filled national ski magazines and regional tourism publications with advertisements for ski areas, ski equipment, ski fashions, and other products. These ads offered images and ideals that defined an easily recognizable ski culture built on beauty, fashion, leisure, health, and athleticism. Socializing with members of the opposite sex was practically required in this culture, a fact which crumbled many of the barriers placed in front of women who tried to participate in more "masculine" sports.[16] Like many popular images in the 1950s, ski industry advertisements featured blonde women and handsome white men achieving fulfillment through the purchase of a certain brand of ski, jacket, or package tour. As yearly vacations became the norm rather than the exception, and ski areas grew along with America's burgeoning tourist industry, visiting destination ski resorts and participating in the accompanying consumer culture took on new meaning. Unlike a day trip to a local ski area, where images of consumption had less power and relevance, resort skiing after World War II had become a symbol for a lifestyle, a means of expressing oneself and impressing others. Success for skier-tourists hinged on having the physical ability and financial wherewithal to live that lifestyle.

The images that defined this "ski culture" came wrapped in representations of ethnicity. Given the sport's historical context, such representations made sense—in the 1930s, most good skiers learned in Europe, and afterward they learned from Europeans who had emigrated to the States. Practical concerns also supported the appeal of European images: St. Moritz,

St. Anton, Val d'Isère, and Garmisch–Partenkirchen attracted skiers from all over the world; the most knowledgeable and experienced ski instructors came from Europe; Europeans consistently dominated international competitions; and European countries developed the newest technology in lifts and ski equipment. Images from Austria, Norway, and Switzerland took on even more appeal in postwar America because of those nations' resistance to Hitler. In 1944, for example, it was easy for Americans to visualize Austrian ski instructors or Swiss mountaineers guiding the family Von Trapp across the Alps to freedom. Norwegian skiers represented ideals of health, fitness, and masculinity, and things European seemed generally cosmopolitan, sophisticated, and sexy. European and Scandinavian images thus appealed to American skier-tourists on moral, physical, and aesthetic levels.

Rather than emphasize specific national identities, however, American ski culture eventually lumped all Europeans and Scandinavians together under a lily-white "European" image. Austria, Switzerland, Germany, Italy, France, Norway, and Sweden all produced excellent skiers and ski products, so fostering a general European Alpine image proved more useful from a marketing standpoint than concentrating on particular national identities. This European ski ideal—which emphasized a geographical region, in this case the Alps, over political ones—allowed American skiers to accept German instructors and lift engineers who had fought against the United States in World War II.[17]

The prominence of European ethnic images in American ski culture may have proved even more evocative than advertisers could have hoped. Sociologists have pointed out that in the mid- to late twentieth century, fewer societal barriers and cultural distinctions existed to differentiate white ethnic groups, and the broad extent of ethnic intermarriage among whites has produced a large group of Americans with ethnically mixed ancestries. As a result, white Americans have the ability to choose a particular ethnic identity and express it to varying degrees whenever and wherever they want. These developments, one sociologist argues, have caused the emergence of a broad ethnic option based on European ancestry—a generic white ethnicity.[18] White Americans identifying themselves as "European" rather than as a combination of distinct ancestries could easily accept the ski culture's images and ideals as their own.

While it is difficult to know how American skiers in the 1930s through 1960s identified themselves, there is no doubt that the ski industry tried to capitalize on the appeal of things European. Ski industry businesses created ethnic images in material forms fit for consumption—they made it possible and appealing literally to buy a European identity while remaining physically in the American West. Marketing western mountains, clothes, restaurants, hotels, and ski instructors as European enabled the ski industry to legitimate its products in the international ski world at the same time that it helped its clientele acquire a culturally constructed white identity through their behavior as skiers, tourists, consumers.

As early as 1936, the new Sun Valley resort compared itself to St. Moritz, suggesting that skier-tourists could experience the same activities and ambiance in Idaho that they could in Switzerland. Indeed, Sun Valley founder Averill Harriman's goal was to re-create a Swiss resort. Before he had even heard of Ketchum, Idaho, he wrote a note to a friend saying, "It has occurred to me that some day there will be established a ski center in the mountains here, of the same character as in the Swiss and Austrian Alps." "I believe it is worthwhile," he went on, "for us to investigate the present centers of the sport in our [Union Pacific Railroad] territory, having in mind we might assist through our advertising and otherwise in promoting these places." When Count Felix Schaffgotsch, sent to find a suitable winter sports center, came upon Ketchum, Idaho, he wrote Harriman, "This is it. Among the many attractive spots I have visited, this combines more delightful features than any place I have seen in the United States, Switzerland or Austria." The publicity and Hollywood movie stars such as Claudette Colbert and Robert Young that Harriman attracted to Sun Valley contributed to its feel as a European resort, where the rich and famous gathered for socializing and sport.[19]

Transforming the Rockies into the Alps proved quite popular among ski industry promoters, and they followed the lead of tourism boosters who had been performing this feat since the mid–nineteenth century. In 1869, for instance, Samuel Bowles published an account of his summer vacation in Colorado under the title *The Switzerland of America*.[20] Earl Pomeroy noted that many nineteenth-century tourists sought the Old World in the New. "Senator Benton had compared the Colorado Rockies to the Alps," he wrote, "and thereafter Alpine similes . . . helped the traveler to transport himself in fancy to more famous scenes."[21] Swiss mountaineer Andre Roch applied this idea to skiing when he visited the mountains near Aspen in 1936 and wrote, "It is easy to see that America could find here a resort that would in no way be inferior to anything in the Alps." Local boosters clung to and repeated those words for over a decade.[22] Even the state of Colorado launched a campaign that advertised the Rockies as "the

The "other" Alps. And then some!

Our great mountains have finer, lighter, more dependable snow, our apres-ski a more genuine western camaraderie. And nowhere else in U.S. skilands will you find more huge alpine bowls, gentle and forest-sheltered broadways, regiments of chairs, gondolas, every high-capacity lift. Complete ski villages, too, with dog sleds to druggists, ski schools to discotheques, movies to pools — and atmosphere. Glamor, charm, history, action and pizza. Sunswept by nature, year-round. Lucky enough to have a choice? You're smart to ski Colorado. Coupon brings a color preview of what's happening. It should happen to you.

Colorado!

STATE OF COLORADO
Division of Commerce & Development
365 State Capitol Building, Denver, Colorado 80003
Please send free ski information packet, including big new Ski Country USA Manual with complete, current details, pictures and prices on all areas, accommodations, winter sports events, transportation.

(please print)
Name_____
Address_____
State_____ Zip____
Zip Code essential. Thank you.

6.1 *"The 'other' Alps. And then some!"* Following the lead of western tourism boosters in the nineteenth century, the state of Colorado hoped to attract tourists to the Rockies by comparing them to the Alps. "Alpine" landscape and atmosphere gave Colorado ski resorts legitimacy and appeal in the steadily growing destination-resort ski culture. *Ski* 22 (December 1967): 89.

'other' Alps," featuring alpine bowls, gondolas, and even ski villages to go with the state's high-quality snow and "genuine western camaraderie." (See Figure 6.1.) A number of Rocky Mountain resorts have tried to alter the identity of their mountains since then, constructing them—both physically and culturally—as a European landscape and implicitly limiting access to that ethnic space in the process.

Referring to the Rockies as the American Alps allowed "European" westerners access to faraway places; ski fashion let them look the part. Clothes from Europe, like European ski equipment, transferred a sense of legitimacy and style to their owner. Klaus Obermeyer's clothes and German ski boots were popular in America, and he stressed their Bavarian roots in images as well as words by posing a St. Bernard dog next to his model in one ad. (See Figure 6.2.) Norwegian sweaters approached the status of uniforms for any self-respecting skiers, and Bogner's stretch

6.2 *Obermeyer Ski Fashions* Beautiful women and European references—Scandinavian-style sweaters, a St. Bernard dog, and "Made in Bavaria" tags—sold many white Americans on skiing and the social ski culture of places like Aspen, Colorado, where Klaus Obermeyer ran his business. *Ski* 24 (November 1959): 49.

pants revolutionized American ski fashion altogether. Bogner's pants didn't *look* especially German—what mattered was that they *were* German, and they were much more sexy than the older "baggy look" fashions. For women skiing in the late 1950s and 1960s, they were almost mandatory. Scandinavian Ski Shop ads (see Figure 6.3) highlighted their Bogner parkas and "s-t-r-e-t-c-h pants" in the text and on their blonde model, nonchalantly converging ethnicities by advertising German clothes for a "Scandinavian" ski shop that was located in Midtown Manhattan. American

6.3 *Scandinavian Ski Shops* Offering to fulfill "all your skiing needs," this advertisement emphasized the sexy aspects of ski vacations at the same time that it merged the German identity of its product with the Scandinavianness of the store. Consumers could thus go to a "Scandinavian" place (in Midtown Manhattan) and purchase items that would give them the ethnic (and sexy) images they "needed" to ski. *Ski* 24 (November 1959): 17.

designers accepted this convergence along with the status of European clothing styles and produced their own variations on the theme.

Restaurant and hotel owners at western ski resorts also shouted their ethnic intentions. Names such as the Hotel St. Bernard, the Alpenhof, the Innsbruck Lodge, and the Edelweiss resonated with meaning even in the unlikely locale of Taos, New Mexico. Copies of European architecture visibly reinforced ethnic images conjured up by business names, restaurant menus, and general ambiance. Warren Miller described the St. Bernard when it opened in the late 1950s as being "more European than Europe." "They had all French dishes," he said, "and silverware, and the service was exactly like a small place in Chamonix or Val d'Isere."[23] Kaarlo Jokela's Finnish Thunderbird Inn, complete with sauna, rounded out the European flavor of Taos Ski Valley.[24] In the early 1960s, the developers of Vail similarly emphasized Europeanness by building a Bavarian village at the base of the area. The Lodge at Vail exuded Austrian flavor, and the Vail Village Inn was eager to compete. When he hired Ed Kilby, a local construction-crew cook who had an Indian wife and specialized in chicken-fried steak, the owner of the Vail Village Inn announced that French chef Pierre Kilbeaux had arrived to preside over their kitchen.[25] When cooks from Minturn transform into French chefs and Taos, New Mexico, attracts skiers with its European hospitality, you know that European images have acquired a market value.

The most visible and powerful ethnic images in the ski industry were people—the European ski instructors who imparted their knowledge of the sport (as well as their good looks and foreign accents) to their pupils. Ski resorts made certain to hire as many European ski instructors as possible and to publicize the Europeanness of their ski schools. Sun Valley was the first resort to capitalize on this ethnic image; Averill Harriman established an entirely Austrian ski school in 1936 and encouraged the instructors to wear native costumes—it seemed at any moment they would start to yodel and burst into song. Through the 1960s, western resorts touted foreign ski school directors and instructors, including Willy Schaeffler, Friedl Pfeifer, Fred and Elli Iselin, Alf Engen, Otto Lang, and Jean Mayer. Stein Erikson, Olympic gold medalist and director of the Aspen Highlands ski school, returned to Norway regularly in the late 1950s and brought at least fifteen skiers from his homeland to instruct with him in Colorado. Just as been the case for others before him, Erikson's expertise and success as a competitor, enhanced by his European heritage, helped him embark on a successful career as a professional skier and instructor in America. In the 1960s, he helped American skiers seek his advice on technique by writing a number of articles and books, encouraging them to "come ski with me." Other European competitors-turned-professionals, including Fred Iselin and Jean Claude Killy, took on similar roles, becoming noted spokespeople for their ski school programs or ski equipment.[26] European ski instructors may have immigrated before the war for political reasons, but they continued to immigrate afterward because American ski culture created such a demand for their image that they could be sure of employment, if not fame. Once in America, these instructors became icons of the ski culture, and their labor itself became an imported commodity crafted around ethnic images—a transformation that resort owners were quick to recognize, encourage, and market.

As members of the ski industry—tourism boosters, clothing manufacturers, ski school and resort owners, and hoteliers and restaurateurs— used the language of ethnicity to attract customers, the historical memory of European skiing and immigration dwindled in importance and became detached from the ethnic images and references themselves. Owners and advertisers blithely made the conscious choice to "go Bavarian."[27] Vail marketers emphasized European image over all else in an ad that began in German. (See Figure 6.4.) This ad tempted readers to discover Europe in Vail, where the skiing, continental flavor, and "the kind of name-your-game aprés that never quits" would provide a vacation that "comes off like it just came in from the Alps." Consumers, of course, did not expect to find all of Europe happily ensconced in Vail. They responded to the ad and embraced these aspects of European ski culture because they gave priority to the image associated with their purchases, not to the origins or practical use of those purchases. This is what happens when commodities acquire social meanings through advertising and marketing: they become cultural more than functional goods, with symbolic meanings that grow separated from and more important than the reality of the commodity's production. Taking a lesson from a handsome Swiss instructor, in other words, mattered more than actually learning how to ski, and eating a *filet de boeuf au poulet frit* prepared by Pierre Kilbeaux was far different from eating Ed Kilby's chicken-fried steak.

Skier-tourists accepted their role as consumers. Buying a ski lesson, staying at a particular hotel, or wearing Bogner stretch pants made a statement about one's personal identity and allowed individuals to feel a part of the "European" ski culture. Participation in this culture grew continuously more expensive as fashion, ski technology, and the hotel and restaurant

6.4 *"Wohin ist Europa gegangen?"* Built from the ground up as a resort town, Vail has capitalized on the marketing appeal of European ski images, from the German language in this ad to the alpine restaurants and hotels that line the brick streets of its Bavarian-style Vail Village. *Skiing* 21 (October 1968): 41.

business grew along with ski resorts. The language of ethnicity thus became the language of class as well: Bogner pants, after all, cost a pretty penny; and one employee explained the plethora of European instructors at Sun Valley by saying the resort "had a lush clientele."[28] Residents of western mountain towns and people who moved there to work and ski— true "ski bums," some athletes, and many Europeans themselves—made up a gradually declining segment of destination resort skiers who existed outside the upper class.[29]

As images of ethnicity and class converged and grew stronger in American ski culture, they eventually overpowered the culture's physical origins. Skiing itself, in other words, became optional. A social sport from its beginning, skiing vacations could consist mainly of drinking on the mountain and visiting local night spots in the evening. This schedule maximized opportunities to show off achievements of consumption and minimized the need for physical exertion. Pretending to ski and looking the part was enough. One advertisement for (European) indoor footwear claimed that "some of the best skiing is done right here," reclining by a coffee table. (See Figure 6.5.) The ad went on to explain, "Half the fun of skiing is in the telling and half the fun of the telling is in the snug warmth of these Swiss-made after-ski boots." Talking and wearing imported clothes thus took precedence over skiing. Earl Pomeroy noticed this trend occurring as early as the 1930s and 1940s. He wrote, "Since [the opening of Sun Valley in 1936] visitors who come to the ski resorts simply to wear the latest in

6.5 *"Some of the best skiing is done here. . . ."* As the power of consuming ethnic images grew in resort ski culture, skiing itself withdrew into the background. As this advertisement claims, telling your friends about your skiing was half the fun. This ad implies, therefore, that if you had the right (Swiss-made) après ski boots and lounged around silver-plated mugs of cocoa, you could claim legitimacy in the ski world, no matter your skill level. *Ski* 27 (October 1962): 22.

6.6 *"Stand in the lift line looking cool"* Looking cool, this ad declares, is four-fifths of what visits to ski resorts are all about. Perhaps more in the nineties than ever before, being seen is the goal. In a sea of fashion objects and spectators, destination-resort skiers constantly compare themselves and their feats of consumption to those around them. *Ski* 60 (October 1995): 23.

ski clothing from Abercrombie and Fitch, ride the chair tow, and recuperate from the trip over hot buttered rum or moose milk have sometimes exceeded the skiers."[30] The Italian clothing line Fila appealed to more recent performances of consumption by emphasizing the significance of "stand[ing] in the lift line looking cool." (See Figure 6.6.) "Lift lines aren't all bad," it declared, "they give everyone a chance to admire your *new* Fila skiwear." If ski culture lost sight of the sport's ethnic roots and even of the sport itself, it nonetheless retained ethnic images as crucial signifiers of exclusivity and status.

Recently, yet another layer in this increasingly removed ski culture has emerged: that of people visiting resort towns to spectate—to watch upper-class and often famous people pretend to participate in the ski culture. Sun Valley, Aspen, and more recently Telluride have acquired some rich and famous residents, visible people who have helped create a sparkling atmosphere in those destination resorts. This atmosphere, foreign to most Americans' daily lives, has appealed to skier-tourists by offering tantalizing images of wealth and fame; and recalling the number of movie stars they spotted has become part of the vacation ritual for many skier-tourists. Spectators thus consume wealthy ski culture wanna-bes so they can identify with wealth and fame, in the same way that the wealthy consume commodified European images in order to identify themselves as members of ski culture.

These sometimes mystifying dynamics have created the stark reality of ski slopes on which only white people have found a welcome. Ski images that emphasized "Europeanness" established, in effect, a new ethnicity—full of savoir faire and glamour—with which many white Americans wanted to identify. They could become "discriminating skiers," that is, by purchasing la Dolomite ski boots (see Figure 6.7), an act that granted—or reaffirmed—their access to brandy served on silver trays. As they consumed products of the ski industry and internalized the ethnic symbols surrounding those commodities, white skiers purchased Europeanness and demonstrated the convergence of ethnicity and class in the ski culture. At the same time this generic whiteness emphasized class and broke down divisions among white ethnic groups, however, it established less flexible barriers around race. White Americans have a relative freedom to choose an ethnic identity that Americans of color do not, and American ski culture continues to exist as an increasingly wealthy culture exclusive of minorities.

Disabled ski programs demonstrate most compellingly the power of white ethnic images and loyalties in the modern ski industry. During the 1970–71 season, Winter Park took over the disabled ski program begun two years earlier at Arapahoe Basin. Run by the ski school and volunteers, Winter Park fully supported the program financially for thirteen years, after which fundraising and individual participants took over most of the burden. Even in 1989, however, the ski area gave $40,000 and $600,000 worth of services to the program.[31] This program and others like it operate in order to give disabled people the opportunity to empower themselves and gain self-confidence through skiing. Because skiing can elicit feelings of freedom and power at almost any skill level, virtually everyone can enjoy the sport and benefit from those feelings in their life off the

6.7 *La Dolomite Ski Boots* Equating upper-class taste with the purchase of la Dolomite ski boots, this ad implies that "discriminating" skiers identify not only with the European image of their equipment but also with wealth. An appealing image for some, this convergence of ethnicity and class further limited access to American resort ski culture. *Ski* 33 (Holiday 1968): 29.

slopes as well. The success of Winter Park's program testifies to that fact. Comparable programs for minorities or urban youth, however, are few and far between. Those that do exist are funded by outside organizations, not ski areas.[32] Surely city kids and ethnic minorities would benefit from a ski program in ways similar to physically disabled people; why hasn't the ski industry responded to them?

My argument focuses on why white people have been attracted to skiing, not what has kept minorities from it, so I have not addressed why many black people have chosen not to ski. The two main barriers I see, however, are the financial costs involved in taking a ski vacation and the extent to which skiers are bombarded with images of whiteness. The first barrier makes skiing difficult for all but upper-class minorities; the second makes it a potentially alienating experience for all. The National Brotherhood of Skiers, an organization made up of black skiers, has recognized these barriers and articulated one goal: to help minority children learn to ski and ultimately to produce a black skier on the U.S. Olympic ski team. As of January 1993, the twenty-year-old National Brotherhood of Skiers had seventy-five ski club affiliates in sixty-two cities and twenty-two states, with an total membership of over fourteen thousand. Despite their numbers and the fact that members spent an estimated $36 million skiing during the 1993–94 season—which does not include the other estimated one hundred thousand black skiers in the country—advertisers and manufacturers have yet to support the organization in particular and black skiers in general.[33] One spokesman noted that black skiers spend nearly $200 million a year on skiing. "If you look at the advertising here," he said, "you don't even see photos of blacks skiing in their brochures."[34] Only a tenacious attachment to whiteness could explain this behavior by such a thoroughly opportunistic industry.[35]

Today, the ski industry still speaks the language of ethnicity through European symbols, and the expanse of whiteness and wealth it has created—especially in the West—has approached the absurd. The Game Creek Club currently under construction at Vail costs between $20,000 and $75,000 to join and will "create a warm atmosphere and a retreat for members reminiscent of some of the fine mountain restaurants found on the high slopes of the Alps—not unlike the Eagle Club in Gstaad or the Corviglia Club in St. Moritz." Another spokesman for Vail said, "We don't want this to be an elitist thing, but there was a large specialized market for this service."[36]

This large specialized market has created some unforeseen circumstances in western resort areas. Continued growth of the ski industry and its accompanying culture created the need for a separate working class to support them and also generated housing, day-care, and transportation crises. The days of entirely local "ski bum" workforces are over; white college students and so-called trustafarians account for a declining percentage of ski resort service workers. Mexican Americans, Mexicans, Eastern Europeans, and even Africans, meanwhile, have been filling manual labor and service jobs, joining a growing multiethnic labor force that supports American ski culture. During the 1980s, Mexican immigrants and their families began coming to the Roaring Fork Valley because Aspen businesses recruited them as seasonal labor. As of 1994 there were at least eight thousand Hispanics living in the valley and an estimated seven thousand undocumented workers at different resorts between Leadville and Aspen. At least twenty Africans ended up in Summit County, Colorado, after signing up with a particular employment agency in Manhattan. Some live as far as sixty—often treacherous—miles away from their work, cleaning hotel rooms and moonlighting at fast-food restaurants in an effort to make ends meet.[37]

One of the many ironies surrounding the western ski industry is that these workers—no matter their racial or ethnic identities—cannot afford to live in or even near the resorts their work supports. Thirty-nine of Vail's forty-eight policemen and firefighters cannot afford to live in town.[38] Ski resort workers live in broken-down trailers, government-subsidized housing, cheap apartments two mountain passes away from their jobs, tents on National Forest land, and even vans parked in maintenance garages.[39] Housing problems—and other problems associated with a new, largely immigrant workforce—have made much of Colorado's ski country look like part of the Third World. Even the Catholic Church took notice. Sister Annette Carrica of the Ohio-based Sisters of Charity came to Colorado ski country to help foster a sense of community among Latin American immigrants. She joined Roman Catholic archbishop J. Francis Stafford, who started the Villa Sierra Madre housing project in Silverthorne to help poor Hispanic workers on the Western Slope. Sisters Mary Jo Coyle and Mary Ellen Beyhan run a similar low-income apartment complex in Glenwood Springs for the Denver Archdiocese, and plans are underway for another in Carbondale and one near Winter Park.[40]

One look at modern ski resort workers proves that the American West remains a region of racial and ethnic diversity. Increased diversity in the resort service industry over the past fifteen years, however, has had little impact on the consumer side of the equation. Western ski slopes and resorts continue to exist largely as islands of whiteness, where the likes of Peter Totemoff and George Sisneros are few and far between. Exceptions to the rule—and there have been a few—have found it difficult to muster the economic or cultural power to alter this course. In 1966, Meadow Mountain ski area, for example, opened two miles north of the Hispanic community in Minturn, Colorado. In contrast to the ethnic overtones of its chalet-style day lodge (which seems to have become a mandatory fixture at every ski area), the owner worked to attract locals to his ski area with easy skiing and low prices. Hispanic families from all over the county learned to ski at Meadow Mountain, with grandmothers and babies looking on. Their business failed to sustain the ski area, however, and Meadow Mountain closed after only three seasons.[41] Small family ski areas like Meadow Mountain—without the exclusive atmosphere of destination resorts—might have helped dissipate the ethnic whiteout pervasive in so many resorts. Lack of business and competition from larger ski areas, however, have stilled their lifts.

The increasing competition for tourist dollars that has closed down small local areas and encouraged growth in resorts such as Aspen, Vail, and Telluride has effectively perpetuated the ethnic and economic exclusivity of those resorts as well. George Sisneros, who taught his wife to ski at Meadow Mountain and worked on the ski patrol there, said, "If Meadow Mountain had survived for another five or ten years, there might be more Hispanics skiing. They didn't want to ski Vail," he went on, "that was a totally alien situation and they didn't feel comfortable there, so skiing became foreign to them."[42]

Some small, local ski areas have survived—mainly because they lack competition from large resorts nearby—and they offer the most compelling contrast to the white, wealthy ski culture prevalent at destination resorts. At least two ski resorts, in fact, are owned and run by American Indian tribes. The Mescalero Apaches bought neighboring Sierra Blanca ski area in New Mexico, now known as Ski Apache, in 1963.[43] The tribe sought employment opportunities for its members more than a vacation spot and added the ski area to their motel and gas station businesses already in operation.[44] Though they hired experienced ski-area managers and directors, the Mescaleros have successfully employed tribal members as ski patrollers, lift operators, maintenance workers, and in other positions both on and off the slopes.

The Mescaleros' emphasis on jobs and the discomfort Vail's Hispanic workers felt skiing at that resort both point to the conclusion that for people of color in the West, ski areas have more meaning as employment opportunities than as outlets for consumption and participation in resort ski culture. Mescaleros ski at their area, but Ski Apache also attracts business—and outside money—from West Texans and wealthy Mexicans. Here is an example of Native Americans selling a historically white sport to wealthy Mexicans—a curious scenario. By virtue of their whiteness (on the Texans' part) and their wealth (on the Mexicans'), these skiers have become invested in the sport of skiing to at least some degree. Proximity of Ski Apache to their homes would encourage them to favor it over other areas for weekend trips, when Ski Apache is open. Those with the financial ability may then travel elsewhere for a longer, more expensive, full-fledged dive into resort ski culture.[45] Ski Apache thus represents an instance of ethnic diversity within the western ski industry, one that contrasts sharply with what might have been a similar area, Taos Ski Valley.

Ernie Blake, the original owner of Taos Ski Valley, made a point to hire Native Americans, but he hired them as maintenance men and manual laborers. (How many Pueblo Indians, one might ask, knew how to ski?) Peter Totemoff's experience becoming a ski instructor there testifies to the ethnic dominance of whiteness on the slopes. Blake—a Swiss-German Jew who left Europe before the onset of World War II—came to New Mexico and encouraged other Europeans to join him in creating a thoroughly continental ski resort there. Taos Ski Valley thus developed as a resort claiming "the best in Alpine runs, American accommodations, Mediterranean sun, Continental cuisine, French wines, Finnish sauna, Bavarian gemülichkeit and Utopian lack of lift lines."[46] Blake turned Taos Ski Valley into a destination resort competing directly with European areas and big resorts such as Aspen, Sun Valley, and later Vail for business. Ski Apache, however, has remained a weekend resort whose clientele must still travel miles to the town of Ruidoso for food and lodging.

These differences meant that Taos Ski Valley would become a bastion of wealthy European ski culture and Ski Apache's atmosphere would feel more like Meadow Mountain, though both remained situated among a Native American population. The ethnicity of their respective ski cultures would further influence not only how owners marketed each area but relations between the area and the local population as well. Since Taos Pueblo existed physically, culturally, and economically outside Taos Ski Valley, marketing executives understood Native Americans as "other" and advertised them as such. Pueblo Indians thus became foreigners in their own home, sightseeing attractions in a place where skier-tourists could participate in one set of ethnic cultures and observe another on the same trip. For their part, the Pueblo Indians developed methods to control tourists and to maintain their native culture at the same time that they took advantage of increasingly popular "cultural tourism."[47] They had to walk the fine line between, on the one hand, marketing themselves as what they thought tourists expected "Indians" to be and, on the other, what they as Pueblo Indians envisioned for themselves.

The Mescalero Apaches have faced fewer cultural conundrums in this regard. Though they did change the name of their ski area from Sierra Blanca (!) to Ski Apache, the Mescaleros have resisted marketing the area as stereotypically "Indian." The Apaches are hardly "other" in relation to skiing there; they are neighbors, owners, operators, instructors, patrollers, and even consumers. Neither the location of the area (central New Mexico) nor its volume of business merited efforts to make Ski Apache competitive with large destination resorts, and the owners themselves have little cultural connection to the Alps. The very name of the ski area anchors the place both physically and culturally. At Ski Apache, the Mescaleros act as a referential "self" rather than "other."

The ability to claim a sense of belonging at ski areas—to acquire or retain "selfhood"—depends largely on questions of economic power. Issues of class and ethnicity thus intersect not only in terms of consumption but in terms of management as well. Control over marketing campaigns often translates to control over constructions of ethnic identity both within and outside American ski culture. Few Native American or Mexican American groups exercise enough of that power to define themselves as part of the western ski industry, and as a result, they are often defined outside of it. Mexican Americans from Minturn thus feel like aliens a few miles down the road in Vail; the Ute Indians visit the same resort to perform a "snow" dance and become a tourist attraction in the process; and the "Indian" in one Taos Ski Valley ad goes by the ridiculous name of "Chief Geronimo Pumpernickel."[48]

Similar power relations have endangered the cultural identity of some people living near ski resorts. As Sylvia Rodriguez has shown, Hispanos and Chicanos in Taos who hold agriculture central to their ethnic and cultural identity see escalating resort development at Taos Ski Valley as a threat, "because it converts farmland to recreational and residential uses controlled and enjoyed mostly by outsiders."[49] If Hispanos and Chicanos either disappeared or behaved politely as objects for those outsiders to view, the implication is, they would not have this conflict. Neither would they have this conflict, the Mescalero Apaches might point out, if they owned the resort and felt a cultural kinship with its clientele. One end result would require succumbing to a white resort's construction of ethnicity and the landscape; the other would demand huge amounts of capital and cultural change. People of color who ski at, work at, compete with, or live near destination resorts in the West all face a hegemonic ski culture that shows few signs of slowing down.

Understandings of ethnicity in the western ski industry thus remain contested and hinge on definitions of class at a variety of levels. At destination resorts, minorities' increasing presence in ski resort kitchens and

6.8 *Steamboat's a Comin'* Steamboat has used more western images to market its skiing than any other resort. Consciously borrowing from Frederic Remington, one of the most influential image makers of the American West, Steamboat ad makers replaced these rough riders' guns with skis and encouraged readers to imagine their ski vacation as part of a John Ford movie. A bolder analysis might question the relationship between these men's skis and the message they carry. *Ski* 40 (October 1975): 102.

maintenance sheds stands in juxtaposition to the whiteness that still prevails on the slopes and in the meeting rooms and accounting offices. Even those marketing executives who advertise their resorts as part of the American West rather than as European enclaves resist the racial and ethnic implications of their ad campaigns and ignore people of color. Jackson Hole and Steamboat Springs use western images to attract customers, but they rely on the mythic image of the cowboy—a distinctly white image—

to do so. In one advertisement (see Figure 6.8), three ski-totin' rough riders cavort in an manner reminiscent of Frederick Remington, hawking promotional posters titled "barn," "stagecoach," and "horseman." Like Taos Ski Valley's incorporation of local Pueblo Indians as exotic others, Steamboat's marketing strategies capitalize on the image of "the Wild West"—an image as white, and as far removed from reality, as that of western alpine villages and Pierre Kilbeaux. Members of the ski industry created these mythic images at large western ski areas as part of an emerging destination resort ski culture that linked the construction of a European white ethnicity to the consumption of status and image. This process "whitewashed" destination ski resorts in the West and transformed local people of color into either invisible workers or exotic objects of tourism. Skier-tourists are left with a choice ultimately of their own making: down one slippery slope, Bavarian villages; down the other, Billy the Kid. Both images quietly perpetuate the unbearable whiteness of skiing.

Notes

This essay is reprinted by permission from *Pacific Historical Review*, 65, no. 4 (November 1996): 583–614. Copyright 1996 by American Historical Association, Pacific Coast Branch.

1. June Simonton, *Vail: Story of a Colorado Mountain Valley* (Denver, 1987), 167.
2. The tribe agreed to perform a rain dance and let it be called a snow dance. It worked. Ibid., 84.
3. Rick Richards, *Ski Pioneers: Ernie Blake, His Friends, and the Making of Taos Ski Valley* (Helena, Mont. 1992), 58.
4. Historians have produced amazingly little scholarship on tourism in the West since Earl Pomeroy's *In Search of the Golden West* (Lincoln, Neb., 1957). Hal Rothman's forthcoming book titled *Devil's Bargains: Tourism and Transformation in the Twentieth Century American West* (Lawrence, Kans.), promises to explore the economic and environmental impact of tourism in the West. See also Kerwin L. Klein, "Frontier Products: Tourism, Consumerism, and the Southwestern Public Lands, 1890–1990," *Pacific Historical Review* 62 (1993): 39–71. Klein's article explores the relationship between economics, environment, and western culture; Patricia Nelson Limerick gave another regional and cultural interpretation of tourism in "Seeing and Being Seen: Tourism in the American West," a speech given at the Clark Library, UCLA, March 11, 1994. As tourism and skiing have shaped western culture, so has culture shaped tourism and skiing, especially in Aspen,

Colorado. James Sloan Allen articulates the connections between Walter Paepcke's Container Corporation of America, advertising, modernism, Great Books, Goethe, and the Aspen ski culture in his book *The Romance of Commerce and Culture: Capitalism, Modernism, and the Chicago-Aspen Crusade for Cultural Reform* (Chicago, 1983).

5. Elliott West, *The Way to the West: Essays on the Central Plains* (Albuquerque, 1995).

6. See Noel Ignatiev, *How the Irish Became White* (New York, 1995); David R. Roediger, *Towards the Abolition of Whiteness: Essays on Race, Politics, and Working Class History* (New York, 1994) and *The Wages of Whiteness: Race and the Making of the American Working Class* (New York, 1991); Ronald T. Takaki, ed., *From Different Shores: Perspectives on Race and Ethnicity in America* (New York, 1994) and *Iron Cages: Race and Culture in Nineteenth-Century America* (New York, 1979); Eric Lott, *Love and Theft: Blackface Minstrelsy and the American Working Class* (New York, 1993); Alexander Saxton, *The Rise and Fall of the White Republic: Class Politics and Mass Culture in Nineteenth-Century America* (New York, 1990); chap. 7 in Phyllis Palmer, *Domesticity and Dirt: Housewives and Domestic Servants in the United States, 1920–1945* (Philadelphia, 1989); and chaps. 5–7 in Elizabeth V. Spelman, *Inessential Woman: Problems of Exclusion in Feminist Thought* (Boston, 1988).

7. Kenneth Bjork, "'Snowshoe' Thompson: Fact and Legend," *Norwegian-American Studies and Records* 19 (1956): 62–88.

8. See Jack Benson, "Before Skiing Was Fun," *Western Historical Quarterly* 7 (1977): 431–441; John B. Allen, *From Skisport to Skiing: One Hundred Years of an American Sport* (Amherst, Mass., 1993); Abbott Fay, *Ski Tracks in the Rockies: A Century of Colorado Skiing* (Evergreen, Col. 1984); John L. Dyer, *The Snow-Shoe Itinerant: An Autobiography of the Reverend John L. Dyer* (Cincinnati, 1890); Leif Hovelson, *The Flying Norseman* (Ishpeming, 1983); Anne Gilbert, "Re-Creation through Recreation: A History of Aspen Skiing from 1870–1970," 1995, Ski Collection, Aspen Historical Society, Aspen Colorado (hereafter cited as AHS).

9. See the sources in note 8, above; and Jack A. Benson, "Before Aspen and Vail: The Story of Recreational Skiing in Frontier Colorado," *Journal of the West* 22 (1983): 52–61; E. John B. Allen, "Sierra Ladies on Skis in Gold Rush California," *Journal of Sport History* 17 (1990): 347–353.

10. Friedl Pfeifer, with Morten Lund, *Nice Goin': My Life on Skis* (Missoula, Mont., 1993), 14; see also Paul P. Bernard, *Rush to the Alps: The Evolution of Vacationing in Switzerland* (New York, 1978); and Charles M. Dudley, *Sixty Centuries of Skiing* (Brattleboro, Vt., 1935). There is also some evidence that inhabitants of the Bloke Plateau and Vipava region of Slovenia had a highly developed ski culture before the nineteenth century and perhaps as early as the sixteenth century. See Dolfe Rajtmajer, "The Slovenian Origins of European Skiing," *International Journal of the History of Sport* 11 (1994): 97–101.

11. City of Aspen Proclamation, n.d., Andre Roch biography file, AHS.

12. Schneider and Pfeifer were Austrians politically opposed to Hitler; Blake was a Swiss-German Jew. See Pfeifer and Lund, *Nice Goin'*; Richards, *Ski Pioneers*.

13. David Emmons emphasized the significance of European immigrants to the history of the American West during the mining era in his book *The Butte Irish: Class and Ethnicity in an American Mining Town* (Urbana, Ill., 1989) and called for further exploration of the variety of European immigrants and their roles in western economy and culture in "A Trip through Western Time and Western Space: A Review Essay," *Montana: The Magazine of Western History* 45 (Spring 1995): 64–68. Skiing offers one avenue through which historians can see the cultural impact of certain European immigrant groups—and of their immigrant identities—on the West.

14. This raises an as yet unexplored issue: the degree to which skiers "fled" to European-styled resorts in response to growing racial tension in American cities. Ski resorts may have represented an escape from a "corrupted" society, mirroring a much older characterization of the West as pristine, pure, and the place where Easterners could get away from it all. Indeed, the very function of destination resorts—whatever their ethnic or racial makeup—has been to offer their clientele a rather isolated setting for rest and relaxation, from which they could return to their "real" lives rejuvenated. I have, as yet, little evidence to support the conclusion that white vacationers used ski resorts to escape urban or eastern racial tension, but the question deserves more study.

15. See Richard Wightman Fox and T. J. Jackson Lears, eds., *The Culture of Consumption: Critical Essays in American History, 1880–1980* (New York, 1983); and Martyn J. Lee, *Consumer Culture Reborn: The Cultural Politics of Consumption* (New York, 1993).

16. Skiing thus offers historians a way to explore the relationships among gender, sexuality, consumer culture, and sport. For a recent examination of gender, sexuality, and sport, see Susan K. Cahn, *Coming on Strong: Gender and Sexuality in Twentieth-Century Women's Sport* (Cambridge, Mass., 1994).

17. Artur Kuen, a German engineer, came to Buttermilk and Snowmass in Colorado to build lifts after having built them for German officers during World War II; Willy Schaeffler also fought for Germany during the war before emigrating and becoming director of the ski school at Arapahoe Basin, as had Sepp Uhl before he came to instruct in Aspen. Artur Kuen, interview by the author, July 13, 1994, tape recording, AHS; Mary Eshbaugh Hayes, "Longtime Aspenite Sepp Uhl Dead at 76," *Aspen Times*, August 28, 1993, 18B. Slovenian competitors were also welcomed under this rubric, and Yugoslavian competitors in the 1950 Fédération Internationale de Ski (FIS) Championships were especially welcomed in Aspen, because a number of mining families were from the same region as the skiers (*Rocky Mountain News*, February 4, 1950). These examples demonstrate the cultural power of geographical boundaries and how they can override those drawn

by governments and armies. Walter Paepcke, a Chicago businessman largely responsible for Aspen's revival as a cultural/tourist mecca, worked explicitly to reunify German and American culture by organizing a lavish and highly publicized celebration of Goethe at Aspen in 1949. While not a personal interest or part of his initial plan, skiing came to play an integral role in Paepcke's re-creation of Aspen as a cultural center. He probably approved highly of Kuen and Uhl's incorporation into the Aspen skiing scene. See Allen, *Romance of Commerce and Culture.*

18. Mary C. Waters, *Ethnic Options: Choosing Identities in America* (Berkeley, 1990); Richard D. Alba, *Ethnic Identity: The Transformation of White America* (New Haven, 1990), 1–21; Werner Sollors, *Beyond Ethnicity: Consent and Descent in American Culture* (New York, 1986).

19. Pfeifer and Lund, *Nice Goin'*, 61–62, 65; see Bernard, *Rush to the Alps*, for a discussion of early Swiss resorts.

20. Samuel Bowles, *The Switzerland of America: A Summer Vacation in the Parks and Mountains of Colorado* (Springfield, Mass., 1869).

21. Pomeroy, *In Search of the Golden West*, 33.

22. Andre Roch, "A Once and Future Resort: A Winter in the Rocky Mountains of Colorado," trans. Ernest Blake, *Colorado Heritage* 4 (1985): 17–23; originally published as "Un hiver aux Montagnes Rocheuses du Colorado," *Der Schnee-Hase* (1937). Roch was describing Mt. Hayden and the resort the Highland Bavarian Corporation was hoping to build near the ghost town of Ashcroft. The project fizzled out with the onset of World War II, after which Aspen Mountain became the area's focus.

23. Richards, *Ski Pioneers*, 103.

24. Ernie Gay, "Tough, Beautiful Taos," *Ski* 28 (February 1964): 82.

25. Simonton, *Vail*, 72.

26. Mary Eshbaugh Hayes, "Norwegian Invasion Brought New Blood to Skiing and Aspen," *Aspen Times*, December 6, 1984, C1. See Stein Erikson, *Come Ski with Me* (New York, 1966); Fred Iselin and A. C. Spectorsky, *The New Invitation to Skiing* (New York, 1958); and Jean Claude Killy, with Doug Pfeiffer, *Skiing . . . the Killy Way* (New York, 1971). Ski movies became popular in the 1930s and showed Americans the winning form of European skiers such as Otto Lang, Friedl Pfeifer, Stein Erikson, and Fred Iselin, contributing to their fame and status. These skiers appeared on film as instructors of technique, promoters of resorts, and stunt doubles for bigger stars in the ever-popular ski chase scenes.

27. Timothy Egan, "Kellogg's Journal: Mining Town Given Lift in Effort to Be a Resort," *New York Times*, July 13, 1989.

28. Kingsbury Pitcher, in Richards, *Ski Pioneers*, 145.

29. My argument applies to destination ski resorts such as Aspen, Vail, Taos, and Sun Valley. Many ski areas in the West, however, including Colorado's Wolf Creek, Eldora, Loveland Ski Basin, and Cuchara Valley, catered to local skiers or

day visitors from urban centers. These areas, in contrast to destination resorts, did not concern themselves as much with the European ski culture, generally charged less for lift tickets, and so were more accessible to middle-class skiers.

30. Pomeroy, *In Search of the Golden West*, 209.

31. Grand County Historical Association, *Winter Park: Colorado's Favorite for Fifty Years, 1940–1990* (Winter Park, 1989), 155.

32. The Slippers-N-Sliders Ski Club, a primarily African American ski club and affiliate of the National Brotherhood of Skiers, supports an annual program called Ski For Kids in which inner-city kids take lessons at Keystone resort. The Slippers-N-Sliders provide transportation, equipment, lunch, and clothing for the kids, over one thousand of whom learned to ski between 1972 and 1994. See Robert Jackson, "Inner-City Kids Learn to Ski, Thanks to Slippers-N-Sliders," *Rocky Mountain News*, October 30, 1994, 28A.

33. Robert Jackson, "Make Pitch to Black Skiers, Industry Told," *Rocky Mountain News*, February 14, 1995, 12A.

34. Ibid. See also Robert Jackson, "Lack of Sponsors Puzzles Ski Group," *Rocky Mountain News*, February 15, 1994.

35. I should remind readers, perhaps, that emphasizing white images and courting white clientele are not the same as actively or consciously excluding minorities. I have no evidence of ski resorts explicitly discouraging or preventing minorities from skiing beyond the alienation that George Sisneros and Peter Totemoff reported. My conversations with resort developers support the view that they saw the whiteness of their resorts as normal and didn't question the lack of minority skiers.

36. Chance Connor, "Vail Plans Mountain Social Club," *Denver Post*, September 14, 1995, 1C.

37. Guy Kelly, "Picking Up a Spanish Accent," *Rocky Mountain News*, September 4, 1994, 12A; Bruce Finley, "'A Better Life': New Wave of Immigrants Lured by Resorts," *Denver Post*, October 30, 1995, 1A, 13A; Ray Ring, "The New West's Servant Economy," *High Country News*, April 17, 1995, 10, 12; Deborah Frazier, "Undocumented Workers Tax Ski Counties," *Rocky Mountain News*, November 9, 1993, 8A. A recent sweep the Colorado Immigration and Naturalization Service made of the Aspen and Vail areas netted thirty illegal aliens; see "Aspen-Vail INS Sweep Nabs Thirty," *Denver Post*, December 7, 1995, 9B.

38. Ring, "New West's Servant Economy," 1.

39. Ibid.; Ray Ring, "Ski Bums Wrapped in Concrete," "Pedro Lopez, Entrepreneur," and "The Leadville-Indy 500," *High Country News*, April 17, 1995, 8–10; Gary Massaro, "Aspen Workers Commute from 'Edge of Hell,'" *Rocky Mountain News*, September 4, 1994, 13A; Deborah Frazier, "Privacy Exacts Price in Telluride," *Rocky Mountain News*, February 15, 1995, 10A; Guy Kelly, "Resorts Face Urban Woes," *Rocky Mountain News*, September 4, 1994, 12A, 18A.

40. Ring, "New West's Servant Economy," 1; Ray Ring, "He Came to Ski and

Stayed to Help," *High Country News*, April 17, 1995, 13; Kelly, "Resorts Face Urban Woes," 12A, 18A; Guy Kelly, "Church Housing Is a Godsend," *Rocky Mountain News*, September 5, 1994, 17A; Gary Massaro, "Nun Steers Hispanics to Shelter," *Rocky Mountain News*, September 5, 1994, 17A, 26A.

41. Simonton, *Vail*, 166–67.

42. Ibid., 167.

43. The resort's first owner, Robert O. Anderson (owner of the Hondo Oil and Gas petroleum empire), was eager to boost tourism in New Mexico and opened it for business in December 1962. He sold Sierra Blanca to the Mescalero Apaches for $1.2 million, even though the area was valued at more than $2 million; Hondo Oil and Gas presented the difference to the tribe as a gift. See Ernest Gay, "Renaissance Man of the Southwest," *Ski* 28 (December 1963): 194–195. Sunrise ski area, near the Fort Apache Indian Reservation in Show Low Arizona, is owned by the White Mountain Apache tribe.

44. Gay, "Renaissance Man," 195; and Ray Heid, phone interview by the author, October 3, 1995. Throughout the 1960s, various Indian tribes sought economic opportunity through Indian-owned businesses, so purchasing a ski area was consistent with contemporary strategies for increasing tribal autonomy.

45. Heid interview, 1995.

46. Taos Ski Valley advertisement, *Ski* 32 (December 1967): 97.

47. See Jill D. Sweet, "'Let 'em Loose': Pueblo Indian Management of Tourism," *American Indian Culture and Research Journal* 15 (1991): 59–74; and Hal K. Rothman, "Devil's Bargains: Tourism and Transformation in the American West" (unpublished manuscript, 1994).

48. Taos Ski Valley ad, 1967. This is the same ad that promoted the European atmosphere and amenities of Taos Ski Valley.

49. Sylvia Rodriguez, "Ethnic Reconstruction in Contemporary Taos," *Journal of the Southwest* 32 (1990): 549.

Chapter Seven

"We Want a Pennant, Not a White Team"
How Boston's Ethnic and Racial History Shaped the Red Sox

Sharon O'Brien

There'll be no niggers on this team as long as I have anything to say about it.
—Boston Red Sox manager Mike Higgins

We Want a Pennant, Not a White Team
—Protester's sign outside Fenway Park, June 1959

I teach courses in U.S. cultural diversity in the American Studies Department at Dickinson College in which we explore the ways in which race is a
social construct and whiteness is privileged. I tell my students that when I
was growing up in the Boston area in the 1950s, I had no idea that I was
white: middle-class Irish were so assimilated by then that our whiteness
was no longer a matter of discussion or contestation. The O'Briens were
three generations away from my Famine Irish great-grandparents, who left
Ireland in late 1840s and 1850s, came to Massachusetts, and confronted a
Yankee aristocracy who viewed them as members of an inferior race, similar to African Americans. The project of upward mobility worked for
those Irish Americans who ascended to the middle or upper middle class
only because this ascent was linked with racial transformation; the Irish
needed to be reimagined as white if they were to succeed according to
dominant American values.

In becoming white, the Irish were aided by minstrel-show performers such as my grandfather Handsome Dan Quinlan (the Prince of Interlocutors), who enacted stereotypic versions of what he called America's "culled chillun" as interlocutor for George Wilson's Minstrels and, later, Al G. Fields Big White Minstrels. Blackface minstrelsy was a way for my grandfather to make a living and move up in social class, far away from his illiterate immigrant father, who worked in the rolling mills. It was also a way to deny economic and political allegiance with African Americans and to pursue assimilation—and whiteness—by enacting a racial drama that elevated Irish above blacks. Minstrelsy was also a way, as Eric Lott and other historians have shown, for Handsome Dan Quinlan and his fellow Irish minstrels to demonstrate their covert connection with, and even attraction to, black people and what blackness signified: resistance to the very assimilation they craved.[1]

My grandfather's generation had sufficiently succeeded so that my father could be one of the few Irish Catholics to attend Brahmin Harvard in the 1920s, although he could not live in the dormitories and commuted in every day from Lowell on the train. And my father's generation had sufficiently succeeded in moving up and erasing any nineteenth-century stains of blackness so that by the 1950s I could live in Belmont, a snooty Boston suburb (although in a rented apartment on the working-class Watertown line), attend high school with the children of Harvard and MIT professors, and not even think it strange that, until 1960, when Victor Gonzalez and his parents moved to town, there were no black kids in the Belmont public schools.

You also need to know that I am a lifelong Red Sox fan, probably irredeemably damaged by the 1986 World Series with the Mets, when—I hate even writing these words—the Sox lost the sixth game even though, in the top of the ninth, they were four runs ahead and one out away from victory, and Miller Lite had already made Marty Barrett Player of the Game (the kiss of death, in my view). This was the infamous game when the ground ball—which could so easily have been handled—skittered through Bill Buckner's creaky legs into right field, and it was all over.

I started being a Red Sox fan when I was six. It was 1951, and my father was working for the advertising agency that handled some of the Red Sox's sponsors—Narragansett (Brewed by the shores of Lake Cochituate), Atlantic (Keeps your car on the go!), Chesterfields. Sometimes my dad would get complementary sky-view seats and take me and my brother to Fenway—I still remember looking down on the green diamond and white bases and thinking there was nowhere else I'd rather be in the whole world. When we'd drive around New England on our summer vacations, we'd always pick up the Sox on a local radio station, and if the signal started to waver and grow dim, I'd implore my father to pull over to the side, just so we could get through a crucial inning while the signal lasted. (You'd often have traffic jams in front of Boston's Callahan Tunnel on summer days if the Sox were in a pennant race: people weren't going to lose their radio signals in the tunnel if the game was close.)

I stayed a fan throughout the fifties and sixties when the Sox were often worse than mediocre, taking the MTA (Metropolitan Transit Authority) into Fenway for Saturday-afternoon games with my semi-bored girl friends. They'd look through the program, trying to decide if they'd rather have a date with Pete Runnels or Frank Malzone, while I'd score the game, a skill I'd learned from my father. My friends and I weren't that different, though—we never noticed that we were gazing at an all-white team. The Sox didn't hire their first black player until 1959, and even then Pumpsie Green hardly ever played, so Fenway's green-and-white color scheme was hardly disturbed at all.

In later years, when I was suffering over lost Series in 1967 and 1975, it never occurred to me that my team might have had a Series chance, way back in the fifties and sixties, if they'd only gone after the amazing black ballplayers who were leading the Dodgers and the Giants and, later, the Yankees: Jackie Robinson, Willie Mays, Don Newcombe, Roy Campanella, Monte Irvin. It never occurred to me, when New Englanders would start chanting the ritual September lament, *What's the matter with the Red Sox?* to say, "Racism," or even to think that race had anything to do with baseball.

Now, of course, it's a whole different ball game.

When you grow up in New England, you grow up with stories about why the Red Sox haven't won the World Series since 1903—why the team is doomed, why a black cloud hangs over Fenway. If you read the Boston *Globe* or the *New Yorker* sometime when the team is in contention for the Series, you'll get high-class, mythic explanations, the kind academics like. It's not bad pitching, it's original sin: the curse of Puritan New England just won't allow Bostonians to be happy. The same culture that gave you Nathaniel Hawthorne and *The House of the Seven Gables* and all those stories about limitation and inherited darkness just isn't going to give you a World Series winner. Massachusetts is all about suffering: why else would we have to wait in three-hour traffic jams at the Sagamore Bridge to get onto the Cape in July, listening to the Sox lose on the car radio? And we weren't just listening a baseball game, we were listening to Greek tragedy. "They [the Sox] were worthy of the Sophoclean stage, actors in traditional and poignant myth, in the long conflict between the larger-than-life hero and inexorable time, native brilliance and predestined ruin. . . . Our hearts were with the Trojans in that war, and with the Sox in this. The hero must go under at last."[2]

Don't give us a long-lost World Series: give us Calvinism, give us pre-destination, give us the Red Sox as tragic heroes.

Give us a break.

You'll get a better story about what's wrong with the Red Sox by listening to the callers to Boston sports talk shows over the last decades.

No pitching. *Bob Stanley? Give me a break, I coulddoabettahjahb.*

The Red Sox management, who traditionally have been obsessed with buying right-handed sluggers who can conquer the Wall, the Green Monster, the short left-field wall that's a target for right-handed hitters. *Why don't they look somewheres else besides down the left-field line? They hire these guys who hit home runs when the Sox are eight runs up and strike out in the clutch.*

No interest in baserunning, hit-and-runs, base stealing. *Whadda they need, home runs to get around the bases? Those guys have molasses on theiyah shoes.*

Bad coaching (this in the era of Mike Higgins and Don "the Gerbil" Zimmer). *Wheahda they get those guys, in a bahgain basement?*

Tendency to buy up used-up famous players in their thirties who come to Boston and hit .233.

The Sawx? Theyah chokahs.

And of course, the curse of the Bambino. *If they hadn't sold Ruth to the Yankees, we wouldn't be having this cawnversation, Jack, ya know what I mean?*

Let me give you another explanation. I'll start with two names: Jackie Robinson. Pumpsie Green. If you were putting together a World Series contender, who would you rather have on your team? Jackie Robinson tried out for the Sox in 1945, but everyone knew it was a setup. Robinson's daughter, Sharon, was asked to join Green to throw out ceremonial first pitches at Fenway in April 1997, the fiftieth anniversary of her father's breaking major league baseball's race barrier. She was still angry at the fact that "my father could come up to Boston and be turned back around. It wasn't a true tryout."[3]

In fact, the Sox were the *last* team to integrate, bringing Elijah "Pumpsie" Green up to the majors in 1959. And so, while teams like the Dodgers and the Yankees were winning the World Series throughout the fifties and early sixties with players like Robinson and Willie Mays and Roy Campanella, the Sox were coming in fourth and fifth with their almost all-white teams.

In 1962, the last year Pumpsie Green played for the Sox, the team included some of these long-forgotten white players: Rudy York, Len Okrie, Arnold Early, Hal Kolstad, Carroll Hardy, Chet Nichols, Done Gile, Gary Geiger. Of the twenty-nine players who signed the official American League ball that year, the only white players Bostonians remember are Carl Yastrzemski, Bill Monbouquette, Pete Runnels, and Frank Malzone. There was one other black player on the team besides Green: the pitcher Earl White, called up from the minors a week after Green because of the informal quota system that required each team to have an even number of black players so that they could be paired together as roommates on the road.

So what is it about Boston? Why *were* the Red Sox the last team to integrate? Can there be a connection between the city and the Red Sox's reluctant, long-delayed hiring of an average black player in 1959, by which time every other team in both leagues had been at least partially integrated? And then the Sox's slowness in hiring players of color, so that the team was not significantly integrated until the 1980s? To understand why the Red Sox were the last team to integrate—and a slow team to fully integrate—we have to understand the history of the baseball franchise as well as the larger context of Boston's ethnic and racial history.

The Red Sox had the chance to sign both Jackie Robinson and Willie Mays. Along with two other black players, also stars from the Negro Leagues—Marv Williams and Sam Jethroe—Robinson was allowed to try out for the Sox in April 1945. General Manager Eddie Collins was responding to pressure from City Councilman Isadore Mushnick, a white member from Roxbury (by then a largely black section of Boston). Unless the Red Sox agreed to a tryout for the Negro League players, Muchnik told Red Sox management, he would lead a campaign to deny the team's permit for Sunday baseball. (These were the days of Massachusetts' famed "Blue Laws," when public activities were restricted on Sundays.) To appease Mushnik and keep their Sunday permit, the Red Sox agreed to a tryout. The three men were turned away from Fenway twice, finally achieving the tryout on the third day after *Daily Record* columnist Dave Egan—who had needled the Sox for over two decades to hire a black player—wrote a satiric column:

> If [the three players] cannot make the grade with that classy aggregation of Red Sox we espied the other day [in 1945 the Red Sox finished seventh] room might be found for [them] in the shabbiest and lowest league in organized baseball in order that [they] might be given the opportunity to work their way up the ladder.[4]

While Robinson was trying out, according to Glenn Stout, someone yelled, "Get those niggers off the field."[5] Used to racial harassment, he ignored the hecklers and played baseball. "Robinson was fantastic. At the plate, he peppered the Wall with line drives and hit several over it. He showed a great arm and was all over the infield gobbling up ground balls and pop flies."[6] Fourteen years later, Isadore Muchnick still remembered Robinson's tryout well: "I'm telling you, you never saw anyone hit The Wall the way Robinson did that day. Bang, bang, bang: he rattled it."[7] According to sportswriter Peter Golenbock, batting coach Hughie Duffy— who, back in 1894, gained a .440 batting average as a member of the Boston Red Stockings, a major league record—told the Red Sox management to hire Robinson, exclaiming, "What a ballplayer!" But Duffy was an old man with no real influence, no authority to sign a player, and no ability to challenge the status quo. "Too bad he's the wrong color," Duffy reportedly added.[8] Owner Tom Yawkey and manager Joe Cronin had no intention of hiring a black player, and Robinson and the other players never heard from the Sox again. Shortly after his insulting experience at Fenway, Robinson tried out for Branch Rickey, president of the Brooklyn Dodgers, and made baseball—and American—history.

By the 1950s, when other teams were hiring black stars from the Negro Leagues, Texas-born Mike "Pinky" Higgins was manager of the Sox. The man who was quoted as saying, "There'll be no niggers on this ballclub as long as I have anything to say about it," let Willie Mays go without a backward glance. (Higgins went on to guide his all-white team to two third-, two fourth-, one sixth-, one seventh-, and two eighth-place finishes during his eight years as manager.)[9] In 1949 the seventeen-year-old Mays was playing for the Birmingham Black Barons, a Negro League team that used the all-white Birmingham Barons ballpark when the team was out of town. "In return, the Barons had first refusal on any of the Black Barons' players."[10] The Barons were Boston's Double A farm team and had told the Red Sox that Willie Mays was a hot player. The Red Sox sent Larry

Woodall to scout Mays, and he returned to Boston without ever having seen Mays play. As even sportswriter Al Hirshberg—a patriotic supporter of the Sox and Tom Yawkey—was forced to conclude, "Someone in authority obviously felt no pressure to sign Negroes. Only when the Tigers obtained [Osvaldo] Virgil did the Red Sox feel the pressure to bring a black player into the fold."[11]

When the Red Sox finally brought Pumspie Green up to the majors in 1959, it was because of "pressure" of being the last all-white team in baseball—not because the Sox management was convinced that Negro League stars and rising young black players could help them win ball games. But by 1959, Jackie Robinson, Roy Campanella, and Don Newcombe had sparked the Dodgers' pennant races in 1947, 1949, 1952, 1953, 1955, and 1956, and Willie Mays had led the New York Giants to pennants in 1951 and 1954. "You didn't have to be a genius," observes Peter Golenbock, "to see how disadvantaged were teams that continued to exclude blacks."[12]

Sportswriter Howard Bryant would have had the Sox management, "for a moment, forget the idea of racial pioneering and just think baseball." If the team had hired Robinson and Mays, in 1950 the Red Sox could have had this lineup:

Catcher: Less Moss
First base: Walt Dropo
Second base: Bobby Doerr
Shortstop: Jackie Robinson
Third base: Vern Stephens
Left field: Ted Williams
Center field: Willie Mays
Right field: Dom DiMaggio

Read this and weep, Sox fans.

"There's no telling what I would be able to do in Boston," Willie Mays said recently. "To be honest, I really thought I was going to Boston. They had a good team. . . . But that Yawkey [team owner]. Everyone knew he was a racist. He didn't want me."[13]

You could eat your heart out over that racially mixed 1950 team the Sox couldn't create or imagine. The problem was, in the 1940s you couldn't "just think baseball" without also thinking "racial pioneering"—because to "just think baseball" as major league club owners had done for decades was to think *white* baseball, without ever acknowledging that was what you were doing. Branch Rickey knew he was thinking both baseball and racial breakthrough, and no Red Sox owner or general manager could ever join those two concepts.

The Red Sox signed Pumpsie Green in 1955, and in the middle of the 1959 season he was called up to the ball club. He played respectably but not sensationally as a utility infielder until 1962, when he was traded to the Mets. His lifetime batting average was .246. Joining the Sox was "the hardest thing I've ever done in my life," Green said in 1997. "The baseball part was the easiest. The rest was hard." The "rest" meant being excluded from the team hotel in Scottsdale, Arizona, during spring training and staying by himself in Phoenix, fifteen miles away. "I stayed by myself living and eating," Green said later. "You learn to live with it." The "rest" meant being sent back to the minors by manager Mike Higgins, even though Green had hit .444 during spring training. The Boston chapter of the National Association for the Advancement of Colored People (NAACP) then filed discrimination charges against the Red Sox; Joe Cronin, president of the American League and former Boston manager, defended team owner Tom Yawkey against these charges, saying that Yawkey "has colored help on his plantation in South Carolina, takes excellent care of them, pays good salaries and they are all very happy."[14] Then, after Green was called up in mid-summer, the "rest" meant being isolated until black pitcher Earl Wilson joined the team and became Green's roommate on the road. (The Sox's scouting report on Wilson described him as "a well-mannered colored boy, not too black.")[15]

The racism in Boston was "no worse than other places I'd been," Green said in 1997. "That was not different." Dealing with racism meant handling the insults and harassment. "Unprintable things," Green remembers. "Statements. Anything you could think of. Talking about my family, friends, and relatives. You turn a deaf ear and try to hit the ball a little harder. If you let it, it could get to you."[16] What *was* difficult was being the only black player: "Every time I was out there, I was more or less an exhibit. . . . As far as I'm concerned, baseball is a tough enough game to play without extra added pressure."[17] "I can't think about racial things and try to get a jump on a curveball."[18]

Clearly, the all-white Red Sox management found no reasons—not even self-interested ones—to challenge the racism that had kept baseball segregated. Owner Tom Yawkey, who actually maintained an estate in South Carolina called "The Plantation," did not provide leadership. Nor did the mostly Irish American general managers he hired—Collins, Cronin, Higgins.

And yet, we can't look solely at the Red Sox front office if we want to understand why the team was the last to integrate. We need to take account of the larger social and historical setting for the team: the city of Boston's ethnic and racial history.

It's important to note that although Boston was the site for abolitionist activity in the nineteenth century, home to William Lloyd Garrison and his anti-slavery journal *Liberator*, the African American population was extremely small: "Through most of its history, Boston had one of the smallest African-American communities of all major American cities."[19]

In the middle of the nineteenth century, blacks numbered between eighteen hundred and two thousand; by 1940, the number had risen only to twenty thousand. The Great Migration north after World War I, which caused the black populations of Washington, Baltimore, and New York to expand significantly, did not bring many southern blacks to Boston. In fact, during the heyday of the Negro Leagues, Boston never had enough of a black population to support a Negro League team, while hosting two major league teams (the Braves and the Red Sox). By contrast, Negro League teams flourished in other Northeast baseball cities, such as New York, Philadelphia, Baltimore, Pittsburgh, and Washington, D.C., as well as smaller cities throughout the Middle Atlantic states and the Midwest, like Toledo, and Harrisburg. This absence is an important reason why the Red Sox management could drag its feet for so long: the city itself had not been exposed to black baseball players; there was no history of fandom among the African American community, and there were no local black stars to recruit during the early years of baseball integration.

During World War II, however, black workers came to New England to take up jobs in war-related industries, and Boston's black population doubled to over forty thousand by 1950 and continued to rise throughout the 1950s and 1960s. Roxbury, Boston's traditionally black community, could not house all these migrants.

The expanding black population literally burst out of its traditional boundaries and began settling along the fringes of formerly all-white (and predominantly Irish Catholic) neighborhoods such as Dorchester, Jamaica Plain, Roslindale, and Hyde Park. For the first time on any large scale, people from one community were moving out of "their own" neighborhoods into other communities. The whites saw the influx of blacks as a direct threat to their welfare and security.[20]

When we think about Boston in the last decades of the twentieth century, phrases like "the most racist city in America" may come to mind. The source of this image was the busing crisis of the 1970s, when Irish American Louise Day Hicks, born in the Irish enclave of South Boston, came to stand for the Irish community's insularity and racism. The busing riots in Charlestown and South Boston, when Irish Americans threw stones at black children being bused in from Roxbury, don't tell us why the Red Sox were slow to integrate (although they may suggest why, even to this day, few African Americans can be seen at Fenway Park). But the busing riots do reflect the ethnic history of Boston, in which Irish and Yankees had been intertwined in struggle since the mid–nineteenth century; and this ethnic history can help us understand the particular nature of Boston Irish racism, which was linked to the working-class Irish sense of being an oppressed minority themselves. This, in turn, forms the larger context for thinking about the Red Sox's slowness in hiring players of color.

It's a historical irony that the Boston Irish, later to be anti-black, were at first considered both black and inferior by the Anglo-Saxon elite, who were both anti-Irish and anti-Catholic. During the nineteenth century as more and more Irish immigrants fled their famine-ridden homeland and came to New England, prejudice against these "Irish niggers" grew.[21] Caricatures and cartoons in both England and the United States showed the Irish as apelike, with large lips and sloping foreheads and simian features. "The Irish were imagined as . . . 'a race of savages,'" observes Ronald Takaki, "at the same level of intelligence as blacks."[22] During the first years of post-Famine emigration, the Irish—considered a "race" rather than a nation—were often referred to as "niggers turned inside out," while blacks were sometimes termed "smoked Irish."[23]

The Boston area became sprinkled with the infamous "No Irish Need Apply" signs, as in this newspaper advertisement:

> Wanted: A good, reliable woman to take care of a boy two years old, in a small family in Brookline. Good wages and a permanent situation given. No washing or ironing will be required, but good recommendations as to character and capacity demanded. Positively no Irish need apply.[24]

Giving a sermon on "The Dangerous Classes," Boston's Rev. Theodore Parker reflected the view of the city's elite class when he classified the Irish as one of the "inferior peoples of the world," along with "negroes, Indians, Mexicans."[25] As Thomas O'Connor notes in his history of the Boston Irish, Boston was a city that rejected the Irish from the very start: the Yankee elite could not imagine this lower race being assimilated into American culture. This antagonism between Yankee and Irish marked the Boston Irish experience forever:

> Other major American cities, to be sure, shared many of Boston's social, cultural, and religious characteristics, but few to the same extent and none to the same degree. Yankee Boston was unique in the depth and intensity of its convictions. The generations of bitter and unyielding conflict between the natives of Boston and the newcomers from Ireland would forever mold the social and political character of the Boston Irish in ways not found elsewhere.[26]

If one could have picked a city in late-twentieth-century America where blacks should not migrate, it might well have been Boston. But, as O'Connor argues, if one could have picked "one city in the entire world where an Irish Catholic, under any circumstance, should never, *ever*, set foot," that city was also Boston:

> an American city with an intensely homogenous Anglo-Saxon character, an inbred hostility toward people who were Irish, and fierce and violent revulsion against all things Roman Catholic, and an economic system that precluded most forms of unskilled labor.[27]

As a result of their experience of discrimination in hostile Yankee Boston, O'Connor contends, even to this day the "Boston Irish are *different*"—different not only from the Irish in New York, Philadelphia, and Chicago but also from the Irish in Springfield, Worcester, and Lowell, other cities in Massachusetts that did not share Boston's Brahmin heritage. The Boston Irish, despite the political power they came to enjoy, have a deep-felt belief that they are a beleaguered minority, combined with a need to consider themselves higher in the social and economic scale than African Americans—and an inability to see the ways in which their class position in fact links South Boston with Roxbury.

The busing crisis of the 1970s needs to be understood in this context. In his powerful memoir of growing up in South Boston, *All Souls*, Michael Patrick MacDonald shows how his friends and relatives in Southie viewed the desegregation of the Boston schools and busing as a WASP plot and allied the Yankee elite with Ireland's English oppressors. "The English themselves weren't completely absent from our struggle, though. They ran the *Boston Globe* and were behind the whole thing. . . . The *Globe* was the enemy." One of MacDonald's friends showed him the names of the *Globe's* owners and editors: "Winship, Taylor. All WASPS," he says. "White

Anglo-Saxon Protestants, forever gettin' back at the Irish for chasing them out of Boston."[28] Meanwhile, Judge Arthur Garrity, the federal judge who had mandated busing, took the place of an English tyrant in Southie's fight songs: like Boston mayor Kevin White, he was viewed as a traitor to working-class Irish Boston, having left the inner city for the suburbs, upward mobility, and—an irony not lost in South Boston—mainly white schools.

There had been signs of a potentially revolutionary alliance between African Americans and Irish during the nineteenth century, forged by leaders who recognized their common interests as members of dispossessed classes. Haunting signs of this lost alliance include Frederic Douglass's trip to Ireland and discovery of important connections between Irish laments and Negro spirituals; Irish leader Daniel O'Connell's call for Irish support for ending slavery; and the 1841 *Address from the People of Ireland to Their Countrymen and Countrywomen in America*, signed by thousands of Irish men and women, which called up all Irish emigrants to "treat the colored people as your equals, as brethren."[29] The address was first given to an American audience in Fanuel Hall, Boston, in 1842, and an advertisement taken in the Boston *Pilot*, the Catholic paper.

But this sense of kinship with slaves was lost when the Irish emigrated to America and found themselves at the bottom of the heap, at times viewed as more dispensable than slaves because they did not even have the economic value of property. Given the discrimination they faced and the competition with blacks for jobs, the Irish sought to promote their own whiteness—and, as historian David Roediger observes, to insist on white supremacy. "They sought to become insiders, or Americans, by claiming their membership as whites. . . . Thus, blacks as the 'other' served to facilitate the assimilation of Irish foreigners."[30]

In the Boston area, however, despite the Irish success in achieving "whiteness," the working-class Irish who remained within the city limits in Charlestown or South Boston—instead of moving "up" to suburbs like Belmont, Arlington, and Wellesley—"continued to see themselves as an embattled minority," dominated by a Yankee power elite:

> Continuing political cultivation of ethnic grievances had clear consequences for race relations in the city during the second half of the twentieth century. When the migration of large numbers of African Americans to Boston after World War II pushed the question of racial discrimination to the fore, the city's Irish leaders refused to address it. South Boston City Councilman Michael Kinsella summed up the prevailing view in 1943 when

he insisted that the Irish rather than the blacks were the true "minority race" in Boston.[31]

It was Boston's unusual ethnic history, in which the largest ethnic majority thought of themselves as the "minority race" despite their political control of City Hall throughout the twentieth century, that created the social and cultural climate that shaped the history of the Boston Red Sox. The prevailing ethos in Boston during the years when other major league teams were recruiting black players simply did not support this kind of outreach. Not only did the city have only a relatively small African American community with no baseball history, but the dominant Irish sensibility had no interest in promoting integration in sports, schooling, or neighborhoods.

I don't think it's an accident that in Irish Boston, the Red Sox upper management who failed to move the team toward integration were, by and large, Irish American: Eddie Collins, Joe Cronin (later vice president of the American League), Mike Higgins, Dick O'Connell. Looking back, too, at my father's brief glory days with the Red Sox in the 1950s, I think it's no accident that Red Sox chose to hire the only Irish American advertising agency in New York City: Cunningham and Walsh. And again, no accident that Cunningham and Walsh then picked my father, Norbert O'Brien, Harvard-educated but born and bred in Massachusetts, the grandson of a Famine immigrant, to be their liasion with the Red Sox.

Perhaps one reason the Boston Celtics, despite their name, were far and away more open to African American players was that the guiding leader in the 1950s, Red Auerbach, had no allegiance to Irish Boston. Under his leadership, the Celtics were the first team in the NBA to hire a black player—Charles Cooper, in 1950. As Auerbach built his championship team throughout the 1950s, he brought in black players such as Bill Russell, K. C. Jones, and Sam Jones to join white players Bob Cousy, Tommy Heinsohn, and Frank Ramsey. When Pumpsie Green joined the Red Sox, it was Bill Russell—having already established himself as a Boston sports star—who befriended him.

My own private theory is that the curse preventing the Sox from winning the World Series in the twentieth century did not derive from what the team *did*—trade the Bambino and focus too much on the Wall—but from what the team *didn't* do—challenge Boston's Irish-tinged racism by hiring Jackie Robinson in 1947 and moving ahead with hiring black and Latin American players in the 1950s and 1960s.

Now it's the twenty-first century, and there are signs everywhere that the team and the city are changing. I like all the signs of mixed and multiple identities I see in Boston—a team of mainly African American basketball players called the Celtics, wearing green and white, symbolized by shamrocks and pipe-smoking leprechauns; a racially diverse Red Sox squad, with a popular black player named Troy O'Leary and names like Martinez and Garciaparra stitched across their shirts; a growing allegiance between the city's poor working-class Irish and African Americans, who are beginning to realize the class allegiances that transcend race. I like reading Michael Patrick MacDonald's poignant memoir of white working-class Irish despair and learning that the author works to create allegiances between working-class blacks and Irish.

I moved back to Southie after four years of working with activists and victims of violence, mostly in Roxbury, Dorchester, and Mattapan, Boston's largely black and Latino neighborhoods. In those neighborhoods I made some of the closest friends of my life, among people who too often knew the pain of losing their loved ones to the injustices of the streets. Families that had experienced the same things as many of my Southie neighbors. The only difference was that in the black and Latino neighborhoods, people were saying the words: *poverty, drugs, guns, crime, race, class, corruption.*

In his memoir, MacDonald tells a story about his Southie neighbor Mrs. Coyne that shows the links between working-class Irish and African Americans, links forged from the same experience of dispossession—unconscious, perhaps, but full of potential for new and surprising allegiances. During the busing crisis, Mrs. Coyne got up on her roof and started calling the police "nigger lovers," recalling the post-Famine Irish who tried to become white by separating themselves from blacks. But then, MacDonald tells us, she started dancing and singing James Brown songs. *"Say it loud, I'm black and I'm proud,"* she chanted at the cops, "Say it loud, I'm black and I'm proud."[32]

General Manager Dan Duquette hasn't asked me, but if the Sox want to win the World Series in this new century, I have two pieces of advice.

Pitching. As my friend Nick Bloom, ten years old and a savvy fan, says, "At the moment Boston's win-loss record goes like this: 'Martinez, Lose, Lose, Lose. Martinez, Lose, Lose, Lose.'" Don't rely on one or two aces who are going to throw their shoulders out during the season. *Get a good pitching rotation.*

History. Your "Special Moments in Boston Red Sox History" on your Web site erases the team's racial history. Between 1941 and 1967 you have only two entries: June 18, 1953 (Red Sox score seventeen runs in one inning against the Tigers), and September 26, 1960 (Ted Williams hits a home run in his last major league at bat). You need to add these two dates:

July 21, 1959: Pumpsie Green, the first African American to wear a Red Sox uniform, plays his first game at Comiskey Park, twelve years after Jackie Robinson played his first game for the Dodgers.

June 26, 1962: Earl Wilson pitches a 2–0 no-hitter against the Los Angeles Angels, becoming the first African American pitcher in the American League to throw a no-hitter. He helps his cause by hitting a home run.

Many people know about Pumpsie Green and the Red Sox's shameful history on race, but few know that Wilson was the first American League black pitcher to throw a no-hitter. Certainly no mention is made of this fact on the Red Sox Web site. I hope the Red Sox management will create a fuller and more honest history of the team, coming to realize that racial history and baseball history cannot be separated, which sometimes can be cause for pride as well as regret.

Go Sox.

NOTES

1. Eric Lott, *Love and Theft: Blackface Minstrelsy and the American Working Class* (New York: Oxford University Press, 1993). Also see William J. Mahar, *Behind the Burnt Cork Mask: Early Blackface Minstrelsy and Antebellum American Popular Culture* (Urbana and Chicago: University of Illinois Press, 1999).

2. Emily Vermeule, "It's Not a Myth—They're Immortal," *The Red Sox Reader,* ed. Dan Riley (Boston: Houghton Mifflin Co., 1991), 287.

3. Jimmy Golen, "First Black Player on Red Sox Honored before Home Opener," April 12, 1997, *The News-Times* (www.newstimes.com/archive97/apr1297/spg.htm).

4. Peter Golenbock, *Fenway: An Unexpurgated History of the Boston Red Sox* (New York: G. P. Putnam's Sons, 1992), 222. In telling the story of the Sox's rejection of Jackie Robinson and Willie Mays, in addition to Golenbock I have drawn on Al Hirshberg, *What's the Matter with the Red Sox?* (New York: Dodd, Mead,

1973); Larry Moffi and Jonathan Kronstadt, *Crossing the Line: Black Major Leaguers, 1947–1959* (Iowa City: University of Iowa Press, 19); and Arnold Rampersad, *Jackie Robinson: A Biography* (New York: Random House, 1997).

5. Golenback, *Fenway,* 222.

6. Hirshberg, *What's the Matter,* 145.

7. Rampersad, *Jackie Robinson,* 120.

8. Hirshberg, *What's the Matter,* 145; Rampersand, *Jackie Robinson,* 120.

9. Golenback, *Fenway,* 226.

10. Hirshberg, *What's the Matter,* 146.

11. Ibid.

12. Golenback, *Fenway,* 230.

13. Howard Bryant, "1959: Boston Red Sox Last to Integrate," *ESPNET SportsZone* (www.espn.go.com/editors/gen/features/robinson/timeboston.html).

14. Moffi and Kronstadt, *Crossing the Line,* 211.

15. Golenback, *Fenway,* 225.

16. "One on One," *USA Today Baseball Weekly* (www.usatoday.com/sports/baseball/bbw/sbbw6553.htm).

17. Golenback, *Fenway,* 225.

18. Moffi and Kronstadt, *Crossing the Line,* 211.

19. Thomas H. O'Connor, *The Boston Irish: A Political History* (Boston: Northeastern University Press, 1995), 239.

20. Ibid., 241.

21. Ronald Takaki, *A Different Mirror: A History of Multicultural America* (Boston: Little, Brown and Co., 1993), 150.

22. Ibid., 149.

23. Noel Ignatiev, *How the Irish Became White* (New York: Routledge, 1995), 33.

24. O'Connor, *Boston Irish,* 69.

25. Takaki, *Different Mirror,* 149.

26. O'Connor, *Boston Irish,* xvi.

27. Ibid.

28. Michael Patrick MacDonald, *All Souls: A Family Story from Southie* (Boston: Beacon Press, 1999), 80.

29. Takaki, *Different Mirror,* 150.

30. Ibid., 151.

31. James J. Connolly, *Triumph of Ethnic Progressivism Vision: Urban Political Culture in Boston, 1900–1925* (Cambridge: Harvard University, 1998), 193.

32. MacDonald, *All Souls,* 7.

Chapter Eight

Whose Broad Stripes and Bright Stars?
Race, Nation, and Power at the 1968 Mexico City Olympics

Amy Bass

Oh man, I never felt such a rush of pride. Even hearing the "Star Spangled Banner" was pride, even though it didn't totally represent me. But it was the anthem which represented the country I represented, can you see that? They say we demeaned the flag. Hey, no way man. That's my flag . . . that's the American flag and I'm an American. But I couldn't salute it in the accepted manner, because it didn't represent me fully; only to the extent of asking me to be great on the running track, then obliging me to come home and be just another nigger.[1]

—Tommie Smith

On December 14, 1967, Harry Edwards, leader of the Olympic Project for Human Rights (OPHR), announced the final demand of his organization at New York's Americana Hotel: the removal of Avery Brundage, whom Edwards declared "a devout anti-Semitic and anti-Negro personality," as head of the International Olympic Committee (IOC). This request joined several others: the desegregation of the New York Athletic Club; the expulsion of South Africa from international competition; the restoration of Muhammad Ali's boxing title; the addition of two black coaches to the U.S. Olympic team; and the addition of two black members to the U.S. Olympic Committee (USOC). Edwards pledged that a boycott of the

Mexico City Olympics by African American athletes would take place the following year unless all demands were met.[2]

Edwards made his announcement standing next to prominent civil rights leaders Martin Luther King Jr. and Floyd McKissick, both of whom lent an elevated credibility to the OPHR. The presence of the two helped fix the boycott as a proposal with the potential virility of past protest actions, such as the Montgomery Bus Boycotts in 1955 and the March on Washington in 1963, both of which solidified a national gaze on the racial inequities deeply embedded in American society. The OPHR's specific terms connected the boycott to a broader international forum of racialized politics, particularly those issues surrounding independent African nations and South African apartheid, as well as the Mexico City student social movements ongoing in this period, and developed a critical and widely articulated relationship between the black athlete in the United States and a global discourse of human rights. Thus, the OPHR became rapidly incorporated into broader movements of civil rights, and Edwards, an instructor at San Jose State and doctoral candidate at Cornell University, emerged, at least momentarily, as a principal player within the movement.

Edwards's promise of a boycott was especially threatening in light of Cold War politics, as Olympic organizers and U.S. statesmen alike appreciated the importance of black athletes in the incessant medal race with the Soviets. As observed by *Ebony* magazine, in the six Olympics since World War II, African Americans had won 34 percent of all U.S. track-and-field gold medals. In 1968, Dick Drake, managing editor of *Track and Field News*, predicted the United States could win 33 medals in Mexico City and calculated that "a net of 15" would be lost "should the Negroes boycott."[3] Undoubtedly recognizing such a loss, Brundage resolutely opposed the boycott, maintaining that the Olympics were "the one international affair for Negroes, Jews and Communists" rather than a place to rally for human rights.[4] His statement encompassed a spuriously color-blind, humanist rhetoric imagined the Olympics transcended politics and yet unwittingly validated the increasingly internationalist mien of the OPHR, mandating that the group be considered in any kind of diasporic understanding concerning the ongoing struggles of citizenship in the sixties, as it exemplified a lengthy tradition of black politics carried out with worldly consciousness.[5]

Such a trend found roots early in the twentieth century with Marcus Garvey and crystallized in 1941 with A. Philip Randolph's proposed March on Washington over the desegregation of wartime production.[6] Richard Wright, as Nikhil Singh points out, articulated such sentiment from afar. From France, Wright clearly enunciated the global centrality of U.S. civil rights struggles: "Isn't it clear to you that the American Negro is the only group in our nation that consistently and passionately raises the questions of freedom?" Wright asked. "The voice of the American Negro is rapidly becoming the most representative voice of America and of *oppressed people anywhere in the world.*"[7] In like fashion, the OPHR encompassed an objective that incorporated international politics to better define and improve U.S. citizenship. This stance built on the antecedent role of Muhammad Ali, who repudiated Vietnam, for example, because he had "no quarrel" with the Vietnamese people.[8] Thus, the powerful significance of the black athlete in American culture, which the OPHR utilized, largely emanated from the media circus that enveloped Ali's position.

The black athlete has continually served as a critical racialized subject, occupying an undeniably crucial place in the American imagination, whether on the television screen, sports page, or cereal box.[9] The development of a historical understanding of the complex manifestations of sport, race, and civil rights in the post–World War II period, then, is a complex but imperative project. Since Jackie Robinson stepped up to bat in 1947, the black athlete has become *the most visible* integrated racial subject in postwar society—seen in all facets of media, cheered by millions of fans, teamed with white counterparts, and situated as both understood and accepted. Building on the tenets of Black Power largely popularized by the Student Nonviolent Coordinating Committee (SNCC), the OPHR ensured that the black athlete, in a collective, politicized effort, played an increasingly significant role in the manufacture of racial and national identity.

Yet it was the use of the black athlete as an effective Cold War diplomatic instrument that inadvertently created the field on which the OPHR could stake its petition. There is a historical pattern of configuring sport as the basis for America's "official" portrait to the world as a racially harmonious country, with Jesse Owens and Jackie Robinson continually heralded to validate service to democratic ideals.[10] President Dwight Eisenhower was anxious to display integrated athletic talent in "developing" nations, particularly as the Soviet Union devoted so much attention to this area. In 1954, Congress appropriated funds to sponsor international tours of athletes, prompting one congressman to declare proudly that athletes were "some of the best salesmen for the American way of life."[11] Baseball, with its well-publicized blueprint for integration, remained one of the most prominent facets of such cultural diplomacy.[12] Perhaps the most instructive case was Jesse Owens's "goodwill tour" to India in 1955, sponsored by the State Department. On his return, *Life* magazine published photos of Owens wearing a madras shirt and Sikh turban and deemed him "a practically perfect envoy in a country which has violently exaggerated ideas about the treatment of Negroes in the U.S."[13]

Sport lent itself easily to this kind of rhetorical display, stretching the idea of a level playing field as a metaphor for racial and national equity. As C. L. R. James demonstrated with his treatment of cricket, sport subsists as a fundamental model for other forms of social existence.[14] It potentially serves as a stage with tremendous symbolic power, one literally—physically—focused on human possibility, transforming the quest for speed and power into a broader pursuit for equality. With the OPHR, it became an archetype for social action. In the midst of the Cold War elevation of sport as America's great success story, a field for restructuring the perception of the black athlete emerged. While the early postwar period presented sport as an effective diplomatic instrument, in the 1960s it became a vehicle for identity politics. The evolution of militant political visibility was critical to this shift. While many observers remained skeptical of the ability of black athletes to mobilize successfully, Harry Edwards, for one, realized the significance of an increasingly "black" presence. "They were no longer dealing with the 'Negro' athlete of the past," asserted Edwards. "Confronting them now was the new black athlete and a new generation of Afro-Americans."[15]

As a facet of the radical political transformations associated with Black Power, the OPHR forcefully recast the role of the black athlete, making it integral to both local and global struggles surrounding race and human rights as it couched its claims in specific terms of blackness. Further, this role evolved in a period in which displays of race were cultivated against the backdrop of far-reaching youth movements, with tactics that played well on television. Centered at the politically volatile campus of San Jose State, the OPHR grew in terms of sophistication and visibility, establishing ties with campaigns against apartheid and the widespread student movements in Mexico City. With its initial proclamation to boycott the Olympics in a stance of *human* rights, the group tried to transform the athletic arena into a source of black empowerment, rather than a forum in which racist suppositions ran rampant.

While the OPHR was inarguably the brainchild of Edwards, such a use of sport did not originate with him; as many recognized, perhaps nowhere else did Jim Crow clash more with ideologies of democracy than on the purportedly level playing fields of sport.[16] However, by 1968 the proliferation of increasingly revolutionary civil rights movements, which did not bring African Americans onto an equal footing with white in the national sphere but rather rehabilitated and completed the broader definitions and implications of citizenship itself, made it possible for more aggressive ideologies of equality to foray into sports, ensuring that the Mexico City Olympics would not be reported solely on the sports page because they held far greater potential as news. The OPHR understood that potential and attempted to redesign the rules of the game, in hopes of procuring a different kind of victory for both the individual athlete and the community represented.

Although the Olympic Charter emphasizes individual athleticism, each athlete physically embodies a nation's collective identity in global competition. Few, if any, events achieve the global nature of the Olympics. In the contemporary games, almost two hundred nations are represented. The Olympic Broadcast Analysis Report, published in 1997, deemed the Olympics "the premier world event in terms of viewer interest," stating that the Atlanta Games in 1996 had 19.6 billion television viewers in 214 countries, averaging 1.2 billion daily.[17] The OPHR recognized the global magnitude of the games.[18] On July 23, 1967, the idea to boycott Mexico City surfaced at the first National Conference of Black Power in Newark, New Jersey, but did not generate much interest until adopted by Edwards that fall.[19] On October 7, 1967, a group met with Edwards to discuss the problems of black athletes, as well as those of the larger black community, and formed the OPHR.[20] With standout sprinters Tommie Smith and Lee Evans, as well as basketball phenom Lew Alcindor, attached to it, the profile of the organization quickly grew. After the OPHR organized a successful boycott of the New York Athletic Club's (NYAC's) annual track meet early in 1968, it appeared that a boycott of the Olympics was indeed attainable.[21] Yet, for many athletes, the question of Olympic participation remained largely unresolved, foundering on a painstaking examination of the role of the individual within a political community and the consideration of endorsements and professional contracts that often accompanied a gold medal.

By the Olympic trials that summer, the question of how best to present a unified political front centered on a "black" identity was pivotal yet seemingly unsolvable.[22] Divisions in the OPHR as well as outside it made it difficult for the movement to maintain what Robin Kelley calls a "collectivist ethos" and effect a unanimous decision to boycott.[23] One of the most conspicuous internal difficulties of the organization, for example, was the lack of input from prominent *female* athletes such as Wyomia Tyus, who aimed to defend her 100-meter track championship in 1968 and become the first athlete—male or female—to do so. With Edwards as the leader and the overwhelmingly male readers and writers of the sports press as the central audience, there seemed little room for African American women in the movement geared toward achieving *human* rights. As the Olympics loomed closer and the OPHR faced its toughest and most direct question—whether or not to go to Mexico—the parameters of the black athlete fell into place as a political, racialized, and *unequivocally masculine* identity, invariably weakening the movement and the likelihood of a full-blown boycott.[24]

The boycott never came to fruition. Yet the Mexico City Games became indelibly linked to Black Power on October 16, 1968, when Tommie Smith and John Carlos raised black-gloved fists during the medal ceremony of the 200-meter track event to the tune of the "Star Spangled Banner." The spectacle created by the two solidified a politicized notion of "black athlete" in spite of the continuous fragmentation and reinvention the label had undergone. With their gesture, they created a moment of resistance and confrontation with dominant and existing forms of racial identity, borrowing pervasive and normative conceptions of the nation and substituting new representations by replacing the dominant image of the American flag with black-gloved fists. With individual predecessors such as Robinson and Ali, the arena of sport had already become highly politicized when Smith and Carlos took their places. Their protest, then, exemplified a *collective* transformation from "Negro" to "Black," one that mediated various internal identities of political consciousness and enunciated a new cohesiveness to its expansive audience.

The intense focus of television ensured a substantial stage on which they could articulate their point, just as it had for civil rights activists throughout the previous decade. The unprecedented attention the American Broadcasting Company (ABC) gave Mexico City, creating the first large-scale broadcast of an Olympics, produced a vehicle by which a revolutionary black athletic figure could, literally and figuratively, take the stand. Under the tutelage of Roone Arledge, ABC procured the rights to the Mexico City games with a blueprint for an unprecedented forty-four hours of programming, making the games a more lucrative venture, augmenting their importance within the corporate structure of network television, and broadening the political capacity of the event.[25] With a vast audience secured, the action of Smith and Carlos, with gold and bronze medals around their respective necks, proved to be the zenith of the mission of the OPHR. In a seemingly simple move, the duo shocked the world with their Black Power protest, an action designed to use their moment in front of a global audience of approximately 400 million people to denounce racism in the United States, creating a cultural strategy effective in its attempt to change or shift, in the words of Stuart Hall, the "dispositions of power."[26]

Yet Smith and Carlos, the focus of much of the American press prior to arriving in Mexico, had not waited for a victory ceremony to stake their symbolic claim; rather, they had cultivated the image of the militant athlete throughout their tenure in Mexico. For example, in their qualifying heats for the 200-meters, the duo wore noticeably tall black socks—what *Newsweek* magazine dubbed "pimp socks."[27] Jesse Owens, a constant media reference point throughout the controversies surrounding the OPHR, advocated a pragmatic disdain for the socks, ostensibly depoliticizing their overtly "black" symbolism. Bearing a persistent label of "Uncle Tom" by OPHR members, Owens advised the young men from San Jose to cut the black socks below their calves so as not to impede circulation while running. Watching Carlos strip down for his semi-final to reveal much shorter socks than those worn in previous heats, Owens smiled to one sportswriter—"Maybe they're listening to their uncle"—but continued with the position he had held since the OPHR boycott was first declared. "I'm old enough to be their uncle," he acknowledged, "but I won't be their Tom. We don't need this kind of stuff. We should just let the boys go out and compete."[28]

Smith also ensured a maximum audience for the 200 meters by running his first qualifying heat in 20.3 seconds, tying the Olympic record and provoking widespread buzz as to what he might do in the final. However, a pulled abductor muscle in his groin from his semi-final heat created speculation about whether he would even be able to run the final. Yet, once in the starting blocks, Smith gave no sign of discomfort and shattered the world record in an awe-inspiring 19.83 seconds.[29] But despite his extraordinary feat, it was the medal ceremony of the race that proved historic. Smith and Carlos stood on the dais in black stockings but wearing no shoes, each wearing a black glove, and Smith with a black scarf around his neck. The athletes turned, as expected, to face the American flag. As the "Star Spangled Banner" began, Smith and Carlos bowed their heads and simultaneously raised black-gloved fists. The crowd slowly but steadily greeted the action by booing and jeering. As the two left the stadium, the booing grew again in volume, to which both athletes responded by raising clenched fists once more.

While intentionally vague immediately after the protest, the response of the USOC became decidedly clear the next day. Emerging from a five-hour emergency session, Everett Barnes, acting executive director, delivered what the Associated Press described as a "veiled threat" to other athletes, indicating that any further actions of political agitation would not be tolerated.[30]

With words of enmity and intimidation dispatched, sportswriters began to devote more columns to the protest. In one day's time, the significance of the Black Power action overtook the significance of the world-record race itself, with reporters scrambling to determine how everyone and anyone in the Olympic athletes' village viewed Smith and Carlos. While not all the athletes supported the mode in which Smith and Carlos made their statement, many athletes, regardless of the stance taken by the USOC and IOC, supported what they considered to be a "pro-black" rather than an "anti-American" statement. One poll found that of twenty U.S. athletes, "white and black," thirteen supported Smith and Carlos, while only five were absolutely opposed to their action. Decathlete Tom Waddell said that he was "disappointed more Negro athletes backed down," while the irreproachable Al Oerter contended, "It's a free country. Perhaps if I felt as strongly about it as they do, I'd do the same thing." An opinion from the other side of the Atlantic concurred. "We all thought it was a bloody good show," remarked British distance runner John Wetton, with teammates Andrew Todd and John Davis in nodding unanimity. "It's bully that these blokes had nerve enough to express their feelings."[31]

As reporters increased the spotlight on the black-gloved fists, whatever magnanimity that remained within the Olympic administration vanished. With intense pressure from the IOC, the USOC revoked the credentials of Smith and Carlos and expelled the duo from the Olympic Village. While they were not stripped of their medals, the loss of their credentials gave them forty-eight hours to leave Mexico and forced them to go home, where they unilaterally were denied the housing, employment, and respect they had sought through their silent protest gesture.

The image of two black men engaged in an expression of defiance was instrumental in causing the eventually harsh "official" response. Henry Louis Gates Jr. has argued that the image of the black male is in itself a threatening one—an "already-read text" that evokes fear as a force that must be contained and controlled.[32] Rather than actors staging political actions, the bodies of athletes, particularly black athletes, are to be just that: bodies.[33] The sporting arena is unusual as a quarter where African Americans often are urged to be superior in the name of nation, whether by acquiring the most Olympic medals, taking part in a "goodwill tour," or, as with Joe Louis's rematch against Germany's Max Schmeling in 1938, to preserve global democracy. However, this arena closes when "misused" politically, as was the case with Smith and Carlos.

Paramount to the potency of the protest gesture was its appropriation from the Black Power movement of the black-gloved fist, a visual image that held weighty significance for audiences both within and outside the world of sports. Crucial to the development of any political movement is an understanding of its various audiences, all of which are inherently complex, depending on their social locations. Distinct communities, both marginal and dominant, are inextricably intertwined and dependent on one another to provide meaning. Thus, what was characterized as "black" in 1968, both by those attaching self-meaning to the designation and those assigning it to another, lent much to the import of the gloved gesture by Smith and Carlos and worked to knit together the expansive black political community.

This community, which the OPHR tried to represent, did not merely exist but rather made itself; or, as Kobena Mercer usefully argues, it was "culturally and politically *constructed* through political antagonism and cultural struggle." Observably, the black community emerged as an oppositional force in postwar America. But, asks Mercer, "if the 'black community' was not always there but something that had to be constructed, what did people use to construct it with?" In this case, the OPHR relied on symbols of the "black" community that had already been identified because of the instrumental rise of SNCC and the Black Panther Party. Beginning in 1966, the Panthers nurtured what Mercer designates a "highly visible oppositional appearance."[34] At the suggestion of friend and adviser Louis Lomax, Edwards himself had taken up such an appearance quite handily, sporting the requisite dark sunglasses, beard, work boots, jeans, and black leather jacket, which his cohort effectively imitated.

The ability of Edwards and the OPHR to cultivate this confrontational, militant appearance had varied ramifications. While historian William Van Deburg argues for the value of empowerment that the very appearance of Black Power provided, for a broader audience it carried a different weight that potentially held far less pressing meaning.[35] Thus, while it benefited the OPHR, situating the organization within a sweeping political landscape of racialized radicalism, it also made it possible for many critics—particularly those, such as Brundage, who believed the Olympics transcended politics and all forms of particularity—to dismiss the group, as well as its demands, as a source of mere political posturing.

Yet the action of Smith and Carlos created a political image that vividly remains in our imagination regarding race and sports and, indeed, among the images of broader movements of civil rights. Its resonance lies in the content of the action. After the victory ceremony, Smith explained the significance of the action in an interview with Howard Cosell:

> The right glove that I wore on my right hand signified the power within black America. The left glove my teammate John Carlos wore on his left hand made an arc with my right hand . . . to signify black unity. The scarf that was worn around my neck signified blackness. John Carlos and me wore socks, black socks, without shoes, to also signify our poverty.[36]

Thus, spectators and viewers alike listened to the national anthem while watching two American athletes display both their connection to and criticism of the United States, using no signs or banners but rather visual beacons of discontent. Without words, the focus became the two athletes themselves, as they physically occupied their statement and became, in essence, the core of the OPHR movement and all it stood for.[37]

The consequences for such an action were far-reaching. Although the IOC handed down no other suspensions to athletes—some of whom, including Lee Evans, who shattered the world record at 400 meters, wore black berets, OPHR badges, and black socks during the various medal ceremonies—all African American members of the track team, whether involved in the OPHR or not, were somehow associated with it. Despite the excessive haul of gold and the numerous world records set by the American squad in 1968, none became millionaires. On his return home, Smith lost his contract with the Los Angeles Rams, and teammate Jim Hines lost his endorsement contract—valued in the millions—with Adidas. And unlike the Olympic teams that both preceded and followed, the squad received no invitations to the White House in 1968.

Additionally, the racialized pride and renegotiated national identity that Smith and Carlos performed *within* the national borders produced consequences *outside* the national borders. Associations established before the opening ceremony between the demonstrating Mexican college students and the OPHR, as well as the pan-African alliances that surrounded issues of South African athletic participation, struck chords with struggles of people who existed outside the physical boundaries of the United States. However, because of the swelling position of American (inter)national power, both political and cultural, Smith and Carlos's gesture erased some of the very connections it was built on, creating what has become one of the most enduring images in the collective memory of American sports, as well as a definitive image of Black Power. In doing so, it became a somewhat perverse form of cultural imperialism, inadvertently complicit with the very "Americanness" the OPHR would expressly condemn in efforts to achieve *human* rights.

For example, before Smith and Carlos took their positions on the victory dais, *Sports Illustrated* already had determined that the massacre of Mexican students at the hands of Mexican soldiers at La Plaza de Las Tres Culturas days before the opening ceremony was "the scene that was to leave its mark on the 1968 Olympics."[38] However, by the closing ceremony, there was nary a mention of what became known as *La Noche Triste*, as the international media scoured the Olympic community for reaction to the two banished Americans, producing an almost despotic extirpation of the slain students. Harry Edwards, for one, reveled in such secure political preeminence, later observing that Smith and Carlos were "banished for having committed the ultimate Black transgression in a white supremacist society . . . to become visible, to stand up for the dignity of Black people, to protest from an *international* platform the racist inhumanity of American society."[39]

Once home, the cultural authority and power of the gesture persisted, continually reshaped and resituated as a political image. The prevalence of the protest in the mass-mediated discussions that followed the Mexico City Olympics secured it a substantial legacy for years to come. As John Carlos stated in an interview twenty-three years later, "The juice, the fire of '68, that scared a lot of people. All of us were such strong personalities, and that scared people. It scared government and business, everybody. It still scares them."[40]

The resonance implied by Carlos initially was evident in the year-end wrap-up program, "Highlights of the Sixties," on ABC's *Wide World of Sports*. As explained by program host Jim McKay, "The political turmoil that swept the world in the 1960s did not spare the field of sport." McKay noted that the protests of the Mexican students in 1968 jeopardized "the very existence" of the Olympics, as did the possible readmission of South

Africa. Lastly, he explained, a "threatened American Negro boycott" endangered the games. "Eventually . . . blacks came, but two . . . caused world wide controversy by this symbolic gesture of protest. . . . Now it seems that sport has become a stage for protest. . . .It's been a time of trouble all right."[41]

The political legacy of the Black Power action in Mexico City continued at the Munich Games in 1972, with another series of so-called scandals regarding black athletes. In what many considered an extension of the purported "introduction" of politics into the Olympics by Smith and Carlos, the IOC banned U.S. sprinters Wayne Collett and Vince Matthews from further competition for failing to pay adequate and deferential attention during the "Star Spangled Banner" at the medal ceremony for the 400 meters. On the podium, the pair talked, twitched, and chafed throughout the ceremony. Walking off the field, Matthews took off his medal and spun it around his finger, leading many—including the jeering crowd—to speculate whether it held any significance for him. For his part, Matthews refuted all accusations of protest. "If we did have any ideas about a demonstration," he told the press, "then we could have done a better job than that." Collett's statement, however, belied Matthews's assertion: "I couldn't stand there and sing the words because I don't think they're true," he said. "I wish they were. I think we have the potential to have a beautiful country, but I don't think we do."[42]

Of course, the alleged disrespect of Matthews and Collett was by no means the defining image of Munich. Far more horrifying was the massacre during the games of eleven members of the Israeli team by the Black September movement on September 5, 1972, as part of an attempt to procure the release of two hundred Arabs and Palestinians in Israeli prisons. The terrifying hostage situation came to a close in one of the starkest moments of any Olympic broadcast. After bringing American viewers through the siege, McKay grimly told his audience, "Our worst fears have been realized. They're all gone."[43] The episode forever scarred the Munich Olympics, which had been staged by the West Germans largely as an event that would erase the enduring memory of Hitler's Berlin Games in 1936 and demonstrate the nation's recovery from war.

Before the Montreal games in 1976, ABC broadcast a documentary titled *Triumph and Tragedy* in an obvious attempt to reinvigorate viewer interest in the Olympics after the violence and terror of Munich, as well as definitively to ostracize those who did fully represent the games' true spirit, at least in the opinion of the network. The first half of the program celebrated "triumphant" figures such as track legend Jesse Owens, projecting his gold medals in Berlin as a conquest over the racism inherent in Nazi ideology. The program then quickly moved through the war era, when the Olympics were canceled, to their celebrated revitalization in a war-ravaged London in 1948, and into the colorful sixties. Images of the space launch, John F. Kennedy, Vietnam, the Super Bowl, Vince Lombardi, "Mrs. Robinson," and the Beatles chronicled the decade, while the network excluded the identity politics—civil rights, women's rights, anti-war movements—that personified the period for many. Rather, the "triumphant" treatment of Mexico City included runner Jim Ryun's heartbreaking loss, Bill Toomey's victory in the decathlon, and Bob Beamon's magnificent record-breaking long jump victory, with no mention of his black-stockinged feet on the victory dais.

The program also made no reference to the world record–breaking achievements of OPHR members Smith and Evans. The eradication of their superior marks from a catalog of "triumphant" feats in Mexico City lent to their manufacture as "tragic." Indeed, the second segment— "Tragedy"—dispensed a discussion on Smith and Carlos alongside a revisitation of the purported turpitude of Matthews and Collett in Munich. Legendary sports commentator Howard Cosell judiciously situated the two cases of banished black athletes in a somewhat longer time line, noting that the "prevailing notion that protests in the Olympic Games really began in Mexico in 1968 . . . is untrue." As an example, Cosell reviewed the case of U.S. Olympic flag bearer Martin Sheridan, who refused to dip the flag before the king of England in 1908, as was customary, because he would not "dip the . . . flag before any earthly king." Yet Cosell did not stand his ground, rather continuing, "But *it is true* that the . . . Games became a forum for international protest in . . . Mexico City in 1968."[44]

Cosell's use of "forum" spoke to an intentional politics of protest, as well as parlaying Black Power as "tragic" rather than "triumphant." The source of strength that Smith and Carlos symbolized with their gloved fists was lost in the ruination of sport that Cosell implied had occurred.[45] The segment failed to recognize the possible social locations of the audience to Smith and Carlos's action, among whom the black clenched fist could well be triumphant in its capacity to create pride. Further, Cosell linked the Black Power gesture, as well as the banishment of Collett and Matthews in Munich, to the only other in-depth investigation of the "Tragedy" segment: the Black September movement. With Cosell's segue from the Black Power stances to the massacre, Smith and Carlos became fortuitously, and yet by design, linked to and blamed for the most horrific invasion of politics into the Olympic arena: "And so the use of the Olympic Games as a forum for protest, which really gained international attention in 1968, grew even further in 1972 and to some may be regarded as the *genesis* for the most horrible thing that's ever happened in any Olympiad: the grotesque massacre of 11 Israelis."[46]

The direct correlation created by Cosell's statement, part of ABC's active construction of Olympic tragedy defined solely in terms of Mexico City and Munich, held Smith and Carlos directly responsible—"the genesis"—for the massacre of the Israeli team.[47] Such a connection has persevered as the Black Power protest continues to be heralded as the political turning point of the Olympics—a sporting event based on national teams and thus inherently political in nature. The inclusion of Smith and Carlos's gesture in various inquests of critical Olympic moments, and amid the turbulent politics of the sixties in general, indicates that it remains a vital and multi-faceted window on the confluence of athletics, politics, and race.

An example of the gesture's resilience occurred when the National Basketball Association (NBA) suspended player Mahmoud Abdul-Rauf for failing to stand at attention with his Denver Nuggets teammates during the national anthem, as dictated by his contract.[48] The dispute evoked a fleeting yet revealing debate regarding race, nation, and sport.[49] Abdul-Rauf, a Muslim, backed his stance with a religious argument, contending that his rights of freedom of speech and religion, as ordained by the U.S. Constitution, enabled him to refuse to stand for a flag he felt, based on his reading of the Koran, represented "tyranny" and "oppression." Yet he encountered an overwhelming objections to his alleged breach of patriotism, particularly in an arena that paid him so well.[50] Retorting that the American flag stood for freedom and democracy, the *New York Daily News*, echoing Abdul-Rauf's fellow NBA Muslim Hakeem Olajuan, roared, "Show some respect!"[51]

As evidenced by the posture of the *Daily News*, Abdul-Rauf received little public support, despite the backing of the players' union and the American Civil Liberties Union. A notable exception in the sports press was Frank Deford, who questioned why the national anthem remains a part of any sporting event, a ritual during which "itchy patriots in the stands start screaming 'Dee-fense' along [with] . . . 'whose broad stripes and bright stars.'"[52] On the court, amid the racket, it was Shaquille O'Neal who most succinctly acknowledged the history of the storm: "Last time someone disrespected the national anthem they talked about them for about 20 years and that was those brothers in the 1968 Olympics Mexico City," O'Neal advised. "I wasn't even born yet, and I heard about it."[53]

The image of the Black Power protest remains, as verified by O'Neal, because of its political malleability and potency. Members of the OPHR understood the elemental stakes involved in sports, demanded racial equality to accompany them, and threatened an Olympic boycott if demands were not met. They went to Mexico City with the intention of demonstrating their pursuit of racial equality, human rights, and black identity individually, exemplified by the black-gloved fists of Smith and Carlos, when the collective strategy of a boycott proved too difficult to obtain. It was a moment that would have heavy consequences for all it chose to represent. While the 1968 squad, arguably the greatest U.S. track team ever assembled, did its country proud with record-breaking achievements, the protest also established the degree to which some were dissatisfied with their prescribed circumstances. A so-called embarrassment to the red, white, and blue, Smith and Carlos were thrown out of the Olympic Village, although their medals remained around their necks and were counted as part of America's success. Their place in society, however, was more uncertain. When Carlos left the Olympic Village, a reporter asked him where he was going. To his response "Home," someone yelled, "Do you mean the United States?"[54]

In 1992, during the NBC broadcast of the Barcelona Olympics, a "Where Are They Now?" segment featured Smith, examining his life decades after his controversial moment on the victory dais. At the end of the segment, sports anchor Jim Lampley stated, "Among many dramatic changes since 1968, one concrete one strikes us tonight: World Record holders no longer go hungry, and it's entirely likely they never will again."[55] While Lampley was able to assure his audience that black athletes finally could cash in their medals as well as anyone, there are few assurances regarding the general state of racial oppression.[56] In 1968, the Black Power salute challenged the flag, contesting and claiming a denied national identity and producing dramatic reaction and consequences. Yet in 1992, the result of a protest that took place in Barcelona with basketball's "Dream Team" was far different. When Michael Jordan, among others, under contract to Nike, refused to don his U.S. team sweat suit because it was manufactured by Reebok, his solution was easier to come by than a black-gloved fist: he wrapped himself in an American flag to cover the Reebok logo, indicating that past global signifiers of black cultural politics had been replaced by a corporate emblem.[57]

It is difficult to imagine a world without an individual like Jordan reaping the gigantic financial benefits of athletic excellence. But as historian Glenda Gilmore warns, one of the hazards of historians is "that what is past to them was future to their subjects."[58] As Tommie Smith remembered on the thirtieth anniversary of his protest, "It's not something I can take off and lay on the shelf . . . it's a whisper—it's gone, and I continue . . . it's been a lot of years . . . and my heart and soul is still on that team, still in that stand, still in what we believed in the '60s for social change."[59] The role of the black athlete, particularly as cultivated by the OPHR, emerged as an overt attempt to make America fulfill its promises, understanding that while sport allows for the location of a black face in one of the most important social arenas, it also exists as a space accompanied by devastating implications, often alleviating America's racial culpability within the consequential framework of popular culture. Hence, while a figure such as Jordan might overshadow and erase the structural reality of racism, the memory and call of a black-gloved fist linger.

NOTES

1. "Gloved Fist Is Raised in Defiance," *Daily Telegraph*, October 11, 1993, 38.

2. "Brundage Ouster Demanded," *San Jose Mercury News*, December 15, 1967, 73.

3. Further, the feature pointed out, African Americans were responsible for 18 percent of U.S. gold in *all* sports. "Should Negroes Boycott the Olympics," *Ebony* 23,5, March 1968, 112.

4. "Brundage Ouster Demanded," 73.

5. In her important study on African Americans and U.S. foreign affairs, Brenda Plummer acknowledges that "an essentialist perspective on race, combined with the belief that the United States has little in common with other mixed societies," created little scholarly attention on black politics in an international arena. What exists, according to Plummer, largely focuses on Africa, rather than what she describes as "Afro-American political behavior." Yet the meaningful manner in which a global discourse centered on issues of decolonization and human rights informed African American pursuits for civil liberty is a critical project and certainly an important facet of the OPHR. As Nikhil Singh details, "Black struggles . . . [became] the 'trigger struggle,' or switch point for a host of other minority discourses and contestations and relay station for emancipatory impulses of decolonization from around the world." See Brenda Gayle Plummer, A Rising Wind: Black Americans and U.S. Foreign Affairs, 1935–1960 (Chapel Hill: University of

North Carolina Press, 1996), 1; Nikhil Pal Singh, "Toward an Effective Antiracism," in *Beyond Pluralism: The Conception of Groups and Group Identities in America*, ed. Wendy F. Katkin, Ned Landsman, and Andrea Tyree. (Urbana: University of Illinois Press, 1998), 230.

6. Randolph's tactics, which directly acknowledged the racial hypocrisy embedded in America's fight against fascism, left little doubt as to the fashion by which World War II would recast domestic politics, particularly as he warned of a coalition of "the darker races" in its aftermath. Perhaps clearest of all was the NAACP's Walter White, who concluded his provocative report *A Rising Wind* (1945) with a solemn prediction of a global race war if racist and imperialist circumstances did not change.

7. Quoted in Singh, "Toward an Effective Antiracism," 228; emphasis mine. Throughout the 1960s, groups such as the Student Nonviolent Coordinating Committee (SNCC) echoed Wright's sentiments, connecting, for example, domestic and international situations with overt opposition to the Vietnam War and a series of staunch anti-imperialist declarations. See George Lipsitz, "'Frantic to Join . . . the Japanese Army': Beyond the Black-White Binary," in *The Possessive Investment in Whiteness: How White People Profit from Identity Politics* (Philadelphia: Temple University Press, 1998), 94.

8. Quoted in Thomas R. Hietala, "Muhammad Ali and the Age of Bare Knuckle Politics," in *Muhammad Ali: The People's Champ*, ed. Elliott J. Gorn (Urbana: University of Illinois Press, 1995), 138. Before Ali, Vietnam was a virtual nonissue for athletes—amateur and professional—as they discreetly served on their respective National Guards to avoid combat service. Yet, once Ali declared his resolute opposition to the war, it became a central issue for athletes, building on his controversial conversion to the Islamic faith and his name change—"Cassius is not my name no more"—years earlier.

9. Some popular constructions of blackness, such as those of hip-hop artists and gang members, create "menacing" images. Yet the athlete is designed as a benign and "natural" figure, ideally intended for consumption by a mass media audience. For example, in the mainstream press, while the black male often is visible on the front page in a criminal capacity, on the sports page the black male body is transformed into heroic form. Kobena Mercer elaborates this process in his discussion of Robert Mapplethorpe's work, elevating the status of the athlete as the "most commonplace of stereotypes" because the figure stands as "mythological endowed with a 'naturally' muscular physique and an essential capacity for strength, grace and machine-like perfection." A complex exception, of course, is when the black athletic hero, such as Mike Tyson upon his conviction for rape, leaves the sports page to take his place among other black figures. In many ways, American media are better equipped to deal with Tyson as a criminal, because the reference points are far more extensive. See Herman Gray, "Black Masculinity and Visual Culture," in *Black Male: Representations of Masculinity in Contemporary*

American Art (New York: Harry N. Abrams, 1994), 176–177; Kobena Mercer, "Reading Racial Fetishism: The Photographs of Robert Mapplethorpe," in *Welcome to the Jungle: New Positions in Black Cultural Studies* (New York: Routledge, 1994), 178-179.

10. As the United States reshaped itself in the aftermath of World War II as the so-called leader of the free world, it became clear that, as Jules Tygiel contends in his work on Robinson, "America's most visible example of interracial harmony had quickly become a weapon of Cold War politics." For example, in 1949, the House Un-American Activities Committee instructed Robinson publicly to condemn Paul Robeson's statement to a French audience that African Americans were unwilling to take up arms against the Soviets. Although Robinson's statement included a powerful attack on prejudice in the United States, he fulfilled his prescribed role and denounced Robeson's Paris speech. The use of Robinson in the U.S. government's persistent battle against Communism laid a precedent for the usage of sport as a Cold War tool, exemplifying the transformation of "blackness," as expressed by Paul Gilroy, into "a matter of politics rather than a common cultural condition." See Jules Tygiel, *Baseball's Great Experiment: Jackie Robinson and His Legacy* (New York: Oxford University Press, 1983), 334; Martin Bauml Duberman, *Paul Robeson: A Biography* (New York: Ballantine Books, 1989), 360; and Paul Gilroy, *The Black Atlantic: Modernity and Double Consciousness* (Cambridge: Harvard University Press, 1993), 27.

11. Quoted in Mary Jo Festle, *Playing Nice: Politics and Apologies in Women's Sports* (New York: Columbia University Press, 1996), 84–85. According to Festle, the money came from the $5 million Emergency Fund for International Affairs and was part of a larger domestic program emphasizing physical fitness.

12. One of the clearest examples of the central role of baseball was the use of the *Sporting News* and its photographs of black baseball players by Catholic missionaries in Africa. In 1953, the publication became a staunch supporter of the idea to send the Brooklyn Dodgers and Cleveland Indians on a world tour. Though the tour never took place, the role intended for black players was clear: to display "living evidence of the opportunity to reach the top, which America's No. 1 sport gives all participants regardless of race." See Tygiel, *Baseball's Great Experiment* 335.

13. "A Famous Athlete's Diplomatic Debut," *Life*, October 31, 1955, 49. Further, in the 1950s, the United States Information Service delivered articles with headlines such as "Negro Hurdler Is Determined to Win Olympic Event" to various African destinations, emphasizing the feats of African Americans as a direct outcome of a staunchly democratic system. Even more famously, the Harlem Globetrotters toured Berlin, Indonesia, Burma, and Italy, playing, in the words of owner-coach Abe Saperstein, an "unusual role in helping combat the spread of communism." See Penny M. Von Eschon, *Race against Empire: Black Americans and Anticolonialism, 1937–1957* (Ithaca: Cornell University Press, 1997), 128, 177.

14. C. L. R. James, *Beyond a Boundary* (Durham: Duke University Press, 1993). James's work is one of the most fruitful studies for this kind of consideration, illustrating how sport subsists as a fundamental model for other forms of social existence. James found the cricket pitch to be the consummate locale for the examination of the contestations among race, class, and nation in conjunction with the politics of colonization. When his gaze shifted from the playing field to the role of learned scholar and public intellectual, he found he was more than prepared. "Cricket had plunged me into politics long before I was aware of it," he wrote. "When I did turn to politics I did not have too much to learn." James's ability to extend sport to another level provides an important methodological foundation, removing sport from those who know it—and perhaps only it—best and putting it in an arena with different questions and an alternative charge. Didactically, he eloquently prefaces his work as "neither cricket reminiscences nor autobiography" and famously poses the question that directly outlines the necessity of such inquiry: "What do they know of cricket who only cricket know?"

15. Harry Edwards, *The Revolt of the Black Athlete* (New York: Free Press, 1969), 57.

16. As demonstrated by Donald Spivey, an early example of the effective coupling of sport and civil rights in overt political athleticism occurred in October 1940, when New York University students protested the so-called gentleman's agreement in sports after African American football player Leonard Bates was forbidden to travel with the team to play against the University of Missouri. The protest expanded when members of the Council for Student Equality were suspended for circulating a petition regarding Bates, rousing support from Paul Robeson, the NAACP, the Urban League, the council on African Affairs, and the Communist Party. See Donald Spivey, "'End Jim Crow in Sports': The Protest at New York University, 1940–1941," *Journal of Sport History* 15 (Winter 1988): 282–299.

17. According to the Amateur Athletic Foundation (AAF) in Los Angeles, California, the closest contender to the Olympics, the World Cup, held 618 million daily viewers in 1994 in 188 countries, for a total of approximately 19.2 billion. According to NBC, the Atlanta Games maintained an *American* viewing audience of 209 million viewers—91.7 percent of all people in the United States with televisions. Despite the apparent greater global merit of the Olympics, the AAF emphasizes that the final game of the World Cup is the most watched ninety minutes of sports programming in the world. For example, on June 15, 1998, the World Cup Web site set a record, with 59 million hits recorded in a single hour. I am grateful to Wayne Wilson at the AAF for his help in compiling these statistics.

18. Because of such global capacity, the OPHR obviously was not the first to view the political possibilities of an Olympic boycott. In 1956, for example, Egypt, Lebanon, and Iraq refused to send teams to Melbourne in protest of the British-French-Israeli invasion of Egypt. A boycott by African Americans is generally

credited to comedian/activist Dick Gregory, former track standout at Southern Illinois University, who suggested a boycott in 1960 and then encouraged African Americans to boycott a U.S.-Soviet Union track meet. The idea gained further momentum when Mal Whitfield, triple Olympic medalist, made a passionate plea for black athletes to boycott Tokyo in 1964 "if Negro Americans by that time have not been guaranteed full and equal rights as first-class citizens." See Donald Spivey, "Black Consciousness and Olympic Protest Movement: 1964–1980," in *Sport in America: New Historical Perspectives* (Westport: Greenwood Press, 1985), 239–240.

19. According to Edwards, one of the pivotal turning points in the fledgling movement was a rally at San Jose State, protesting the treatment of black students. Over seven hundred people attended the rally, producing the United Black Students for Action. The new organization threatened to block an upcoming San Jose–UTEP football game if its demands were not fulfilled. While the school met the demands, at the urging of California governor Ronald Reagan it also canceled the game because of the upheavals on campus. As the first collegiate athletic event canceled because of racial unrest, the San Jose–UTEP game formed a critical juncture; in Edwards's succinct recollection, "We had learned the use of power—the power to be gained from exploiting the white man's economic and almost religious involvement in athletics." See Edwards, *Revolt of the Black Athlete*, 41–47; idem, *The Struggle That Must Be* (New York: Macmillan, 1980), 161.

20. Edwards, *Revolt of the Black Athlete,* 50.

21. The NYAC boycott, which took place in February 1968, coincided with the IOC decision to allow South Africa to compete in Mexico City, after the team had been banned from the Tokyo Olympics in 1964 because of apartheid policies. After substantial international protest and debate and the threat of a boycott by independent African nations, as well as much of Eastern Europe, the IOC reinstated the ban on South Africa. The South Africans would not appear in the Olympics until Barcelona in 1992.

22. As Stuart Hall cautions, an essentialist "black" political appellation is not adequate in defining "progressive politics." Stuart Hall, "What Is This 'Black' in Black Popular Culture?" in *Black Popular Culture*, ed. Gina Dent (Seattle: Bay Press, 1992), 195.

23. Robin D. G. Kelley, "'We Are Not What We Seem': The Politics and Pleasures of Community," in *Race Rebels: Culture, Politics, and the Black Working Class* (New York: Free Press, 1994), 39.

24. Of course, the exclusion of women from the dialogue of civil rights was not isolated to the foray of Black Power into the sports arena. In his seminal work on SNCC, Clayborne Carson posits that while the group made some attempts to address the existence of sexual discrimination within its ranks, the budding feminist movement induced female members to recognize and to challenge the inequities they encountered. According to Carson, SNCC "had not developed an

egalitarian ethic regarding sexual relations similar to racial egalitarianism," as was exemplified when Stokeley Carmichael responded, "Prone," to a question regarding the suitable *position* of women in the organization. Whether stated jokingly, as he claimed, or not, Carmichael's notorious rejoinder mirrored the dearth of regard paid toward feminist preoccupations. See Clayborne Carson, *In Struggle: SNCC and the Black Awakening of the 1960s* (Cambridge: Harvard University Press, 1995), 147–148.

25. See Amy Bass, "Race and Nation in Olympic Proportions: Televising Black Power at the Mexico City Games," *Spectator* 19,1 (Fall/Winter 1998): 8–23.

26. Hall, "What is This 'Black' in Black Popular Culture?" 24–25.

27. "The Olympics' Extra Heat," *Newsweek*, October 28, 1968, 74.

28. Steve Cady, "Owens Recalls 1936 Sprinter's Ordeal," *New York Times*, October 17, 1968, 59.

29. Smith's race was the fastest 200 meters in the history of the timed track; no one else would run the distance in under twenty seconds until Carl Lewis in Los Angeles in 1984.

30. "U.S. Apologizes for Protest by Blacks," *Chicago Tribune*, October 18, 1968, III:1; "U.S. Apologizes for Athletes' 'Discourtesy,'" *Los Angeles Times*, October 18, 1968, III:1.

31. "Reactions among Athletes," *New York Times*, October 18, 1968, 55; "Black-Fist Display Gets Varied Reaction in Olympic Village," *Los Angeles Times*, October 18, 1968, III:1. Among the numerous voices that spoke out regarding Smith and Carlos, Waddell's support was particularly notable. While his sixth-place finish in Mexico did not make headlines, his life eventually did. Born Tom Flubacher, Waddell was a physician who came under terrific scrutiny for the various political battles he fought throughout his tragically short life. In 1966, he was drafted into the armed services but registered as a conscientious objector and was assigned a domestic medical post. Such political awareness undoubtedly enabled him to demonstrate a nuanced understanding of the Smith-Carlos action. For example, when asked by the international press if the pair had disgraced the American flag, he responded, "I think they have been discredited *by* the flag more often than they have discredited it. . . . This can only help." After both his army service and athletic career ended, he traveled the world as a physician. However, Waddell, who died in 1987 of AIDS, is likely best known for the "Gay Games," which he founded in 1982 in a heavily criticized attempt to use sport as a vehicle for the acceptance of gay and lesbian culture into mainstream society, an idea with many parallels to the ideas of Harry Edwards. Waddell spent much of the last years of his life in a prolonged legal battle with the USOC, which objected to his use of the word *Olympics* in his enterprise. See Tom Waddell and Dick Schaap, *Gay Olympian: The Life and Death of Dr. Tom Waddell* (New York: Knopf, 1996), 104–109.

32. Henry Louis Gates Jr., preface to *Black Male: Representations of Masculinity in Contemporary American Art* (New York: Harry N. Abrams, 1994), 13.

33. Deeply embedded in racism is what Kobena Mercer describes as "a logic of dehumanization in which African people were defined as having bodies but not minds: in this way the super-exploitation of the black body as a muscle machine could be justified." See Kobena Mercer and Isaac Julien, "True Confessions," in *Black Male: Representations of Masculinity in Contemporary American Art* (New York: Harry N. Abrams, 1994) 197.

34. Kobena Mercer, "'1968': Periodizing Politics and Identity," in *Welcome to the Jungle*, 292–302.

35. William L. Van Deburg, *New Day in Babylon: The Black Power Movement and American Culture, 1965–1975* (Chicago: University of Chicago Press, 1993), 306.

36. Archived Olympic footage, October 17, 1968 (tape 16, 8:39–8:41) American Broadcasting Company, New York, New York.

37. As John MacAloon submits in his work on symbolism and the Olympiad, through the athlete's body the Olympic medal ceremony reinforces the results of competition but also reinforces nation and Olympiad through flags, anthems, and medals. The athlete assumes a dual personality because he or she stands on the dais as a member of both a nation and what MacAloon designates as "a wider human community." Such symbolism works well in a realm where, according to Stuart Hall, the body has been used to such degree that individuals become "canvases of representation." See John J. MacAloon, "Double Visions: Olympic Games and American Culture," in *The Olympic Games in Transition*, ed. Jeffrey O. Segrave and Donald Chu (Champaign, Ill.: Human Kinetics, 1988), 279–280; Hall, "What Is This 'Black' in Black Popular Culture?" 27.

38. Bob Ottum, "Grim Countdown to the Games," *Sports Illustrated*, October 14, 1968, 38.

39. Edwards, *Struggle That Must Be*, 204; emphasis mine.

40. Kenny Moore, "A Courageous Stand," *Sports Illustrated*, August 5, 1991, 60.

41. "Wide World of Sports: Highlights of the Sixties," American Broadcasting Company, aired December 27, 1969, Museum of Radio and Television, New York, New York. McKay also remarked that such protest was not limited to Black Power: Czech gymnast Vera Cáslavská bowed her head on the victory dais during the playing of the Russian national anthem in order to protest the invasion of her country, a move that reportedly put her in political trouble at home. The role of the seemingly slight gesture by Cáslavská should not be symbolically underestimated, even though she was not punished by the IOC. As one of the most celebrated gymnasts in history, she shared first place in 1968 in the floor exercises with Soviet gymnast Larissa Petrik. The tie meant that the two athletes stood alongside each other during the playing of each nation's anthem. After the Czech anthem played, Cáslavská bowed her head and turned away for the duration of the Soviet anthem.

42. Quoted in David Wallechinsky, *The Complete Book of the Olympics* (New

York: Penguin Books, 1988), 22. According to Wallechinsky, Matthews told the *New York Times* why he stripped off his medal: "I took it off to tell them this was my medal. A lot of people had forgotten about me and given up on me. . . . Twenty years from now, I can look at this medal and say, 'I was the best quarter-miler in the world that day.' If you don't think that's important, you don't know what's inside an athlete's soul."

43. In a millennium list of the "100 Greatest Moments" in television history, *Entertainment Weekly* magazine ranked the Munich tragedy at number sixty-five, arguing that it transformed the Olympics from "glorious escapist TV fare" to something much different. McKay remembered of the incident, "At some point I learned that one of the athletes was [originally] from Shaker Heights, Ohio. . . . And I realized that it was very likely that the young man's parents would be hearing from me whether he was dead or alive" (*Entertainment Weekly,* February 19–26, 1999, 65).

44. *Triumph and Tragedy: The Olympic Experience,* American Broadcasting Company, aired January 5, 1976, Museum of Radio and Television, New York, New York; emphasis mine.

45. Juxtaposed with Smith and Carlos was the gold medal of boxer George Foreman, who, to the chagrin of OPHR members, carried an American flag around the ring in Mexico City after defeating Soviet opponent Ionas Chepulis; he subsequently was labeled a "triumph" in ABC's documentary.

46. *Triumph and Tragedy*; emphasis mine.

47. Further, the network made no mention of the massacre that took place in Mexico City at the hands of the host city's soldiers.

48. Section II of the official *NBA Guide,* "Basic Principles," states in section J, rule 2: "Players, coaches and trainers are to stand and line up in a dignified posture along the sidelines or on the foul line during the playing of the national anthem."

49. The debate took place throughout the sports press and appeared on a wide range of television programs, from ESPN's *Sportscenter* to CNN's *Crossfire.* See "The Reuter Television Daybook," March 13–14, 1996.

50. As a member of the Denver Nuggets, Abdul-Rauf was paid $2.6 million per season, or approximately $31,707 per game.

51. "Hakeem Tells Abdul-Rauf: Show Some Respect," *New York Daily News,* March 14, 1996.

52. Frank Deford, "Of Stars and Stripes," *Newsweek,* March 25, 1996, 64.

53. Donna Carter, "Mutombo Goes to Bat for Suspended Guard," *Denver Post,* March 13, 1996, D:4.

54. Arthur Daley, "The Incident," *New York Times,* October 20, 1968, 25.

55. "Where Are They Now?" National Broadcasting Company, Barcelona Olympic Coverage, 1992. Lampley's cohost, Hannah Storm, insipidly added, "It's about time."

56. As Nikhil Singh dramatically asserts in his important discussion on anti-racism, "Yet today, as we sit on the threshold of the twenty-first century, the condition of poor communities of color, particularly black communities, is as dire as any time in recent history." See Singh, "Toward an Effective Antiracism," 222.

57. "Don't Like the Sponsor? Just Zip It," *New York Times*, August 5, 1992, B13; "Dream Team Will Dress in Reebok Suits," *San Diego Union-Tribune*," August 5, 1992, D6; Scott Ostler, "Dropping the Other Shoe on the Olympics," *Los Angeles Times*, August 10, 1992, B1; Jay Mariotti, "Even on the Medal Stand, This Team Is a Dream," *Chicago Sun-Times*, August 9, 1992, 2; Jay Mariotti, "Sweatsuit Solution Pleases Jordan," *Chicago Sun-Times*, August 5, 1992, 96. I am grateful to Nikhil Singh for helping me formulate this understanding of the Dream Team "protest."

58. Glenda Gilmore, *Gender and Jim Crow: Women and the Politics of White Supremacy in North Carolina, 1896–1920* (Chapel Hill: University of North Carolina Press, 1996), 1.

59. National Broadcasting Company (NBC) transcript of interview with Tommie Smith, by Scott Boggins, June 19, 1998, New Orleans, Louisiana. I am grateful to Scott for sharing his work with me.

Chapter Nine

Documenting Myth

Racial Representation in Leon Gast's *When We Were Kings*

Julio Rodriguez

In decolonising the image of "the black male," while re-
constructing themselves, Black people have, of course,
exposed its pernicious origins in the preoccupations and
desires of white men. But white men cannot take back
the desire they have projected onto Black men, and also
maintain their traditional image of themselves. In challenging the images of Black masculinity, Black men
threaten the centrality of white masculinity. As Black
people, like women and gay men, dissect and reject the
conceptual hierarchies which construct them as subordinate, and struggle to transform the power relations they
express and maintain, the mantle of white manhood, its
preeminence once so seemingly obvious, looks increasingly frayed and threadbare.

—Lynne Segal[1]

The 1910 heavyweight championship bout between the white challenger
Jim Jeffries and the black champion Jack Johnson was supposed to be an
easy victory for the undefeated Jeffries. Jeffries's superior intellect and
Anglo-Saxon masculinity were supposed to vanquish the black brute.
Johnson thrashed Jeffries, and race riots occurred in numerous cities. Late
Victorian culture identified the powerful, large male body of the heavy-
weight prizefighter as the epitome of manhood, and hence of evolution.

The Johnson–Jeffries bout concerned evolutionary as much as racial supremacy. The possibility that a black male could be the epitome of manhood set off waves of panic across white America. Theatrical replays of the bout were outlawed. Johnson was hounded by authorities for consorting with white women and was finally forced into exile on trumped-up charges.

Sport often renders critical sociocultural moments clearly and concisely because in its ideal form it is the unsullied province of fair play and equality. Regardless of the real-world conditions of professional and amateur sports, the idea of the sporting contest—that the participants have engaged each other willingly as autonomous equals on a level playing field, with a set of rules that favor neither competitor—assumes that the outcome is indicative of some substantive form of resolution. A clear victor is supposed to emerge. However, since sporting contests are never conducted in the abstract, the contestants are saddled with variant discourses. Rather than providing a simple escape, a repudiation of serious issues, sport, due to its rules and assumptions, provides an ideal venue for debating matters of cultural import.

Some sports fit certain discourses more readily than others. By design, boxing pits two men in hand-to-hand combat before a crowd. It has been charged with sociocultural import on numerous occasions throughout Western history, most frequently addressing questions of racial superiority. After blacks came to dominate the ranks of heavyweight title holders, a long list of "Great White Hopes" ensued: Max Schmeling, Primo Carnera, Rocky Marciano, Jerry Quarry, and Gerry Cooney among others. Each white fighter carried "white hopes" of regaining supreme masculinity. Informing the rhetoric that changed their bouts into discourses on race, as opposed to simple sporting contests, is the popular misconception of Darwinism. As most Americans understand Darwin, the world is shaped through conflict and adaptation. A creature either adapts to shifts in its environment or perishes, thereby leaving only the fittest alive. When misapplied to race in the form of Social Darwinism, logic dictates that since the Anglo-Saxon race leads the world, it is the most highly evolved. This specious reasoning has been employed to justify any number of injustices, ranging from slavery to the lack of minorities in managerial positions in sports. In keeping with prior notions of masculinity, the heavyweight champion is construed as the "baddest man on the planet" and the pinnacle of evolution; hence the need for a white champion. More so than any other sport, boxing lends itself to the framework of "survival of the fittest" and is historically dotted with matches that celebrate the latest racially loaded incarnation of supreme masculinity.

Leon Gast's 1997 Academy Award–winning documentary *When We Were Kings* records such a historical moment. The film captures the October 30, 1974, "Rumble in the Jungle" title bout between George Foreman and Muhammad Ali, the concert that coincided with the bout, and the events leading up to the fight. The Foreman-Ali bout marked seven years since Ali had been stripped of his title for his refusal to be drafted into the military on the grounds of religious convictions. After a three-and-a-half-year layoff and a handful of uneven performances since his return, this was Ali's first opportunity to vie for what he had always considered his title. Foreman, at age twenty-five was seven years younger than Ali and had brutally taken the title from Joe Frazier in 1972. A year later, in his only serious title defense, Foreman had demolished Ken Norton in a two-round rout, and he was coming into this defense the heavy favorite. *Time* had categorized Ali's cause as an "apparently hopeless" one, and odds makers had Ali as a three-to-one underdog.[2] Ali had provided only flashes of his former brilliant self in the years since his return, and there seemed to be a consensus about his lost skills and fading aura. In his coverage of the January 28, 1974, Ali-Frazier fight, the marquee bout of the Ali comeback to that point, *Sport Illustrated*'s Mark Kram characterized the bout as "largely . . . a script of pride, profit, and decline, two men on a precipice, and possibly only one will pick up the remnants of his talent and go on."[3] Kram argued that Ali's "messianic aura" was no more. Even though the fight turned out to be a memorable one, with Ali being the one to pick up the "remnants of his talents," the prevailing feeling leading up to the "Rumble in the Jungle" was that Ali was genuinely in danger. Only Ali displayed any confidence in his chances, and the only chance anyone gave him was based on his ability to dance in the ring.

Once in the ring, Ali proceeded to stun the world. Rather than dance, Ali shuffled to the center of the ring, raised Foreman's ire with a pair of right-hand leads, and then backpedaled to the ropes and stayed there.[4] Foreman, surprised and pleased, moved in for the kill and began hammering Ali mercilessly with body blow after body blow. Not even Ali's corner knew of his plan. After spending the first round on the ropes, the corner urged Ali to dance and stay off the ropes. Ali countered with "Don't talk. I know what I'm doing."[5] The second and third rounds were replays of the first. By the fourth, everyone, including Foreman, knew Ali simply planned to let the champ punch himself out and then pick him apart.

There wasn't much Foreman could do. The plan seemed to work by default. Foreman kept coming forward, and by the eighth round, he was out of gas. With a pair of crisp combinations, Ali sent Foreman to the canvas and fixed the term *rope-a-dope* in popular consciousness forever.

Presumably, the moment that *When We Were Kings* captures is Ali stunning the boxing world once again. Were it simply a chronicle of the evening and the event it certainly would not have been an Academy Award winner. The moment captured by Gast is worthy of distinction because of how he recasts the bout. In recording the crowning of the latest incarnation of supreme masculinity, Gast revisits notions of racial superiority and Social Darwinism. Needless to say, this was not a fight between two opponents of differing races; yet the film sets up the black-white dichotomy that was familiar to fight fans and aficionados drawn to those white-black bouts specifically because of the racially charged atmosphere. The "We" in the title refers not to Ali and Foreman, as one would think, but to George Plimpton and Norman Mailer, who are the film's primary narrators, and, by extension, to Gast. The film is not about the Foreman-Ali bout but really concerns itself with the significance of the moment as seen through the eyes of Plimpton and Mailer. Ali comes to represent a particular moment in racial evolution. The film preserves the moment when *they* (Ali, Mailer, Plimpton, Gast) were kings, when they achieved the title of "fittest."

With *When We Were Kings*, Gast has made a specific kind of documentary. The film is a response to a sense of loss, a lack of wholeness, the passing of white masculinity. Not only have white males become second-tier athletes, but their previously unquestioned cultural authority and power has been or is being stripped along both racial and gender lines. Through taxidermy and the practices of ethnographic cinema, Gast recreates Ali's victory over Foreman as the defining moment in the evolution of Ali and white masculinity, an instant when the two shared sensibilities and delivered a final blow before ungracefully fading from the limelight. Since no cinematic representation can ever be fully objective, Gast has captured the Ali-Foreman bout as he, primarily through the reminiscences of Plimpton and Mailer, thought it had been. Fatimah Rony terms this impulse to capture things as the filmmaker perceived them to have been "taxidermy." "Taxidermy seeks to make that which is dead look as if it were still living."[6] Paradoxically, in order for the subject to seem most alive, it needs to be presented as having existed in a former era. Obviously, Muhammad Ali and George Foreman are not dead so the film's exclusion of their remembrances of the fight and the events leading up to it serve the same purpose. Ali and Foreman are present, but only in film clips of the event. The fact that their nineties embodiments are absent leads one to the realization that the film is not about them but about the narrators, or at least the narrators' experience of them. Since the subjects aren't dead, what becomes clear is that which *is* dead is the moment in October 1974. That moment has come to mean enough in the minds of Gast, Plimpton, and Mailer that it deserved to be preserved in a particular state.

To comprehend fully the Ali-Plimpton/Mailer connection, we need to digress into a brief and incomplete sketch of the liberal left in the early seventies. Comprised mostly of white artists, writers, journalists, commentators, and academics, the liberal left came out of the heady idealism of the late sixties and for a brief period boasted the embodiment of the interests of ordinary, mainstream United States. Both Plimpton and Mailer were among this white liberal elite. But there was a backlash against the liberal left in the years prior to the Ali-Foreman fight. Lyndon Johnson's Great Society programs were blamed for the economic stagnation that plagued the United States in the early seventies. The programs were accused of creating a cycle of poverty and a dependency of the poor on the welfare state. Through a combination of fact and political manipulation, liberal notions of economic justice and equality were interpreted as a smoke screen designed to serve the ambitions of a narrow social elite.[7] In response to this attack, writers turned to the company of boxers and boxing as metaphor to connect them with something real, something they indulgently perceived as working- or lower-class.[8] This shift from elite whiteness to working-class blackness was nothing new for Mailer. In *The White Negro,* subtitled *Superficial Reflections on the Hipster* (and Mailer considered himself one), he argues that in the Hip lies a wedding of white and black. To this marriage the white brought social activism in the form of the bohemian and the juvenile delinquent; the black provided the cultural dowry. Mailer argued:

> The Negro had stayed alive and begun to grow by following the needs of his body where he could. . . . The Negro could rarely afford the sophisticated inhibitions of civilization, and so he kept for his survival the art of the primitive, he lived in the enormous present, he subsisted for his Saturday night kicks, relinquishing the pleasures of the mind for the more obligatory pleasures of the body, and in his music he gave voice to the character and quality of his existence, to his rage and the infinite variations of joy, lust, languor, growl, cramp, pinch, scream and despair of his orgasm.[9]

As high-minded as Mailer thinks himself to be, this presentation of the Negro is simply an extension of the racist dichotomy that associates white with the mind and black with the body. By appropriating the black body, Mailer attempts to inject a degree of authenticity and masculinity to the Hipster. The process was much the same in the early 1970s. Instead of producing something "useless, indulgent, overly cerebral, elitist . . . the embattled writer" now feels involved with something of relevance to his audience.[10] This appropriation of the black masculine/boxing metaphor is taken to a new level in the fight sequence of Gast's film. Gast's taxidermic approach, in which Ali embodies Plimpton and Mailer's struggle, marks another instance of white effete masculinity appropriating "blackness." There is no real Ali in the film, only white writers.[11]

Fundamental to the process of taxidermy is the idea that one is preserving an evolutionary moment in one's history. In her discussion of the film representation of Nanook in *Nanook of the North*, Rony suggests that Nanook served as "something of a mirror for the white audience: he too was from the North, and . . . was seen as embodying the Protestant values of patriarchy, industriousness, independence and courage."[12] At the time of the film's release, the Nordic race, a term used to refer to whites of Northern European descent, was fearful of being eradicated by racial mixing. The untainted figure of a robust Nanook calmed some of those fears. Gast's reliance on the memories and interpretations of Plimpton and Mailer works in much the same manner. Rather than relying on the memories of the participants, framing the evening's events through the white male narrators allows for Ali to become an embodiment of white masculinity. Gripped by fear that their time as figures of cultural and social power has passed, white masculinity in the form of Plimpton and Mailer turns to representations of Ali and Foreman to calm their fears. This process is heightened in Mailer's retelling of the first round of the fight, a key segment that will be discussed shortly.

To further present the quixotic moment as an evolutionary one, Gast relies on romantic primitivism. Zaire, the site of the fight, and Zaireans are depicted as violent, cannibalistic, simple, and childlike. The film opens with a montage of African children singing and dancing in the streets, Ali at different moments in his career talking about boxing and beauty, scenes from Zaire's revolution, stills from civil rights demonstrations in America, clips of the concert that accompanied the fight, and a Ku Klux Klan (KKK) rally. The opening sequences establish a continuum between the struggles of blacks in the United States and in Africa, placing Ali as an intermediary between the two. The connection between Africa, Ali, and blacks in the United States is underscored throughout the film. Malik Bowens, an African artist present during the "Rumble in the Jungle," identifies Ali as being the more African of the two boxers despite Ali's lighter skin color. According to Bowens, Africans interpreted Ali's anti-Vietnam stance as a statement on behalf of the Third World. This was not the first time Ali had identified with the Third World. A year prior, in 1973, he defeated Dutch heavyweight Rudi Lubbers in the former Dutch colony of Indonesia. Economics was at the heart of choosing Jakarta as the site for the Lubbers bout (as it was whenever Ali fought abroad). Lubbers clearly became representative of Dutch colonialism, and Indonesians were eager to see their political victory replayed in the ring. Crass commercialism aside, Ali always enjoyed the hometown advantage when he fought in the Third World.

Conversely, Foreman becomes identified with the First World. His arrival in Zaire is a public relations disaster. Foreman gets off the plane with his German shepherd, the same dog the Belgians used to police Africans when Zaire was a Belgian colony. Even Foreman's name proved troubling. Aside from its obvious First World connection when compared to Ali, Foreman "in dialect sounded vaguely like a word that means `Flemish,' thus fostering the notion that somehow Ali had lured into the ring the embodiment of Belgian colonial repression replete with swagger stick."[13] Foreman's connection to years of empire and his status as "their" champion effectively dismiss him as representative of Africans or black Americans. No doubt, the memory of Foreman's performance at the 1968 Olympics helped cement his connection to the First World. Against the backdrop of Tommy Smith and John Carlos protesting against white oppression in the United States by offering the black power salute from the medal stand, Foreman's jaunt through the ring waving the Stars and Stripes seemed particularly ill-timed and Uncle Tom–ish. The six-year lag did little to fade that memory, particularly when juxtaposed with Ali's status abroad.

It would be most fortuitous if the First World–Third World dichotomy were simply a filmic creation, but the reality is that the 1974 press coverage played this angle up considerably. *Newsweek* noted that on his first trip to Kinshasa, Zaire's capital, Foreman's manager, Dick Sadler, "noted the primitive landscape, the poverty and the heat, and he cracked, 'Thank God our grandpappies caught that boat!'"[14] Aside from being astoundingly thoughtless and glib, the comment underscores the connection between

Foreman and the West. *Newsweek* was also kind enough to relate the tale of one of Foreman's sparring partners, who was enjoying "an interlude with one of Kinshasa's bargain-priced prostitutes when he noticed a huge butterfly fluttering near his head. To his shock, the girl plucked the butterfly out of the air and ate it. 'A delicacy,' she explained. The fighter promptly got sick."[15] By contrast, the stories told of Ali, and Ali himself, played up his connection to the Zaireans. Ali enhanced his training sessions with bongo drums and dances. Immediately after Foreman's dismissal of Ken Norton, Ali began working the Zaire connection by taunting Foreman with "If you behave like that my African friends will put you in a pot."[16] Not one to waste an opportunity to create a home-court advantage, Ali characterized Foreman as a "Belgian oppressor" as he diligently courted the Zaireans. What finally cements the real-world connections the film highlights is a spectacular bit of prose by Plimpton. What follows is the final paragraph of Plimpton's report of the fight:

> Kinshasa is a city symbolically appropriate to the fall and shifts of dominance and power. Everywhere, usually at the end of a broad avenue, or in front of a government building, are the great bare stone pedestals, now flat on top, with weeds growing in the cracks, on which once stood the imposing statues of Belgian colonial rule. On the promontory above the stretch of the Zaire which is still called Stanley's pool, the famous statue of the explorer once stood, peering up the river under the palm of one hand like an Indian chief. It too has been pulled down and lies in a giant shed near the National Museum in a jumble of cast-iron horses and kings. The roof of the shed is tin. On the dawn of the day the heavyweight crown shifted hands, the sound of the rain on the roof must have been deafening.[17]

What becomes clear in Plimpton's extended metaphor is that the First World–Third World connections were present in 1974 and that the press, if not the American populace, was sensitive to Ali's identification with the Third World and the cultural significance of his victory. Additionally, all the press coverage of the fight exhibits a willingness to paint Africa, Zaire, and Zaireans as primitive and barbarous. This depiction is not only represented in *When We Were Kings*, but it is a key component of Gast's overall purpose.[18]

The connection between a primitive rendering of Africa and Ali is mediated and furthered through the presentation of the musicians performing at the concert accompanying the bout. The film constitutes the musicians as mirror images of Africans. Repeatedly, shots of the musicians dancing, rehearsing, performing, packing, traveling, and partying are jux-taposed with images of Africans dancing, singing, eating, drumming, car-rying goods on their heads, and performing in tribal dress. The juxtaposi-tion of images of Zaireans and live grubs and insects, which the audience surmises will be food for the Zaireans, enhances their representation as primitives. Ali enters this relationship through the musicians. After a morning run, Ali tells the camera he's going to listen to some soul music, gives a small speech on the importance of black music to black Americans, and later attends the concert. Earlier, he greeted the musicians when they arrived in Zaire, and his speech on the importance of black music is framed between clips of B. B. King's concert performance. Furthering the connection to primitivism is the rendition of Ali: "It is always the gregari-ous, quick-witted Ali who performs for Gast's camera."[19] The black male as congenial entertainer ready to break out in song and dance at a mo-ment's notice, the Sambo, is an old stereotype rooted in the depiction of American slaves as simple and happy. Collectively, the musicians, Africans, and Ali render blacks paternalistically as childlike, playful, and primitive. However, Ali's composition as essentially black is not that simple, and herein lies the film's brilliance. For all his "blackness," Ali's identity is slip-pery enough for him to represent "whiteness" as well. The shift enables Ali to become as much a mirror for Gast, Plimpton, and Mailer as he is for Africa and black America, and quite possibly an evolutionary stage from "blackness" to "whiteness."

Curiously enough, Ali first becomes identified with "whiteness" through Foreman. In the film, Foreman is described as a destroyer, a mummy, a monster, a nightmare, and as possessing negritude—the flip-side of the Sambo stereotype. Ali, by contrast, is, according to Spike Lee in the film, "a beautiful specimen, a fighting machine. Handsome, articu-late, funny, charismatic, and whoopin' ass too." In this trope, Foreman be-comes the blacker of the two, embodying white America's fears and open-ing Ali to the possibility of being something other than black. In Lee's de-scription of Ali, his beauty, intelligence, and power particularly are attributes that hegemonic white masculinity uses to describe itself and gives as evidence of its inherent superiority. This wasn't the first time Ali slid up and down the color line or open to interpretation. In fights against Sonny Liston and Joe Frazier, Ali deployed the kind of dehuman-izing language whites have historically aimed at black males to build up prefight hype and to get inside the head of his opponents. On another oc-casion, Ali tried to "out-black" Frazier, calling him an Uncle Tom "and an 'honorary white,' when in fact Frazier had grown up dirt poor in South Carolina."[20]

Twenty years has softened the harshness of America's response to Ali's refusal to fight in Vietnam. Contemporary public discourse on the Vietnam conflict coincides with Ali's 1967 view. Over time, Ali came to represent white society at large by virtue of his position as "their" champion even as he enjoyed the adulation of black America. After his victory in Kinshasa, he visited Gerald Ford in the White House and later campaigned for Jimmy Carter. Even in 1974, his anti-integrationist views echoed the beliefs of much of mainstream America.

Mainstream culture may have appropriated Ali long ago, but what cements Ali's "whiteness" in the film is the fight sequence. Mailer and Plimpton speak for Ali. Both give a rendition of what was going through Ali's head during the fight. Gast has choreographed fight footage to coincide with Mailer and Plimpton's statements, creating a virtually seamless representation of the "truth" of the fight. By dismissing with any inclusion of Ali's or Foreman's rendition of the evening's events, what Gast has created is a film based on a true story. The fight did occur and Ali did vanquish Foreman, but the narrative surrounding the fight is a fiction created by Plimpton, Mailer, and Gast. Of particular importance is Mailer's narration of the fight. Mailer explains Ali's use of the "right-hand lead" as a tool designed to knock Foreman out in the first round that fell short and, in the process, infuriated Foreman. In what may be the film's defining moment, Mailer describes Ali's soul-searching between rounds. Mailer contends that Ali has come face to face with a personal nightmare and, in the break between rounds one and two, must muster a new resolve to vanquish his greatest foe. With each statement attributed to Ali, Gast crops shots of Ali standing in his corner tighter and tighter, until the resolve is found and Ali unveils the rope-a-dope and surprises the world.[21]

The mirroring of Plimpton and Mailer in Ali returns us to Rony's concept of taxidermy. An additional aspect of romantic primitivism is a lust for the native body. Clearly, Mailer's description of the physical pleasures available to the Negro borders on desire. Gast's cinematography is equally lustful. Among the shots that connect the musicians to Africans and to Ali is one detailing the baring of a performer's breasts to the audience. This erotic display is in keeping with footage of Ali training and with blacks' reputed superiority in carnal matters. Whereas Foreman is not shown without a shirt until fight night, Ali's training is nearly always bare-chested. Spike Lee already commented on Ali's beauty, but so do Mailer and Plimpton. Much is made of Ali's form. Plimpton and Mailer's appropriation of it can be readily interpreted as lust. For Rony, however, this lust is conjoined with images of impending death.[22] This holds true for *When We Were Kings* as well. While death is not visually invoked, Mailer comments that after the fight in Zaire, Ali "harmed" himself in the twenty-two bouts he fought prior to finally retiring. This comment follows a montage of stills from Ali's prime, set to the tune "When We Were Kings." The invocation of loss, if not death, is palpable.

The harm Ali did was obviously physical; Parkinson's cannot be blamed for all of Ali's current state. But the harm Mailer refers to is to Ali's mythic power. As a boxer, Ali hung on too long. By the end of his career, Cassius Clay and Ali circa 1974 were distant memories hazed by nostalgia. The "messianic aura" was lost in a slew of sparkless bouts, needless comebacks, and embarrassing defeats. *When We Were Kings* is an effort to undo the harm Ali did to himself, to bring him back to life—and, by extension, Gast, Mailer, and Plimpton. "The irony is that in order to look most alive, the 'native' must be perceived as always already dead."[23] The taxidermic approach to documentary filmmaking is expressive of a desire to preserve the purity of a life unspoiled by the advance of civilization. While certainly civilized, the mid-sixties marked the high point for the liberal left, and, even though the Zaire fight came nearly a decade later, the Ali presented in the film is one circa 1967. Aside from his anti-Vietnam stance, Ali is not politicized. His figure is not complex. His problematic Muslim identity is not discussed. He, Plimpton, Mailer, and Gast are frozen in time. In the cinematic re-creation of Ali as an embodiment of "whiteness," then, what has also perished, the thing that civilization has soiled, is that moment where Plimpton, Mailer, and Gast were evolutionary spearheads. Good intentions and past political leanings notwithstanding, the "harm" done to them is, of course, their ungraceful ouster from cultural dominance. As middle-aged white males, they symbolize besieged white masculinity. Imaginary though that siege may be, the early nineties were rife with tales of the demise of white masculinity. Now that power has supposedly shifted Third World–ward, other-ward, the film revisits the moment and reframes it with the good guys (read "white") firmly allied with a Third World–identified Ali. Perhaps Gast (and Mailer and Plimpton) performs a rope-a-dope of his own, coming off the cultural ropes after taking a pounding from women and people of color to deliver a lasting blow for the white male.

Muhammad Ali was an anachronism during the majority of his life-time. He steadfastly refused to conform to any stereotype of the black American male. As a Black Muslim, he embodied the fears of mainstream white America—a powerful and militant black caucus—at the same time speaking out against integration and racial mixing. He used the rhetoric of racist whites to berate black opponents and mercilessly punished Floyd Patterson, who was a staunch supporter and practitioner of integration. He spoke out against the Vietnam War before it was fashionable, popular-izing himself in international circles yet damning himself at home. To fur-ther his career, he played up his blackness as well as his appeal to main-stream white America. In 1980, he went on a mission to Africa on behalf of President Carter to drum up support for an Olympic boycott; African leaders informed Ali that they regarded the boycott of the games as Cold War posturing. In 1984 he backed Reagan for office, but in 1988 he was in Jesse Jackson's camp.[24] Gast uses Ali's fluidity to his own advantage, capi-talizing on white America's ambivalence and confusion regarding its feel-ings toward black America.

In triumph or tribulation, in celebration or contempt, Ali was invested with white America's conflicts and contradictions.

"For us white liberals he helps assuage our guilt for having negative feelings about blacks," wrote Ali biographer Henry Korn. "For other whites, he may represent confirmation of their favorite notions about blacks: pushy, uppity, exploitive of others, radical, potent, even magical."[25]

Using Ali as a mirror for Plimpton, Mailer, and the white liberal left is not a stretch. As each heads into his twilight years, the film may be, more than anything else, a final example of a particular type of white male artist granting himself relevancy in a world that continues to fragment away from the grand ideal narratives he espoused in his youth.

An individual who watches a sporting event live constructs and derives any number of meanings from the experience. These result from the inter-action between the meanings the contest has built into it (rules, history, myth) and the beliefs and values the individual carries to the event. How-ever, viewing a televised/filmed/recorded event is a different experience. Any meanings derived are affected by the framing of the event by an-nouncers, various mediators, and cinematographers and directors.[26] In the case of *When We Were Kings*, the framing language is the rhetoric of civi-lization. Ali's connection to the "primitive" Africans and "barbarous" mu-sicians sets him up as a stepping-stone to a more evolved human stage: whiteness. In keeping with Spencerian interpretations of Darwinian thought, "human races were assumed to evolve from simple savagery, through violent barbarism, to advanced and valuable civilization."[27] Of course, the only people to achieve "valuable civilization" were Anglo-Saxons. Ali is consistently framed as being between primitive and fully evolved civilizations.

Since the turn of the century, Social Darwinism has slowly lost its grip on the rhetoric of civilization. However, given the ideal conditions of the boxing ring, "survival of the fittest" has never been more apt. With white masculinity all but absent from the upper echelons of the sporting world, white males have lost a key facet of their superiority. Through their identification with Ali, Gast, Mailer, Plimpton, and white middle-aged film viewers are able to attain a quality of masculinity increasingly denied them and to continue to fancy themselves the spearheads of evolution.

Notes

1. Lynn Segal, *Slow Motion: Changing Masculinities, Changing Men* (New Brunswick, NJ: Rutgers University Press, 1990), 204.

2. "Muhammad on the Mountaintop," *Time*, November 11, 1974, 84–85.

3. *Sports Illustrated*, January 21, 1974, 23.

4. The right-hand lead is an insult to an opponent. Delivering a straight right-hand punch takes a fraction of a second longer than a left. Leading with a right implies disrespect for your opponent's skills.

5. George Plimpton, "Breaking a Date for the Dance," *Sports Illustrated*, November 11, 1974, 26.

6. Fatimah Rony, *The Third Eye: Race, Cinema, and Ethnographic Spectacle* (Durham, NC: Duke University Press, 1996), 101.

7. Barbara Ehrenreich, *Fear of Falling* (New York: Harper Perennial, 1989).

8. Gerald Early, *The Culture of Bruising* (Hopewell: Ecco Press, 1994) 22.

9. Norman Mailer, *The White Negro: Superficial Reflections on the Hipster* (San Francisco: City Lights Books, 1957) 4.

10. Ibid.

11. Ali's connection with the left goes deeper than metaphor. For many on the left, Ali represented the political concept of blackness. During his exile from boxing, Ali earned a living giving lectures at colleges, winning support from student radicals.

12. Rony, *Third Eye*, 108.

13. George Plimpton, "They'll Be Swinging in the Rain," *Sports Illustrated*, September 30, 1974, 37.

14. "It Takes a Heap of Salongo," *Newsweek*, September 23, 1974, 72.

15. "Ali—You Gotta Believe," *Newsweek*, November 11, 1974, 71.

16. "Five Minute Massacre," *Time*, April, 8, 1974, 57.

17. Plimpton, "Breaking a Date for the Dance," 28.

18. For a more complete discussion of the fight's political overtones, see Grant Farred's "Feasting on Foreman: The Problematics of Postcolonial Identification," *Camera Obscura*, 39 (1996): 53.

19. Ibid., 58.

20. David Remnick, "American Hunger," *New Yorker*, October 23, 1998, 57.

21. Gast chooses to ignore Ali's remarks in interviews after the fight that the right-hand lead and rope-a-dope were part of a calculated strategy Ali had prepared months before the actual bout.

22. See Rony's discussion of Nanook's igloo scenes in *Third Eye*, 113.

23. Ibid.

24. For a more complete sketch of Ali's shifting allegiances see Mike Marqusee's "Sport and Stereotype: From Role Model to Muhammad Ali," *Race and Class* 36,4 (1995): 1–29.

25. Frederic Cople Jaher, "White America Views Jack Johnson, Joe Louis, and Muhammad Ali," in *Sport in America: New Historical Perspectives*, ed. Donald Spivey (Westport: Greenwood Press, 1985), 180.

26. Michael Messner et al., "Separating the Men from the Girls: The Gendered Language of Televised Sports," *Gender and Society* 7,1 (1993): 219–233.

27. Gail Bederman, *Manliness and Civilization: A Cultural History of Gender and Race in the United States, 1880–1917* (Chicago: University of Chicago Press, 1995), 25.

Part III

Sports and Race in the Post–Cold War Era

Chapter Ten

The Silence of the Rams
How St. Louis School Children Subsidize the Super Bowl Champs

George Lipsitz

When the St. Louis Rams defeated the Tennessee Titans on January 23, 2000, to win the Super Bowl, the team's players, coaches, and management deserved only part of the credit. Sports journalists covering the game cited the passing of Kurt Warner and the running of Marshall Faulk as the key factors in the Rams' victory. Others acknowledged the leadership of head coach Dick Vermeil, the player personnel moves of general manager John Shaw, and the financial acumen of team owner Georgia Frontiere. But no one publicly recognized the contributions to the Rams' victory made by the 45,473 children enrolled in the St. Louis city school system. Eighty-five percent of these students are so poor that they qualify for federally subsidized lunches. Eighty percent of them are African American. They did not score touchdowns, make tackles, kick field goals, or intercept passes for the team. But revenue diverted from the St. Louis school system through tax abatements and other subsidies to the Rams made a crucial difference in giving the team the resources to win a Super Bowl.

Children in St. Louis attend underfunded schools staffed by underpaid and inexperienced teachers. Beginning teachers in the district receive salaries of $26,501 with a B.A., $26,511 with an M.A., and $29,443 with an Ed.D. or Ph.D. The average salary for teachers in the district is $33,269 per year.[1] Compensation is so meager in St. Louis that teachers' union president Sheryl Davenport reports that the district cannot even attract qualified *substitute* teachers in competition with neighboring school systems. Consequently, teacher assistants frequently staff classrooms when the primary instructor is absent. Out of 104 school districts in the region, the pay scale for teachers in St. Louis is the seventy-third lowest.

During the 1990–1991 academic year, more Black students dropped out of the city's high schools (1,421) than graduated from them (966).[2] For every hundred students who begin the ninth grade in St. Louis schools, only thirty graduate.[3] The total dropout rate from the city schools in 1998–1999 was 18.7 percent, the highest in Missouri and more than three times the state average of 5.5 percent.[4] During the 1999 Missouri School Improvement Program review, the city's schools met only three of the state's eleven performance standards. Yet, at the same time, tax abatements for profitable businesses, including the Rams football team, deprived St. Louis children of $17 million annually in educational funding.[5]

St. Louis's school-age children suffer a class injury because of the subsidies received by Rams. Students from low-income families lose access to educational dollars so that these can be spent guaranteeing the millionaire owner of the Rams the largest possible profits. The injury in this case is also a racial one, and not merely because most of the students in the city school system are Black. The starkly unequal educational opportunities offered to students in different districts within the St. Louis metropolitan area stem directly from carefully designed and deliberate discrimination against African Americans. The diversion of funds to the Rams is only the latest in a series of measures designed to prevent Blacks in St. Louis from competing fairly with whites by relegating them to separate and unequal segments of the area's housing, labor, and educational infrastructure.

In 1983 as a federal judge ruled in the St. Louis school desegregation case (1972), Black students in city schools have had their constitutional rights violated systematically by the city of St. Louis and St. Louis County, by the state of Missouri, and by the federal government for more than fifty years. The concentration of Black students in city schools with "high poverty" populations is the cumulative effect of the ways in which school district lines have been drawn, the location of low-income housing projects in the city solely in Black neighborhoods, the county's use of zoning to reject public housing, steering people with vouchers for subsidized housing to Black neighborhoods, the subsidies for "white flight" granted by the Federal Housing Authority, and the refusal by the state's housing development corporation to publicize, promote, or even adhere to federal fair housing regulations.[6] The subsidies to the Rams not only augment the power of rich people over poor people; they are also an illustrative example of what I have referred to elsewhere as "the possessive investment in whiteness."[7]

The Rams are not the only St. Louis corporation to receive tax abatements or other subsidies, and some of the money that the city loses through tax abatements is recouped from increased revenue to the city from sales and earnings taxes. But because school funding remains largely dependent on property taxes, the recouped revenues cannot be spent on education. According to one conservative estimate, for every dollar the city abates in property taxes, the schools lose fifty-seven cents.[8] In addition, despite extravagant claims about tax abatements and other subsidies as investments that increase the general wealth of cities, the St. Louis case shows clearly that subsidies for professional sports teams and other corporations do not "trickle down" to the majority of the population but instead function largely as a means for transferring wealth and resources from the poor and the middle class to the rich.

To attract a football franchise, St. Louis's business and political leadership secured approval from taxpayers to spend $270 million of public money (actually more than $700 million, counting interest payments over thirty years) to build a domed stadium as an addition to the city's downtown convention center.[9] The facility, constructed completely with public funds, stands twenty-one stories high and contains eight hundred thousand square feet of concrete block, a five hundred thousand-square-foot roof covering twelve acres, 595 miles of wire and cable, thirty-two escalators, and twelve passenger and freight elevators.

The great costs involved in building the stadium made it imperative for local officials to secure a team. After being denied a franchise by the National Football League's expansion committee, they turned their efforts toward convincing the Rams to move to St. Louis from Los Angeles. As part of their inducements, $45 million of tax revenues raised in St. Louis were given to Rams owner Georgia Frontiere to pay off debts incurred by the Rams in Los Angeles and to build a new practice site for the team in St. Louis. Paying off the mortgage on the Trans World (TWA) Dome in St. Louis will cost city, county, and state treasuries $24 million a year, or $55,000 per day for thirty years.[10] St. Louis County imposed a new hotel tax to pay its share of the debt, but the city of St. Louis and the state of Missouri make their contributions out of general revenues.[11]

The state of Missouri's contribution to the TWA Dome is particularly offensive because state agencies and officials have played a primary role in imposing impediments to educational opportunity on St. Louis's Black children. Missouri has the lowest per-capita taxation of all fifty states and ranks forty-third in educational spending per pupil.[12] Consequently, Missouri's schools depend more than schools in other states on local funding from property taxes—the source that most reflects the inequalities shaped by housing discrimination.[13] By minimizing the state's contribution to education, Missouri's government increases the value of segregated housing in suburban communities—where the presence of shopping centers and the high value of property allow for large expenditures on education with low tax rates—while decreasing the value of housing in inner cities or the largely Black suburbs of North St. Louis County, where low property values and high taxes are the rule.[14]

The specifically racist malice of state officials toward St. Louis's Black children became most evident in response to the remedies mandated by the courts in the St. Louis school desegregation case. Ruling that the city, county, state, and federal governments had violated the students' constitutional rights by collaborating to maintain an illegally segregated school system, the courts supervised the creation of a voluntary cross-district busing program that included the establishment of new magnet schools in the city of St. Louis. The courts also ordered the state of Missouri to encourage local governments to enforce fair housing laws and to promote integrated housing. Attorney General and later Governor John Ashcroft used the powers of office to lead massive resistance to the court's orders at every turn. He delayed the implementation of court orders, appealed even minor rulings to higher courts, and opposed every magnet school proposal. Ashcroft demonstrated an unusual understanding of the concepts of personal responsibility and respect for the law by arguing that the state should take no responsibility for the harm done to Black children by the segregated educational system that the state had helped to create. Most egregiously, he repeatedly lied to the people of Missouri, claiming that the state had never been found guilty of any wrongdoing when the clear finding of the federal judiciary was that the state of Missouri was obliged to pay most of the costs of the St. Louis desegregation program precisely because it had violated the constitutional rights of Black children.

Under Ashcroft's leadership, the state of Missouri spent nearly $4 million to fight desegregation and resist accountability for the damages perpetrated on Black children by the state's illegal actions.[15] Ashcroft's Missouri Housing Development Commission even refused the token step of drawing up a plan to enforce fair housing laws, as the court ordered it to do. In fact, the agency acquiesced to local resistance to new integrated housing so thoroughly that it did not even encourage local governments to enforce the fair housing laws already on the books.[16] Thus, a state unwilling to spend money on educating Black children showed itself to be quite willing to spend money to fight federal court orders mandating desegregation. That same state government also found it reasonable to obligate itself to pay subsidies to the Rams football team for thirty years.

State subsidies made the TWA Dome project possible. If huge sports arenas made money, private investors would pool their funds and build them with their own resources. For a domed stadium to be profitable, it must host an enormous number of events. Economists estimate that every $1 million of debt for stadium construction necessitates two dates with large crowds every year. A $100 million stadium requires two hundred football or baseball games, huge concerts, or religious revivals per year. A $270 million project such as the Trans World Dome needs 540 such dates for every 365-day year—a physical impossibility.[17] The Convention Center adjacent to the Trans World Dome hosts 240 events per year, but the size of conventions and car shows is too small to make a dent in the project's debt obligation. In fact, there would be no need for the domed stadium at all if not for the Rams and their eight regularly scheduled games each year. But these eight dates and sporadic exhibition or playoff games actually lose money because they produce so little revenue.[18]

The dome offers lavish accoutrements for select patrons, especially to the owners of 122 luxury boxes. League regulations require home teams to split ticket revenues on a sixty-forty basis with visiting teams, but these rules do not apply to luxury suites, enabling the Rams to keep all this money. The Rams pay only $25,000 in rent per game, an amount aptly characterized by one local journalist as barely enough to cover the cost of turning on the lights.[19] Thus, the team plays its games in a publicly funded stadium on a virtually cost-free basis. The Rams receive all revenue from ticket sales, concessions, and luxury seating. In the event that occupancy ever drops below 85 percent, the city's Convention and Visitors' Commission pledges the purchase of all unsold luxury suites and club seats, ranging in price from $700 to $110,000 per year per ticket. The Rams keep more than $24 million of the $36.7 million paid by Trans World Airlines (TWA) to have the stadium named the Trans World Dome, as well as 75 percent of all other advertising revenue up to $6 million and 90 percent of revenues from advertising above that figure. Business experts estimate that the value of these revenues alone to the Rams approaches $15–$20 million per year.[20]

While the Rams and their fans in expensive luxury suites are housed lavishly inside the TWA Dome, Black children in St. Louis confront the consequences of a segregated housing market. The shortage of affordable housing for all people in the St. Louis metropolitan area is exacerbated by racially discriminatory practices by realtors, lenders, and insurance brokers that confine African Americans to an artificially constricted housing market.[21] A 1990 survey of housing segregation found that St. Louis ranks as the eleventh most segregated city among the 232 largest metropolitan areas in the nation.[22] Some children have to move and change schools so often that they are never exposed to one form of pedagogy or curriculum for very long. St. Louis school administrators and teachers estimate that about half their students move to a new residence during any given school year.[23]

Many African American children in St. Louis live in dwellings with lead-based paint on the interior and exterior walls, exposing them to a strong likelihood of developing toxic amounts of lead in their bloodstreams. One out of every four children tested in St. Louis in 1998 was found to be lead-poisoned. Medical authorities discovered 1,833 *new* cases of lead poisoning in that year alone. Moreover, the full dimensions of lead poisoning in St. Louis remain unknown because the city has only enough funds to test 40 percent of preschool-age children.[24] National studies show that lead poisoning is even more of a racial injury than a class injury. Among the poorest families, Black children are almost twice as likely to contract lead poisoning as white children. Among the working poor, Black youths are three times as likely to develop lead poisoning as their white counterparts.[25]

The Trans World Dome was not the first gigantic structure in St. Louis built with public funds. The 630-foot-high Gateway Arch on the banks of the Mississippi River celebrates Thomas Jefferson's purchase of the Louisiana Territory and the westward expansion that followed it. Local residents ruefully note that it cost the U.S. government more to build the arch commemorating the Louisiana Purchase than it did to purchase the territory in the first place. But the construction and management of the Trans World Dome is more than a matter of local excess. Properly understood, the history of the Trans World Dome can help us understand some of the dynamics of contemporary urban economics and politics in cities all across the nation at the start of a new century.

Why would the political and business leadership of a city faced with crises in public education and public health extend such lavish subsidies to a spectator sport? What happens to a city or a society that neglects the education of its children in order to build sports arenas? Why is the racial injury done to Black children in St. Louis not just their problem but also a manifestation of how racial inequality in our society encourages a misallocation of resources, with ruinous consequences for the majority of the population?

Despite their high public profile, professional sports are not a significant sector of the U.S. economy. As colorful southern politician Sam Ervin once noted, the national sports industry is no larger than the pork-and-beans industry as a locus of economic activity and a generator of profit.[26] A study commissioned by the mayor of Houston found that the local sports industry in that city (including all nonsporting events held at the local domed stadium) had a smaller economic impact on the city than the Houston Medical Center, amounting to less than 1 percent of the local economy.[27] But professional sports teams play a privileged role in public-private partnerships for urban redevelopment everywhere, and their utility for such projects tells a great deal about the general priorities and practices of our society.

Justifications for projects like the Trans World Dome in St. Louis generally revolve around two related claims: (1) the benefit of professional sports to the economic and social health of the city and (2) the need to protect the competitive position of the local team in relation to wealthier franchises. These claims are worth investigating, not because they are true but rather because their blatant and obvious mendacity serves to occlude the actual role played by subsidies for sport in the urban economy in particular and in consumer culture more generally.

Discretionary spending on sports and other entertainments is limited. Subsidies for new arenas and entertainment districts tend to shift spending from one part of a city to another, but they do not often generate new wealth. The subsidies supplied to sports entrepreneurs create artificial advantages for some profit-making firms over others, misallocating resources away from more productive and more socially beneficial investments and imposing indirect burdens on small business owners and on middle- and lower-income taxpayers.

The experience of the Rams in St. Louis exemplifies the economic advantages available to team owners. Sports franchises generate a flow of cash that can be invested in many ways. They provide long-term appreciation as well. The cartel/monopoly status of sports ensures a shortage of franchises, inflating the value of all teams so that owners always make a profit when they sell the team to someone else. Sometimes they make money by selling the team to themselves, forming a separate corporation that now "owns" the club. This enables the owners to lend money to the team and receive the principal and interest back in return payments from the team. The payments appear as a debit on the club's financial records, but they provide the owners with a flow of cash from the operation. In addition, owners can provide themselves with large salaries and expense accounts as team executives.[28] But the most significant economic benefits that accrue to professional team owners come from tax benefits. The tax advantages available to owners of sports teams provide secret subsidies to professional franchises and impose secret burdens on taxpayers unable to take advantage of the favored treatment afforded team owners.

Financial institutions capable of selling thirty-year bonds for stadium construction profit directly from the municipal subsidies that make feasible the creation of new sporting venues. Other corporate executives can take their clients and coworkers to football games and deduct a large part of the expense from their taxes by claiming it as business-related entertainment. Nearly half of the gate receipts of most National Football League franchises now come from sales to corporations.[29] In addition, returns on municipal bonds to investors are not taxed by the federal government, a subsidy that costs the federal treasury more than $2 million a year for a project the size of the Trans World Dome.[30] As a writer in *Fortune* magazine concluded, "Professional sports teams qualify for so many tax benefits as to render their 'book' profit or loss figures meaningless."[31]

Sports teams can also claim players' salaries as depreciable assets for five years after buying a franchise, even though the cartel-like nature of professional football guarantees that the value of players on the roster does not actually depreciate. Depreciation credits can be extended by forming a new corporation and transferring ownership of the team to it, even when franchise ownership remains essentially in the same hands.[32] At the Trans World Dome, nearly $2 million a year of the cost of luxury boxes and club seats will be written off as business-entertainment deductions. Nearly $6 million a year will be lost to the federal treasury because profits on municipal bonds are tax free.[33]

Claims about the value of sports franchises to cities are often articulated but rarely investigated. The studies that have been conducted provide ample room for skepticism about the economic value of sports to the average worker, consumer, or business owner. One study of seventeen cities during the 1994 baseball players' strike found that sales of nondurable goods actually *increased* in thirteen of the cities without the revenue usually brought in by major league baseball. Another longitudinal study examined nine cities between 1965 and 1983 and found no significant correlation between building a stadium or attracting a new franchise on the one hand and economic growth on the other. In all but two of these cities, the opposite took place—the municipal share of regional income actually declined after the opening of a new stadium or the relocation of a team. Yet another study of fourteen cities hosting professional sports franchises could find no positive economic gain attributable to sports in most cases.[34]

Economist Robert Sorenson of the University of Missouri–St. Louis points out that no one has done a thorough study on the revenues generated by the Trans World Dome; "I don't think the city really wants to," he notes, observing, "they'd be embarrassed by what they'd find."[35] Seven hundred and twenty million dollars invested over thirty years could make an enormous difference in the economy of a city the size of St. Louis. Loans for housing renovation and acquisition could stabilize neighborhoods and offer individuals opportunities to accumulate assets that appreciate in value and could be passed along to future generations. Throughout the nineties, for example, the city of St. Louis lacked funds for assisting middle-income families interested in buying houses inside the city limits.[36] Loans to small businesses could increase employment opportunities and stimulate the local economy by generating wage earnings and profits almost certain to be spent in local stores, invested in local banks, spent on local goods and services, and used to increase municipal revenues.

A massive domed stadium, however, does none of this. It occupies a huge amount of tax-abated land, surrounded by freeways and parking garages that inhibit rather than enable the development of new businesses. It drains resources from the rest of the city through its needs for police protection, traffic control, and the construction and maintenance of electrical power, water, and sewer systems. It provides windfall profits for millionaire players, investors, and owners, almost none of them people who live in or even invest in the city. Moreover, its hidden subsidies shift tax burdens away from the wealthy, thereby imposing new (albeit unacknowledged) tax burdens on middle- and low-income workers.

In the past, stadium construction in St. Louis has failed to generate the revenues promised by city boosters. The Civic Center Redevelopment Corporation justified spending $20 million of public money (80 percent of the total cost) to build Busch Stadium for the St. Louis Cardinals base-ball team in 1966. They promised that tax abatements for the stadium would enable the Cardinals to give the city $540,000 in payments, in lieu of taxes, within ten years. But the team paid only $269,324 to the city in lieu of taxes in 1976, while downtown retail establishments discovered no increase in business because of the stadium. In 1981, the Anheuser-Busch brewery that owned the Cardinals (and which enjoyed the free publicity that came from having a stadium with the same name as one of their brands of beer) threatened to move the team out of St. Louis unless the Civic Center Redevelopment Corporation gave them full ownership of the stadium and control over parking, concessions, adjacent offices, and ho-tels. Waging what he later described as "a skillful public relations cam-paign," the brewery's president claimed that the increased holdings would enable the team to compete for better players. But he knew what the pub-lic did not: that concerns about the competitive position of the Cardinals were only a smoke screen, that the heart of the matter was "essentially a real estate deal, a very big real estate deal. And, for Anheuser-Busch . . . a very good deal."[37]

The brewery offered a ridiculously low bid of $30.2 million for the en-tire package, which was valued at somewhere between $75 and $90 mil-lion. When a competitor offered a bid of $58.9 million, the brewery broke off negotiations and used its influence behind closed doors, eventually succeeding in gaining a controlling interest over the properties in ques-tion. The brewery paid $3 million to purchase the team in 1953, added $5 million toward the cost of the new stadium in 1976, and may have paid as little as $53 million in 1981, to emerge in control of most of the real estate in the southern part of downtown St. Louis.[38]

In the mid-1990s, Anheuser-Busch sold the Cardinals to a new group of investors that included the corporation that owns the city's only daily newspaper, the *St. Louis Post-Dispatch*. Pointing to the revenues available to the Rams, the new ownership group immediately began to complain about "antiquated" Busch Stadium (then only thirty years old) and started using their influence to get the state of Missouri to pass enabling legisla-tion for a new baseball stadium, to be financed with $120 million in cash and real estate contributions from the Cardinals and $250 million in pub-lic money. The plan called for tax abatements that would cost the city and its public schools an additional $600,000 every year.[39]

St. Louis's subsidies to the owners of sports teams, while neglecting the educational and health needs of its children, may seem the product of the particular problems of that city: a metropolis devastated by capital flight, deindustrialization, and economic restructuring and left with few other feasible options for urban renewal and redevelopment. Certainly, distinctly local factors inflect every aspect of the Trans World Dome deal. But the significance of the ways in which African American St. Louis school children and some of their poor white classmates have been forced to subsidize the professional football franchise in their city lies less in local factors than in larger transformations that have taken place in the United States over the past thirty years, which have decisively altered the meanings of local place, politics, and property. However extreme, the St. Louis experience is a representative part of a larger pattern.

In their generative study of urban economics, John Logan and Harvey Molotch argue that urban investors try to trap capital in the areas they own in order to win advantages against competitors elsewhere in the city. Downtown real estate investors and owners try to enhance the value of their property by making their part of town the locus of profitable activity. They increase their profits considerably when they secure public assistance for land acquisition, development, and construction, as well as for tax abatements.[40] In addition, inequalities among as well as within cities force small local units to compete with one another for capital to such a degree that few can afford to withhold subsidies from developers.

During the late industrial era when Keynesian economics prevailed (1933–1980), urban redevelopment in North America coalesced around pro-growth coalitions led by business leaders, managed by elected officials, but supported largely by urban voters. These coalitions often pursued disastrous policies that destroyed inner-city homes in order to build highways, office buildings, and cultural attractions oriented toward the interests of suburban commuters.[41] Yet, to secure better spaces for large corporate headquarters and to build the kinds of cultural institutions required to recruit top-rank executives (symphony halls, art museums, theaters), local elites had to offer concessions to a broader population. Banks with money invested in conventional mortgages; industrialists in need of a healthy and educated workforce made charitable contributions to social service agencies; and politicians needing voter approval for the bond issues that financed new developments made sure that their constituents received services from the city. Bankers, business leaders, and politicians all found themselves (for different reasons) attentive to "place" in the local region on which their well-being depended.

The postindustrial era helped "delocalize" capitalism. Mergers made local corporations part of transnational conglomerates. Deregulation made it easier for banks to neglect local investment. Computer-generated automation allowed for "outsourcing," turning high-wage skilled jobs that had to be performed by educated workers in urban areas into low-wage unskilled tasks that could be done by virtually anyone in virtually any place. Containerization and capital flight enabled management to ship industrial production overseas; forty-four thousand manufacturing workers in St. Louis alone lost their jobs between 1979 and 1982. Even before the Reagan presidency, government programs established to aid urban areas were restructured and began funneling benefits away from the inner city and toward the suburbs, especially funds to develop infrastructures for new (often racially segregated) developments.[42] An astounding increase in the use of industrial-development bonds and tax-increment financing treated private for-profit developments as if they were public services, shifting resources away from taxpayers and toward businesses that found themselves strapped for capital. State and local governments sold only $6.2 billion of bonds for commercial projects in 1975, but that total climbed to $44 billion by 1982. Because these bonds are tax exempt, they cost the federal treasury $7.4 billion in 1983. At the same time, bond sales for the construction of schools, hospitals, housing, sewer and water mains, and other public works projects in cities tapered off.[43] Direct federal aid to urban areas fell by 60 percent between 1981 and 1992.[44]

After the election of Ronald Reagan to the presidency in 1980, the nation's business and political leadership built on themes developed during the Nixon, Ford, and Carter years in advocating policies that cut federal expenditures on cities in order to "return" money to state and local governments. This "new federalism" emphasized "revenue sharing" and block grants rather than direct federal spending and administration of programs targeting particular needs. Revenue sharing enabled municipalities to take money originally intended for the sick, the old, the very young, and the poor and instead use it to cut property taxes for the wealthy, subsidize corporate development projects, and increase security and police protection in the new zones of wealth surrounded by blocks and blocks of desperately poor people.

Federal funds for water, sewage treatment, and garbage disposal declined by more than $50 billion per year during the 1980s. State aid to cities dropped from 62.5 percent of local urban revenues to 54.3 percent during the decade. The corporate share of local property tax burdens counted for 45 percent of such revenues in 1957 but fell to 16 percent by 1987.[45] These changes helped redistribute wealth upward, but they also fractured the fabric of local life in urban areas, pitting each governmental unit against every other unit and creating the preconditions for the kinds of subsidies secured by the Rams in St. Louis.

Proponents of the new federalism proclaimed their intention to return power to the people at the local level. But in reality, these policies were designed to remove local obstacles to capital investment and to break the power of inner-city social movements and political coalitions. First, the new federalism transferred resources and decision-making authority to county, suburban, and rural governments. Second, it left the "public" represented by a plethora of administrative units too small to resist the demands of capital by themselves. Suburban growth, for example, strengthens the hand of big investors by enabling them to play off one small unit of government against another.

While purporting to make local connections to place more meaningful, the new federalism and revenue sharing did the opposite, creating deadly competition between places for scarce resources and diminishing the power of those most dependent on local places for residence, work, and community. It also increased the power of those approaching local places as sites for speculation and profit. In short, it delocalized decision making about urban life in order to create new circuits for investment capable of generating massive returns. This pattern not only requires no concessions to urban residents of the kinds made by pro-growth coalitions in the Keynesian era, but it even discourages philanthropy and the reinvestment of profits back into the sites that produced them. Rather than giving back to urban areas to show themselves good citizens, today's transnational investors expect cities to supply them with subsidies for the privilege of profiting from local sites and resources. In fact, the business coalitions such as Civic Progress in St. Louis, which often speak for the city when establishing subsidies for public-private development, are usually dominated by the local firms most responsible for disinvestment in the local economy and most responsible for the flight of capital to more profitable places.

Tax cuts for the wealthy and transfer to the states of programs such as Aid to Dependent Children and General Assistance have exacerbated the delocalization of decision making in urban areas. Every time a unit of government cuts necessary services, it increases the pressure on the unit just below. Cuts in federal spending on infrastructure and social welfare put pressure on the states. State cutbacks impose new demands on counties, in turn squeezing the resources of cities. As Sidney Plotkin and William Scheuerman point out, under these conditions "every unit in the sub-national government system must preserve, protect, and expand its tax base at the expense of every other unit."[46] Municipalities within a region compete for low-risk wealthy populations and high-yield establishments such as shopping centers while avoiding high-risk poor and disabled populations and low-yield, high-cost institutions such as hospitals and schools. But this competition only produces new inequalities that can be used by capital to pit one unit against another in bidding wars that reduce taxes and other obligations while increasing subsidies and the provision of free services.

The subsidies offered to sports structures like the Trans World Dome proceed from this general pattern. In the Keynesian era, St. Louis financial institutions invested in their own region. But since the 1980s they have been shifting investments elsewhere, exporting locally generated wealth to sites around the world with the potential for rich and rapid returns. Building the Trans World Dome offered financial institutions an opportunity to create a potential source of high profit for outside investors in their own region. Large projects like the Trans World Dome generate some new local spending for construction, financing, and services, and they clear out large blocks of underutilized land for future development. But because they are so heavily subsidized, they wind up costing the local economy more than they bring in, although they offer the prospect of windfall profits to wealthy investors from other cities.[47]

Although basing their actions on capitalist principles of profit making and risk, investors in the Trans World Dome and its surrounding area actually counted on the government to neutralize their risk by passing off debt obligations to the city, county, and state. Profits projected as a result of the dome's development lay not in new consumer spending and the ripple effect it might have on the local economy but rather on profits made for a few from real estate speculation. Here again, federal tax policies encourage speculation and discourage broad-based investment in the local economy by treating income gained from long-term investment more favorably than income generated from the production of actual goods and services. In addition, mortgage interest payments can be deducted from income, depreciation allowances can be taken for property, and, in abatement zones, property taxes are waived.[48] The tax structure makes developments that are unprofitable for the local region quite profitable for individual speculators and investors.

Business leaders often claim that the presence of professional sports franchises gives a city a "big-league" image and consequently makes it easier to attract capital and corporate relocations. But no evidence supports this claim. It is true that individual corporations find it easier to recruit top-flight executives when they can offer them the use of tax-subsidized luxury boxes at sporting events, but nothing indicates that this is a wise investment for the entire area or that it means more to fiscal health of the region than adequate housing, medical care, and schools.

Even if it somehow becomes an economic success for someone, the Trans World Dome will almost certainly be a disaster for the residents of St. Louis. The Rams can always move again; after all, they were the Cleveland Rams before they were the Los Angeles Rams. Even in Los Angeles, the team moved from the Los Angeles Coliseum to Anaheim Stadium after officials in that suburban city expanded the size of their facility from 43,250 to 70,000 seats, constructed new executive offices for the team's use, and built one hundred luxury boxes for use by Rams fans. But when Georgia Frontiere found a better deal somewhere else, the Rams left Anaheim too.[49] The team's lease at the Trans World Dome even contains a provision stipulating that the Rams can move to another city or demand a whole new round of upgrades on the stadium if it does not remain among the best stadiums in the NFL for the next ten years.[50]

Subsidies to previous franchises did not prevent St. Louis from losing the basketball Hawks to Atlanta or the football Cardinals to Phoenix. In fact, by using subsidies to provide the Rams with more profit in a metropolitan area with 3 million people than they could get in one with more than 9 million, the backers of the Trans World Dome in St. Louis have increased the number of their potential competitors. With subsidies like these, professional football franchises can move virtually anywhere and make a profit. The Tennessee Titans defeated by the Rams in the 2000 Super Bowl previously played in Houston as the Oilers, until a subsidized stadium in Nashville persuaded team owner Bud Adams to move his operations there.

As long as the federal courts and Congress allow the National Football League to use its "labor exemption" to evade anti-trust laws, the league will make sure that franchises are limited and that teams always have leverage with the cities in which they play simply by threatening to move somewhere else. As long as the tax system encourages speculative investment over the production of goods and services, resources will be misallocated into projects like the Trans World Dome. As long as the federal government abdicates its responsibilities to states and cities, capital will have a free hand and the public interest will be represented by fragmented units too weak to resist the concessions demanded by corporate interests. As long as urban political coalitions and social movements remain more poorly organized than the representatives of corporate and suburban interests, poor children will continue to pay for projects like the Trans World Dome out of funds originally intended for education, medical care, and transportation.

Yet even if the Rams remain in St. Louis, even if the Super Bowl championship they won in 2000 is the first of many, and even if new stores, restaurants, and hotels surface near the Trans World Dome, the vast majority of people in St. Louis will be no better off. Recreational discretionary spending will just shift from one part of town to another, and entrepreneurs in the newly marginalized areas will then demand the same kinds of concessions and subsidies supplied to their competitors. As long as urban real estate investment projects are dominated by global investors, local political leaders will simply be administrators of austerity and supervisors of the subsidies sought mostly by out-of-town investors.

Inequalities among cities and within them make it possible to play off one part of town against another and to provoke political leaders from different jurisdictions into bidding wars to obtain high-profile projects. But rather than reduce inequality, urban developments like the Trans World Dome exacerbate it. They not only take money out of education and health care to service debts incurred by speculators, but they also drain resources away from the precisely targeted "demand-side" expenditures (loans for housing and small business, public works projects) that might lessen inequality and increase opportunities and life chances for inner-city populations.

The delocalization of decision making about urban spatial relations leaves residents with little stake in the cities in which they live. It fractures the social fabric, encouraging individuals and communities to monopolize high-yield and low-risk economic activities in areas they control while dumping low-yield and high-risk obligations onto others. Inequality generates poverty and its attendant costs: underutilization of human resources, increased expenditures for health care, impediments to local investment, and the diversion of resources toward increased policing and incarceration. Such practices are not only unjust; they are also inefficient. Cities with the lowest economic and social polarization have less crime and experience faster growth. They utilize human resources more efficiently and provide a better quality of life for more people.[51]

At a time when cities should be imposing *more* taxes on profitable ventures like the Rams, when sports arenas should come with long-term leases and large penalties for moves to other cities, the opposite seems to be the case. Whether it is the sports business or the pork-and-beans business, it has become increasingly difficult to "trap" capital and secure a fair share of the tax burden from business enterprises. But the costs of inaction are far greater than the risks of action on these matters. Efforts to lessen the leverage of the NFL by asking Congress to remove the limited anti-trust exemption it enjoys, a revision of the tax code to discourage speculation and encourage more productive spending, and measures to reverse the new federalism's fracturing of political authority by displacing decision making on to small units that are powerless to resist the demands of concentrated capital are measures that would all help residents of St. Louis and other cities resist the plundering that is now taking place in the name of development.

Yet we need to understand as well the role that culture plays in the politics of stadium subsidies. Relentless attacks on public schools, libraries, parks, gyms, transportation systems, and other services over the past thirty years have left people with few public spaces that promote mutuality and commonality in urban areas. The delocalization of decision making has undermined local political organizations and leaders, while the mobility of capital has undercut the critical force of trade unions and other community organizations. The creation of new specialized markets and the emergence of new "lifestyle" differences based on seemingly trivial consumer preferences divide families and communities into incommensurable consumer market segments.

Under these conditions, professional sports fill a void. They provide a limited sense of place for contemporary urban dwellers, offering them a rooting interest that promises at least the illusion of inclusion and connection with others. This illusion is not diminished by contrary evidence, by the fact that every St. Louis Ram would become a Tennessee Titan and every Tennessee Titan would become a St. Louis Ram tomorrow if they could make more money by doing so, by the fact that team owners preach the virtues of unbridled capitalism while enjoying subsidies that free them from the rigors of competition and risk, by the fact that impoverished and often ill school children are called upon to subsidize the recreation of some of their society's wealthiest citizens.

Entire communities pay the price for the profits secured by speculators and investors from subsidized sports developments. But the aggrieved racial minorities who need public services the most because of rampant discrimination in the private sector suffer most of all. Cruelly enough, the success of Black athletes in St. Louis on the football field every Sunday helps build public identification with a project that systematically deprives Black children of needed educational resources.

The denial of educational resources to Black children in St. Louis because of the TWA Dome is not a peculiar aberration in an otherwise just society. It represents just one of the many forms of systematic inequality and injustice that underwrite "business as usual" in our society. Despite claims that the 1964 Civil Rights Act "ended" racism, our society continually devises new ways of rewarding racism and subsidizing segregation. St. Louis students receive meager resources for their educations, but even that small amount is too much for the team owners, developers, and business leaders who use their power to divert resources away from the schools in pursuit of even more wealth for themselves.

For her skill at securing public funds for private purposes, Rams owner Georgia Frontiere was rewarded with a Super Bowl trophy. For his efforts in blocking the implementation of a federal court order and refusing to take responsibility for the obligations that the law imposed on the state of Missouri, John Ashcroft has become attorney general of the United States, the nation's chief law enforcer. Black students and parents in St. Louis, however, who have broken no laws and who turned to the federal courts to secure the educational opportunities guaranteed to them by the Fourteenth Amendment, have not received the rewards available to Frontiere and Ashcroft; in fact, their victimization played an essential part in Frontiere's and Ashcroft's successes.

Every Rams victory will be celebrated loudly, but the despair of students deprived of decent educations will be kept quiet. People speaking the language of democracy broadcast the illusions of "trickle-down" economics to us at high volume. But ever so quietly, they produce only a plutocracy that sacrifices the rights of citizens in order to subsidize the profits of speculators. In the case of the TWA Dome, trickle-down economics send a clear message that our society values entertainment more than education, that the pursuit of unlimited profits for the wealthy counts for more than the basic needs of the poor. The exploits of the Rams on the football field make their fans cheer and fill the TWA Dome with joyous and high-decibel noise. But quiet as it's kept, the echoes of educational inequality will be heard long after the fans' cheers have died down.

NOTES

1. "St. Louis Public School District Facts, 1999–2000," St. Louis Public Schools, at http://dtd1.slps.k12.m0.us/articles/schlfact.htm.1-2. Peter Downs, "Tax Abatements Don't Work," *St. Louis Journalism Review* (February 1997): 5.

2. Amy Stuart Wells and Robert L. Crain, *Stepping Over the Color Line: African American Students in White Suburban Schools* (New Haven: Yale University Press, 1997), 337.

3. John Portz, Lana Stein, and Robin R. Jones, *Institutions and Leadership in Pittsburgh, Boston, and St. Louis* (Lawrence: University Press of Kansas, 1999), 118.

4. Rick Pierce, "St. Louis Schools Get Year Reprieve while Kansas City Loses Accreditation," *St. Louis Post-Dispatch*, October 22, 1999.

5. D. J. Wilson, "The End of Desegregation as We Know It," *Riverfront Times*, January 6, 1999, 12, 13.

6. Dennis R. Judd, "The Role of Governmental Policies in Promoting Residential Segregation in the St. Louis Metropolitan Area," *Journal of Negro Education* 66, 3 (1997): 216–17.

7. George Lipsitz, *The Possessive Investment in Whiteness: How White People Profit from Identity Politics* (Philadelphia: Temple University Press, 1998).

8. Arthur Denzau and Charles Leven made these estimates in 1985 in a report to the St. Louis Board of Education's Community Advisory Committee.

9. Matthew Ulterino, "The Great American Give-Away: Are Cities Selling Themselves Short for the Sake of Redevelopment?" Center for Urban Research and Policy, Columbia University School of International and Public Affairs, 1998, at http://sipa.columbia.edu/CURP/resources/metro/v01n0401.html.

10. Mike Meyers, "L.A. Rams Finally Win Big but Most of Us Stand to Lose," *Minneapolis Star-Tribune* online, January 20, 1995. Melinda Roth; "At the Trough," *Riverfront Times*, September 17, 1997, 16.

11. Ulterino, "Great American Give-Away," 3.

12. Wells and Crain, *Stepping Over the Color Line*, 313.

13. Kern Alexander, "The Impact of Fiscal Inequality on At-Risk Schoolchildren in St. Louis (Testimony of Kern Alexander)," *Journal of Negro Education* 66, 3 (1997): 304.

14. Judd, "Role of Governmental Policies," 226.

15. Wells and Crain, *Stepping Over the Color Line*, 312.

16. Judd, "Role of Government Policies," 217.

17. Charles C. Euchner, *Playing the Field: Why Sports Teams Move and Cities*

Fight to Keep Them (Baltimore and London: Johns Hopkins University Press, 1993), 67.

18. D. J. Wilson, "The Deal of the Century," *Riverfront Times* February 23, 2000.

19. "Trans World Dome By the Numbers," at http://www.transworlddome.ord /fact01.html. D. J. Wilson, "Ballpark Frankness," *Riverfront Times*, March 10, 1999.

20. Toby Eckert, *Indianapolis Business Journal* 18, 5 (April 21–27, 1997).

21. Reynolds Farley and W. H. Frey, "Changes in Segregation of Whites from Blacks during the 1980s: Small Steps toward a More Integrated Society, *American Sociological Review* 59 (1994): 23–45.

22. Wells and Crain, *Stepping Over the Color Line*, 24.

23. Portz, Stein, and Jones, *Institutions and Leadership*, 119.

24. Anthony J. Scalzo, "What the Companies Knew and When They Knew It," *St. Louis Post-Dispatch*, April 23, 2000; Alliance to End Childhood Lead Poisoning, at http://www.aeclp.org/5/companies.html.

25. Robert D. Bullard, "Anatomy of Environmental Racism and the Environmental Justice Movement," in Robert D. Bullard, ed., *Confronting Environmental Racism: Voices from the Grass Roots* (Boston: South End, 1993), 21.

26. Senator Sam Ervin's quote appears in Euchner, *Playing the Field*, 65.

27. Joanna Cagan and Neil deMause, *Field of Schemes: How the Great Stadium Swindle Turns Public Money into Private Profit* (Monroe, ME: Common Courage, 1998), 63.

28. Gerald W. Scully, *The Market Structure of Sports* (Chicago: University of Chicago Press, 1995), 116.

29. Euchner, *Playing the Field*, 34.

30. Roger G. Noll and Andrew Zimbalist, "Sports, Jobs, Taxes: Are New Stadiums Worth the Cost?" *Brookings Review* 15, 3 (Summer 1997): 1, at http://www .brook.edu/pub/review/summer/97/noll.html.

31. Ibid., 45.

32. Euchner, *Playing the Field*, 46.

33. Cagan and deMause, *Field of Schemes*, 61.

34. George Cothran, "Hook, Line, and Sinker," *San Francisco Weekly*, May 1, 1996, 11.

35. Ulterino, "Great American Give-Away," 3.

36. Judd, "Role of Governmental Policies," 234.

37. August A. Busch III, quoted in Peter Hernon and Terry Ganey, *Under the Influence: The Unauthorized Story of the Anheuser-Busch Dynasty* (New York: Simon and Schuster, 1991), 390.

38. Michael N. Danielson, *Home Team: Professional Sports and the American Metropolis* (Princeton: Princeton University Press, 1997), 256; George Lipsitz, "Sports Stadia and Urban Development: A Tale of Three Cities," *Journal of Sport and Social Issues* 8 (Summer/Fall 1984): 6.

39. Ray Hartmann, "Stadium Sale: The Name of the Game Is Deceit," *St. Louis Riverfront Times,* March 10, 1999, 2.

40. John Logan and Harvey Molotch, *Urban Fortunes: The Political Economy of Place* (Berkeley: University of California Press, 1987).

41. John Mollenkopf, *The Contested City* (Princeton: Princeton University Press, 1993); Kenneth Jackson, *The Crabgrass Frontier: The Suburbanization of the United States* (New York: Oxford University Press, 1985).

42. Logan and Molotch, *Urban Fortunes,* 173: "By 1977, with Carter in the White House, urban aid benefits now directed toward the suburbs and growing sunbelt cities; Dallas's receipts alone had grown tenfold in four years."

43. Euchner, *Playing the Field,* 64; Logan and Molotch, *Urban Fortunes,* 177.

44. Walden Bello, *Dark Victory: The United States, Structural Adjustment and Global Poverty* (London: Pluto Press, 1994), 91.

45. Sidney Plotkin and William E. Scheuerman, *Private Interest, Public Spending: Balanced Budget Conservatism and the Fiscal Crisis* (Boston: South End, 1994), 22–24.

46. Ibid., 21.

47. Logan and Molotch, *Urban Fortunes,* 206–7. Euchner, *Playing the Field,* 63.

48. Logan and Molotoch, *Urban Fortunes,* 280.

49. Euchner, *Playing the Field,* 83.

50. Cagan and deMause, *Field of Schemes,* 61.

51. Randy Abelda and Chris Tilly, "Unnecessary Evil: Why Inequality Is Bad for Business," *Dollars and Sense,* no. 198 (March–April 1995): 20.

■

Chapter Eleven

Warriors and Thieves

Appropriations of the Warrior Motif in Representations of Native American Athletes

John Bloom and Randy Hanson

North American sports teams have long used the image of a Native American warrior as a mascot to symbolize fierceness and competitive zeal. A broad spectrum of Native Americans, from activists in the American Indian Movement (AIM) to Republican senator Ben Nighthorse Campbell, are united in their opposition when teams don names such as Redskins, Braves, and Warriors. Their protests illustrate some of the important ways in which Native North Americans have been and continue to be harmed by the racial stereotypes used to characterize them. Yet, even in the face of this opposition, sports teams in the United States, from the high school level to the professionals, continue to inspire fans by using Native American mascots.

Why does the dominating sports culture in the United States have such an affinity for the image of Native Americans? Why does this image have such lasting power, even in the face of angry protests? A part of the answer can by found by examining an aspect that is central to almost all Native American sports mascots: the image of the warrior. The significance of the warrior motif lies not only in its ubiquitous association with mascots but also in the very ways in which sports journalists, coaches, and institutions actively deploy it to motivate players, to inspire the imaginations of fans, and to represent Native Americans and Native American athletes themselves. The warrior motif makes not only an explicit statement about popular representations of Native American identity but also an implicit one about the relationship of mainstream sports culture in the United States to public understandings of race, American exceptionalism, and the cultures of United States imperialism.

This chapter focuses on two relatively recent deployments of the Native American warrior motif in sports. The first is a 1991 article about high school basketball on the Crow reservation in Montana that appeared in the popular magazine *Sports Illustrated*. The second is Phil Jackson's use of Lakota warrior traditions, popularly chronicled in his 1995 book *Sacred Hoops* and more recently recalled in a 1999 television profile by the cable sports network ESPN. These two representations of the warrior motif, at first glance, seem very different. When examined carefully, however, they are two sides of a coin, one that suggests how the image of the Native American warrior serves as a representation of social tensions and ambivalence in mainstream society.

Dying Warriors on the Hardwood

A two-page photo spread unfolds to reveal to readers a bleak, barren, treeless road in a colorless neighborhood. Boxy, one-story government houses are set back about twenty-five feet on either side of the street, while rusty cars and pickups are parked in driveways and along the road. Just before the first house on the left-hand side of the photo stands a basketball hoop with a rusted pole and backboard. Its shadow angles toward the reader, the backboard stretching out on the pavement and extending from the left-hand page to the right. The title of the article, "Shadow of a Nation," floats in the sky above the hoop on the left-hand page and frames the image below as an ironic metaphor, the rusted hoop presented as a symbol for a lost nation. Below the headline, the subheading reads, "The Crows, once proud warriors, now seek glory—but often find tragedy—in basketball."

On the top of the next page, over both columns of text, is an italicized epigraph, provided without any information as to why or in what context it was written or uttered, credited to "Plenty Coups, Chief of the Crows, 1930":

> I have not told you half that happened when I was young. I can think back and tell you much more of war and horse stealing. But when the buffalo went away the hearts of my people fell to the ground, and they could not lift them up again. After this nothing happened. There was little singing anywhere. (Smith 1991, 62)

This article, written by Gary Smith for the February 18, 1991, edition of *Sports Illustrated*, tells of basketball's popularity among the Crows, focusing on the story of Jonathan Takes Enemy, a former star on the Hardin High School boys basketball team. It recounts the tragic fate of several star players who either died in drunk-driving accidents or dropped out of school only to face a life of menial labor and anonymity. Yet one need not read beyond the opening photograph, headline, and epigraph pieced together by magazine staff to get the story's core message. Basketball has become a vehicle for the expression of a warrior culture, or even instinct, among the Crow, a people who the article and layout suggest have fallen from glory and are hopelessly tied to the past.

The article begins with a description of the scene looking out from the Hardin High School team bus in March 1983: a traffic jam extending across the Valley of the Big Horn, where people were coming from miles outside Billings to watch the state tournament. In the article's opening sequence, writer Gary Smith recounts the fate of four players on the team bus that day. One would drop out of school shortly before cirrhosis killed his mother and would end up working as a restaurant janitor on the reservation. The second, who "had grown up with no father," also had a mother recently die of cirrhosis and in a few weeks would himself be unemployed and drinking heavily. The third would be killed in a drunk driving accident in two years, and in sixteen months the fourth would also be dead, after falling asleep at the wheel of a car after a night of drinking (62).

Takes Enemy, the article notes, was the tribe's basketball hero, who had been richly rewarded with trophies and awards at national and state athletic banquets. He had been recruited by several top, Division I university teams. Yet, by his junior year in high school, he was already drinking and was the father of two children. His sister had died from liver disease. He was, Smith states, "the newest hero of the tribe that loved basketball too much" (63).

The article identifies basketball as the opiate of the Montana Indian masses. With a 75 percent unemployment rate, severe poverty, alcoholism, and a reservation that, through broken treaties and land fraud, had shrunk to less than 3 percent of its size in 1851, the article notes, the Crow had become, along with the other tribes in Montana, the state's top basketball force. Even though they comprised only 7 percent of the state's population, the Crow had won ten Class A, B, and C state high school basketball titles between 1980 and 1990. "Somehow, in the mindless way that rivers sculpt valleys and shame shapes history," Smith writes, "the Montana Indians' purest howl against a hundred years of repression and pain had become . . . high school basketball" (65).

Smith goes on to explain how basketball had become, for the Crow, a modern vehicle for maintaining warrior traditions, such as the ritual of counting coup, that were a central part of the tribe's rituals of manhood:

> Of all the perplexing games that the white man had brought with him—frantic races for diplomas and dollar bills and development—here was the one that the lean, quick men on the reservation could instinctively play. Here was a way to bring pride back to their hollow chests and vacant eyes, some physical means, at last, for poor undereducated men to re-attain the status they once had gained through hunting and battle. Crow men had never taken up the craftwork, weaving or metallurgy that males in other tribes had. They were warriors, meat eaters, nomads whose prestige and self-esteem had come almost entirely from fulfilling an intricate set of re-quirements—called "counting coup"—while capturing enemy horses or waging battle. (64)

The article continues in this vein, discussing the legacy of this warrior tradition among the Crow and its relationship to basketball. For example, Smith notes how Takes Enemy's family celebrated his success on the court with the same rituals that the Crow had used to celebrate a successful raid.

The *Sports Illustrated* article directly addresses important problems that have characterized life on many Indian reservations for over a century. It discusses alcoholism, poverty, a lack of job opportunities, poor education, and high rates of psychological depression. Yet, importantly, it approaches these problems almost entirely out of any historical context. In the place of history, the article provides a narrative of a Native American culture mired in the past, unable to escape from its mythic warrior traditions, which are inept at dealing with modern institutions. In fact, the author identifies the Crow connection to basketball through its warrior past as not even cultural but essential—basketball as a game that they could "instinctively play."

Such narratives reveal less about the Crow than they do about the racial discourses of the commercial, media, audience, and entertainment complex that is *Sports Illustrated*. The stories of tragedy that Gary Smith recounts in his article may be sad ones, and they may even lead many readers to yearn nostalgically for a romanticized image of what was lost when Native Americans made contact with Europeans. Yet, by attributing problems among to Crow to cultural or even "instinctive" factors, *Sports*

Illustrated readers need not feel any connection to, benefit from, or responsibility for that loss themselves. In fact, most readers could read this story and feel satisfied with their society—proud of the ability of its corporately owned media outlets, such as Time-Warner, to address compassionately the problems of people like the Crow.

This discussion of Crow basketball, then, is connected to a number of discursive threads. It resonates with centuries-old traditions in the popular representation of Native Americans. The image of noble warriors that the article highlights is something that has long been part of a standard formula, from George Catlin paintings in the mid–nineteenth century, to James Fenimore Cooper's novels, to "Buffalo Bill's" Wild West shows, to a century of Hollywood films (Berkhoffer 1979; Bird 1996; Rogers 1981).

Thus, the article focuses on a people with a particularly significant military history. As the article acknowledges, many different Native nations in Montana and around the United States have been particularly successful in basketball on the high school level. The Crow, however, are most well known to non–Native Americans because of their military history. After settlers and rail companies began exterminating buffalo, the Crow had to compete more intensely with neighboring tribes for hunting grounds. They chose to side with the United States military against their traditional enemies, most famously as scouts for George Armstrong Custer during the Battle of Little Big Horn (Calloway 1999, 288).

The article notes this history with sad irony. Smith recounts how Takes Enemy would sometimes watch movies on television that depicted Custer's last stand and would cheer for the Indians, only later realizing that those he was rooting for would have been fighting against the Crow. In times of uncertainty, Takes Enemy would drive out to the Little Big Horn monument, only a few miles from his house, to sit and reflect about the past and the future. Such images present the contemporary Native American athlete as a sad reflection of the defeated Native American warrior.

Yet, just as important, the article weaves such images into a racial discourse that emerged in the neoconservative and neoliberal political climate of the 1980s and 1990s. This political rhetoric tended to address racial inequalities in the United States by framing them as the result of cultural or even biologically inherited "deficiencies" among nonwhite sectors of society (Gray 1995; Lipsitz 1998). Such ideas resonate with a long tradition of European American thinking about Native American social formations as backward, never having evolved or "advanced" to a supposedly higher level of European society (Hoxie 1984). Like social reformers of the late nineteenth century who advocated severality of Indian lands and boarding-school education for Native American children, neoconservatives of the late twentieth century argued that government agencies perpetuated social inequalities by making racially defined minorities "dependent" on federal handouts. This rhetoric had a particularly gendered tone, presenting aggrieved populations as emasculated by government dependence and in need of strong nuclear families, father figures, and strong male role models who would personify individual upward mobility.

The *Sports Illustrated* text presents just such an image, particularly portraying Crow traditions surrounding family as harmful to Takes Enemy. For example, the extended family and clan system of the tribe is presented as enabling the basketball star's drinking. When Takes Enemy and his friends needed money for alcohol, they would go from relative to relative, collecting enough from uncles, cousins, and others to buy what they wanted at a liquor store off the reservation. "Jonathan and his friends would each ask a relative or two for a buck, and all of the sharing and family closeness in which the Crows pride themselves would boomerang" (Smith 1991, 69). Similarly, the article notes a deep distrust of educational institutions on the reservation, something Smith attributes to memories of children being sent to federally operated boarding schools. This distrust, he argues, has ended up making rising stars reluctant to leave their reservations behind and is therefore a barrier to individual mobility and success.

Basketball is presented as a part of this cultural malaise, but not because of the game or the social structures that support it generally in the United States. The article does not critically analyze the scholarship structure of college basketball, for example, or the institutional barriers that might specifically block Native American players from becoming professionals, or even the local media hype that exposes very young people to public fame. Rather, basketball is a problem only insofar as it has become, according to the article, a modern replacement of a continuing warrior tradition that makes Crow men ill equipped to handle upward mobility and success.

Dale Old Horn, head of the department of Crow studies and social sciences at Little Big Horn College, is quoted as saying that the game has become an empty promise on the reservation:

> For us, a victory in a high school basketball game is a victory over everyday
> misery and poverty and racism . . . but it's not a *real* victory. It doesn't de-
> crease bigotry. It doesn't lessen alcoholism. It doesn't remove one Indian
> from the welfare rolls or return a single acre of our land. It gives us pseudo
> pride. It hasn't led us on to greater things. (65)

Old Horn's criticism of basketball could be interpreted as a larger criticism of the overemphasis on success in sports in the United States. Such
an interpretation would necessarily also open up criticism of the privileges
and prestige that athletic heroism affords disproportionately to men. Instead, Smith reads Old Horn's commentary as evidence of the inability of
Native American men to achieve, by contrasting the Crow with successful
individual basketball players who have come from other minority groups.
Smith writes, "The game that was a highway into mainstream America for
black men . . . was a cul-de-sac for red ones" (65).

Although magazines such as *Sports Illustrated* more commonly associate sports with masculine character, among the Crow basketball is equated
with addiction, one of the ultimate symbols of emasculating dependence.
Smith writes that "the way the Crows were using" basketball on the reservation had turned it into a "drug" (70). The article follows Takes Enemy
into a decline after he is barely able to graduate from high school. He is
unable to succeed at a junior college and soon returns to the reservation,
where he collects welfare, drinks, and gains weight.

The article ends with a sense of hope, however, based on Takes Enemy's
assumption of independence and paternal responsibility. He moves off the
reservation with his wife and two children and begins to attend Rocky
Mountain College where he plays basketball in order to get an education.
He says, in one of the few quotes that come directly from him in the article,

> I finally realized that I was running out of time. It's not that the reservation
> is a bad place. There are many good people there. But it's just not a place
> where you can become what you want to become. It's not a place where you
> can achieve your dreams.(74)

The article concludes with Takes Enemy leaving the reservation early one
morning in his Mustang, on his way to Billings. He leaves alone. "He wants
to go back to the reservation someday and help the kids to take the risk, to
see both the beauty and the danger of the circle. But he may never live
there again" (74).

In his 1970 manifesto, *Custer Died for Your Sins*, Vine Deloria Jr. took
aim at a theory expressed by a prominent anthropologist of the late 1960s

that poor education performance on the Pine Ridge Reservation was the result of a pent-up, unexpressed warrior tradition. He quipped, "Every conceivable difference between the Oglala Sioux and the folks at Hyannisport was attributed to the quaint warrior tradition of the Oglala Sioux." He went on to suggest that "a wagon train be run through the reservation each morning at 9 A.M. and the reservation people [be] paid a minimum wage for attacking it" (Deloria 1988 [1970], 91).

As humorous as Deloria's comments are, they underscore the relationship of such theories to a broader culture of imperialism. The warrior imagery deployed by the *Sports Illustrated* article, like the one that Deloria ridiculed, takes images and stereotypes already familiar to readers and reframes them. It effectively presents social problems brought about by a history of colonial power relations as the product of timeless cultural traits that, in the challenges they pose to mainstream assumptions about social norms, become "defects." At issue more than Crow basketball is Crow manhood, which, in the world that *Sports Illustrated* creates, has failed in its adherence to its warrior past. As Peter Van Lent has argued in his discussion of the Native American warrior as a male sex symbol during the 1990s, "Deeply imbedded in the mystique of the fearless warrior is an air of tragic destiny, the potential for defeat and death" (Van Lent 1996, 213–214).

Not all representations of the Native American warrior in sports are presented in terms of defeat, however. One of the most popular has been that deployed by former Chicago Bulls and current Los Angeles Lakers coach Phil Jackson, widely celebrated for having drawn on New Age imagery and warrior traditions to motivate players and win championships.

Phil Jackson as Lakota Warrior

The second-winningest coach in NBA history, Phil Jackson has a seemingly contradictory place in the world of American sports. A hard-nosed coach disliked by many in the NBA, Jackson's coaching style is physically and psychically demanding, and he is infamous for deploying psychological warfare against his opponents. For his part, Phil Jackson fashions himself as a distinctly New Age man, one whose putatively compassionate sensibilities derive from the influences he came into contact with during the 1960s. Accordingly, Jackson's use of American Indian material and spiritual culture is typically framed in terms of an outsider being culturally knowledgeable, intimate, and empathetic. His fusing of these strands of Native culture with other elements is projected as a creative harnessing of a premodern bonding and a peaceful aggression, a kind of postmodern primitivism that is simultaneously hip, savvy, and serious.

The following examination of Phil Jackson's self-fashioning and the mass-media framing of his uses of American Indian material and spiritual culture reveals a surprising cultural sleight of hand. Indeed, in contradistinction to the ways in which the warrior image is discussed in relation to the Crow basketball players (Indian students reclaiming a warrior tradition playing basketball, but, ultimately, the process becoming a drug, an addiction, a symbol of emasculating dependence), Jackson's deployment of these images and concepts in fashioning his Chicago Bulls champions is celebrated as salvaging the warrior culture of the Lakota Sioux. We begin with a discussion of Jackson based on his autobiography, *Sacred Hoops: Spiritual Lessons of a Hardwood Warrior*, proceeding to contextualize his self-presentation within broader cultural and historical trends. We then turn to an examination of the 1999 television profile "The Native American Sports Experience," an episode in the ESPN special series *Outside the Lines*. This critical appraisal of the ways in which Phil Jackson borrows from American Indian traditions demonstrates a surprising but, in the end, familiar theme: white appropriation of American Indian material and spiritual culture seen as reclamation, better use than that of the very Native culture that fostered it.

As Phil Jackson explains in his autobiography, he grew up in a family of strict Pentecostalists in North Dakota and Montana. He writes that his mother instilled in him at an early age the necessity of being an "exceptional" Christian, in preparation for the imminent Apocalypse. This absolute necessity to triumph at being a Christian, coupled with the sibling rivalry he experienced with two older brothers, made "winning a matter of life and death" (Jackson 1995, 31). Yet speaking in tongues was apparently not young Jackson's calling, and he experienced a crisis of faith in his early teenage years. As he puts it, "The unfulfilled legacy of my devout childhood had left an emptiness, a yearning to connect with the deeper mysteries of life" (43). This yearning was to be answered in his coming of age amid the mid–1960s counterculture at the University of North Dakota. Dabbling in a variety of experiences that were in stark contrast to the strict, ascetic world of his upbringing, Jackson was able to find "a way to express myself spiritually without giving up my newfound freedom" (44). Of the various strains of counterculture of the 1960s, what resonated with

Phil Jackson was not the collective political demands of the era but an emphasis on individual freedom. Again quoting from his autobiography, he states that "what I carried away with me when it was over . . . was the emphasis on compassion and brotherhood, getting together and loving one another *right now*" (33).

Jackson's autobiography proceeds to tell his tale of becoming an NBA player with the New York Knicks, where he was part of a championship team; how his playing career ended; and how he ultimately ended up coaching professional basketball. Throughout all this fame and fortune, Jackson struggled to reconcile his upbringing with the many spiritual traditions in which he dabbled, creating a fusion of disparate influences along the way. He eventually got a call from the Chicago Bulls, for whom the already-famous Michael Jordan played, and despite having been "disenchanted with the way power, money, and self-glorification had tainted" basketball, he took the coaching position offered (4). From there he proceeded to craft a highly competitive and successful team that went on to win six championships.

And so we arrive at this postmodern, New Age guru in the middle of one of the most financially profitable and competitive franchises in sports history, whose self-fashioning from disparate influences is apparently readily transferable to all arenas. As he puts it, "Creating a successful team—whether it's an NBA champion or a record-setting sales force—is essentially a spiritual act" (5). Indeed, while his ethos is putatively spiritual, his pliable words of wisdom are also instrumentally crafted to win in whatever way is needed, in whatever arena one inhabits. Such an understanding of the fusion between the highly competitive goals of contemporary American society in business and professional sports and a spiritual, indeed, religious platform is clearly a sign of our times for a segment of the U.S. population. In many ways, Phil Jackson reflects the contemporary pragmatic orientation that David Brooks so aptly describes in his new book *Bobos in Paradise: The New Upper Class and How They Got There*, namely, the new elite sensibility of being a bourgeois bohemian, able to embrace the rebellious, anti-establishment attitudes of the 1960s and the social-climbing, cutthroat competitiveness of the 1980s. As his book explores, the "bobos" represent a new upper class that "has combined the counter-cultural 60's and the achieving 80's into one social ethos" (Brooks 2000). Brooks provides numerous examples that demonstrate the seemingly contradictory stance of this group wanting to have it both ways: powerful but projecting a rebelliousness against power, wealthy yet affecting a negative attitude toward materialism. In this world, as Brooks notes, "the one realm of American life where the language of 1960's radicalism remains strong is the business world," where this consummate road to U.S. power is cast as the domain of the outsider.

This description seems to fit the contradictory place that Phil Jackson occupies as one of the highest-paid and most-sought-after coaches in professional sports. Interestingly, the mode of rebelling against his station in life while inhabiting the central place in his profession involves uses of American Indian material and spiritual culture. In particular, Jackson inculcated Lakota material and spiritual culture into the environs of and interactions with his players. As he explained in the ESPN interview, Jackson had some contact with Native peoples growing up in Montana, and he maintained that connection in his basketball coaching, holding basketball camps on the Pine Ridge Reservation in South Dakota since 1973. Jackson felt a deep psychic connection to Native culture, as he recently explained: "There's something that speaks to you from another culture that says, You've been here before, or you belong to us. . . . Where I grew up it was cowboys and Indians. I always had a bow and arrow in my hand, I was always playing the Indian" (ESPN 1999) Jackson put this ostensible kinship to the service of his coaching. He decorated the Bulls' training room and his office with Native American relics, drums, an arrow, a headdress, symbols and folklore, paintings with Native American motifs, a sketch of Crazy Horse. He regularly burned grasses and sage to cleanse the souls of his players and the buildings in which they played of negative energy. As Rick Telandar, the narrator in the ESPN documentary explains, these materials and practices gave Jackson an emotional edge over his players.

The component Phil Jackson was most interested in isolating in his understanding of Lakota culture was the "warrior tradition," transforming it in the service of the Chicago Bulls' pursuit of basketball championships. As Jackson framed it, "They [Lakota warriors] respected their enemies for giving them the opportunity to have this chance to be a warrior" (ESPN 1999). In his own creative way, Jackson saw many possibilities for this approach:

> It struck me that the Lakota way could serve as a paradigm for the Bulls, because there were so many parallels between a warrior's journey and the life in the NBA. A basketball team is like a band of warriors: a secret society of rights and initiation, a strict code of honor, a sacred quest: the drive for a championship trophy. (ESPN 1999)

Many of the Bulls' players were initially highly skeptical of Jackson's use of American Indian rituals and materials, but when Michael Jordan began to go along with it, other Bulls' team members followed suit. As former Bulls' team member Will Perdue put it:

> You know, if we don't win the championship, and Phil is still trying to push the ideals of the Native Americans, he might be seen as a little bit off his rocker. Guys would sometimes make jokes that, you know, he smoked too many peace pipes you know back in his old days. (ESPN 1999)

In collecting and disseminating the bits of Lakota material and spiritual culture, Phil Jackson sought to combine them with his other religious or spiritual leanings, creating a literal and conceptual postmodern fusion suited to his needs. Part of this was done with new media technologies of the late twentieth century. Indeed, in his cultivation of the Bulls as Lakota warriors, Jackson made extensive use of the film *The Mystic Warrior*, which depicted young Native boys in the nineteenth century going on a vision quest. *The Mystic Warrior* (1984), as it turns out, is a four-part made-for-television miniseries based on the epic novel *Hanta Yo*, by Ruth Beebe Hill, a devotee of Ayn Rand who, according to one critic, "feels that the United States has gone sour, sacrificed individual freedoms for mis-guided social responsibility." First published in 1979, this novel drew enor-mous negative responses from Lakota people and Indian communities more generally across North America for its simultaneous claims to au-thenticity and projections of Ayn Rand–like traits onto the nineteenth-century Sioux. Such criticism suggests that Hill makes nineteenth-century Sioux look much like the "bobos" in late-twentieth-century middle Amer-ica. Jackson was aware of the quite negative appraisals that many Native people had of the film, but he brushed them aside, stating that "my friends at Pine Ridge dismissed the film, pointing out the inaccuracies in it. But I sharply illustrated the importance of making personal sacrifices for the good of the group" (48). Indeed, Jackson's use of the films didn't necessar-ily demand American Indian acceptance of it; nor did he, for all his pre-tense toward compassionate bonding with Native peoples, require that the depictions he used be accurate. For him, their power lie in motivating his players. These contradictions seem to fly from Hill's introduction to her book:

> The American Indian, even before Columbus, was the remnant of a vary old race in its final stage, a race that attainted perhaps the highest level of indi-

vidualism ever practiced. . . . His view was never that of the altruist; he was a
trader in spiritual values . . . he never answer to anyone but himself, never
answer for anyone but himself. (Cited in Churchill 1991, 70)

In reviewing and analyzing game footage, Jackson would intersplice
segments of *The Mystic Warrior* into a particular play or game segment,
fusing the made-for-TV imitation of American Indian traditions with the
ready-for-prime-time exploits of his star Bulls. In doing so, Phil Jackson
recreated a late-modern primitivism that resonates with many instances of
a broader Euro-American appropriation of Native American cultures.

In the ESPN video, David Plume, high school principal of the Pine
Ridge Reservation, speaks of being flattered that Jackson was using his understanding of selected parts of Lakota material and spiritual culture
(ESPN 1999).Yet this is not a universal response from American Indian
peoples, many of whom see such appropriations as a projection of Euro-
American values onto Native traditions, as well as a commodification of
Indian traditions. As the Osage religious scholar George Tinker points out,
most of the Euro-American representations of Native spirituality are
highly selective or patently false. As he puts it, many Euro-American notions of Native spirituality "are centered on the self, a sort of Western individualism run amok, whereas Indian spirituality focuses on the larger
community, the tribe, and never on the individual" (cited in Whitt 1999,
n. 8). Certainly this description fits the novel *Hanta Yo* and its filmic version, *The Mystic Warrior*.

Laurie Anne Whitt, a Choctaw scholar, levels a far more serious charge
against such phenomena. She writes that this kind of cultural appropriation, whether conscious or unintentional, serves to extend the political
power, secure the social control, and further the economic profit of the
dominant culture. The commodification of indigenous spirituality is a
paradigmatic instance of cultural imperialism. As such, it plays a politically vital diversionary role, serving to colonize and assimilate the knowledge and belief systems of indigenous cultures. Ultimately, it facilitates a
type of cultural acquisition via conceptual assimilation: Euro-American
culture seeks to establish itself in indigenous cultures by appropriating,
mining, and redefining what is distinctive and constitutive of them (Whitt
1999, 170).

This phenomenon of appropriating Indian ways is not recent but has a
deeper connection to American culture. Indeed, Philip J. Deloria explores
this tradition in his book *Playing Indian*, which charts a European/Euro-

American ambivalence about and fascination with American Indians since colonial times (Deloria 1999). More specifically, he examines a deeply American tradition of masquerading as Indian, selectively appropriating aspects of Indian culture and identity that have served to fill the void that American identity has long been experienced; being (selectively) Indian has been to be authentically American, something haughty, superior Europeans have lacked the opportunity to do. Deloria traces this tradition across U.S. history, from the Boston Tea Party to the late-1990s New Age penchant for so-called Indian spirituality. In the present context, many variations on this theme can be cited, ranging from the "men's movement" to New Age movements more generally to corporate executive retreats that seek to reclaim the wild man, the primitive within oneself, channeling that "power" toward late-modern instrumental ends (Deloria 1999).

Of all the possible components of American Indian culture, it is useful to ask why the warrior tradition is isolated for use. In *What This Awl Means*, the feminist archeologist Janet Spector discusses how, from the point of view of archaeology, (western) knowledge of American Indian societies generally has tended to focus on war, a warrior tradition, and weaponry. According to Spector, focusing on these elements of Native history and culture provided ideological justification for making war on Indian societies. Indeed, this was an important function, since Euro-American society was always making war on Indian societies to acquire their land and thereby "producing" and elevating the place of warriors in their societies. Thus, the image of American Indians as warriors is an ossified image, cast from many possible images.

In twentieth-century American culture, the warring Lakota and the Apache have served as the classical "western movie Indians," trumping other possible depictions of Native societies. While it may be true that Lakota and Apache peoples were more warlike than many other American Indian societies, due to their geographic location, their mobility, and their internal cultural dynamics, these images became the overall image of American Indians writ large in the emerging American western genre as it took shape in dime novels, circuses, and Wild West shows. The genre of the western in American culture is perhaps the most sustained national myth in the American tradition, a retelling for adults and children alike of the conquest of indigenous peoples in the advance of western civilization. As the last tribal peoples to capitulate fully to Euro-America in the late nineteenth century, Lakota and Apache societies (and individuals in these societies, such as Geronimo, Cochise, and Crazy Horse) were seized on to justify certain violent treatment but also for entertainment. Indeed, according to anthropologist Renato Rosaldo, there is in U.S. culture, and in western culture more generally, a nostalgic mourning for something once it has been destroyed, and from that mourning developed an ossification of that (dynamic) thing as the thing itself, be it Nature in national parks or Native peoples in the western genre (Rosaldo 1993). In sum, then, we might say that the warrior tradition is rooted in the culture of imperialism, both in its active form and in its more passive, nostalgic form. As Philip Deloria puts it, "Playing Indian represented, evaded, and perpetuated those [asymmetrical power] relations. Indianness was the bedrock for creative American identities, but it was also one of the foundations (slavery and gender relations being two others) for imagining and performing domination and power in America" (186).

Phil Jackson, an eminently creative man, has since taken over the Los Angeles Lakers basketball team, with its young superstars Shaquille O'Neal and Kobe Bryant. When asked if he would use his Native American motifs and practices in his coaching of the Lakers, Jackson replied: "Hey, this is the city of the Crips and Bloods after all. . . . LA is a place where gang behavior is the only way you survive on the streets. . . . The Sioux and the Oglala and the Lakota are all branches of gang behavior—it's tribalism. We're all part of some kind of tribe" (ESPN 1999). And in an interview on *The News Hour with Jim Lehrer* on June 16, 2000, Jackson spoke more flippantly about his use of American Indian traditions, laughingly stating that at least these tactics didn't bore his players (*The News Hour* 2000).

In the end, then, it's a case of "whatever works." What we have termed Phil Jackson "postmodern primitivism," a latter-day version of a long tradition of "playing Indian" in Euro-American culture, may give way to another homegrown tradition. Whatever pastiche can be culled from wherever to motivate someone is seized upon, whether by Jackson or by any number of corporate CEOs in their vision quests for becoming better warriors in an increasingly competitive global market. In our postmodern world, would-be "warriors" turn to ancient treatises and traditions. From the ancient Chinese Sun Tzu, to the Prussian Klauswitz, to the homegrown, authentic American traditions appropriating American Indian cultures, we shall overcome. As Phil Deloria notes:

The disconnections of the 1960s and 1970s may have reached peak development in the activities of the New Age, a movement for an aging counterculture. . . . In New Age identity quests, one can see the long shadows of certain strands of postmodernism: increasing reliance on texts and interpretations, runaway individualism within a rhetoric of community, the distancing of native people, and a gaping disjuncture between a cultural realm of serious play and the power dynamics of social conflict. (1999, 170)

And so, while the appropriation of Indian imagery in the 1960s may have served the oppositional and rebellious nature of that period, just as it continued to serve its many spin-offs, it hid the much more serious reality of appropriation, which has its roots deep in U.S. history. As the anthropologist John Borneman observes, "In the American context the constructed category 'Indian' occupied the space of the quintessentially 'foreign'"(Borneman 1995, 665). While it was historically accepted that Indian peoples were native to North America, it was also widely assumed by Euro-Americans (and by many American Indians as well, albeit for different reasons and to different ends) for a good deal of U.S. history that Indian peoples were foreign to the United States, a notion that was important in justifying the alienation of Indian lands and the formation of reservations. In other words, "the formidable cognitive and emotional task for white Americans was to (re)create oneself as and occupy the category 'American,' though fully 'foreign' oneself, through the expropriation of native lands and the liquidation of those natives" (Borneman 1995, 665). We see that task continuing in a more playful arena but in a no less serious way. While Phil Jackson salvages American Indian warrior traditions, Crow basketball players succumb to defeat. The Indian wars continue.

Jackson's use of the Native American warrior motif and the *Sports Illustrated* article representing Crow basketball as the product of a warrior culture are two sides of a cultural coin. Together they reveal an important ambivalence toward a continually changing contemporary society that is the real product and legacy of United States imperialism. The *Sports Illustrated* piece, for example, flatly positions Crow traditions of sharing, selflessness, and strong kinship as antithetical to success, individual mobility, and the possibility of a meaningful life in the contemporary world. Yet the key words in Jackson's success narrative convey precisely the ideals embodied in a Crow value system that *Sports Illustrated* credits with the downfall of its basketball stars: compassion, family unity, human connection, respect, and mutuality. In other words, Jackson draws on a set of cultural ideals that, in the *Sports Illustrated* article, modern society has worked to destroy and deploys these values in a way that has allowed him (the individual) to win.

As George Lipsitz has observed in his work on the ethnic television situation comedies of the 1950s, commercial popular culture often draws on collective memory as a source of entertainment—an entertainment that provides legitimacy for new social formations that demand everyone's allegiance while simultaneously destroying the foundations of past social arrangements (Lipsitz 1990). Jackson's narrative draws on cultural fragments in a way that helps provide a powerful sense of legitimacy to corporate capitalism in the competitive global marketplace. However, one cannot read his book alongside the *Sports Illustrated* article without noting the irony that they reflect on each other. As Lipsitz often has noted, collective memory evoked to provide legitimacy can also become the seed for more criticism. Sports and the warrior motif combine as a powerful vehicle through which Jackson is able to evoke desires for human connection, community, and compassion in the service of masculine victory on the corporate battlefield. But, reading his book, one might also ask why Jonathan Takes Enemy had to sacrifice these same values to become a "winner."

REFERENCES

Berkhoffer, Robert. 1979. *The White Man's Indian: Images of the American Indian from Columbus to Present.* New York: Random House.

Bird, Elizabeth, ed. 1996. *Dressing in Feathers: The Construction of the Indian in Popular Culture.* Boulder: Westview Press.

Borneman, John. 1995. American Anthropology as Foreign Policy. *American Anthropologist* 97, 4: 663–672.

Brooks, David. 2000. *Bobos in Paradise: The New Upper Class and How They Got There.* New York: Simon and Schuster.

Calloway, Colin G. 1999. *First Peoples: A Documentary Survey of American Indian History.* Boston: Bedford/St. Martin's Press.

Churchill, Ward. 1991. *Indians Are Us? Culture and Genocide in Native North America.* Monroe, ME: Common Courage Press.

Deloria, Philip. 1999. *Playing Indian.* New Haven: Yale University Press.

Deloria, Vine Jr. 1988 [1970]. *Custer Died for Your Sins: An Indian Manifesto.* Norman: University of Oklahoma Press.

ESPN. 1999. The Native American Sports Experience. *Outside the Lines.* Broadcast November 16.

Gray, Herman. 1995. *Watching Race: Television and the Struggle for Blackness.* Minneapolis: University of Minnesota Press.

Hill, Ruth Beebe. [1979]. *Hanta Yo.* New York: Doubleday.

Hoxie, Frederick. 1984. *A Final Promise: The Campaign to Assimilate the Indians, 1880–1920*. New York and Cambridge: Cambridge University Press.

Jackson, Phil, with Hugh Delehanty. 1995. *Sacred Hoops: Spiritual Lessons of a Hardwood Warrior*. New York: Hyperion.

Lipsitz, George. 1998. *The Possessive Investment in Whiteness: How White People Profit from Identity Politics*. Philadelphia: Temple University Press.

———. 1990. *Time Passages: Collective Memory and Popular Culture*. Minneapolis: University of Minnesota Press.

The News Hour with Jim Lehrer. 2000. Public Broadcasting System (U.S.). June 16.

Rogers, Phyllis. 1981. *The Image of the American Indian Produced and Directed by "Buffalo Bill."* UCLA Museum of Cultural History Pamphlet Series, no. 13.

Rosaldo, Renato. 1993. *Culture and Truth: The Remaking of Social Analysis*. Boston: Beacon Press.

Smith, Gary. 1991. Shadow of a Nation. *Sports Illustrated*, February 18, 60–74.

Spector, Janet. 1993. *What This Awl Means: Feminist Archaeology of a Wahpeton Dakota Village*. St. Paul: Minnesota Historical Society Press.

Van Lent, Peter. 1996. "Her Beautiful Savage": The Current Sexual Image of the Native American Male. In Elizabeth Bird, ed., *Dressing in Feathers: The Construction of the Indian in Popular Culture*. Boulder: Westview Press.

Whitt, Laurie Anne. 1999. Cultural Imperialism and the Marketing of Native America. In Duane Champagne, ed., *Contemporary Native American Cultural Issues*. Walnut Creek, CA: AltaMira Press.

Chapter Twelve

Running with Her Head Down

Oprah Winfrey and Middle-Class Black Women's Discourses of Fitness

Connie M. Razza

In the wake of popular women's sports victories such as the 1996 U.S. women's Olympic basketball victory and the 1999 World Cup triumph of the United States women's soccer team, writing about women's sports has gained a wider audience. *Sports Illustrated* and *Outside* have spun off women's magazines. Books have appeared offering surveys of women's sports history, accounts of particular teams, biographies of star players, and works of fiction.[1] Much of the recent writing has emphasized an intimate relationship with one's body and with teammates, coaches, opponents.

However, fitness literature offers none of these relationships. Rather than presenting the protagonist working with her body and teammates, fitness literature isolates the heroine in a battle against her body and the world. Although fitness magazines, manuals, and autobiographies may occasionally feature sports activities, the values they present differ fundamentally from those of sport. Although both fitness and sport emphasize hard work and discipline, fitness ideology places a premium on individual self-reliance, rather than drawing attention to the group context of personal effort.

In 1994, Oprah Winfrey established herself as the icon of women's fitness. Having fought an epic and quite public war with her weight, Winfrey marked her victory over fat by running the Marine Corps Marathon. She then published a book and produced a video with her exercise physiologist Bob Greene in order to help others win their battles.[2] Her identification as a model for women's fitness generally, rather than for black women's fitness in particular, suggests a project of deracination that is a common part of her public persona.[3] Winfrey's project of moving a black woman's experience into the mainstream of American womanhood exemplifies this most important goal of the black women's fitness movement: assimilation. It is, then, fitting that Winfrey would be the icon for black women's fitness precisely because she positions herself as an everywoman.[4] This chapter is concerned with the machinations of Winfrey's project of self-creation, of self-reliance, of the American dream.

I'm Everywoman

Winfrey's universalized position requires that she present herself as an individual like other individuals rather than as an individual within a specific context. Winfrey is a rich and successful black woman in a career dominated by white men. She has strong ties to a legacy of Southern black foodways, which grew out of the social and economic caste system of slavery. Her first dramatic weight gain took place during her transition between these two contexts. However, she chooses to downplay her positions in these (and other) historical, social, and economic contexts in order to highlight her own power, her self-determination.

For example, instead of allowing herself to be read as a black woman specifically, Winfrey presented Harpo Productions' valet, Louise. While Winfrey was shooting the video *Make the Connection*, Louise committed to lose weight. A year later, during the taping of the show introducing the video, Louise had lost seventy-eight pounds, and Winfrey featured her as the first guest.[5] Winfrey told Louise and the audience:

> I think you're classic, culturally classic in that you're like my mother, my auntie, my grandmother, all of the ma'dears who like smothered chicken for dinner, macaroni and cheese everyday, not just on Sunday. I know Louise in the morning used to have some stuff at the table. I'd pass on my way to the work out room and go, "You gonna have doughnuts and smothered pork chops?" Before ten o'clock.

Winfrey's connection to the tradition with which she identifies Louise's eating habits is delicate. Although her elders ate like Louise, Winfrey does not indicate that this is *her* tradition. The well-known strain on her family relationships distances Winfrey from the women she names who resemble

Louise.[6] Further, Winfrey frequently mentions her long-standing low-fat diet.[7] The story that Winfrey tells highlights her difference from Louise by directly juxtaposing Louise's excesses with Winfrey's discipline. Louise, then, stands alone in representing the poor eating habits of Southern food traditions. Ultimately, this gesture offers Winfrey a figure (of a domestic, notably) on whom she can pin a uniquely black identity for the episode. Louise carries the weight of history and sociology, freeing Winfrey to be everywoman.

Winfrey most often replaces historical or sociological contexts with the language of spirituality. She writes, "The biggest change I've made is a spiritual one. It comes from the realization that taking care of my body and my health is really one of the greatest kinds of love I can give myself. Every day I put forth the effort to take care of myself. And there's no question I'm living a better life" (MC 32). On the show introducing the video she preaches, "That's what I really want people to get. That it's a spiritual change that happens after you take control and that it's exactly what God, the universe, intended for you." In both statements, Winfrey suggests to her audience that the daily discipline needed to lose weight will lead to individual spiritual growth. Further, she promises that this spirituality will improve her readers' lives generally. The spirituality to which she appeals offers the individual as the solution to her own problems. Through discipline and self-focus, each person takes responsibility for and resolves those factors that lead to her weight issue. By regaining control of her life, each individual is able more generally to better her life.

This emphasis on spiritual growth and indifference to historical context serve to further the conception of the American dream that Winfrey advocates. True to talk-show form, Winfrey uses "Oprah's Story," the autobiographical introduction to *Make the Connection: Ten Steps to a Better Body—and a Better Life,* to reshape the American dream for her readers.

God Bless the Child Who's Got Her Own

Winfrey's strong emphasis on self-reliance extends both a long tradition of self-dependence in African American letters and the recent rise in self-help literature generally. Booker T. Washington's 1901 autobiography, *Up from Slavery,* provides a well-known articulation of this emphasis on self-dependence.[8] Throughout his autobiography, Washington advises his readers of the important role that self-reliance and struggle play in forming one's strength of character. Washington's pedagogical model comes to depend on the physical labor that had been required of slaves, because he believes that it prepared one to be "self-dependent," whereas, he says, "the slave system on our place, in a large measure, took the spirit of self-reliance and self-help out of the white people" (*US* 170). Because of the trials of slavery, blacks have the tools necessary to be truly self-reliant.

In the aftermath of slavery, Washington's prioritization of industrial training seems grounded in the fear that to stray too far from one's place (i.e., blacks' manual and domestic labor) will result in atrophying muscles of self-reliance. Washington ties these priorities not only to individual success but to the aggregate well-being of the race. In this, he differs from Winfrey's desire to assimilate black women into an American mainstream. Washington instead aims to establish a separate black middle class.

To achieve this goal, Washington argues, the trials of physical labor encourage the "self-dependence" necessary for blacks' advancement. The category "self-dependence" implies that one must rely primarily on him- or herself to succeed, rather than that one can live detached from all others. One who is self-dependent can make his or her own way in the economic world without being an undue burden on his or her community. Those individuals can then earn success for both themselves and their race by proving their irreplaceability.

Usefulness is an important rubric for Washington. When black men and women prove their usefulness to the economy, Washington insists, their success will be guaranteed. And, he argues, blacks have already proven their usefulness in manual labor and domestic positions. Thus he insists that blacks accept as organic a division of labor that was previously maintained through constraint. This prioritization of usefulness highlights the irony of black women's fitness literature's adherence to a Washingtonian evaluation of self-reliance and struggle. Washington emphasizes physical labor (notably not exercise) as both the most socially acceptable kind of labor for blacks and the most likely to build character.

But black middle-class women's fitness literature engages Washington's tradition of self-dependence and presents its readership with an opportunity: the literature offers specific directions for *constructing* an obstacle course that is supposed to build the character necessary for making oneself. The need for black middle-class women's fitness literature to help construct obstacles to build muscle and character suggests a simultaneous adoption of Washington's terms of character building and denial of the superiority of physical labor. Physical leisure is more desirable for this

group. Through facing self-made obstacles, black fitness readers are encouraged to construct themselves uniquely. They also are able to establish
a context for themselves that, although largely free of others, does call
back to this tradition of self-reliance in black letters and black lives.

Winfrey's emphasis on individual success without regard to socioeco-
nomic context highlights each individual's responsibility for (and ignores
social and historical forces that contribute to) the obstacles that face her.
First, one is most obviously responsible for creating the challenges that
will help her lose weight. She must, for example, set fitness goals that push
her capabilities. She must avoid eating some foods that she is used to enjoying. She must be a vigilant exerciser. But she is also responsible for the
biggest obstacle of all: her weight problem itself. By reciting her own
binge-and-diet habits, Winfrey insists on her accountability for her excess
weight, whether or not she knew the problems she was causing. She makes
no gesture toward the roles that historical, regional, professional, or social
pressures might have played on her weight gain. The adoption of full responsibility is important if black women's fitness fans are ever to live up to
this standard of self-making.

Victoria Johnson, one of the earliest black fitness instructors to have
her own series of instructional videotapes, exemplifies this part of the
project of the black women's fitness movement. She opens her book *Victoria Johnson's Attitude* with an autobiographical introduction in which
she recalls her youth as the daughter of migrant farm workers.[9] Having
never known stability because her family was constantly on the move, she
found security and comfort in food. She would seek food out when she
felt unsafe. Motivated by her parents' "search for racial equality," she
started going to school with white students. However, she became very
self-conscious of her large body and began practicing disordered eating
(namely, extreme dieting and bulimia). Importantly, she states that it was
her body size, not "the color of my skin that made me feel different" (*VJA*
5). She is able to erase this difference through fitness. Although she insists
on her total comfort with her white peers, she later catalogs an intense
alienation from other blacks because she has an active interest in school
(*VJA* 7–8).[10]

The story Johnson writes traces two parallel paths: (1) the move from
poor and unstable to financially secure and comfortable and (2) the transformation from unhealthy and unhappy to fit and self-confident. As the
title of her book suggests, Johnson places a great deal of emphasis on one's

attitude, emphasizing the triumph of individual will over individual problems. Although Johnson's class position influences her relationship to food, her narrative constructs that influence as psychological rather than sociological. As such, both the problem and the solution are based in the individual. So, rather than trying to distance herself from the black community in particular, Johnson's aim is to become part of the aggregate of the American mainstream.

Like Johnson, Winfrey's stories reflect a firm commitment to self-reliance. Indeed, Winfrey advocates a degree of isolation in order to achieve the weight-loss goals and spiritual growth that her program values. The individual focus of fitness, as opposed to the community focus of health in the World Health Organization's sense, helps achieve this isolation.[11]

Both Johnson and Winfrey forgo Washington's attention to historical moment, sociological context, and racial advancement in favor of an individualized project consistent with contemporary self-help literature. According to a study by Adrian Furnham and Mark R. McDermott, "the public perceives strategies of will power and self-reliance to be the most effective ways of overcoming a *self-indulgence* problem."[12] The authors explain the implications of this perception:

> Such an insistence on the primacy of self-reliance . . . suggests: first, subjects' willingness to individualise and decontextualise the causation of the problem, designating aetiology intrapersonally rather interpersonally (Brown, 1986); and secondly, subjects' willingness to take responsibility for overcoming these problems, despite any additional assistance obtained via seeking help from others. ("LB" 405)

This extreme individuation is present in Winfrey's texts. Rather than addressing, for example, the impact of Southern black foodways and poor health-care access[13] or the pressures of being an isolated black woman working in a largely white, male-dominated field, Winfrey focuses much more exclusively on herself as the source of the problem as well as the only source of the solution. However, Furnham and McDermott criticize the accuracy of these self-focused perceptions. While they acknowledge that individuals must commit to alleviating their own problems, they argue that the lay beliefs reflected in their study place too much emphasis on self-help strategies and not enough on professional assistance.

Gerald M. Rosen, a frequent critic of self-help literature, has noted that self-help treatments cannot ensure proper self-diagnosis or application.

Therefore, especially in the case of failed attempts, "there may be risks of negative self-attributions, of anger toward self or others."[14] This self-attribution of negative results indicates a heightened emphasis on individual responsibility, largely to the exclusion of seeking outside help.

Winfrey emphatically advocates for self-reliance, even as she illustrates the failures of that strategy. Throughout "Oprah's Story," Winfrey recounts her failed efforts at losing weight by herself. She finally does lose the weight, with the help of a staff.[15] However, despite her employment of both a chef and an exercise physiologist, Winfrey insists that she and she alone is responsible for her "change." In claiming herself as the exclusive source of her success, Winfrey hyperbolically reflects the importance of individual commitment to a project of self-improvement. Her assertion of her self-making—which both encourages her audience and belies the function of her staff—is necessary to her claim for a new American dream that is available to all women regardless of race.

Like other narratives of self-made success, Winfrey's story encourages her readers to believe that everyone enters the weight-loss game on equal footing, with the same resource: one's own will. If an individual wants *it* badly enough and works for *it* hard enough, she can and will attain *it* (whether *it* is the perfect body or the perfect bank account). Indeed, contrary to appearances, Winfrey argues that she faces more obstacles than the common fat person: she is on television, so her shame is always exposed; she has an extraordinarily full schedule, so she must schedule her workouts at uncomfortable times. But she has done *it*, and so can you.

Her insistence that she alone did *it* effaces the work of her trainer and chef. Both her video and her book imply that all the information her trainer, Bob Greene, shared with Winfrey has been collected and packaged and that, apart from providing that background information, Greene served primarily as a workout buddy. Greene's suggestion that readers work out with a friend combines with the information in the book to simulate for readers Greene's total function in Winfrey's program. By denying the role of her staff in the success of her program, Winfrey further encourages her readers to assume full responsibility for overcoming their weight problems. Although *Make the Connection* may serve as an important tool in their effort, readers' success or failure rests wholly on their own shoulders.

Winfrey's insistence on individual responsibility is consistent with her frequent reference to her overeating as an addiction. After her first indepth description of a desperate binge, Winfrey writes, "Now, looking back, I see no difference between myself and a junkie, scrambling for a needle and whatever dope might be around. Food was my dope" (*MC* 9). Winfrey's language of addiction provides an understanding of overeating within a medicalized discourse with which much of the public might be familiar. However, just as she advocates for fitness rather than health, Winfrey ignores medical approaches to eating disorders in favor of a self-help model. By employing the discourse of addiction that twelve-step programs such as Alcoholics Anonymous use, Winfrey inflects traditional connotations of obesity as "moral failure, the inability to delay gratification, poor impulse control, greed, and self-indulgence."[16] The discursive affinity between overeating and drug or alcohol addiction both reflects a popular perception of the problem and creates a way to understand and articulate the problem and solution that does not simply dismiss the overeater but offers the opportunity for rehabilitation.[17]

On the video, Winfrey carefully highlights the process of recovery, which demands the vigilant attention that twelve-step programs advocate. When she says, "Beyond a doubt if I had not worked out every day for the past three years . . . I would have, beyond a shadow of a doubt, put all the weight back on," she highlights the discipline that "making the connection" requires for her.[18] However, on the show announcing the video, Winfrey more comfortably speaks as though the project is completed. Winfrey speaks of the "struggles with weight" as behind her. Contextualizing a clip of the video in which she says, "I just thought, 'You've got to change,'" Winfrey reports to her audience, "And change I did." The shift to a past-perfect tense suggests Winfrey's increased trust that her new weight will remain constant. Despite occasional lapses like this, Winfrey continues throughout the show to recognize the need for hard work. She engages a discourse of recovery that is very much like the twelve-step process.

Winfrey writes that when she was overweight, "I was feeling no stress, because I was eating it all" (*MC* 19). Now, she is committed to exercising and eating healthily because "I never want to be anesthetized by the extra weight again" (*MC* 224). Like Winfrey, "Martin," a case study in an article about Alcoholics Anonymous (AA), identifies the first process of AA as understanding "that you're feeling something."[19] Both Winfrey and Martin identify their addictions as attempts to escape their feelings. Both addicts see "remembering their spirit" as a key component to their recovery.[20] However, unlike the twelve-step process to which Winfrey often alludes, Winfrey's plan does not require a program of mutual support with others. Two psychotherapists of substance abuse treatment have noted that "if it were the individual (self) who was doing the helping, there would be no need for a group" in AA.[21] Winfrey articulates no such need for a group. The message she sends is that we make ourselves.

Reframing the Dream

Winfrey certainly moves from poverty to wealth, but (like Victoria Johnson) she posits the significant success of her transition from fat to fit. This shift of the relevant realm of success draws her audience into the narrative because it allows readers to imagine Winfrey's success as possible for themselves. Winfrey is already simultaneously read as both exceptional and ordinary because of her talk show. Her on-air sincerity and openness about her own life have led to her talk show's success. At the same time, too much attention to her social context would destroy the identification Winfrey is trying to create. Although Winfrey is more economically successful than most can ever expect to be, and although she has already become fit, she writes her personal narrative as if she is "one of us." In her opening, Winfrey immediately shifts the story away from herself:

> "And the nominees for Best Talk-Show Host are. . ." Those five seconds when the announcer is calling your name—no matter who you are or what you've been told about what an honor it is to be nominated—at that moment, when your name is announced before the world, you want to win. Except for me, this night. I honestly didn't care.
> I was sitting in the front row trying to keep my too-fat knees together in a ladylike position. (*MC* 1)

Although she writes about receiving a Daytime Emmy, Winfrey draws her readers into a relationship of identification rather than awe or alienation by shifting to a generic second-person pronoun. Even in a moment of exceptionalism, Winfrey connects herself to her readership. But not completely. She differentiates herself from her audience, not because she was nominated for the Emmy but because she does not care if she wins it.

This alienation-identification dynamic empowers Winfrey's readers. As the reader identifies with Winfrey in a largely alien context or sees her negative self-image as both exceptional (i.e., extremely severe) and exemplary (i.e., representative), so she reads Winfrey's victory over her weight as both extraordinary and ordinary. She imagines Winfrey's accomplishments as possible for herself. Positioning the reader in this way, Winfrey hopes to help readers gain control. It is not, however, control over weight that is at stake. As the subtitle of the book suggests, her close reader will take control of her life. In the project of weight loss, the reader can become a self-made woman.

Her shift from fat to fit requires that her lack of control metamorphose into discipline. Her opening anecdote reveals an utterly out-of-control Winfrey. She waits to hear the decision of the Academy in the contest for best talk-show host. Despite all that she has done to achieve a Daytime Emmy nomination, her telling focuses on her inability to control her situation or herself. She has been trying to lose weight; she is unable to control that. She is so anxious about her weight that she dreads the possibility of winning the award; she cannot control this. "The weight," she writes, "was consuming me" (*MC* 1).

As we turn the page, we see a picture of Winfrey after having won the Emmy that night juxtaposed with an image of post-*Connection* Winfrey winning a later Emmy. The look of shock in the first picture is replaced with a look of self-confident pleasure. Under the picture of the 237-pound Winfrey she writes, "I felt so much like a loser, like I'd lost control of my life. And the weight was symbolic of how out-of-control I was" (*MC* 2). Setting the tone for the rest of the book, Winfrey expresses that her weight, which had seemed to be the problem, was in fact only a symptom of the larger inner conflict in her life. Above this articulation of her desperation, a shocked Winfrey's bronze jacket pulls at her breasts as she grasps the award in one hand with the other hand outstretched. Her posture and expression suggest disbelief.

On the facing page, we see the slimmer Winfrey and we read, "The next day, I met Bob. That's when my life began to change" (*MC* 3). In this picture, Winfrey displays in one hand the trophy and in the other her gown. Her newly buffed arms and corseted dress exhibit the spoils of her discipline. This seems to be the message of her narrative as a whole: *I was unable to enjoy the rewards of my disciplined professional life until I was able to get my physical and personal life under control.* Her newly disciplined body exhibits that accomplishment. Her body becomes the window to her soul. When she is fat, she is unable to feel successful and she makes a habit of self-destructive behavior. When she is fit, she feels more in control of her life but also better able to enjoy her life.

Winfrey's focus on her movement from fat to fit, from out of control to disciplined, simultaneously interrogates and affirms the American dream. Winfrey describes the financial success promised by the American dream as empty. She is unable to appreciate her economic achievement until she successfully navigates the road to fitness. Of course, without her fame and fortune, markers of traditional success, Winfrey would only sound disgruntled with the American dream. Only as one who has fulfilled the American dream is Winfrey authorized to change it.

Winfrey's proposal that fitness replace fortune as the manifestation of the realized dream bears out Naomi Wolf's thesis in *The Beauty Myth*.[22] Wolf identifies the "affluent, educated, liberated woman of the First World" as the subject of the beauty myth (*BM* 9). Wolf highlights that

> the qualities that a given period calls beautiful in women are merely symbols of the female behavior that that period considers desirable: *The beauty myth is always actually prescribing behavior and not appearance.* (*BM* 13–14)

The fitness ideal for which Winfrey advocates and strives shares the values and behaviors of the more traditional American dream. Hard work, discipline, and self-denial form the means through which both financial and fitness American dreams are fulfilled. Because Winfrey has achieved financial success, and because she has a faithful following of women, regardless of their races, she has the authority to "redefine" success for women. She has license to note that material wealth cannot be fulfilling in the absence of personal, spiritual, and physical achievement. Wolf's understanding that the beauty myth prescribes behaviors that inscribe the body offers a lens through which to see Greene and Winfrey's subtitle, *Ten Steps to a Better Body—and a Better Life*. The better body does not simply lead to a better life; it visually represents the better life that is being achieved. On the show introducing the video, Winfrey underscored the meritocracy of the American dream in this fitness context when she said "You get out of this exactly what you put in." Importantly, Winfrey does not suggest that the more traditional American dream is unimportant. Rather, women should aim to achieve both.[23] By thus encouraging women, Winfrey's "redefinition" in fact underscores, rather than offers an alternative to, societally prescribed "feminine" behaviors.

Although Wolf's analysis is limited by her focus on middle- to upper-middle-class white women, this limitation precisely marks how Winfrey's redefinition works. Winfrey makes her new American dream available to black women, but not by appealing specifically to them. Instead, Winfrey offers success to all women. This decision against specifically identifying black women as her audience reflects a larger push by middle-class black women to assimilate into a broader American middle class.

Veronica Webb, the first black model to have an exclusive contract with a major cosmetic company, illustrates the force of this assimilationist agenda. She recounts losing her contract with Revlon because the company's market research showed that the middle-class black women it was targeting did not want to see themselves as different from any other consumer or, more accurately, any other member of the middle class (93–94). Webb was already associated with Revlon's line specifically for black women and so was dismissed in favor of a fresh face, Halle Berry. Like Berry's role in more recent Revlon campaigns, Winfrey models African American women's opportunities in a larger (seemingly deracinated) middle-class women's context.[24]

Winfrey's role in this Revlon campaign is emblematic of the problem with her approach to black women's inclusion in the (old or revised) American dream. After losing sixty-seven pounds on a liquid diet, Winfrey posed for a Revlon advertisement. However, once she resumed eating solid food, she rapidly regained her lost weight and more. Her ability to keep the weight off was undermined by the very process by which she lost it. She had lived for months ignoring her physiological needs—as a relatively healthy person, she needed food and exercise. However, she was able to create the illusion of success. Likewise, her new approach to weight loss and her new vision of the American dream isolate individuals from her social context, producing the illusion of success by distracting women from external contributors to their weight problems (i.e., regional, professional, sociological pressures) and systemic limitations on their economic success (i.e., sexism, racism, prejudice against overweight women). Winfrey offers black women the illusion of equality and inclusion by focusing exclusively on individual responsibility and ignoring external factors.

In an article about fiction writing of the 1970s and 1980s, Ann Folwell Stanford has written that black women writers "insist that individual disease is inextricably bound up with broader social ills—sexism, racism, classism, and heterosexism, to mention but a few."[25] I would extend this argument to contemporaneous nonfiction health literature by black women.[26] Winfrey's choice to focus on fitness extracts her readers and herself from the social context provided by a concern with health or with sport. Her description of her victorious marathon run seems an accurate summation of her philosophy of the American dream itself: "I was focused and determined. I spoke to almost no one . . . I never looked up" (*MC* 30). Winfrey's participation in the Marine Corps Marathon reinforces her emphasis on discipline. However, the Marine

Corps requires and acknowledges the necessity of others for the success of a mission.

1. I thank Richard Yarborough, Valerie A. Smith, Michael North, Debbie Banner, Tracy Curtis, Jim Lee, and David Witzling for their insights regarding this chapter.

Examples of these texts include: Susan K. Cahn, *Coming on Strong: Gender and Sexuality in Twentieth-Century Women's Sport* (Cambridge, MA: Harvard University Press, 1994); Sara Corbett, *Venus to the Hoop: A Gold Medal Year in Women's Basketball* (New York: Doubleday, 1997); Madeleine Blais, *In These Girls, Hope Is a Muscle* (New York: Atlantic Monthly Press, 1995); Jackie Joyner-Kersee, with Sonja Steptoe, *A Kind of Grace: The Autobiography of the World's Greatest Female Athlete* (New York: Warner Books, 1997); Cynthia Cooper, *She Got Game: My Personal Odyssey* (New York: Warner Books, 1999); Nina Revoyr, *The Necessary Hunger* (New York: Simon and Schuster, 1997); Joli Sandoz, ed., *A Whole Other Ball Game: Women's Literature on Women's Sport* (New York: Noonday Press, 1997).

2. Oprah Winfrey and Bob Greene, *Make the Connection: Ten Steps to a Better Body—and a Better Life* (New York: Hyperion Books, 1996); hereafter cited in text as *MC*, with page numbers. See also Oprah Winfrey, *Make the Connection . . . It's about Changing Your Life* (Burbank: Buena Vista Home Video, 1997).

3. In identifying Winfrey's project as one of deracination, I mean that she aims to prove that race is not important, not that she wants to deny that she is black. Janice Peck notes that "Winfrey has been described as a comforting, nonthreatening bridge between black and white cultures—a perception . . . link[ed] to popular accounts of Winfrey that minimize and/or depoliticize her race, presenting her instead as an exemplar of American success" ("Talk about Racism: Framing a Popular Discourse of Race on *Oprah Winfrey*," *Cultural Critique* [Spring 1994]: 89–126).

4. Throughout the episode of *Oprah* on which Winfrey announces the release of the video *Make the Connection . . . It's about Changing Your Life*, Winfrey speaks as an everywoman. An early exchange on the show between an audience member and Winfrey demonstrates the workings of this dynamic:

> *Audience member:* I feel the same way. I mean, that whole video was me. Totally.
> I could relate to everything you said.
> *Winfrey:* Like what? Wasting time?
> *Audience member:* Oh, yeah. And every morning you think you're going to start over and—I'm gonna cry just saying it—the whole thing was me.
> *Winfrey:* The whole thing was me, too. But, it's everybody, that's what I thought. You know what's so interesting I—you know, I have a very big and full life,

you know. I'm on TV everyday but what I am really interested in people knowing is that the only difference between being famous and not is that more people know you, that your pain is the same.

In this conversation, the (white) audience member affirms Winfrey's ability to represent other women, regardless of race. Winfrey's response to this license simultaneously claims the right ("it's everybody, that's what I thought" and "your pain is the same") and asserts the individual nature of *her* story ("the whole thing was me, too" and "I have a very big and full life. . . . I'm on TV everyday"). The tension in these statements suggests an ambivalence in the project of sharing her story. On the one hand, she wants to speak as everywoman; on the other, she does not want to give up the self-focus on her own weight-loss project.

5. "Making the Connection," *The Oprah Winfrey Show*, aired 3 December 1997.

6. See, for example, Merrell Noden, *People Profiles Oprah Winfrey* (New York: Time, Inc., 1999); 23–31.

7. Rosie Daley, *In the Kitchen with Rosie: Oprah's Favorite Recipes* (New York: Knopf, 1994).

8. Booker T. Washington, *Up from Slavery*. (1901; reprint, New York: Penguin Classics, 1986); hereafter cited in text as *US*, with page numbers.

9. Victoria Johnson, with Megan V. Davis, *Victoria Johnson's Attitude: An Inspirational Guide to Redefining Your Body, Your Health, and Your Outlook* (New York: Penguin Books, 1993); hereafter cited in text as *VJA*, with page numbers.

10. Like Johnson's awareness of her difference from her schoolmates, Winfrey recalls getting the job that led to *The Oprah Winfrey Show* and realizing that she did not look like anyone else who'd ever hosted a show. In her book, Winfrey acknowledges that she is different from her colleagues because she is both fat and black (*Make the Connection*, 5–6). However, on the video, Winfrey focuses exclusively on her weight.

11. The World Health Organization defines health as "a state of complete physical, mental, and social well-being and not merely the absence of disease or infirmity" (quoted in Michael S. Goldstein, *The Health Movement: Promoting Fitness in America* [New York: Twayne Publishers, 1992], 5).

12. Adrian Furnham and Mark R. McDermott, "Lay Beliefs about the Efficacy of Self-Reliance, Seeking Help and External Control as Strategies for Overcoming Obesity, Drug Addiction, Marital Problems, Stuttering, and Insomnia." *Psychology and Health* 9 (1994): 398. This source hereafter cited as "LB" in text, with page numbers.

13. For a discussion of the impact of these factors on black women's health status, see Angela Y. Davis, "Sick and Tired of Being Sick and Tired: The Politics of Black Women's Health," in Evelyn C. White, ed., *The Black Women's Health Book: Speaking for Ourselves* (1990; reprint, Seattle: Seal Press, 1994), 18–26.

14. Gerald M. Rosen, "Self-Help or Hype? Comments on Psychology's Failure to Advance Self-Care," *Professional Psychology: Research and Practice* 24, 3 (1993): 341.

15. I write about her weight loss as final because the autobiographical introduction freezes that accomplishment as final, despite any post-*Connection* weight gain.

16. Sharlene Hesse-Biber, *Am I Thin Enough Yet? The Cult of Thinness and the Commercialization of Identity* (New York: Oxford University Press, 1996), 4.

17. Hesse-Biber, a sociologist of eating disorders, warns that this addiction model has political consequences, such as the decontextualization of eating disorders from outside social forces (*Am I Thin Enough Yet*, 43).

18. According to Winfrey's personal trainer and coauthor, Bob Greene, "making the connection" is that "change in perspective" that allows a person to see the "excess weight is merely a symptom of a larger problem and losing it is a side effect. . . . It is really about increasing self-confidence, inner strength, and discipline. It is about feeling better on a daily basis, having control over your life, and caring about yourself. Ultimately, it is about self-love" (*Making the Connection*, 50–51).

19. E. J. Khantzian and John E. Mack, "How AA Works and Why It's Important for Clinicians to Understand," *Journal of Substance Abuse Treatment* 11, 2: 82.

20. "Remembering the Spirit" is a daily five-minute segment on Winfrey's talk show that explores how individuals have changed their spiritual lives in obvious and not-so-obvious ways.

21. N. Peter Johnson and John Chappel, "Using AA and Other Twelve-Step Programs More Effectively," *Journal of Substance Abuse Treatment* 1, 2: 137.

22. Naomi Wolf, *The Beauty Myth: How Images of Beauty Are Used against Women* (New York: Anchor Books, 1992); hereafter cited in text as *BM*, with page numbers.

23. Winfrey's success according to the new dream was largely achieved through her success by the old dream's standards. She was able to hire a personal chef and an exercise physiologist. Although Winfrey constantly reminds her viewers and readers that they do not need the staff she had in order to succeed, her ability to hire these specialists certainly helped her.

24. Veronica Webb, *Veronica Webb Sight: Adventures in the Big City* (New York: Miramax Books/Hyperion, 1998). This connection is illustrated by the fact that when Winfrey lost much of her weight on a liquid diet, Revlon featured her in ads for their general makeup line.

25. Ann Folwell Stanford, "Mechanisms of Disease: African-American Women Writers, Social Pathologies, and the Limits of Medicine," *NWSA Journal* 6, 1: 28.

26. For example, see White, ed., *Black Women's Health Book*.

Chapter Thirteen

Saving Face, Place, and Race
Oscar De La Hoya and the "All-American" Dreams of U.S. Boxing

Gregory S. Rodríguez

In the last quarter of the twentieth century, Mexican and Mexican American boxing industries must be seen as both historical realities and as contemporary continuums that have revealed, and still reveal, the construction of ethnic and national identities among U.S. Mexicans. By the mid-1980s the weekly spectacles of prizefighting arenas in southern California were the domains of Mexican Americans and Mexican nationals whom together I refer to as ethnic Mexicans or U.S. Mexicans. Throughout the twentieth century, southern California had been the center of ethnic Mexican boxing. Boxing contributed to a sense of ethnic and national belonging, much like flags, anthems, religious icons, geographical boundaries, commonality of language, political structures, and the ideas of a shared culture. Like nationalism, boxing divided and united people. As movements for ethnic, national, and racial self-determination in the United States heightened awareness of group difference, nationalistic expressions in boxing permitted the blurring of differences and helped unite a multiethnic people behind a single sporting ideal. The great unifying quality emerging in commercial sport was that it offered a community of involvement that provided a place for everyone, whatever her age or station, whether fan or player. Nevertheless, by the 1980s, new ethnic Mexican boxing idols emerged within a postindustrial, postmodern era where an ever-expanding media network manufactured their celebrity and shaped their ethnic and national identities.

The new generation of ethnic Mexican boxing heroes emerging in southern California by the turn of the twentieth century is instructive of many important contemporary debates related to identity politics. World champion Oscar De La Hoya offers a particularly apt case for developing insights into the broader social and cultural concerns related to racial and national identity politics. By examining the evolution of his career and the discourses that surround it, I hope to provide insights into the ways ethnic Mexicans define, contest, and reproduce their identities at the new millennium. I begin by examining structural changes in the boxing industry, in its production and consumption, and then turn to the experiences of ethnic Mexican boxers and fans. I focus particularly on De La Hoya, who I argue has been read by whites as transcending his racial status at the same time that ethnic Mexicans have made "race," place, gender, and class the key issues of his career.

As it had done throughout the twentieth century, boxing continued in the 1980s and 1990s to provide a common language for a wide array of groups comprising the increasingly diverse ethnic Mexican community. Ethnic Mexican social groups often otherwise at odds over issues of U.S.-Mexican identity politics nevertheless continued to hold in common a special identification with ethnic Mexican boxers. The sport represented the dreams of ethnic Mexicans of all colors, classes, generations, and sexual and political orientations. Even local politicians became enthusiastic about the possibilities of using boxing to get in touch with their constituents. For example, Congressman Edward Roybal, the moderate representing East Los Angeles, became a big supporter of local boxing. Roybal—who worried in public about the rising militancy of East Los Angeles youth in the 1960s, especially their willingness to "riot" for recognition—offered the violence of the ring as a panacea. He bought an old church in East Los Angeles and turned it into the Resurrection Boxing Gymnasium, which became home to many world champions. In 1996 welterweight champion Oscar De La Hoya, himself a product of Roybal's gym, bought the building and made it the Oscar De La Hoya Youth Center. He refurbished the gym, adding coed facilities, and made it not only a place for both males and females to box but also a place for them to study, get tutoring with their schoolwork, learn about computers, and engage in family activities of various sorts.[1]

As a result of boxing's expanding appeal to more heterogeneous groups, the sport became widely known as a proven way for a select group of ethnic Mexicans to "make it" in southern California society. By the early

1980s another generation of local Mexican American and Mexican national boxers were ready to become "main eventers" at Los Angeles' world-famous Olympic Auditorium—or so they thought.

Although ethnic Mexicans mobilized themselves to dominate local championship boxing, producing more champions in the 1970s than in any previous decade, by the early 1980s corporate forces and technical change would transform the production and consumption of boxing, unmooring the sport from its local context. Whereas in the 1970s gate receipts were the primary revenue generated by southern California boxing, by the 1980s promoters were perfecting their use of television to reach wider audiences and increase their profits. The power of television gave rise to a new kind of promoter, free of the attachments that had chained his predecessors to specific venues. Boxing promoters such as Don King and Bob Arum sought contracts with the fighters directly and then worried about negotiating sites and television rights. They staged fights in exclusive locations, such as Las Vegas, where they soon could charge $1,000 a seat, then beamed the fights to local theaters, where everyone else paid to watch. With the California Athletic Commission firmly on their side, southern California boxing venues had successfully locked out renegade promoters like King and Arum until the 1980s. In that decade, Arum and King began snatching up fighters the moment they made names for themselves as promising amateurs. The new boxing capitalism these promoters represented coincided with a renewed interest in boxing at the national level, largely as a result of the success of U.S. boxers in globally televised Olympic competition. The new corporate prizefighting promoters virtually guaranteed Olympic boxing champions huge television contracts from the start of their professional careers.

For young ethnic Mexican males in East Los Angeles, the sport now offered the dream of instant boxing credibility, international acclaim, and a chance to become fabulously wealthy. Indeed, largely as a result of the new boxing capitalism introduced by Don King and Bob Arum, by the mid-1980s, East L.A. boxers wanted to fight for "Olympic gold" more than they did for the local ethnic Mexican audiences that attended fights at the Olympic Auditorium. In the 1970s and 1980s, Mexican Americans took notice when African American Olympians such as Floyd Patterson, Muhammad Ali, George Foreman, Joe Frazer, Sugar Ray Leonard, Evander Holyfield, and others used boxing to win acceptance as "Americans" and made a lot of money in the process. The allure of big bucks in Los Angeles boxing and the high cost of maintaining amateur status kept virtually every ethnic Mexican champion from competing in the Olympics until the 1980s. In the 1980s, however, young boxing prospects found new sources of sponsorship, especially among the slowly expanding Mexican American middle class. For example, East L.A. Olympians Paul Gonzáles and Oscar De La Hoya realized their Olympic dreams by drawing on the resources of the East Los Angeles Mexican American middle class. The tremendous growth of the ethnic Mexican population in Los Angeles, from about 1.1 million in 1970 to 3.7 million in 1990, fueled economic growth that benefited ethnic Mexican entrepreneurship.[2] And it was this middle-class minority that found ways to sustain the amateur status and Olympic dreams of young boxing prospects.

Meanwhile, local L.A. promoters tapped into the expanding audiences of recently arrived or commuting Mexican nationals. As more and more local youth set their sights on the Olympics in the early 1980s, the Olympic Auditorium came to rely almost exclusively on Mexican national boxers, who filled the house with Mexican immigrant fans. In January 1984 the *Los Angeles Times* announced that the "Olympic Auditorium's weekly-boxing era ha[d] ended." It had been a rough four years. In 1980, Los Angeles' famous "Dragon Lady," Aileen Eaton, retired after thirty-two years of promoting weekly boxing at the Olympic. In 1981 the Los Angeles Athletic Club sold the property—fifty-seven years after designing and building the arena—citing rising property taxes as their main problem. In the next three years the arena would have three different boxing promoters, who steadily began losing money. By 1984 the Olympic was losing $5,000 to $6,000 on its weekly shows. "The grind of weekly boxing just did [us] in," argued Don Fraser, the promoter in 1984:

> You just can't make it with small [nontelevised] shows anymore. It was possible once, when boxers could be built up in small money-losing shows and then put in a big-draw show that would recoup the losses. But those days are over. As soon as a boxer becomes an attraction, the networks or some big promoter swoops in to take advantage of the free buildup. You take a kid like Lupe Aquino. We put him on two shows, he gets two wins and seems like an attraction. The next thing I know I'm sitting in my living room and there he is on the network TV, fighting on the Larry Holmes–Scott Frank card. It was possible to hold on to them once, but now it just doesn't make sense.[3]

The year 1984 also marked the closing of the Main Street Gym, a victim of urban "renewal." City renovators razed the gymnasium, making it into a parking lot. Bennie Georgino, manager of champions Little Red Lopez, Jaime Garza, and Albert Davila, believed the recent structural changes in Los Angeles meant the sport was likely to wither away. "I was in the gym the other day and a kid comes up to me and asks about me taking him in. Good kid. Might have been interested before. But now? What would I train him for? I told him to stick with his job."[4] Georgino lamented, as did the *Times*, that whatever boxing competition persisted in Los Angeles would be dominated entirely by Mexican nationals. As Richard Hoffer noted for the *Times*, boxing at the Olympic would "end up showcasing Mexican fighters [who] draw big and fight well but [whose] presence slows the development of the local fighters."[5] Nonetheless, in the early 1980s the extent to which Mexican national fighters and fans virtually took over boxing at the Olympic Auditorium indicates the extent to which the newest Mexican immigrants were now sustaining boxing as part of an expanding parallel, Spanish-speaking universe in southern California. In 1984 the *Times* reported:

> This month's World Boxing Council title fight between Mexican contenders Mario Martinez and Julio Cesar Chavez was largely a secret to L.A.'s Anglos. There was no prefight coverage in The Times that week, and there were no interviews on any of the three network TV affiliates. . . . The fighters are almost exclusively from Mexico, big-name fighters who may be past their prime but who still excite a homesick following.[6]

Indeed, according to the *Times*, as an attempt to stay in business in the early 1980s, the Olympic's promoters began serving the expanding ethnic Mexican community of southern California, using its newspaper and radio outlets as house organs and getting more exposure than they ever got with the English-language media. Coverage of boxing and other sports became part of the everyday experience of ethnic Mexicans actively engaging in what David Gutiérrez has called "the accelerated process of cultural Latinization that began in the 1970s" and has since gathered steam.[7]

This is not to suggest that the "Latino" community was a homogeneous one. Ethnic Mexican communities were themselves increasingly and complexly stratified by gradations of class, generation, and affiliation. For example, Oscar De La Hoya, despite his pride in being Mexican American, chose to emulate an African American as a model of a prizefighting champion. "As a champion, in and out of the ring," he announced, "I want to be like Sugar Ray Leonard. I think he got cut one time, that's it. . . . I want to have as few fights as possible and make the most money. My image is like a star image."[8] Both Paul Gonzáles and Oscar De La Hoya identified with and followed the lead of African American Olympic boxers rather than the Mexican nationals who competed locally in southern California. They did so in part because they, like other Americans, grew to admire African American boxers from watching them fight on television. Indeed, both Gonzáles and De La Hoya were as much products of watching championship boxing on television as they were products of attending boxing at local arenas. In their lucrative, televised careers, African Americans made clear to young Mexican Americans the possibility of making the Olympics into a vehicle for national notoriety and financial success.

One of the first Mexican Americans to follow the African American example of putting off a professional career in favor of taking a shot at the Olympic gold medal was Paul Gonzáles. In 1984, the same year that weekly boxing ended at the Olympic Auditorium, the United States produced its first Latino boxing gold medalist. A flyweight from East Los Angeles, Gonzáles won the gold medal before a hometown crowd at the summer Olympics held in Los Angeles. The son of a single mother, who raised him on welfare in a tough Boyle Heights housing project, Gonzáles ran with a local gang until the day he narrowly cheated death. "I've got these little knots, scars," he claimed. "From buckshot. It hit the window and ricocheted. Or else I'd be dead."[9] He turned to boxing on the advice of Al Stankie, a cop who taught him to fight at Resurrection Gym and the Hollenbeck Youth Center in East Los Angeles. After his Olympic victory, Gonzáles became an instant celebrity in Los Angeles, inside and outside the Latino community. He used his stature to promote education, urging youth to stay in school and become champions academically as he did athletically. He proudly proclaimed that he would retire from boxing a wealthy man in order to pursue a college education. He lent his support in various drug-prevention campaigns. In January 1986, in his third professional fight, Gonzáles became the North American Boxing Federation's flyweight champion. At the conclusion of his decisive victory, Gonzáles handled himself with all the dignity and class he displayed during the Olympics. He praised his defeated opponent and thanked God and "all my fans for praying for me."[10]

Although Gonzáles was an instant "all-American" who was high above average in his concern for community issues, not all Mexican Americans viewed him as a positive symbol of ethnic Mexican American masculinity. "I wanted to be excited for the hero from the Eastside," noted Frank del Olmo in a *Times* editorial, "but I couldn't." A minority of Mexican Americans, such as del Olmo, began questioning the value of expressing manhood in a sport where the Mexican or Mexican American boxers "who are most popular and make the most money are usually not those who fight their opponents with evasive skill, but those who knock the other guy senseless most rapidly and dramatically." In his best fatherly tone, del Olmo worried about Gonzáles's burgeoning career, despite the possibility of it being short and lucrative. "I had to write what I feel about Gonzáles' new pro career *before* anything bad happens," wrote del Olmo. "[His career] is a mistake, and he should quit while he's ahead." But, as del Olmo pointed out, "it would be hard to quit, of course. The television networks want him to fight for a world championship soon, and that's a lot of money to walk away from. And there are many Latinos who will root Gonzáles on because they like pro boxing. But I don't anymore. So if Paul Gonzáles goes on fighting. I won't be watching. Just praying."[11] Unfortunately, Gonzáles's physical problems would torment and inhibit him from ever achieving greatness in his ten-year career.

Nevertheless, as the first Latino Olympic boxing champion, Gonzáles demonstrated that ethnic Mexicans, like African Americans, could use Olympic boxing as a way to enter the lucrative world of corporate sports. Had he distinguished himself in boxing, it seems clear that Gonzáles was in a position to "cross over"—that is, to become a race-neutral hero representing the United States and U.S. citizens everywhere. This was so because, in the 1980s, the prominent place of an increasingly commodified Olympic festival—in television and in the national imagination—emerged simultaneously as ethnic Mexicans mobilized themselves for Olympic competition.[12] The old days of L.A. boxing, as Jim Murray noted, when you "left-hooked your way to the top in grimy little fight clubs, on the undercard, often for a payoff in cheap watches or bouncing checks," were gone for good.[13]

The money to be made in boxing was more attractive than ever to young ethnic Mexican males facing declining opportunities for social mobility. In the 1980s and 1990s the effects of capital flight, deindustrialization, flexible accumulation, increased immigration, and spatial redistribution worked to deny the majority of ethnic Mexicans the avenues for mobility that had been open to earlier generations, much less the kind of prosperity experienced by middle-class, white suburbanites.[14] As the pressures of intensifying globalization and immigration transformed the social geography of southern California, the ethnic Mexican community became both more socially diverse and more economically bifurcated. The flow of

Mexican immigrants into the region's burgeoning low-wage industries made the working class, the foreign born, and their children the majority of over 3.5 million ethnic Mexicans in southern California.[15] By the early 1990s, the new generation's interest in boxing stimulated new local industries, leading to promotions of regular bouts in the greater southern California and northern Baja transborder region. Across southern California, boxing gymnasiums filled with first- and second-generation Mexican Americans, many of whom had transnational ties to Mexico via family, work, or media.

In Mexico, Mexicans thought of the new communities of U.S. Mexicans that grew up in the 1980s and 1990s as part of the Mexican nation settled within the boundaries of the United States. Examples of this emerged in boxing. For example, when the anti-Mexican immigrant initiative Proposition 187 appeared likely to pass, the most powerful of the ruling boxing bodies (headquartered in Mexico City) called for a boycott of California boxing arenas.[16] The call for the boycott came officially from José Sulaiman, an ethnic Lebanese Mexican, who demonstrated that, at least in boxing, Mexicans wielded a certain amount of power and authority in the United States.

The kind of authority that Mexicans and other immigrants possessed in southern California boxing was connected to the steady growth of post–World War II boxing industries in Latin America and Asia, a trend some white commentators worried signified the absolute loss of white, "American," male influence in the sport. Jim Murray noted in 1990, "The control of the sport, if that's the word I want, has passed into the hands of a cast of Third Word characters who seem to invent a new division every time television wants to hang a title label on a fight that would have been a walkout in the old days."[17] What Murray obscured was the fact that ethnic Mexicans, and other "Third World characters," and the proliferation of boxing divisions were representative of the proliferation of global connections in boxing. With the globalization of boxing through television, competitors from around the world were drawn in, making southern California a breeding ground for heroes from diverse ethnic and national groups who, in turn, attracted corporate sponsorship.

As a new generation supplanted the goal of fighting in the Olympic Auditorium with the dream of fighting in the Olympic festival, Los Angeles became a breeding ground for new ethnic Mexican boxers who dreamed of winning an Olympic gold medal. In 1984, after winning his gold medal, Paul Gonzáles visited Resurrection Gym, where he "passed the torch," as he put it, to an eleven-year-old boxer who displayed remarkable ability in the ring. The young boxer's name was Oscar De La Hoya, who proudly announced in English and Spanish that he would follow in Gonzáles's footsteps by winning an Olympic gold medal. Although his wishes would eventually come true, what nobody could predict was the role De La Hoya's career would play in contemporary struggles to define the meaning of ethnic, national, and gender identities in the U.S.-Mexico borderlands.

On the one hand, De La Hoya's career broke with the past in the way he behaved, was promoted, and was read by fans. On the other hand, these "differences" made him a contentious figure in continuing debates over the meaning of ethnic Mexican identity in the United States. He therefore provides a glimpse of both the evolution and juxtaposition of a diversity of group sentiments that stratified the ethnic Mexican community as they resisted or accepted dominant discourses, or did both simultaneously. De La Hoya appealed to many corporate sponsors because he was telegenic, family oriented, and wholesome. He was portrayed as "all-American," the antithesis of the stereotypical threatening "Mexican" masculinity so often represented by the media.

De La Hoya's success and emergence as a racially transcendent, authentic, "American" identity was in part explained by his rise within the context of new right politics in the United States. In this context, specific cultural spaces expanded that afforded the opportunity for a successful Mexican American athlete embodying the right characteristics to "cross over" to or "pass" in a white, male-dominated corporate order. De La Hoya, it could be argued, transcended his ethnic and racial status, despite his explicit pride in being "Mexican," because to be an "all-American" or authentic "American" almost by definition meant subordinating any sense of being a Mexican American or any other "hyphenated American." Becoming an Olympic champion in essence meant becoming an "American."[18]

Oscar De La Hoya was a second-generation Mexican American born in Los Angeles in 1971. Vicente De La Hoya, Oscar's *abuelito* (grandfather), came to Los Angeles in 1956 and, among other jobs, worked as an auto mechanic in a garage at Seventh Street and Central Avenue. In 1957 he had saved enough money to open a small Mexican restaurant half a block away that he named Virginia's Place. Shortly thereafter he entered the demolition business. He would bid on home demolition jobs, knock the houses down, haul the scrap lumber to Mexicali, and sell it. According to one of Oscar's cousins, lots of families live in Mexicali homes that were built of lumber hauled there by Oscar De La Hoya's grandfather. Vicente

De La Hoya, who boxed as an amateur in Durango, Mexico, after World War II, ultimately returned to Mexico, retiring in Mexicali. Oscar's father, Joel De La Hoya, was sixteen when he arrived in Los Angeles in 1956. He went to Roosevelt High School, learned to box in East L.A. gyms, turned pro, and fashioned a 9-3-1 record. Like so many ethnic Mexican fighters before him, he too boxed several times at the Olympic Auditorium. In 1975 he became a dispatcher for an Azusa firm (in Los Angeles County) that made industrial heating and air-conditioning systems, and he remained in that job until his son made sure that he would never have to work again.[19]

In 1979, at the age of six, Oscar De La Hoya began boxing in tournaments at the Pico Rivera Boys Club just south of East Los Angeles. Over the course of his amateur career he won 223 bouts and lost only 5. At Barcelona, Spain, in 1992 he won the Olympic gold medal. In the next seven years he would earn four world titles and establish a record of thirty-one wins and no losses.[20] In 1992 he was estimated to be worth close to $100 million.[21] In 2000, observers had him at roughly twice that amount. He remains the number-one draw in the boxing world today and second only to the recently retired Michael Jordan and Tiger Woods in endorsement earnings by sports figures.

Following the now-proven path of Paul Gonzáles, De La Hoya's advancement through the Olympic Games captured the attention of media moguls and advertising executives. At one time De La Hoya considered turning pro instead of waiting the years it would take to pursue an Olympic medal. Then he met Shelly Finkel, the onetime New York rock promoter, who in the 1980s managed the professional careers of African American Olympic heroes such as Evander Holyfield, Pernell Whitaker, Mark Breland, and Meldrick Taylor. "Oscar and his father talked to me [around 1990] about turning pro then," recalled Finkel, "and I told them that if he did turn pro then, he'd make maybe a few thousand dollars in his first fight. But then I told them that with an Olympic gold medal, I could get him $200,000 for his first pro fight."[22] Waiting for the Olympics would, in fact, pay off dearly for De La Hoya.

In the meantime, he was already becoming a local hero in East Los Angeles as a strong Olympic prospect. Wherever he went in the streets of East L.A., he got slaps on the back and "good luck" gestures from well-wishers. Even the local Maravilla street gang that he had resisted joining gave him a modicum of respect. In 1991, for example, De La Hoya had a run-in with armed members. As he put it:

I was walking to my girlfriend's house one evening, about five blocks from my house. A truck pulled up and about five guys jumped out and three of them put guns to my head. They told me to give them my wallet, which I did. It had $150 in it. They took my camera, too. They didn't know who I was, I had some gold rings on and a nice leather jacket, but they didn't even ask for them. They were amateurs, I guess. That was around 7 pm. By 9, the wallet was on my front porch, the money still in it. I guess they opened it, saw my I.D. They kept the camera, though.[23]

Although De La Hoya's fanfare and popular appeal emerged in East Los Angeles, his successful Olympic bid made him into an instant regional and national celebrity. Despite his origins and because of his origins, commentators saw in De La Hoya a usable past, a befitting example of "assimilation" by white, middle-class standards, thus permitting him to be a symbol of multiculturalism. De La Hoya's popularity among whites captured the contemporary fascination with the athlete who is everywhere and admired by everyone. Particularly in relation to the persistent absence of Mexican American celebrities in U.S. history, De La Hoya's privileged location as a popular Mexican American marked alleged advances in the nation's tortuous race relations. Furthermore, the fact that De La Hoya was a relatively young Mexican American male who was not routinely caricatured or subtly demonized in media representations might indicate widespread cultural accomplishment and progress.

It is impossible for us to understand Oscar De La Hoya's cultural and political significance without recognizing his relationship to the new cultural racism that informed the agenda of conservative administrations of the late twentieth century. Renouncing the devastating influence of centuries of structural racism, conservative politicians insisted on viewing ethnic Mexicans and other urban communities of color as culturally deficient, morally weak, and therefore responsible for unemployment, poverty, urban decay, illiteracy, crime, and a plethora of human troubles. Oscar De La Hoya as a symbol of achievement not only authorized U.S. narratives of melting-pot assimilation but also managed the contradictory relations between white middle-class identities and the lived conditions of aggrieved communities of color.

The celebration of De La Hoya through stories of his success graphically substantiated dominant explanations of the genesis of urban problems by directing popular attention to a perceived lack of personal resolution, will, and enterprise as being the reason for the lack of achievement among vulnerable urban inhabitants. Part of De La Hoya's fanfare involved repetitive references to De La Hoya as a "good Mexican." Reports repeatedly recorded De La Hoya's father as saying, "Oscar's a very good boy, he doesn't smoke, drink, fool around—he's very dedicated to boxing and his schoolwork."[24] Much was made of De La Hoya's dedication of his Olympian quest to his "best friend," his mother, who died a year before he became champion. His promoters encouraged him to speak publicly to "inner-city kids" about the importance of family, as well as education, to instill values necessary for success in life. "The most important thing in life," he once told an elementary school gathering, "is to love and listen to your parents. When you go home, give your mom a big hug and tell her that you love her and tell your parents, 'Thanks for taking care of me.' They'll love you even more."[25] Carol Koshi, De La Hoya's elementary school teacher at Ford Boulevard Elementary School, gave a glowing report of De La Hoya's own school behavior. "He was so nice," she said. "He did everything I asked of him. And he didn't get into fights."[26] The story of Maria Elena Tostado—a former nun and De La Hoya's principal at Garfield High School—circulated in numerous accounts. "He knew what he wanted from Day 1," she was quoted as saying. "He always had a goal and worked toward it. I mean, nonstop. His mother . . . must have seen he had special qualities. He really is a single-minded young man. . . . He's never, ever once complained about what he was doing or how much it was taking of his life."[27] De La Hoya's image was so attractive that he was made into a parody of the quintessential American. Fans deemed him "The Golden Boy of East Los Angeles." "He doesn't look right," an astonished Jim Murray observed:

> Look at him! You ever see a prizefighter like him? Even Dempsey bragged a little. Joe Louis too. Not our Oscar. . . . I mean, who does he think he is, Mother Teresa? So far as anyone knows, Oscar never even stole a Hershey bar. What kind of record is that for a champion? It's un-American. . . . He should learn to scowl a lot. Travel around with an entourage. Trash his opponent. Talking trash has become an American hallmark. . . . It's part and parcel of the way we compete . . . Oscar doesn't have to work on his jab, his uppercut, but he has to work on his vocabulary. He has to learn his opponent is a bum, the referee a crook, and that bad manners sell tickets. I don't say he has to go to prison, but maybe a 2 a.m. difference of opinion with a bartender is indicated.[28]

Perhaps more than anything, De La Hoya was a key figure in the management of paradoxical claims and practices and an instance of dominant rearticulation of assimilationist narrative in the guise of color-blind language that dominated the contemporary popular cultural politics of both conservatives and liberals. In projecting themselves as the protectors of white racial privilege, conservative ideologues used color-blind language that conflated the U.S. population into a homogeneous grouping that supposedly shared the same experiences and problems as a result of the high cost of funding the social welfare of others. Middle-class suburban populations supported redirecting monies into law enforcement and tax reform at the expense of education and job training. It is evident that, while masquerading behind a purported egalitarianism, the last twenty-five years of color-blind social legislation reproduced a "possessive investment in whiteness." De La Hoya's popularity emerged at precisely the same time that California demagogic political leaders launched a series of decidedly racist attacks on communities of color. Ethnic Mexicans faced legal assaults on the rights of immigrants, on affirmative action, on bilingual education, and on the rights of working people in a public sphere increasingly characterized by hatred against poor immigrants and racial minorities. George Lipsitz has identified "the ways in which power, property, and the politics of race in our society continue to contain unacknowledged and unacceptable allegiances to white supremacy," making "California in the 1990s the human rights equivalent of Mississippi in the 1960s."[29]

Given Oscar De La Hoya's location in this context, his presence is implicated in ways of thinking and seeing that deny, and yet extend, the subordination of racial others. De La Hoya assimilated not by conforming to the positive attributes of an American identity or by shedding his particular attachments to his Mexican identity but by proclaiming his pride in being Mexican American. Nevertheless, De La Hoya's emergence in international boxing led to dominant representations that suppressed his Mexican identity, revealing a hegemonic order in which American national identity reinforced white racial and cultural dominance of others. Thus, to assimilate Oscar De La Hoya as a fitting example of national identity, dominant representations tended to erase all traces of his ethnic culture and history. White journalists detached him from his Mexican identity by portraying him as the "West's best boxer ever."[30] As Mike Downey for the *Los Angeles Times* put it:

Out here we really haven't produced that many great ones, you know. Ali was from Kentucky. Marciano came from Massachusetts, same town as Hagler. Louis hailed from Michigan, by way of Alabama. Dempsey, Leonard,

Frazier, Holmes, LaMotta . . . all of these champions were Easterners. I guess this is why I wouldn't mind seeing more of us embrace Oscar De La Hoya now, once and for all. He is our fighter, our Olympian, our champion, and obviously has what it takes to become one of the great boxers. . . . He really is the Golden State's golden boy, this kid.[31]

Articulations of De La Hoya's identity in and through white middle-class myths of melting-pot inclusion provided him with a seductive means of distancing his imaged existence from its potentially troubling connotation of racial otherness. The widely felt need for Mexican Americans to disavow any overt expression of or reference to their Mexicanness, as a strategy for securing—as opposed to alienating—popularity, was indicative of the ingrained racist practices and representations of those who controlled the media industries. In the above quotation, the columnist renders De La Hoya's invasive presence in the public sphere as "race neutral" or "colorless," reinforcing the strategic exclusions and depictions of race that characterized dominant ideologies of the 1980s and 1990s. De La Hoya's depiction as the hero of the "land of opportunity" masked the real struggles ethnic Mexicans faced in a society increasingly characterized by social inequality and economic discrimination. Media and advertising agencies routinely portrayed De La Hoya as someone whose wholesomeness, humility, inner drive, personal responsibility, and success spread the belief that in this country, have-nots can still become haves; that the American Dream is still working. Thus, De La Hoya reinforced national myths and promoted the idealized imagined community. The success of De La Hoya, for some, has come to represent national culture as a vindication of the reassuring persistence of the United States' founding principles, such as freedom, liberty, rights, justice, obligation, and agency.

Yet registering De La Hoya's location in a mass public culture requires understanding ways of thinking about "progress" that deny the social relations and manifestations of postindustrial production. We cannot reduce De La Hoya's popularity, then, to his exceptional fighting skills. Instead, his location is inextricably bound both to signs of a new and improved national context that disavows the aggrieved experiences of most U.S. Mexicans and to the production of prizefighting in order to stimulate and satisfy consumer desire. Yet De La Hoya also matters because a regional community made him and demands that he serve as a public acknowledgment of the achievement of that community in U.S. public culture. Fabricating De La Hoya as quintessentially "American" elides the social and, more important, ethnic realities of both De La Hoya and the national project. Representations of the American Dream and the role of Mexicans in it are abstract, transhistorical, and seemingly apolitical. The rhetorical strategies in which sportswriters celebrated De La Hoya's racially neutral American identity distanced him from the context in which a community made him and assuaged ongoing anxieties around the possible recognition of those conditions.

Representations of De La Hoya reinforced the myth of accessibility to privilege for those willing to assimilate the dominant work ethic and prevailing ideologies, at the same time that they provided middle-class whites with another opportunity for consuming a cultural commodity produced in the *barrio*. Yet, even given his availability as a *barrio* commodity, boxing promoters in the 1990s shied from producing overt expressions of ethnic difference, studiously avoiding them in promotional strategies aimed at nurturing De La Hoya's widespread popular "all-American" appeal. Thus the numerous corporations that sought De La Hoya's endorsement strategically distanced his image from the highly suggestive signifiers of ethnic, racial, and national difference that dominated popular representations of virtually all other ethnic Mexican males. The rhetoric of transcendence in stories about De La Hoya appeared to distance him from the historical conditions and mainstream discourses that locate and position other, nontranscendent ethnic Mexicans. But what about the opinions and attitudes of "nontranscendent" ethnic Mexicans toward De La Hoya? And what of the effect De La Hoya himself had on his own representation?

Dominant attempts to define the meaning of Oscar De La Hoya as a "good East L.A. Mexican," the opposite of the stereotypically deviant "Mexican" male urbanite, arose from an interweaving of presence and absence. While local and national media often represented De La Hoya's achievements as so momentous that they transcended any relation to the social relations in his community of origin, the trace of the stereotypical ethnic Mexican male was an ever-present and telling absence in the promotional discourse's attempt at fabricating De La Hoya's all-American image. Representations of De La Hoya's exceptional feats thus work to displace the unexceptional urban "Mexican" from the assimilation narrative. Mainstream narratives of De La Hoya's success both preclude recognition of and help facilitate the continued denial of a possessive investment in whiteness. Consequently, De La Hoya's success legitimated the reactionary color-blind shift in United States racial politics by perpetuating the myth of an open class structure, racial tolerance, economic mobility, the sanctity of individualism, and the availability of the American Dream for Mexican Americans and, by extension, all other so-called minorities. Read as an athlete who shed his ethnicity to become the embodiment of "American" virtue, De La Hoya reconciled the distance between dominant fantasy and materiality. His public image allowed fans to think of people in trouble as people who cause trouble and who are, as such, worthy of blame for their own impoverishment.

Yet, as part of America's common culture, boxing was nonetheless inseparable from the identities it helped construct and manage. The mass media's disavowal of the problems and effects of racism, the elision of immediate contradictions, and, by extension, the evasion of the social and historical context are integral to the mediated management of a late-capitalist possessive investment in whiteness. Out of such forces, Oscar De La Hoya became a sign of transcendence as both a national and a commercial spectacle. Yet these representations did not emerge from within ethnic Mexican boxing history but from an uncritical acceptance and blithe celebration of the products and practices of contemporary American racism. Dominant reinterpretations of the meaning of De La Hoya's ethnicity did not easily seduce ethnic Mexicans who might have been displaced by them. The project of national media corporations and popular nationalist politics could not easily raid the ethnic Mexican boxing history, culture, and consciousness from which De La Hoya emerged. Even though the Golden Boy may have been living proof of the ability of athletic genius to liberate the individual from group identity, or, more generally, proof of the potential of marginal people, De La Hoya's fans tended to resist his impersonation of an "assimilated Mexican."

Consequently, when De La Hoya made a series of moves away from East Los Angeles—ultimately to the city's most affluent real estate, in Bel Air—he immediately drew the ire of East L.A. fans. That De La Hoya was of Mexican descent was less important to many of these fans than that he came from a particular ethnic Mexican place, in this case East Los Angeles. De La Hoya's move, combined with a series of other events, would finally drive a wedge between him and many of his once-loyal fans in East Los Angeles. By the end of the 1990s, the Golden Boy of East Los Angeles found that he was more warmly received by huge numbers of supportive ethnic Mexican audiences in Texas than in California. What East L.A. fans who turned against De La Hoya refused to accept was that there will never be room in representations of U.S. national identity for Mexicanness except in delimited public spheres. Mexican identity was wonderful, as long as its adherents performed it away from the celebrations of "American" national identity that the promoters of U.S. boxing expected their Olympic champions to enact. De La Hoya's career reflected dominant views of ethnic Mexicans generally: that they should erase all traces of their place of origin in the act of claiming authentic American identities. In winning his authentic American identity in professional sport, De La Hoya exposed dominant thought about racial and ethnic identity that worked to exclude the culture and history of minorities from representations of professional sports. Yet the myopic vision and exclusionary thinking of boxing's promoters was in many respects no different from the "all-or-nothing" litmus test that some East Los Angeles Mexicans applied to Oscar De La Hoya.[32] Ethnic Mexicans who derided De La Hoya because he "crossed over" racial, gender, class, and physical boundaries denied in their own experience the very syncretism that had historically ensured the survival of their ethnic culture.

The refusal of some whites to grant De La Hoya his Mexican identity and the refusal of some ethnic Mexicans to grant him his American identity in essence denied social realities. Oscar De La Hoya is both Mexican and American. He believes he is both Mexican and American. And he believes in being Mexican and American he is more than the sum of the parts. In this respect, De La Hoya, like golf star Tiger Woods, resists being pigeonholed by racist thinking. Frank del Olmo, in the *Los Angeles Times*, noted that the celebration of Woods being the first African American to win the Masters was not entirely accurate: "For Woods is only part African American. He is the son of a black American father and a mother from Thailand." Moreover, del Olmo added, "I suspect [Woods] is smart enough to know that his identity is too complex to easily fit into anybody's stereotype." As for De La Hoya, del Olmo noted, he, too, must know "his identity is too complex to be put into a box labeled 'American' or 'Mexican.'" Del Olmo's most valuable insight, however, was when he noticed "both of these fine young men were raised in the polyglot megalopolis that sprawls across the Los Angeles basin." "Who knows," del Olmo conjectured, "if we older folks just step back and let these skilled young heroes be themselves, along with the rest of their multiracial, multiethnic generation, they just may lead us out of the box that ethnic, racial and cultural rivalries fed by stereotypes have led us into."[33] What del Olmo left out of his otherwise astute observations, however, was that many who took an interest in De La Hoya did so precisely because his career provided an opportunity to emphasize, challenge, and affirm group differences. De La

Hoya's experience proved that those in the "multiracial, multiethnic generation" to which he belonged, but especially the majority of Americans, had
some way to go in order to work through and dismantle the "ethnic, racial
and cultural rivalries fed by stereotypes" that remained central to not only
prizefighting rivalries but also to ethnic, racial, and national rivalries.
Whether they accepted or derided De La Hoya, boxing fans made clear
that racism, xenophobia, and ethnocentrism are alive and well in the
United States.

Sports historian Michael Oriard argues that in the late twentieth century "the hero-making impulse is strong . . . because genuine folk heroes
have not had centuries in which to grow in the minds of the people." Following Oriard's logic, the athlete-hero in the United States has emerged as
a result of this hero-making impulse. Yet sports heroes such as Oscar De
La Hoya have not existed in an "apolitical, asocial, amoral, even timeless,
placeless quality of the athletic contest itself enabling the heroes of the
contest to remain unchanged after decades," as Oriard suggests.[34] Oscar
De La Hoya was a sign read differently by different groups, according to
their social locations. In his community of origin, De La Hoya instilled
pride in some and hatred in others. Among outsiders, he was celebrated as
a widely popular and attractive self-made man or berated as an un-American Mexican. As a site for intercultural communication, De La Hoya's career reflected a multidimensional conversation shaped by unequal relations of reciprocity and mutuality, where groups spoke from positions of
unequal access to power and opportunity. Only after further research is
carried out will we get a clearer understanding of how the desires, wishes,
and expectations of sports fans'—that their heroes accept or change the
social order—might be implicated in the wider national politics of ethnic
relations.

Notes

1. Hector Tobar, "A Fighting Chance: De La Hoya Refurbishing Gym to Help
Youngsters, Neighborhood," *Los Angeles Times*, 12 October 1996, sec. B, p. 1, col. 2.

2. Alejandro Portes and Ruben Rumbaut, *Immigrant America: A Portrait*
(Berkeley: University of California Press, 1996); Ivan Light and Elizabeth Roach,
"Self-Employment: Mobility Ladder or Economic Lifeboat?" in Roger Waldinger
and Mehdi Bozorgmehr, eds. *Ethnic Los Angeles* (New York: Russell Sage Foundation, 1996), 193–214.

3. Richard Hoffer, "Olympic Auditorium's Weekly-Boxing Era Has Ended," *Los Angeles Times*, 8 January 1984, sec. 3, p. 16, col. 3.

4. Richard Hoffer, "Bright Futures May Never Come to Pass," *Los Angeles Times*, 22 January 1984, sec. 3. p. 23, col. 1.

5. Ibid.

6. Richard Hoffer, "Live Shows at the Olympic Auditorium Thrive on Mexican Fighters, Fans," *Los Angeles Times*, 22 September 1984, sec. 3, p. 20, col. 1.

7. David G. Gutiérrez, "Ethnic Mexicans and the Transformation of 'American' Social Space: Reflections on Recent History," in Marcelo M. Suárez-Orozco, ed., *Crossings: Mexican Immigration in Interdisciplinary Perspectives* (Cambridge: Harvard University Press, 1998), 315.

8. Tim Kawakami, "$8 Million Later, Oscar De La Hoya Says He's Still Hungry," *Los Angeles Times*, 30 April 1995, sec. C, p. 8, col. 1.

9. Chris Dufresne, "His Torch Burns Out," *Los Angeles Times*, 10 August 1994, sec. C, p. 1, col. 2.

10. Frank del Olmo, "Watching and Praying for Paul Gonzales," *Los Angeles Times*, 6 February 1986, sec. 2, p. 5, col. 3.

11. Ibid.

12. For an insightful analysis of the Olympic Games as cultural productions of national and international identities, see John J. MacAloon, "Interval Training," in Susan Leigh Foster, ed., *Choreographing History* (Bloomington: Indiana University Press, 1995), 32–53.

13. Jim Murray, "Three Times Now Has Charm," *Los Angeles Times*, 12 January 1993, sec. C, p. 1, col. 3.

14. For a discussion of these processes and their effects, see Edward W. Soja, *Postmodern Geographies: The Reassertion of Space in Critical Social Theory* (New York: Verso, 1989), 190–248.

15. Georges Sabagh and Mehdi Bozorgmehr, "Population Change: Immigration and Ethnic Transformation," in Waldinger and Bozorgmehr, eds., *Ethnic Los Angeles*, 93–100.

16. Chris Dufresne, "Proposition 187 Prompts WBC to Ban Title Fights in California," *Los Angeles Times*, 16 November 1994, sec. C, p. 8, col. 2.

17. Jim Murray, "No ABCs for Real Champs," *Los Angeles Times*, 8 November 1990, sec. C., p. 1, col. 2.

18. Nevertheless, as John MacAloon persuasively argues, the meaning of national identities is always up for grabs and is constantly reconstituted by the athletes themselves. This is especially true in high-stakes international athletic competitions such as the Olympic Games, which provide opportunities to contest or affirm national allegiances. See MacAloon, "Interval Training."

19. Earl Gutskey, "Relative Humility," *Los Angeles Times*, 1 July 1992, sec. C, p. 1, col. 6.

20. Ibid., p. 10, col. 2.

21. Tim Kawakami, *Golden Boy: The Fame, Money, and Mystery of Oscar De La Hoya* (Kansas City: Andrews McMeel Publishing, 1999), 253.

22. Gutskey, "Relative Humility," p. 10, col. 3.

23. Ibid.

24. Earl Gutskey, "Thoughts of Gold in East L.A.," *Los Angeles Times*, 31 October 1990, sec. C, p. 1, col. 5.

25. "Del La Hoya Doesn't Pull Punches on Education during Visit to School," *Los Angeles Times*, 24 June 1997, sec. B, p. 4, col. 3.

26. Ibid., p. 4, col. 4.

27. Tim Kawakami, "Boxing's Twister: De La Hoya Has Stormed the Sport," *Los Angeles Times*, sec. C, p. 10, col. 1.

28. Jim Murray, "He Doesn't Look Right—until He Gets in the Ring," *Los Angeles Times*, sec. C, p. 5, cols. 2–4.

29. George Lipsitz, *The Possessive Investment in Whiteness: How White People Profit from Identity Politics* (Philadelphia: Temple University Press, 1998), xviii–xix.

30. Mike Downey, "Golden State Has True Golden Boy," *Los Angeles Times*, 8 May 1995, sec. C, p. 9, col. 2.

31. Ibid., col. 3.

32. For detailed descriptions of De La Hoya's increasingly tenuous relations with East Los Angeles fans, see Kawakami, *Golden Boy*.

33. Frank del Olmo, "KO the Stereotypes: They're Not OK," *Los Angeles Times*, 20 April 1997, sec. M, p. 5, col. 4.

34. Michael Oriard, *Dreaming of Heroes: American Sports Fiction, 1868–1980* (Chicago: Nelson Hall, 1982), 132.

Chapter Fourteen

Race in Soccer as a Global Sport

Michiko Hase

Over the past fifty years, it has become increasingly common to see for-eign-born players in American professional and collegiate sports: Caribbean, Latin American, and Asian players in baseball, Africans and Europeans in basketball, Northern and Eastern Europeans in ice hockey, to name just a few. At first glance, their presence may not strike observers as anything remarkable or noteworthy. This international presence in U.S. sports might be understood by many as a manifestation of familiar Amer-ican ideals regarding opportunity and assimilation. On closer inspection, however, the increasing presence of foreign players in American sports is not simply a part of this historical pattern. As foreign athletes have been moving to the United States, more and more American players are also moving overseas: to Europe (basketball, American football) and to Mexico and East Asia (baseball). Such transnational mobility of athletes[1] is a part of the process of growing economic, political, and cultural interdepen-dency called globalization, brought about by the transnational flow of capital, labor, and culture.[2]

The trend in transnational migration of athletes is most pronounced in Western European soccer (Maguire and Bale 1994b, 2).[3] Western Europe is the world center of the sport, with the most lucrative soccer industry of all, attracting the most-skilled and highest-paid players not only from within Europe but also from Latin America, Africa, and even Asia. The growing numbers of foreign players in European professional leagues, as in the overall labor force, have forced the European nation-states to reex-amine their laws and policies delineating the boundaries of "citizens"/"na-tionals" and "foreigners." Following decolonization after World War II through the 1960s, the former colonial powers in Europe witnessed the increase in immigration from their former colonies, a trend that has accelerated under intensified globalization in the 1980s and 1990s. As a result, most European clubs and some national teams feature a number of Third World players, many of whom are (sons of) immigrants from former colonies.

The globalization of sports raises important questions about the relationship between athletes and racial ideology. For example, if sport has a symbolic power as a vehicle to express (masculinist) national identity conjoined with individual and collective male identity, what happens when European teams include many players of color who don't look "European"?

In the United States, similar phenomena may be viewed as merely an extension of a historical pattern unique to this country. Yet European soccer presents a striking example of the redrawing of the global racial map as a result of decolonization and globalization. Because sport is often wrapped in nationalist discourses, functioning as a symbol of masculinist nationalism, soccer also is an appropriate site to investigate the tensions and contradictions between "the local (national)" and "the global" and between forces of globalization and nation-states. In this formulation, "race" is a vital component of national identity formation.

This chapter maps out, with broad strokes, issues of race and sports under globalization, with European soccer as a case study. It raises three interrelated issues: questions of citizenship; racism and xenophobia; and economic forces that created and sustain the globalization of soccer, especially the role of U.S. transnational capital and business practices that have helped shape the contemporary sports industry.

Soccer Clubs with "Multinational" Casts and "Multiracial" National Teams in Europe

Two events that happened at the turn of the year 2000 highlighted accelerated transnational migration of soccer players, especially to Europe. One took place in England on December 28, 1999. For the first time in the history of soccer in England, the birthplace of the sport, an English side did not field a British player in its starting lineup—an event the British media called "historic." The starting players in the London-based Chelsea club that day came from France, Romania, Nigeria, Brazil,

Uruguay, Italy, Norway, Spain, and the Netherlands and were managed by an Italian who, according to the *Times* (of London), "made no excuses for his all-foreign cast" (Kempson 2000). The other incident took place a month later, on January 22, 2000, in Nigeria. In the opening match between Cameroon and Ghana in the Twenty-second African Cup of Nations Championships, all twenty-two starting players were based with European clubs ("Cameroon and Ghana Share the Spoils" 2000). In fact, more than half of the players who took part in the African Cup played in leagues overseas, especially in Europe ("Is Europe Stealing Africa's Best Players?" 2000).

These two events also exemplified the two-tier structure of world soccer: domestic and international competitions among professional clubs, on the one hand, and international contests among national teams, on the other. The former includes domestic leagues and championships as well as international competitions among professional clubs. The latter consists of the quadrennial World Cup, the Olympic Games, and regional championships such as the Euro Cup, La Copa America, the African Cup, and the Asia Cup. This dual structure, in my view, adds greater complexity to the issues of the local versus the global and of (national) identity for both players and fans, as is discussed later in this chapter.

In terms of governing and coordinating this complex web of national and international competitions, soccer governing authorities have a hierarchical structure, with the world governing body, FIFA (Fédération Internationale de Football Association, formed in 1904), headquartered in Zurich, Switzerland, at the top.[4] There are six regional confederations, representing Europe, South America, North and Central America, Africa, Asia, and Oceania. Below the regional confederations, each member nation has its own national associations.

Within the dual structure of European soccer, the issue of race and nationality/citizenship under globalization has two interrelated dimensions. One is the increasing presence of "foreign" players, especially men of color from outside Europe. The other is the growing tendency of European national teams to become multiracial, as was clearly seen during the 1998 World Cup. The larger presence of "foreign" players (from the Third World) in the leagues and of "nationals" of "foreign" (especially Third World) origin on national teams complicates discourses about national identity, which in turn are often played out within a racial discourse.

Redrawing the Boundaries of Citizenship

From the perspective of impact of race on European soccer, it is appropriate to distinguish between immigrants from within Europe and those from Latin America, Africa, and Asia, although, increasingly, not all Europeans are white. The former group of immigrants started earlier than the latter and are still numerically the more dominant of the two. Two factors contributed to the acceleration of intra-European migration of soccer players in the 1990s: the greater integration of Western Europe and the collapse of the former Soviet bloc, which unleashed migration from Eastern European countries, including migration of professional athletes. The greater integration of Western Europe and the creation of a new "European citizenship," in particular, has had a profound impact on the redrawing of the boundaries between "citizen" and "foreigner" among European Union (EU) nations. Specifically, the economic integration raised the issue of the freedom of movement for EU soccer players within the EU.

With the creation of the European Economic Community (EEC), citizens of the member nations became entitled to move to and to work in any member state.[5] In soccer, the Bosman ruling of 1995 has had a great impact on the migration of soccer players within the EU, paving the way to accelerated migration of EU players. In a judgment in a suit filed by Belgian player Jean-Marc Bosman, the European Court of Justice ruled that soccer players were workers like any others and entitled to the freedom of movement guaranteed all citizens of the European Union member states. Prior to the Bosman ruling, a club wishing to acquire a player from another club was required to pay a transfer fee to the other club, which could demand a prohibitively high fee to prevent the transfer. In the Bosman decision, the transfer fees were ruled to be in breach of EU law on the free movement of workers. Subsequently, the law was changed to allow players to negotiate their own deals with other clubs when their contracts expired. These changes have enabled players, especially top players, to receive huge signing-on fees and higher pay because of the absence of transfer fees. The changes in the laws have also made more room for sports management agents in negotiations of contracts ("Bosman Summer Holiday" 1999).

Another, related issue arising from the growing presence of "foreign" players is that of quotas. With the increase of "foreign" players in Europe, national soccer governing bodies in most EU member states have imposed limits on the number of "foreign" players allowed to play in the domestic league championships (Duke 1991, 188). Different states adopted varied interpretations and policies regarding the rules on limiting the number of foreign players. Some member nations, for example, interpreted the term *national* liberally, as Portugal did, treating all Brazilian players as Portuguese. Even before the integration of the EEC as a single economic market in 1992, there were "established patterns in Europe of the flow of players from the poorer clubs/countries to the wealthier clubs/countries in football terms," according to Vic Duke (1991, 189). In the 1990s, the leading clubs of Italy and Spain emerged "at the pinnacle of the importers' list and paying the highest salaries" (Duke 1991, 189). By the end of the decade, the English Premier League clubs were also seeking to join "the global search place for top talent" (Maguire 1998, 71). On the first weekend of the 1999/2000 season, more than one-third (37 percent—82 of 220 players) of starting players in Premier League matches were from outside the United Kingdom ("Call to Limit Foreign Footballers" 2000).

Further, players who are citizens of the fifteen EU member states and of Iceland, Norway, and Liechtenstein playing in other EU countries are not considered "foreigners" in soccer terms and not subjected to national quotas on foreign players. To take advantage of this rule, some non-EU players have claimed parentage of an EU member nation to escape quotas, and some soccer officials have expressed concern about "an underworld trade in passports." Hence, in November 1999 it was reported that the UK Immigration Enforcement Agency was investigating the suspected use of fake passports by foreign soccer players signing to British clubs, after an Argentinian striker was found to be traveling on "a bogus Italian passport" ("Foreign Players in Fake Passport Probe" 1999).

In the context of the more expansive definition of "citizen" within the EU and the freedom of movement guaranteed EU citizens, dual citizenship and claims of citizenship based on ancestral connections have gained significance. To take advantage of opportunities in the lucrative soccer industry in Western Europe, more and more players try to gain EU citizenship based on ancestral connections. This trend is aided by the movement of many nation-states toward allowing dual citizenship or loosening citizenship requirements (Faist 2000).[6]

As more than 1 million people gathered on the Champs-Elysées to celebrate the French victory in the World Cup Final in Paris, French media and politicians touted the victory as a symbol of a new, multicultural France, for the French national team included a number of men of color

(Dahlburg 1998). French media threw a spotlight on Zinedine Zidane, the son of Algerian immigrants from housing projects in Marseille, who scored two goals in France's 3-0 upset victory over the favorite Brazil (Vinocur 1999). Even Jean-Marie Le Pen, the head of the National Front, the ultra-right-wing, anti-immigrant party, "was caught flat-footed by the outburst of joyful patriotism, was forced to backtrack on his statement two years [earlier] that immigrants should not be allowed to play on the national team" (Dahlburg 1998). FIFA also highlighted "France's 1998 triumph" as "not only a sporting victory but also a vivid illustration of multi-cultural harmony," calling the sport "The Colourful Game" (2000).

Despite the French media's and FIFA's enthusiasm, it is noticeable that the players of color on European national teams tend to be (sons of) immigrants from their former colonies. In the cases of both professional leagues and national teams, the migration of players from Latin America, Africa, and the Caribbean tends to follow the old colonial ties between former colonies and their colonial powers (Maguire 1991, 106–7). In the case of Britain, the Afro-Caribbean soccer players are sons of immigrants from its former colonies who "were recruited to fill lower-class occupations positions" in the 1950s and 1960s (Maguire 1991, 118). The French national team in the Euro2000 Finals included the largest number of players of color of all the teams: nearly half (ten) of the twenty-two member squad. Among those French players of color were Zidane and black players born in Guadeloupe—a French possession in the Caribbean—French Guiana, New Caledonia, and Senegal (Euro2000 2000; Swardson 1998). By contrast, the other finalist, Italy, did not have any black players in its squad (Euro2000 2000).

This migration pattern is consistent with the larger pattern of global labor migration, which tends to flow from Third World countries to First World economies with colonial ties. Saskia Sassen observes the existence of "regional systems constituted as zones of influence of major economic or geopolitical powers (e.g., the long-term dominance of the United States over the Caribbean Basin) . . . to a good extent major international migration flows have been embedded in some or another variant of these regional systems" (1998, 14). Thus, in soccer players' migration as in other sectors of global labor migration, there is an element of neocolonialism in that the migration patterns tend to reproduce the old colonial ties.

The other side of this global migration of top players from the Third World to Europe is what has been called "talent drain" from the Third World, a cause for concern and debates about "underdevelopment" of soccer in the exporting countries. For example, during the 2000 African Cup the British Broadcast Corporation (BBC) Web site ran a message board titled "Is Europe Stealing Africa's Best Players?" that generated many responses from around the world. The "stealing" and exploitation of African soccer talent has a deep resonance with the broader economic and political issue of the First World's "stealing" and exploitation of Africa's natural resources and the underdevelopment of the African economy.[7]

A similar concern about the underdevelopment of local talent has been raised in Europe. Critics of the growing importation of "cheap" "foreign" soccer labor maintain that this trend has stunted the development of local talent and call for a reconsideration of the Bosman ruling and stricter restrictions on the importation of "foreign" players. For instance, in June 2000, the British government blamed "England's premature departure from Euro 2000 on the influx of foreign stars to the Premier League" and "urged British football to introduce a voluntary quota on the number of foreign players" (Wilson et al. 2000). Such concern may be seen not only as nationalist but also as racist, for there have increased incidents of racially motivated verbal abuse and violence against players and supporters of color on and off the field.

Racism toward and Exploitation of Third World Players in Europe

The visibility of Latin American, African, and Caribbean players in European soccer has grown since the 1960s but especially in the last decade. In 1989–90, according to Maguire, 15.4 percent of players in Division One of the English Football League were black Afro-Caribbean. In the 1988–89 season, the following European soccer leagues had black Afro-Caribbean players in their elite divisions: Portugal (16.6 percent of all players), France (12 percent), Holland (6.7 percent), and Belgium (4.4 percent) (Maguire 1991, 106). By the late 1990s, some estimated that as high as 25 percent of England's elite Premier League players were black (Garland and Rowe 1999, 38). As the number of players of color increased, racism both inside and outside the stadium—racist verbal abuse and violence aimed at players and fans of color—became a serious social problem, recognized by the media, governments, clubs, soccer governing bodies, and fans. Racial slurs come not only from players and fans of opposite sides. For instance, during the qualifying tournament for the 1990 World Cup, the then-Dutch manager made derogatory comments about black players on his own team, calling them "lazy." His comments provoked a "dressing room revolt" that led to the manager's dismissal (Maguire 1991, 107).

Racism in European soccer is often linked to hooliganism and right-wing, neo-nazi movements.[8] Hooliganism, soccer-fan violence sometimes called the "English disease," has spread to the European continent and continues to be a social (and political) problem, especially in international competitions. Researchers, particularly in Britain, have produced a large body of work on hooliganism from a variety of theoretical and methodological positions (Giulianotti 1994; Giulianotti et al. 1994).[9] Much of the research attributes soccer hooliganism to social malcontent among working-class male fans. As racist violence has increased, the link between hooliganism and anti-immigrant racism has been pointed out. The central tenet of right-wing, neo-nazi movements is nativism as a backlash against increasingly multicultural societies. In April 2000, the Rome correspondent for National Public Radio reported that the anti-immigrant sentiment in Europe was most evident in soccer stadiums, where displays of Nazi swastika are a common sight (*Sunday Morning Edition*, 2 April 2000).

The redefinition of citizenship and the ensuing reshaping of the racial composition in European soccer (both players and fans) have complicated the question of fan allegiance, nationalism in soccer, and identity formation through sport. On the one hand, according to Garland and Rowe, a "common puzzle to many in debates about racism in contemporary football is the tendency for spectators to racially abuse black players on opposing teams while remaining loyal and supportive towards black members of their own side" (1999, 37). On the other hand are reports about fans who refuse to accept black players as "true" members of their team. For example, in the 1986 World Cup Finals in Mexico, England made it to the semifinals. After a big victory during which a black player scored one of two goals, the team flew back to England. Some English fans taunted the team, claiming they had really scored only one goal. According to those fans, the one from the black player was not from a "true Englishman" (*Three Lions*).

In addition to racism, the exploitation and human rights abuses of young African, Latin American, and Eastern European players have become a serious political concern in Western Europe. Wealthy European clubs send scouts to discover young talents who are eager to migrate to play soccer in (Western) Europe. Not all young recruits succeed, however, and many are exploited by the clubs with little or no pay. In the worst cases, some have been discarded by the clubs and become "illegal immigrants," with no proper documentation or money to go back to their countries of origin. According to the Nigerian ambassador for sport, who was a professional soccer player in England, some "can find themselves in Israel or Russia, cleaning cars or restaurants, with barely enough money to get back to their country of origin" ("Africa's Worrying Soccer Exodus" 2000).

This problem has become serious enough to draw attention of human rights activists and, later, some governments. In 1990, a nonprofit organization on human rights for athletes, Sport and Freedom, was established in Belgium. It investigates human rights violations for athletes and assists them in legal contests. Additionally, labor unions and governments have become involved in more recent years. In Belgium, for example, as a result of heavy lobbying by human rights activists and labor unions, new rules were passed by the parliament in 1998, forbidding deals with players under age eighteen from outside the EU and making both clubs and agents responsible for the living, medical, and travel expenses of non-European recruits for at least three years after their arrival ("Belgium's Football 'Slave Trade'" 1999). In addition to the Belgian government, the French government has moved to curb what one French official calls "the new slave trade" by outlawing "soccer clubs paying for players under the age of 18 in an effort to halt the trade in young African hopefuls" (Sopel 2000).

Studies have shown that the gap between the rich and the poor, both within a society and between countries, has widened under globalization. This widening gap is evident in world soccer as well. First, among Third World players migrating to Europe, only a handful become multimillionaire stars, while the majority fail to achieve such a spectacular upward mobility and could even become the victims of a "modern slave trade." Whereas successful athletes sustain their spatial mobility, which in turn can bring them economic upward mobility, those who fail to do so lose their spatial mobility, becoming "stuck" in one place and unable to move out of the location and out of poverty. Second, the growing flow of soccer players from the Third World to Europe reflects the widening gap between the two world regions in economic strength and opportunities for players.

Further, even successful Third World players can be abused by soccer authorities and sponsors. Because many top Latin American and African players are with European clubs, conflicts and disputes often arise between the clubs and the national soccer associations of their countries of citizenship. When the latter want their European-based top players to play in international tournaments, the European clubs may be reluctant to let them do so at the expense of regular league matches (Lawrence 2000). This "double duty" can burden top players who have to travel to other continents on a tight schedule, risking fatigue and injury. For example, Brazilian top players are forced to play as many matches as they can, in both professional leagues and on national teams, by both Brazil's football association and Nike, the sponsor of the Brazilian national team (Hughes 2000).

The Media-Sports Complex and the Sporting Goods Industry

Sports sociologists and media studies scholars have coined the term *media-sports (production) complex* to describe the close ties and collaboration among multinational media organizations, sports teams, and sports governing bodies.[10] Also included in this complex are (multinational) sports-marketing and player-management agencies, whose business expertise includes the production of sporting events with a tie-in with sponsors. For example, IMG Latin America, the regional division of U.S.-based giant management firm IMG (International Management Group), "totally restructured the Copa America" (Blount 1997a, 33).

Significantly, the sporting goods industry works closely with the media-sports complex. As Jean Harvey, Genevieve Rail, and Lucie Thibault write, "Sporting goods manufacturers are primary agents in the commodification of sport along with the sports media industry, an industry that is increasingly interconnected with the sporting goods industry through sponsoring and strategic alliance" (1996, 266). The sporting goods industry is one of the most globalized industries, with huge multinational corporations headquartered in the United States, Western Europe, and, on a lesser scale, East Asia, operating or contracting with sweatshops in Third World countries, most of which are in Asia.[11] Not only do these multinationals, such as Nike, Reebok, Adidas, and Fila, make profits from sales of sporting goods, but their operations are increasingly involved in the media-sports complex through the sponsorship of sporting events and of both professional and national teams, as well as through player endorsements. As one reporter writes, "Like few industries, sports has the chance to build a critical mass allowing all aspects of the market to feed off each other and grow. Sports sells TV which sells ads which sells beer and shoes and everything else imaginable and keeps sport in the eye of the fan" (Blount 1997a, 33).

The world sports market was estimated in a 1997 publication at $200 billion (Blount 1997a, 32).[12]

The following Japanese news bulletin not only shows the cutting edge of the linkage between soccer and commerce but also illustrates the ways in which international mobility of star players has a profound impact on the market and on club-fan relationships. On February 14, 2000, it was announced that Hidetoshi Nakata, a Japanese soccer player who plays for AS Roma in Italy's elite league Series A, would participate in a new electronic commerce company that would market sporting goods associated with Nakata. The company had already signed with star athletes in baseball, golf, and tennis and was due to open on the Internet in March. Nakata already had his own Web site, parts of which required fees, and it was reported to have had four hundred thousand daily hits. The Web site of the new company, called E-Players, would be accessible from Nakata's Web site, have an auction page for Nakata-related goods, and market AS Roma–related goods and packaged tours to tournaments. A Japanese newspaper reported that the new company, with Y10,000,000 capital investment, expected to make sales of Y200–300 million in its first year of operations ("Nakata bujinesu shinshutsu" 2000).

From a market viewpoint, AS Roma's hiring of a Japanese top player helped expand the market for the club's sponsors. In terms of club-fan relationships, the club's fan base stretched to Japan, as Japanese fans of Nakata support his Italian club, follow his play via global telecommunications, buy Nakata- and Roma-related goods, and even travel to Europe to watch him (and Roma) play.

Examples of Asian athletes (with huge Asian markets on their backs) playing for European clubs raise intriguing questions about not only identity formation for the players but also fan allegiance, nationalism, and internationalism in a globalized world. Japanese fans support Nakata because of his nationality.[13] At the same time, those supporters' interests, knowledge, and consumer behavior are not limited to Japan but are, rather, increasingly international. This interface of nationalism and internationalism means an expanding global market for sponsors and the media. For the fans, it means a new—fluid and complex—form of allegiance to and identification with athletes and sports teams that simultaneously are bound by and cross national borders.[14] Together with issues of identity formation for transnational migrant players, these questions point to the complex interplay of the local, the national, and the global in a globalized world.

Although major sporting goods manufacturers are a powerful presence in the sporting world, sport is only a part of the business for those corporations. In the 1990s, for example, sportswear became "the big league" (Vallely 1997). According to an Adidas spokesman, "Eighty per cent of our products are used for leisure. Sport has become the pop of the Nineties. Sportswear sales have gone at a phenomenal rate in the past five years" (Vallely 1997). In this context, it is easy to see why the brand-name manufacturers are willing to pay huge sums of money to sign endorsement contracts with star athletes such as Michael Jordan and Tiger Woods and to sponsor international sports competitions. Just as media organizations use sporting events as a vehicle to make profits (by producing media-sport spectacles), the sporting goods industry uses sports events and sports stars as venues and vehicles to advertise and market their products, and such advertising—both direct advertising and advertising through sponsorship—helps corporations access and broaden consumer bases that go far beyond sports fans. It is in this context that FIFA boasted "an accumulated total of around 37 billion viewers in some 200 countries for the 64 matches of the 1998 World Cup." In other words, FIFA and the media-sports complex delivered this huge number of viewer-consumers, admittedly with varying degrees of purchasing power, to their corporate sponsors and advertisers ("Natural Partners" 2000).

Americanization of the Soccer Industry

Although soccer itself is not (yet?) a major sport in the United States, sociologists of sports have pointed out the Americanization of soccer worldwide, especially in the marketing of the sport and related images, goods, and events. This trend is a result of the economic prowess of powerful U.S.-based multinational corporations that form the (global) media-sports complex. The selection of the United States as the site of the 1994 World Cup Finals is widely seen as the epitome of American commercial and financial power and of the commercialization/Americanization of the sport. As two British sociologists put it:

> The staging of the 1994 World Cup Finals in the United States, a country with no established professional soccer league and little apparent interest in the professional game, represents an extraordinary triumph for the dollar

over culture and marks a key shift in the way in which the world game is administered and financed. (Williams and Giulianotti 1994, 1)

Scholars attribute this shift to the former FIFA president (1974–1998), the Brazilian entrepreneur João Havelange, who had personal stakes in global communication and media industries. He reversed the traditional policy of independence from commercial sponsors and actively sought sponsorship from multinational corporations such as Coca-Cola and Adidas (Williams and Giulianotti 1994, 1–2). Interestingly, according to John Williams and Richard Giulianotti, "Havelange rose to power on the basis of his accusations that FIFA favoured Anglo-Saxon countries and through his tireless lobbying of African and Asian FIFA members" for the removal of his "paternalistic British predecessor," who represented the traditional values in the sport (1994, 1).

In defining the term *Americanization*, Peter Donnelly does not limit it to the actions of actual U.S. corporations. Rather, he means it in the sense that "most of the conditions for corporate sport either are American in origin or have been more fully developed in the United States" (1996, 246). Donnelly lists the following as characteristic of Americanization: "the American style of sport has become the international benchmark for corporate sport—'show-biz,' spectacular, high-scoring, or record-setting superstar athletes; the ability to attract sponsors by providing desired audiences; and having the characteristics necessary for good television coverage" (1996, 246).

The awarding of the 1994 World Cup soccer finals to the United States was an example of the country's "extraordinary success in securing the venues" for international games: the 1984 Los Angeles summer Olympics; the 1996 summer Olympic Games in Atlanta, headquarters of Coca-Cola, the event's major sponsor; the 2002 winter Olympics in Utah. David Rowe and his colleagues argue that "the key to these winning bids was the enormous material advantage of the world's largest and most lucrative market for sport on commercial television" (1994, 664). Besides U.S. financial and marketing prowess, some fear "commercially induced modification" of the game itself to make soccer a major media/spectator sport in the United States. "Games schedules, camera angles, rules of play and forms of presentation can all be subjugated to American-dominated business logic and commercial television interests" (Rowe et al. 1994, 664).

Significance of Global Perspectives for the Study of Race in American Sports

One of the paradoxes in American life is the relative lack of interest in the world beyond the borders of the United States, even though the United States exerts enormous power economically, militarily, and culturally in the rest of the world. One might argue that Americans can afford to remain uninterested in, even oblivious to, the rest of the world precisely because of the hegemony the United States enjoys. The same paradox is observable in the studies of sports: while American sports and, more important, the American business practices around sports and the U.S.-dominated sports-related industries have had great impacts on sports in the rest of the world, American scholars of sports have remained relatively focused on domestic issues. It is ironic indeed that while U.S.-based multinational media, sporting goods manufacturers, and management agencies are the main forces of globalization of sports *elsewhere*, the United States has remained "the most isolated sports culture in the world" (Miller 1998, 347).

Closer to the theme of this book, discussions of race and sports in the United States have tended to be framed in both a nationalist discourse and a black-white binary paradigm of race and racism. This isolationist tendency has also been pointed out by Toby Miller, who criticized the "devastatingly intramural gaze" of American sports sociologists. Commenting on the manuscripts submitted by American scholars during his three-year tenure as editor of the *Journal of Sport and Social Issues*, Miller observed "the intense parochialism of local [= U.S.] sport sociology" and asked: "Why do so few scholars write about world sports rather than the minority interests in this country?" (Miller 1999, 372).

In the United States, soccer was historically associated with male immigrants from Europe and never entered the mainstream of American sports, especially as a media/spectator sport. This began to change in the 1960s, when its popularity as a participant sport, rather than as media sports entertainment, rose particularly among the youth from suburban middle-class families. David Andrews and his colleagues (1997) argue that suburban middle-class parents chose soccer for their children to distance and differentiate themselves socially and symbolically from sports such as basketball that were associated with the inner-city black "underclass." In recent decades, soccer's popularity among girls has grown, aided by Title IX of the 1972 Education Amendments Act. In the mid-1990s, the gender ratio among soccer players was sixty-forty male to female (Andrews et al. 1997, 265). By 1998, one observer noted, soccer had become "the most popular game for girls in America," with 7.24 million American women and girls playing the sport (Hirshey 1998, 95–96).[15] The strength of American women's soccer was demonstrated in the U.S. national team's victory in the first Women's World Cup Finals in 1991 and then again in 1999, the latter occasion attracting huge media attention. The majority of players and fans of soccer in the United States in the 1980s and 1990s were from among the white suburban middle classes, as suggested by the media hype about "soccer moms," a presumably significant voting bloc during the 1996 presidential election campaign.[16] This picture of American soccer as a symbol of a white suburban middle-class lifestyle shows a stark contrast with the strong association of the same sport with working-class male identity in the United Kingdom.

Also in recent decades, however, new immigrants from Latin America, where soccer is "the people's sport," have brought their passion for the sport to the United States. Thanks to global communications systems such as satellite television, immigrant soccer enthusiasts can follow the matches of their "homelands" at international competitions. During the 1998 World Cup Finals, a newspaper article reported on a World Cup "frenzy" among immigrants from Latin America in Queens, New York City; the subtitle read "World Cup Kicks Off Frenzy of Fútbol and National Pride" (Toy 1998). These (male) immigrant soccer fans, too, exemplify the complex interplay of globalization, a newly forming immigrant identity, and the connection to the "homeland" through world soccer.

This cartography of race, class, and gender in American soccer presents fascinating questions for future research. If suburban middle-class white families are using soccer to fashion their identity as a suburban American family distinct from the black "underclass," does that identity signify (white middle-class) isolationism from the increasingly multiracial American society under globalization? Is it part of a white middle-class backlash against "multiculturalism"? How would the two forms of engagement with soccer, discussed above, interface with each other, if at all? Where in the raced, gendered international division of labor are the two groups situated? Even in their attempt at retreating from "multiculturalism" and globalization, in what ways are forces and processes of globalization affecting those white suburban families? How is their comfortable lifestyle in

American suburbia made possible in a globalized world where the gap between the rich and the poor is widening?

There appears to be a parallel between the paradoxical absence of interest among American sports scholars in world sports, which are so influenced by American sports and business practices, and white middle-class families' retreat from "multicultural America" while their very lifestyles and privileges depend on the exploitation of working-class Americans and Third World workers. As C. L. Cole warns about the media hyperbole over the recent successes of American women's sports:

> The images of victorious and degenerate athletes encourage ways of thinking about women, race, and sports that *deny the extent to which multinational corporations are reshaping and profiting from sport-related ventures.* Relatedly, *they make it difficult to imagine how these highly profitable megacorporations and we, as consumers, are implicated in the broader struggle faced by those who are economically and politically disadvantaged and vulnerable.* (Cole 2000, 6; emphasis added)

Like Cole, I emphasize the importance of the political economy of sports as we try to analyze the discourses on nationalism, race, and identity in sports in a globalized world. In other words, I suggest that one way to end "American isolationism" in the study of sports is to recognize the economic, military, and cultural hegemony of the United States and to become aware of, and critically analyze, ways in which the American sports industry (including players) and American consumers (fans and academics) are implicated in that hegemony. Not doing so, as Cole points out, is tantamount to being an apologist for the exploitation and oppression of the vulnerable under corporate-driven globalization.

Notes

I would like to thank the editors of this volume, John Bloom and Michael Willard, for their helpful feedback on earlier drafts of this essay. John Bloom, in particular, made valuable comments and suggestions on the theme and focus of the essay, shared his observations and insights about the state of English soccer, and provided editorial assistance. Many thanks to John for helping me complete this essay.

1. For an overview of issues and theoretical frameworks for the study of sports labor migration, see Maguire and Bale 1994a and 1994b.

2. For a survey of theories of globalization, see Waters. For a helpful introduction to and overview of major social theories that have influenced the studies of sport, see Jarvie and Maguire 1994. For exploratory overviews of research in sports and globalization, see Harvey, Rail, and Thibault 1996; Miller et al. 1999.

3. Soccer, like other sports, is a highly gendered activity. This essay concerns *male* soccer, which is the mainstay of world soccer, both in popularity and as a business. Not surprisingly, then, as Maguire points out, "the global migration of 'sports labour' predominantly, though not exclusively, involves men" (1994, 453).

4. For a detailed study of FIFA and its power, see Sugden and Tomlinson 1998.

5. On the conflict between the European Community's free-market policy on labor and the football authorities' "protectionism" before the 1995 Bosman ruling, see Miller and Redhead 1994.

6. In a 1999 publication, Vertovec reported that "around half the world's countries recognize dual citizenship" (455).

7. The theory of underdevelopment and dependency is one of the influential paradigms in the study of sports and globalization. See, for example, Jarvie and Maguire 1994, 237–51.

8. In an overview of the history of anti-racist interventions in British soccer, Garland and Rowe point out that there has been a tendency in the media, government policies, and academic debates to conflate racism solely with fascism or hooliganism, neglecting more subtle forms of day-to-day racism experienced by players and fans of color alike (Garland and Rowe 1999).

9. These approaches include process sociological, Marxist, anthropological, environmental psychological, and cultural studies (Giulianotti 1994).

10. On the media-sports (production) complex, see Jhally 1989; Maguire 1993; and Wenner 1989. David Rowe prefers the term *media sports cultural complex* to stress "the two-way relationship between sports media and the greater cultural formation of which it is a part" (1999, 4).

11. When one takes into account that the majority of the labor force in the manufacturing of sporting goods are women, as are the clerical staff of corporations and other organizations, the gendered international division of labor in the soccer industry becomes even more stark.

12. The importance of sports as an industry is evident also in the media treatment of sports-related items. As McKay and Miller pointed out in the context of the emergence of corporate sport in 1980s Australia, sports-related news items "routinely appear in marketing, financial, computer, and business columns," and "articles on sport and advertisements using sporting themes are increasingly found in leading business magazines" (quoted in Donnelly 1996, 245).

13. Nakata has steadfastly resisted having his achievements framed in terms of his Japanese nationality, insisting that his vision is not limited to being a Japanese player. One might characterize Nakata's attitude as "postnational" (Appardurai 1993), which sharply contrasts with the tense nationalist posture of the Japanese

national team that won the bronze medal in the 1968 Olympics in Mexico. On the history of soccer in Japan, especially its recent development and popularity, see Horne 1996.

14. In the case of Japan, a strong case can be made that "internationalism" is promoted to strengthen nationalism.

15. According to Hirshey, by 1998 the number of Division I women's soccer temas (229) had surpassed that of men's programs (191). See Hirshey 1998, 96.

16. Hirshey notes that the members of the U.S. national team were "products of upper-middle-class suburban homes: privileged, college educated, well scrubbed" (1998, 99).

REFERENCES

"Africa's Worrying Soccer Exodus." 2000. *BBC News Online* 14 January. Available from http://news.bbc.co.uk/low/english/sport/...ns/cup_features/newsid_603000/603845.stm.

Andrews, David L., Robert Pitter, Detlev Zwick, and Darren Ambrose. 1997. "Soccer's Racial Frontier: Sport and the Suburbanization of Contemporary America." In *Entering the Field: New Perspectives on World Football*, ed. Gary Armstrong and Richard Giulianotti, 261–82. Oxford: Berg.

Appadurai, Arjun. 1993. "Patriotism and Its Futures." *Public Culture* 5: 411–29.

"Belgium's Football 'Slave Trade.'" 1999. *BBC News Online* 10 March. Available from http://news.bbc.co.uk/low/english/special_report/newsid_292000/292958.stm.

Blount, Jeb. 1997a. "Name of the Game." *Latin Trade* (May): 32–33.

———— 1997b. "Sporting Life." *Latin Trade* (May): 28–37.

"Bosman Summer Holiday." 1999. *BBC News Online* 16 March. Available from http://news.bbc.co.uk/low/english/sport/football/newsid_297000/297921.stm.

"Call to Limit Foreign Footballers." 2000. *BBC News Online* 18 May. Available from http://news2.thls.bbc.co.uk/english/low/uk_politics/newsid_752000/752678.stm.

"Cameroon and Ghana Share the Spoils." 2000. *BBC News Online* 22 January. Available from http//news.bbc.co.uk/low/english/sport/...ations/cup_news/newsid_614000/614706.stm.

Cole, C. L. 2000. "The Year That Girls Ruled." *Journal of Sport and Social Issues* 24, 1: 3–7.

"The Colourful Game." 2000. FIFA Web site. Available from http://www.fifa2.com/scripts/runisa.dll?m2.65822:gp:418652:67173+fgg/racism.

Dahlburg, John-Thor. 1998. "France: Racially Diverse Team's World Cup Success Spurs Discussion of Virtues of a 'Melting Pot' Nation." *Los Angeles Times*, 25 July, home edition.

Donnelly, Peter. 1996. "The Local and the Global: Globalization in the Sociology of Sport." *Journal of Sport and Social Issues* 20 (August): 239–57.

Duke, Vic. 1991. "The Politics of Football in the New Europe." In *British Football and Social Change: Getting into Europe*, ed. John Williams and Stephen Wagg, 187–200. Leicester: Leicester University Press.

Euro2000. 2000. *BBC News Online*. Available at http://bbc.co.uk/low/english /euro2000.

Faist, Thomas. 2000. "Transnationalization in International Migration: Implications for the Study of Citizenship and Culture." *Ethnic and Racial Studies* 23, 2 (March): 189–222.

"Foreign Players in Fake Passport Probe." 1999. *BBC News Online* 29 November. Available from http://news2.thls.bbc.co.uk/hi/eng...ball/news/newsid_541000 /541981.stm.

Garland, Jon, and Michael Rowe. 1999. "Selling the Games Short: An Examination of the Role of Antiracism in British Football." *Sociology of Sport Journal* 16, 1: 35–53.

Giulianotti, Richard. 1994. "Social Identity and Public Order: Political and Academic Discourses on Football Violence." In *Football, Violence and Social Identity*, ed. Richard Giulianotti, Norman Bonney, and Mike Hepworth, 9–36. London: Routledge.

Giulianotti, Richard, Norman Bonney, and Mike Hepworth, eds. 1994. *Football, Violence and Social Identity*. London: Routledge.

Harvey, Jean, Geneviève Rail, and Lucie Thibault. 1996. "Globalization and Sport: Sketching a Theoretical Model for Empirical Analyses." *Journal of Sport and Social Issues* 20 (August): 258–77.

Hirshey, David. 1998. "Soccer Idols." *Women's Sports and Fitness* (July/August): 94–99, 142, 145.

Horne, John. 1996. "'Sakka' in Japan." *Media, Culture and Society* 18: 527–47.

Hughes, Rob. 2000. "Kyokai, meika ni kokushi sareru burajiru senshu." *Asahi Shimbun* (6 June), international edition, 17.

"Is Europe Stealing Africa's Best Players?" 2000. *BBC News Online* 21 January. Available from http://newsvote.bbc.co.uk/low/english/ta...debates/african /newsid_607000/607285.stm.

Jarvie, Grant, and Joseph Maguire. 1994. *Sport and Leisure in Social Thought*. London: Routledge.

Jhally, Sut. 1989. "Cultural Studies and the Sport/Media Complex." In *Media, Sports and Society*, ed. Lawrence A. Wenner, 70–93. Newbury Park, CA: Sage.

Kempson, Russell. 2000. "British Left Out of Vialli's Winning Blend." *Times* (London). 27 December.

Lawrence, Ken. 2000. "Premiership Managers Prepare for Exotic Hiccup." *Soccernet* 21 January. Available from http://www.soccernet.com/english/news /210100africanpremiership.html.

Maguire, Joe. 1991. "Sport, Racism and British Society: A Sociological Study of England's Élite Male Afro/Caribbean Soccer and Rugby Union Players." In *Sport, Racism and Ethnicity*, ed. Grant Jarvie, 94–123. London: Falmer Press.

Maguire, Joseph. 1993. "Globalization, Sport Development, and the Media/Sport Production Complex." *Social Science Review* 2, 1: 29–47.

———— 1994. "Preliminary Observations on Globalisation and the Migration of Sport Labour." *Sociological Review* 42 (August): 452–80.

————. 1998. "Border Crossings: Soccer Labour Migration and the European Union." *International Review for the Sociology of Sport* 32, 1: 59–73.

Maguire, Joseph, and John Bale. 1994a. "Postscript: An Agenda for Research on Sports Labour Migration." In *The Global Sports Arena: Athletic Talent Migration in an Interdependent World*, ed. John Bale and Joseph Maguire, 281–284. London: Frank Cass.

————. 1994b. "Sports Labour Migration in the Global Arena." In *The Global Sports Arena: Athletic Talent Migration in an Interdependent World*, ed. John Bale and Joseph Maguire, 1–21. London: Frank Cass.

Miller, Fiona, and Steve Redhead. 1994. "Do Markets Make Footballers Free?" In *The Global Sports Arena: Athletic Talent Migration in an Interdependent World*, ed. John Bale and Joseph Maguire, 141–52. London: Frank Cass.

Miller, Toby. 1998. "American Exceptionalism?" *Journal of Sport and Social Issues* (November): 347–49.

————. 1999. "Moving On." *Journal of Sport and Social Issues* (November): 371–72.

Miller, Toby, Geoffrey Lawrence, Jim McKay, and David Rowe. 1999. "Modifying the Sign: Sport and Globalization." *Social Text* 60: 15–33.

"Nakata, bijinesu shinshutsu." 2000. *Asahi Shimbun* (15 February), international edition.

"Natural Partners." 2000. FIFA Web site. Available from http://www.fifa2.com /scripts/runisa.dll?m2.265822:gp:418652:67173+fgg/tv.

Rowe, David. 1999. *Sport, Culture and the Media*. Buckingham: Open University Press.

Rowe, David, Geoffrey Lawrence, Toby Miller, and Jim McKay. 1994. "Global Sport? Core Concern and Peripheral Vision." *Media, Culture and Society* 16: 661–75.

Sassen, Saskia. 1998. *Globalization and Its Discontents: Essays on the New Mobility of People and Money*. New York: New Press.

Sopel, Jon. 2000. "Africa's Football 'Slave Trade.'" *BBC News Online* 14 February. Available from http://news.bbc.co.uk/low/english/world/europe/newsid _639000/639390.stm.

Sugden, John, and Alan Tomlinson. 1998. *FIFA and the Contest for World Football: Who Rules the People's Game?* Cambridge: Polity Press.

Swardson, Anne. 1998. "The French Tricolor: White, Black and Brown National

Soccer Team Finds Prosperity with Racial and Ethnic Diversity." *Washington Post*, 8 July, final edition.

Three Lions. Video documentary.

Tomlinson, Alan. 1994. "FIFA and the World Cup: The Expanding Football Family." In *Hosts and Champions: Soccer Cultures, National Identities and the USA World Cup*, ed. John Sugden and Alan Tomlinson, 13–33. Aldershot: Arena.

Toy, Vivian S. 1998. "For a Month, Soccer Is Life: World Cup Kicks Off Frenzy of Fútbol and National Pride." *New York Times* 10 June, national edition.

Vallely, Paul. 1997. "Shoe Wars: The Struggle for Global Dominance between Nike and Adidas." *Independent* (London) 6 December.

Vertovec, Steven. 1999. "Conceiving and Researching Transnationalism." *Ethnic and Racial Studies* 22, 2 (March): 447–62.

Vinocur, John. 1999. "Just a Soccer Star, After All." *New York Times Magazine*, 14 March, 32–35.

Waters, Malcolm. 1995. *Globalization*. London: Routledge.

Wenner, Lawrence A. 1989. "Media, Sports, and Society: The Research Agenda." In *Media, Sports, and Society*, ed. Lawrence A. Wenner, 13–48. Newbury Park, CA: Sage.

Williams, John, and Richard Giulianotti. 1994. "Introduction: Stillborn in the USA?" In *Game without Frontiers: Football, Identity and Modernity*, ed. Richard Giulianotti and John Williams, 1–20. Aldershot: Arena.

Wilson, Jamie, Patrick Wintour, and Vivek Chaudhary. 2000. "Malaise at the Heart of Football." *Guardian* (London) 22 June.

Chapter Fifteen

Tiger Woods at the Center of History

Looking Back at the Twentieth Century through the Lenses of Race, Sports, and Mass Consumption

Henry Yu

> *Can't you see the pattern?* Earl Woods asks. *Can't you see the signs?* "Tiger will do more than any other man in history to change the course of humanity," Earl says.
>
> *Sports* history, Mr. Woods? Do you mean more than Joe Louis and Jackie Robinson, more than Muhammad Ali and Arthur Ashe? "More than any of them because he's more charismatic, more educated, more prepared for this than anyone."
>
> *Anyone,* Mr. Woods? Your son will have more impact than Nelson Mandela, more than Gandhi, more than Buddha?
>
> "Yes, because he has a larger forum than any of them. Because he's playing a sport that's international. Because he's qualified through his ethnicity to accomplish miracles. He's the bridge between the East and the West. There is no limit because he has the guidance. I don't know yet exactly what form this will take. But he is the Chosen One. He'll have the power to impact nations. Not people. *Nations.* The world is just getting a taste of his power."[1]

The history of sports, a subject garnering little respect two decades ago, has come of age. Partially this has been due to the increasing number of high-quality scholars who have built the field and who have placed it on solid foundations in interdisciplinary enterprises such as American Studies and Cultural Studies, as well as in traditional disciplines such as sociology, anthropology, history, and English literature. But the scholarly importance of understanding sports has also been generated because of large-scale historical developments in the twentieth century. Without understanding how sports changed during the last century—from a set of bodily practices shaped by rhetorical claims of escape from the drudgery of work to a central institution in the spread of global entertainment and leisure industries—historians will have missed one of the key social transformations of twentieth-century history.

My aim in this chapter is not to survey the burgeoning fields of sports studies, nor is it to offer future directions for studying the history of sports; rather, I sketch a few broad developments in twentieth-century history, outlining how interpreting sports as a part of that history is analytically, pedagogically, and aesthetically compelling. This chapter, in other words, is an argument that sports can be useful for thinking about and teaching the history of the twentieth century. In addition, the sheer excitement of understanding sports, a major part of why many academics disdain sports studies, results from the recognition of the central place of sports in the historical changes of the twentieth century. Incorporating the story of sports into our historical narratives is to have a more persuasive synthesis that explains key developments.

This chapter uses the recurring example of professional golfer Tiger Woods as a way to sketch some of these changes in the history of the twentieth century. I am not arguing (unlike his father, Earl Woods, in the quote above) that Tiger Woods as an individual has actually changed the course of history. However, there are reasons that make Woods an interesting example beyond his utility as a recognizable and accessible explanatory device. When Woods left Stanford University in 1996 to become a professional golfer, the widespread confusion over his racial status was highly revealing, and analyzing the difficulties that Americans had in classifying Woods tells us much about transformations in concepts of race and culture during the twentieth century. Understanding how Tiger Woods came to possess such a complicated body also helps illustrate the very complex migrations and movements of human bodies around the globe that marked twentieth-century life. Furthermore, making sense of why Tiger Woods was so loudly heralded as a savior for golf—and, at times, for America and for the world—helps trace the changing politics of racial difference. That Tiger Woods was given in 1996 a $37 million endorsement contract from Nike before he ever played in a single professional golf tournament is a fact that can be understood only within a long-term history involving the increasing importance of entertainment and leisure industries and the expanding reach of corporate business institutions in the social, economic, and political life of the United States. Tiger Woods's very existence, therefore, is the consequence of the transformations in twentieth-century history that this chapter addresses.[2]

In this chapter, I address three points: (1) how contemporary descriptions of cultural difference retain many of the problems of older languages of biological race; (2) how the end of race-based conflict in the United States has been constantly imagined as an act of individual redemption, blinding Americans to the structural bases of racial hierarchy; and (3) how sports and celebrity have become powerful economic and political commodities with the rise of the entertainment industries. As an introduction, I describe quickly how sports is also one of the best ways to understand the broad transformation that occurred during the twentieth century in bodily practices defined as work versus play. Therefore, let us begin with the question of why sports is supposed to be "fun" and not a serious activity.

Much of the lingering disdain for studying sports is itself a legacy of the early-twentieth-century idea that sports was a leisure-time activity to be indulged outside the earnest hours of the industrial workday. Therefore, if sports was a fun activity, how could it be the subject for serious study? However, this ideal of sports as a transcendence or an opting out of industrial time—and the related assumption about intellectual production as a form of rigorous, professional work—was rooted in a particular historical period. Narratives of twentieth-century history that neglect later transformations in sports also miss important changes in the meaning of industrial time, of bodily practices, of what constitutes paid labor, and of what are valuable commodities in an expanding global market. The Olympic movement at the end of the nineteenth century, for instance, was founded on the ideal of amateur athletics. At the time, amateur sports almost exclusively involved men of privilege, whose wealth meant they did not have to exchange labor for money, and therefore their sporting activities were practices exempt from monetary transactions.[3] Early events such as the equestrian clearly reflected the class basis of Olympic sports—the wealthy could afford to own and ride horses. Even when events such as riding and rifle shooting could be connected to the criteria of military prowess (rather than the exclusively noble sport of hunting), they were still the accomplishments of gentlemanly officers. Although the United States seemed to have no hereditary nobility such as Europe had, it was from the ranks of the upper social classes that early Olympic participants were drawn. Rowing had long been an activity associated with student crew races between the gentlemen of Oxford and Cambridge, and in the United States elite students at Harvard and Yale had taken up oars in the mid–nineteenth century in explicit imitation.[4]

The opposition between serious work and playtime was therefore the product of a particular historical moment, when the bodily activities of paid laborers were in explicit opposition to the leisurely, unpaid, and thus amateur activities of the privileged elite. In the United States, the amateur ideal quickly spread and became egalitarian in practice as well as in principle. By the early decades of the twentieth century, American athletes from impoverished roots had achieved fame by representing the United States, their achievements often gained despite great obstacles. Nonwhite athletes such as African American track stars Jesse Owens and Wilma Rudolph and Native American long-distance runner Jim Ryun became popular symbols of how people could seemingly overcome racism through sheer talent and hard work. The amateur ideal, however, often worked against such lower class athletes, since they were not allowed to accept any financial reward for their talent. The famous example is Owens, who lost his amateur status because he was paid for such spectacles as sprinting against horses.

One of the major transformations of the twentieth century in the United States was the blurring of the dichotomy between work and play, so that, on the one hand, sports increasingly became a professional, paid form of labor and, on the other hand, labor became commonly idealized as an activity that should be "fun" or intrinsically rewarding—in other words, like sports. Although the difference between work and leisure remained, the character of the bodily practices that marked each type of activity began to resemble each other. Today, people finished with their day job pay to "work out," mirroring the laborious lifting and exertion that in the nineteenth century would be disdainfully considered the exclusive province of wage laborers. Similarly, professional athletes are paid millions of dollars to perform in games that almost all will admit they would play for free.

Therefore, the early period of sports reflected a time when labor was a paid activity wrenched by financial coercion from the bodies of those who needed the money to live, and play was either the exclusive domain of those who did not have to work or the precious leisure time of workers when their bodily practices were not leased by others. This was the relationship of human labor to production and leisure that Karl Marx described so astutely in the mid–nineteenth century.[5] The twentieth century saw a remarkable transition in the United States and other advanced capitalist nations from a bifurcated world, where work was work and play was play, to one where the difference between work and play seemed much less clear. Whether in the realm of sports, leisure, recreation, or any of the myriad entertainment industries, playing now seems the product of much hard work.

This is not to say that the privilege of working at something fun is at all widespread. Increasingly, the hard work necessary to provide for and support the playful activities of Americans is being performed in faraway or hidden places, whether those be the sweatshops of Southeast Asia or East Los Angeles. The development of the industrial order of mass consumption in the twentieth century and the centrality of leisure and entertainment activities such as sports are crucial for understanding how these transformations in ideas of work and play connect to larger historical changes. The global expansion of capitalism (sandwiched around the anomalous period of the Cold War) has been marked by the spread of a distinction between work and play that has helped justify the social hierarchies of capitalism. No matter how much it seems that working is now less onerous and playing is in the province of more and more people, one's play is still inevitably at the expense of someone else's work.

In addition, the hierarchical relationship between those who work so that others can play has been marked by transnational connections, so that work performed in one nation is connected to the leisure of someone in another. One of the prominent recent examples of the connection of play in the United States with work elsewhere has been the controversy over the low-wage labor, usually performed by young women in Vietnam, Indonesia, or Southern China, who make products for the American sportswear company Nike. Nike's multibillion-dollar sales were fueled by famous athletes such as Michael Jordan and Tiger Woods, who endorsed their products. In trying to understand the phenomenon of Tiger Woods, we can come to realize how it is that the fantasy of racial fair play on the golf courses of America came to be so intimately tied to sweatshop labor on the other side of the world.[6]

When Tiger Woods Lost His Stripes, or How We're Forced to Capture a World of Color Using Black and White Film

As the summer waned in 1996, the world was treated to the coronation of a new public hero. Eldrick "Tiger" Woods, the twenty-year-old golf prodigy, captured his third straight amateur championship and then promptly declared his intention to turn professional. The story became an American media sensation, transferring the material of sports-page head-lines to the front page of newspapers in a way usually reserved for World Series championships or athletes involved in sex and drug scandals. Televi-sion coverage chronicled every step of Tiger's life, debating his impact on the sport and wondering if he was worth the millions of dollars that Nike and other companies, such as Titleist and American Express were going to pay him for an endorsement contract.

Tiger Woods's eagerly anticipated professional debut was hailed in Au-gust 1996 as a multicultural godsend to the sport of golf. As a child of multiracial heritage, Woods added color to a sport that was traditionally preserved for those who were white and rich. For its very significance as a bastion of hierarchy, golf had also become a marker of the opposition to racial and class exclusion. Similar to how Jackie Robinson's entry into baseball symbolized for Americans not just the eventual desegregation of baseball but also that of American society, Woods's entry into golf was heralded as the entry of multiculturalism into the highest reaches of coun-try-club America.[7] A multicolored Tiger in hues of black and yellow would forever change the complexion of golf, attracting American inner-city children to the game in the same way Michael Jordan had done for basketball.

The manner in which observers initially explained Tiger's potential ap-peal was revealing. A *Los Angeles Times* article on 27 August 1996, the day after Woods turned pro, declared that Tiger had a "rich ethnic back-ground," calculating that his father was "a quarter Native American, a quarter Chinese and half African American" and that his mother was "half Thai, a quarter Chinese and a quarter white." How did we arrive at these fractions of cultural identity? Did they imply that he practiced his multi-cultural heritage in such a fractured manner, eating chow mein one day out of four, soul food on one of the other days, and Thai barbeque chicken once a week? Obviously not. The exactness of the ethnic breakdown referred to the purported biological ancestry of Woods's parents and grandparents.

The racial calculus employed by both print and television reporters to explain Tiger's heritage harked uncomfortably to earlier biological classifications. Southern law courts tried for much of the nineteenth and twentieth centuries to calculate a person's racial makeup in the same precise manner, classifying people as mulattoes if they were half white and half black, quadroons if they were a quarter black, octoroons if an eighth, and so on. The assumption was that blood and race could be broken down into precise fractions, tying a person's present existence in a racially segregated society with a person's purported biological ancestry. A single drop of black blood made a person colored, and no amount of white blood could overwhelm that single drop to make a person pure again.[8]

In historical and contemporary conceptions of race, Tiger Woods was African American. The intricate racial calculus that broke Tiger into all manner of stripes and hues was a farce not only in terms of its facile exactitude but also in its purported complexity. According to the calculations, Tiger Woods is more Asian American than African American (a quarter Chinese on the father's side plus a quarter Chinese and half Thai on the mother's side, for a total of one-half Asian in Tiger, versus only half African American on the father's side, for a total of one-quarter black in Tiger . . .).[9] But this is an empty equation because social usage, and the major market appeal of Tiger, classified him as black.

In an earlier essay, I used the phrase "How Tiger Woods Lost His Stripes" to describe the process by which the complexities of human migration and intermingling in this country became understood first in the simplifying classifications of race and then in those of culture.[10] The awkward attempts to describe Woods's heritage bear the legacy of Old South notions of race, but they also arose from the nineteenth-century context of massive international labor migration.[11] The rise and triumph of the concept of culture at the beginning of the twentieth century supposedly eclipsed earlier biological definitions of race, but in some ways the idea of culture is little more than the grafting of nonbiological claims onto preexisting categories of race.

Theories of biological race that arose in the nineteenth century emphasized belonging to some fictive category (for instance, Negroid, Mongoloid, Caucasoid) that collapsed racial type and geographical location. This mythic tie between race and spatial location called forth an epic history stretching back to prehistoric ancestors, tying racial difference to origins deep in time. We still operate with a version of this classificatory scheme when we identify some physical features as "Asian" (straight black hair) and others as "African" (brown skin) or "European" (light skin).[12] For much of the late nineteenth and early twentieth century, racial theories that attributed variations in behavior and in physical and mental abilities to biological differences served as justification for social oppression and hierarchy.

An anthropological conception of culture that came to the fore in the early twentieth century redefined variety in human behavior and practice as a consequence of social processes. Meant to eliminate any association of mental capacity with biological race, the theory of culture proved relatively successful as a way of attacking biological justifications for social hierarchy. The culture concept, however, has mirrored the suppositions of racial theories about the centrality of biological ties to the past. Particularly in how differences in behavior between people whose ancestors have come from Africa or Asia or Europe have been explained as cultural in origin, cultural difference has paralleled the boundaries of earlier definitions of racial difference.

Created by anthropologists visiting exotic locales, culture as an intellectual concept has always been driven by the contradiction that it has come to be an *object* of description (the actual practices of various "cultures") at the same time that it has really only been the *description* of practices. Culture, as it was defined by early theorists such as Franz Boas, was transferred between physical human bodies through social means of communication. Embodied in social rituals and practices, culture was a way of life, reproduced by social groups that were bound together by such acts. As a set of descriptions, ethnographies were claimed by anthropologists to describe actual "cultures"—a whole set or society of people that had strict boundaries. However, the differentiation between what was unique to one culture versus another always depended on the perspective of Europeans or Americans, implicitly comparing their objects of study to other ways of life (sometimes, unwittingly, their own).

Cultural theory worked best with societies that were seemingly static and had little in- or out-migration. Indeed, anthropologists quite consciously limited their studies to what they labeled "primitive" societies. Anthropologists defined "primitive" as those societies that could be studied using their theories about static, bounded cultures. Any social group that had any significant number of human bodies entering or exiting was extremely difficult to describe using cultural theory, a serious shortcoming that nonetheless did not stop cultural theory from being applied eventually to all human societies.

Arising out of a systematic awareness of differences, the concept of culture is undermined when users forget its origin as a description. *Culture* as a word is continually used as if it were an object with causal powers ("Franz did that because his culture is German"). However, culture is the *product* of seeing the world anthropologically ("Franz, in comparison with other people I have known, does things differently, and I make sense of that difference by describing those acts and linking them to my awareness that he and other people I have known who do it all come from Germany"). Unfortunately, in popular language the word *culture* has come to have universal significance at the same time that it signifies less and less.

Despite the ability to perform cultural practices described as being the embodiment of some particular culture (for instance, German culture), we are constantly faced with examples of how cultural membership has very little to do with performance ability. Take, for instance, white American missionaries in Japan and Japanese immigrants in the United States during the nineteenth and twentieth centuries. There were a number of children of American missionaries to Japan who were born and raised in Japan and came to be adept at speaking the local language and understanding and practicing local customs and ways of life. They knew how to use chopsticks; they wore "native" dress; they were allowed to play the same Japanese games as their childhood friends. Were they, by any definition, Japanese? Perhaps with a definition that is restricted to functional ability at performing cultural practices; but in any other sense they are anomalies, freaks of culture who serve to uphold the notion of culture as nonbiological ("they know what Japanese culture is") at the same time that they point to the not-so-hidden reliance of cultural differentiation on legal nationality and biological definitions of race.

Such a reliance is highlighted by the example of Japanese immigrants to the United States at the same moment, parallel émigrés traveling in the opposite direction. Their children born in the United States were invariably raised in American schools and became adept at American customs and the local language of English. They ate hamburgers and french fries; they wore Boy Scout uniforms and shouted the Pledge of Allegiance; they were allowed to play in American games such as baseball and basketball with their childhood friends.[13] Legal standards of national citizenship categorized them as American. But if internment of a whole people on the basis of ancestry during World War II means anything, questions of national loyalty, cultural performance (including sports), and racial biology have been so confused in U.S. history that the maintenance of culture as a separate category of analysis gains little more payback than a perverse sense of irony. Japanese Americans, despite the possibility of being described as culturally similar to other Americans, were still treated as if they were racially different and nationally suspect.[14]

Cultural differentiations, like the biological notions of race they purportedly replaced, relied on a historical narrative of population migration. No matter how much even the most astute observers believed that culture is a purely social phenomenon, divorced from biology, there are easy links to histories of the physical migration of human bodies that lead to generalizations based on physical type. On the whole, these links have practical functions, connecting individual human bodies to histories of population migration. Seeing a body that shares physical characteristics with those descended from individuals who live in Asia allows fairly accurate suppositions about biological ancestors from somewhere in Asia.

Almost inevitably, assumptions are made concerning the cultural knowledge and practices of such a person, and it is these connections, between culture and the body's history of biological origin, that are fraught with presumption. Thus, children of American missionaries in China, never having set foot in the United States until the age of eighteen or nineteen, could get off a boat in San Francisco and instantly be American—not only in the legal sense but in the cultural sense as well. The children and grandchildren and great-grandchildren of Chinese immigrants to the United States are always seen as possessing Chinese culture, no matter how inept they are at what it means to be Chinese in China (and in America)— they are asked whether they know how to translate Chinese characters and how to cook chow mein and to discuss the takeover of Hong Kong. Orphans from Korea who grew up in Minneapolis with Scandinavian American parents, no matter how young they were when they were transported from South Korea, are always linked to Korean culture—they are allowed to discover their real culture, or perhaps more indicative, *re*-discover their culture. At worst, and in a manner too reminiscent of the internment of Japanese Americans, airport security officers and the FBI continue to suspect Arab Americans of being terrorists because of how they spell their names or the clothes they wear or the color of their skin.

At the heart of all these distinctions is not race as a biological category or culture as a nonbiological category but a historical awareness of population migrations. If it really is because someone's grandfather came from

Croatia and someone else's came from Canada that one is different from the other, then the cultural difference of now echoes the national difference of before. Origins and biological heritage are central to the assumption that what makes someone different here in the United States is equivalent to their link to some other place in the world.

As historical narratives defining the origins of difference, theories of cultural and national belonging have linked the politics of the present to a biological genealogy of the individual body's past. If the reason someone has been treated differently in the United States is because his or her grandfather came from China, this tie is important less because of what was unique and native to China (both in the nineteenth century and now) and more because of how racial difference and animosity have been defined in North America—how, in other words, people in the United States have defined "whiteness" and being full American citizens with European origin and have linked otherness in racial and cultural terms with non-European origin. Racial, cultural, and national categorizations, therefore, have been inextricably linked in history, and in the most foundational sense, these linkages have depended on an awareness of population migration.

The fractional nature of the racial and cultural categories in Tiger Woods is as arbitrary as the classification of him as African American. The key factor that undermines Tiger Woods's racial formula is the fiction that somehow his ancestors were racially or culturally whole. When he was broken up into one-quarter Chinese, one-quarter Thai, one-quarter African American, one-eighth American Indian, and one-eighth Caucasian, the lowest common denominator of one-eighth leads to a three-generation history. Tracing a three-step genealogy of descent back to an original stage of pure individuals places us at the end of the nineteenth century. If we were to consider other striped, Tiger Woods–like bodies in a similar manner, they might be described as containing one-sixteenth or even one-thirty-second fractions. But in any case, the individuals who are imagined to live at the beginning point of the calculations are whole only because they have been assumed to exist originally in a shared moment of purity.

The timing of this moment of imagined purity is partly founded on the coincidence of migration with national identity. The illusion of ethnic and racial wholeness of a grandparent's generation marks the importance of nineteenth-century nationalism in defining bodies. Emigrating from specific nations or nation-states coming into being, migrants during the nineteenth and early twentieth century had their bodies marked by nationality—Irish, Chinese, Japanese, Italian, German. That their bodies were whole in a national sense allowed for a consequent holistic definition of their racial and cultural origins.

Both race and culture as categories of belonging have often presupposed a biological genealogy of national origin. This view was legally enshrined in the 1924 National Origins legislation, when each nation was given a maximum quota for migrants to the United States. Every immigrant entering and every body already in the Unites States was defined by a national past. A migrant body was marked as a member of a single nation, and thus a national purity was conveyed, regardless of their heterogeneous or complicated origins. Immigrants may have come from a place that did not exist as a political and legal nation, or they may have gone through numerous national entities before entering the United States, any of which could be defined as their "national origin." For instance, migrants from the area now known as South Korea were in the early part of the twentieth century counted as Japanese nationals. Virtually all Koreans understood, that as a colonized and subject people, they were not Japanese in what might be termed a cultural or even a biological sense, but their legal status under the National Origins Act meant that they had to have a national origin, and like other members of the nation of Japan, they were to be excluded from the United States on the basis of national categories.

Even with the supposed eclipse of biological notions of race in the twentieth century, we cling to definitions of national and cultural origin as shorthand for describing biological origin.[15] The three-generation history of intermarriage that the one-eighth fractions ostensibly revealed in actuality described a family tree arbitrarily truncated. The hypothetical racially whole grandparents, given their own family genealogies of ancestry, would have themselves reached into the past to delineate histories of intermingling population migrations. Further and further back in time, these genealogies would reveal that there has never been a set of racially whole individuals from which we have all descended. Whether in purportedly mixed or pure fashion, biological descent that invokes racially whole individuals in the past is delusional.

When the 2000 U.S. Census no longer restricted individuals to single racial categories (allowing people to check more than one box for categories of racial belonging), it seemed that American views of racial and cultural descent might finally have left behind the notion of racially pure, whole individuals. But the new problem of complex logarithms and formulas to try to convert the new fractions of identity into whole numbers still resulted from a need to produce data that made sense, in other words, that counted humans as racial individuals. How will all those who rely on population calculations from the U.S. Census use totals that are not the sum of whole numbers of individuals but crazy totals like 234,574.375, which themselves reflect the sum of a string of fractions such as three-fourths and one-eighth and one-sixty-fourth?[16] Racial categories have always been fictional, but just because they are fictional does not mean we can either wish them away or simply leave behind their continuing use as politically powerful categories of existence.

By the end of the twentieth century, advertisements in every media displayed a seeming rainbow of skin color, as marketing surveys and political polls responded to demographic changes in the racial and cultural makeup of the U.S. population. A *Newsweek* cover published on 1 January 2000 described "Our New Look: The Colors of Race." But the new look is also an old look, and as Gary B. Nash and other historians have pointed out for years, the history of the United States has been a complex mix from its first moments.[17]

The attempt to see in Tiger Woods the embodiment of all his diverse backgrounds was a valiant attempt to contain within a single human body all the ethnic diversity in the social body that multicultural America claimed to be. The awkwardness of description and its inevitable failure resulted from both the flawed conception of cultural and racial origins described earlier and an inability to leave behind an obsession with the idea that race is a biological category represented by individuals.

It is seemingly possible to describe a person's racial history in terms of fractions because each of those fractions is derived from a supposedly whole person several generations before; however, American categories of racial belonging do conceptual and political work because they fit individuals into larger categories of race, not because racial categories somehow fit together in complicated ways within individuals. Tiger Woods as a single human body could not express the fractions within—like almost all children of supposed mixed heritage in this country, his whole quickly becomes his darkest part. Woods himself as a child, attempting to rebut his reduction by others to a state of blackness, came up with the term *Cablinasian* (CAucasian + BLack + INdian + ASIAN) to encapsulate his mixed makeup. Mentioned briefly by the press, the term achieved no currency or usage. Since the power of racial categories comes from their work of tying a number of people together under a single description, a label such as

"Cablinasian" that serves only to describe Woods's individual admixture had little use. Indeed, though Woods had found a name for his unique brand of mixed-up pain, he might as well have used the term *Tiger* to label what was a singular racial description in practice limited to only himself. Tiger Woods was more politically useful, and understandable, as black.

The incipient power allegedly held by "mixed-race individuals" to herald a new racially mixed millennium lies in the promise that such individuals will lessen the utility of prevalent racial categories. But a quick glance at the history of Latin America shows that social hierarchies of racial classification can coexist for long historical periods with the large-scale existence of racially mixed individuals. Racial categories, in other words, achieve social power by connecting individuals to larger groups, and individuals who are apparently the resulting mix of these larger groups are only limited, temporary aberrations in the racial order.[18] Categories that make sense of biological ancestry inevitably repackage the complexities of the past by providing a group connection in the present. Individuals who cannot be made sense of using existent racial classifications may, if their numbers are large enough, change the nature of the categories, but their very existence as individuals historically has not destroyed the utility of racial categories.

There are three main conclusions to be drawn from the ways in which racial and cultural categories have been defined in U.S. history: (1) that continual migration and biological admixture have been the rule rather than the exception in U.S. history (and therefore so-called race mixing is not a "new thing" that will change the future, since it has always been our past); (2) that this history of migration and mixture has been erased or distorted as much with theories of culture as with racial theories based on biology;[19] and (3) that a key to understanding the twentieth century is how changes in definitions of human difference, from languages of race to those of culture, did not eliminate the use of biological heritage as a way of understanding categories of human belonging. This is not to say that justifications for human oppression based on theories about biological difference were not successfully attacked—one of the great stories of the twentieth century was the large-scale campaign waged against social hierarchy based on theories about biological race. However, new theories about national and cultural belonging were still based on historical narratives of biological origin, and sometimes these categories of cultural or national origin have proved quite useful in justifying, and at the same time in combating, social domination and oppression.

Sports and Military Training: Self-Discipline and the
Black Male Savior, from Jackie Robinson
to Colin Powell to Tiger Woods

The confusion of tongues regarding how to name Tiger's complex heritage was a direct result of the confusion over languages of race that continues to bedevil this country; however, Tiger's fading into black was not just the result of an inability to understand Tiger's complexity. Rather than being a product of a negative phenomenon, a confusion or ignorance, there was also a seemingly positive desire to paint Tiger in a darker shade, a pulling for Tiger to be a heroic black man who would save America from its racist past. In his trek from the sports page to the front page, Tiger Woods quickly became another example of a black man making it in America because of his athletic skill. Woods earned his success through his prodigious accomplishments, but his popular apotheosis as black male hero fit him into generic modes of understanding African American masculinity.

Early commentators, in trying to reflect Woods's complexity, often cited that he would bring a newfound awareness of multiracial and mixed-race children to the American public. Sportswriter Rick Reilly's March 27, 1995, *Sports Illustrated* article, "Goodness Gracious, He's a Great Ball of Fire," became the definitive introduction to Tiger Woods for hundreds of thousands of sports fans. Reilly remarked on Woods's mixed ethnic background, describing how Earl was "a quarter American Indian, a quarter Chinese and half black" and how Kultida was "half Thai, a quarter Chinese and a quarter white." But Reilly also described how Woods's appearances as a young child on television shows such as *That's Incredible* and *The Mike Douglas Show* traced a long history from early childhood as a "Great Black Hope." By the end of 1996, other articles in *Sports Illustrated* were clearly emphasizing Woods's potential in this regard. In September 1996 writer Leigh Montville was asking of Woods: "Who can he be? Pick a name. Arthur Ashe. Jackie Robinson. Colin Powell. . . . "[20]

The strange way in which Tiger Woods was received in September 1996 revealed much about the more general American craving for individual black heroes to redeem its ugly history. Whether it was Jackie Robinson, Michael Jordan, Tiger Woods, or Colin Powell, Americans had learned by the end of the twentieth century to fantasize that a single person would save them from racial problems that were endemic, built into the structure of U.S. society. Through much of the media hype that surrounded Woods's decision to turn professional in the fall of 1996 ran a current questioning of whether much of the hope invested in him was because of the color of his skin.

Because Woods received so much money before winning a single professional golf tournament—a fact that distinguished him from almost any other golfer turning from amateur to professional—observers such as sportswriter John Feinstein placed Woods's race as being a prime factor in his potential marketability. On ABC's television show *Nightline*, the week after Woods turned professional, Feinstein remarked that Woods's race was the major reason Nike was giving him such a rich endorsement contract, somewhat unwittingly plugging Woods into larger debates at the time about affirmative action and the role of merit in distinguishing individuals for their racial identity. Tim Finchem, the president of the USPGA (the Professional Golf Association), countered that Woods was unique only because of the extraordinary amount of golfing talent he possessed, and that he would turn out to be worth every penny that Nike paid him. That both Finchem and Feinstein could turn out to be right was clear only several months later, when Woods won the Masters golf tournament in Augusta, Georgia, in April 1997. For several months, however, nobody could say for sure whether Woods would become merely a well-paid "Great Black Hype."

The Masters ended a period of speculation about the role of race in Tiger Woods's rich endorsement deals, but it also masked the transformation of Woods from a highly paid multiracial body—in the news for switching from amateur to paid professional—into a heroic black male icon. In the weeks before the Masters tournament, the media hype intensified around the question of what impact Woods would have if he won. On April 7, 1997, in a *Sports Illustrated* article titled "One for the Ages," Jaime Diaz wrote that Woods's "African-American heritage would make a victory in the tournament, in which no black was invited to play until 1975 and where every caddie was black until '83, a transcendent accomplishment."[21] The symbolism employed by many writers and observers was clear in regard to a potential Tiger Woods victory: this single act was going to change race relations. Lee Elder, one of the African American pioneers on the professional golf tour, remarked about the possibility that Woods would win the Masters: "It might mean even more than Jackie Robinson breaking into baseball."[22] Woods played his ordained role as the inheritor of the hopes of a long line of black golfers who had paved the way for him, graciously acknowledging his debt to Lee Elder, Charlie Sifford, Ted Rhodes, and other early African American golfers.

When Woods won the Masters in record fashion in April 1997, shooting the lowest tournament score in history, he seemed to fulfill all prophecies of him as, in the words of one sportswriter, "The Chosen One." Rick Reilly described Woods's accomplishment in the grand strokes of epic history:

> Almost 50 years to the day after Jackie Robinson broke major league baseball's color barrier, at Augusta National, a club no black man was allowed to join until six years ago, at the tournament whose founder, Clifford Roberts, once said, "As long as I'm alive, golfers will be white, and caddies black," a 21-year old black man delivered the greatest performance ever seen in a golf major. Someday Eldrick (Tiger) Woods, a mixed-race kid with a middle-class background who grew up on a municipal golf course in the sprawl of Los Angeles, may be hailed as the greatest golfer who ever lived, but it is likely that his finest day will always be the overcast Sunday in Augusta when he humiliated the world's best golfers, shot 18-under-par 70-66-65-69—270 (the lowest score in tournament history) and won the Masters by a preposterous 12 shots.[23]

Reilly went on to say that Woods was "the first black man to win any major" golf tournament. John Feinstein, the writer who had emphasized the role of race in Tiger Woods's endorsement deal with Nike, opened and closed his celebratory article by describing how members of the Augusta National Golf Club, which until recently had excluded African Americans, gave Woods a standing ovation to welcome him after he won their club's annual tournament. Feinstein wrote, "They were welcoming him to their club, not grudgingly, but graciously—even happily."[24] Race relations, according to both Feinstein and Reilly, would forever be changed by Tiger's victory.

At around the same time that Tiger Woods was being hailed as the racial savior of golf, and perhaps of America, retired U.S. Army general Colin Powell, chairman of the U.S. Armed Forces Joint Chiefs of Staff during the 1991 Gulf War against Iraq, was eagerly being courted as a potential vice presidential or even presidential candidate. Powell's popularity at the same moment as Woods's ascendancy marked more than just historical coincidence. Both Tiger Woods and Colin Powell represented a number of standard ways in which African American men were perceived as safe and nonthreatening while offering the possibility of U.S. racial redemption. Like General Powell, Tiger's father, Earl Woods, was a military veteran, a lieutenant colonel in the U.S. Army's Special Forces, embodying the safe black man who sacrifices himself in wartime for the nation.[25]

Tiger's father correctly channeled the violent masculinity that popular imagery at that time ascribed to African American males, forsaking the alleged criminality contained in rap and hip-hop music and videos and in mainstream movies such as *Colors* and *New Jack City*. The drug-dealing, drive-by-shooting, and gang-banging black male represented in such popular media was the negative twin of the black war hero. Better yet, Tiger's father directed the oft-represented dangerous sexual desirability of black masculinity not toward white women but to the safe option of a foreign, Asian war bride. Tiger himself, as the son of a black veteran who applied military discipline to create a black male sports hero, served to connect the appeal of the safe black male body as sports star to a lineage of the black male as a military man.

As the sports-star progeny of the black male military hero and the Asian wife picked up in the United States' foray into Vietnam, Tiger Woods might have seemed an ideal symbol of a racial diversity that went beyond black and white. Media imagery, however, did not quite manage to represent the complexity of Tiger. Besides the added complications of describing his fractional nature, there was a more powerful story to be told. When Tiger Woods won his first professional golf tournament, and again when he won the prestigious Masters, newspaper photographs overwhelmingly showed him hugging his father. His mother, Kultida, was either cropped from the frame or blocked by the powerful imagery of the black American military father triumphantly joined with his black American sports-star son. Along with the disappearing stripes of Tiger's racial complexity, Thai American Kultida Woods faded into black.

The dominance of Earl Woods in representations of Tiger was particularly apparent early in Tiger's professional career. When *Sports Illustrated* chose Tiger Woods as its Sportsman of the Year in 1996 (before Tiger's win at the Masters), writer Gary Smith spent a full page discussing how important Earl Woods's two tours of duty as a Green Beret in Vietnam were for understanding Tiger Woods's development. ("Tiger" was, in fact, the nickname Earl had originally given to his South Vietnamese friend Nguyen Phong during the war.) The theme of Tiger's training—and the remarkable military-style discipline he showed—was eventually parlayed by Earl Woods into a pair of popular books, the first one titled *Training a Tiger: A Father's Guide to Raising a Winner in Both Golf and Life*.[26]

Earlier *Sports Illustrated* articles had reported that Kultida had often been the arbiter of discipline—for instance, making Tiger do his homework—but this narrative had little popular resonance in the first few years. It was Earl Woods and the father-son relationship that dominated not only the bookshelves but renditions of the family dynamic on television and in print. In the same article that described Earl Woods's application of military discipline to Tiger, a picture of Kultida with hands clasped paralleled the article's suggestion that her contribution to Tiger's game was Buddhist serenity. Accompanying the photo was a caption reminiscent of the voice of Obi-Wan Kenobi reminding the young Luke Skywalker to "use the Force" in *Star Wars*: "Tida's eyes close when she speaks, and Tiger can almost see her gathering and sifting the thoughts."[27] The attribution of such soft, feminine, Asian qualities of peace and serenity to Kultida Woods contrasted with the controlled violence of Earl Woods's masculinity:

> This is war, so let's start with war. Remove the images of pretty putting greens from the movie screen. . . . Jungle is what's needed here, foliage up to a man's armpits, sweat trickling down his thighs, leeches crawling up them. Lieut. Col. Earl Woods, moving through the night with his rifle ready. . . . [28]

Golf, like Earl Woods's military career, was portrayed in the article as one of the ways in which both male Woodses had channeled their anger toward white racists. Racism and the response of Earl and Tiger Woods was one of the major themes of the article, whereas the thoughts and responses of Kultida Woods to racism were not even a minor subject.

It is interesting that by the middle of 2000, with Earl Woods in declining health and less of a factor in Tiger's postvictory celebrations, Kultida Woods was increasingly being portrayed as the actual disciplinarian of the two parents. Her maternal contributions to Tiger's winning ways became more prominent in articles, and the military career of Earl Woods was no longer the story line. In the beginning, however, representations of Tiger Woods as a popular hero made extensive use of existing tropes of heroic black masculinity. Perhaps in the light of how popular representations had so overdetermined the meaning of his body, it is hard to imagine how Tiger could not have lost his stripes.

The desire for Woods to be a savior matched a widespread hunger for a great African American redeemer. In twentieth-century American history, a series of black sports heroes achieved mythic status for athletic exploits that transcended the social limitations of their race. From Jack Johnson,

Jesse Owens, and Jackie Robinson to Muhammad Ali, Arthur Ashe, Jim Brown, and all the way through Tiger Woods, American writers have continually fantasized that a single person could save U.S. society from endemic racial problems.[29] These Christlike narratives, heralding the redemption of all through the sacrifice of a single martyr (with historical roots in abolitionist narratives such as *Uncle Tom's Cabin*), powerfully shaped the historical memories of African American sports figures. In particular, descriptions of Jackie Robinson and Hank Aaron often highlighted their suffering on the athletic field as somehow redemptive for the nation as a whole.

Transgression was progressive, and just as working class men tasting the leisure reserved for the nonlaboring classes suggested the democratic spread of privilege, so the very entry of a black male body into a formerly segregated white field of sports indicated a signal social change. The transgression did not always take masculine form; mid-twentieth-century female athletes such as Wilma Rudolph and Babe Henson carved off some of the privileges of masculinity by succeeding at sport. However, the black savior during the twentieth century was almost invariably cast as male.

The symbolic value of the single hero overcoming larger social problems helped define Tiger Woods as a black male. This myth of the individual triumphant over the legacies of the past has had mixed political uses—sometimes helping mobilize historical memories of anti-black oppression for political purposes, sometimes justifying public policies that ignored group-based solutions to historical inequity. In the case of Jackie Robinson, actions on the athletic field translated into popular acceptance of political movements such as the Civil Rights movement. Paradoxically, however, the increasing centrality of sports figures in the economic and cultural life of the nation has led to a seeming decrease in their political impact.[30] Muhammad Ali shook the nation when he resisted the Vietnam War draft. In contrast, Michael Jordan and Tiger Woods seem studiously apolitical in their loyalty to their corporate branding. However, this paradox disappears when we place racial politics in the larger context of an American politics focused on corporate rather than racial identity. This does not mean that racial politics have disappeared; rather, race has come to have new meanings in popular politics. The value of Tiger Woods as a racial hero extended beyond the political and into a larger world of mass consumption and communication that could capitalize on the popular hopes and dreams invested in him.

Tiger Woods as National Hero: Using the Rise of Sports and
Entertainment Industries to Understand How American Life
Became Dominated by Mass Consumption
and the Global Spread of Capitalism

The chances are that our first nonwhite president will be a male athletic hero, rather than a military man such as General Colin Powell. Why? Because of the increasing importance of sports and entertainment industries in the economic and cultural life of the United States through the twentieth century. Racial politics have consistently marked the rise of these multibillion-dollar industries. Developments in communications media have also steadily decreased the importance of military heroes in American political culture, and sports and entertainment celebrity has gradually replaced military heroism in popular definitions of moral character.

Sports as a social and institutional practice, originally created at the end of the nineteenth century as the proving ground for young boys who would someday be soldiers, is now an end in itself. What began as a one-way metaphor, that sports competition was a playful representation of battlefield conflict, has reversed directions. Athletic team play and character traits such as self-sacrifice, acceptance of one's role, and courage in the face of adversity are no longer coded behaviors that predict success on the battlefield but the cliched tropes of television sports programs that have conquered American life.

By the end of the 1990s, media mavens were decrying the declining moral character of American professional athletes. The murder and rape trials of football players, the sexual exploits of basketball stars, the boorish behavior of child superstars—all became symbols of the moral deterioration of athletics. But what such critics missed was the long-term historical trend: the virtue (or lack of it) among athletes was not the subject of intense media scrutiny it would eventually become. What the spotlight's glare on athletics revealed was not just the moral defects of sports stars but also the fact that Americans wanted them to be heroes in ways that were not required fifty years before. Nobody would have accused baseball legend Ty Cobb, a noted bigot and bully, of being a paragon of virtue. For most of the twentieth century, the criteria for sportsmanship on the field did not extend to behavior off it; and as with the sexual peccadilloes of presidents, journalists and ordinary people alike turned a blind eye to questionable private behavior among public heroes.

By the end of the twentieth century, however, in the popular imagination, moral character in a heroic sense was almost monopolized by sports figures. This trend was a product of a mass media geared around the commodity of celebrity. In 1980, when Ronald Reagan (still one of the most popular presidents in American history) entered the White House, many political pundits and public intellectuals derided his motion-picture background as unfit for the leader of the nation. Reagan's popularity, however, and his Teflon-like ability to be untainted by political scandal were both derived from his practiced ability as an entertainer to deliver simple moral messages in front of television cameras. If television as a medium was now scrutinizing celebrities for moral failings, the hunger of viewers for positive signs of moral character was just as intense.

There has been a long tradition of American sports heroes turned politicians. Gerald Ford was a college football quarterback at Michigan long before becoming president; presidential hopefuls such as Jack Kemp, a former NFL quarterback, and Bill Bradley, a college basketball hero at Princeton and a professional star with the New York Knicks, were both former athletes. These men used their athletic notoriety as launching pads for political careers, a celebrity that gave them the initial investment capital of fame so helpful to starting a political life. When they began their political careers, however, they also needed to provide healthy doses of seriousness as an antidote to what was perceived as the frivolous nature of their athletic past. By the 1990s, several congressional representatives, such as J. C. Watts and Steve Largent of Oklahoma, both former professional football players, seemed to make seamless transitions from athletics to politics. Once Reagan had marked the triumph of celebrity as a forum for morality, political hopefuls with athletic backgrounds increasingly found that a character forged on Soldier's Field in Chicago playing professional football was no less valuable than a baptism of fire on a soldier's field in Normandy.

In an age of explosively rapid production of celebrity, the realms where character and sociability were constructed changed. Increasingly, combat heroism found less and less purchase. For over two centuries, the battlefields of U.S. wars had been the places where great leaders were made, but the end of the twentieth century saw a withering of this trend. Colin Powell, Norman Schwarzkopf, and John McCain had much less popular appeal as war heroes than Dwight Eisenhower, Ulysses Grant, and Andrew Jackson. Wars were, by the end of the century, consciously made-for-TV events that were not the arena for the production of heroes but highly crafted representations enlisted to persuade public opinion.

Changes in the actual medium of communication were crucial in determining the heights to which popular apotheosis could be achieved. For Andrew Jackson and Zachary Taylor over 150 years ago, newspaper stories detailed their heroic triumphs. For Dwight Eisenhower, it was newsreels flashing in the dark of movie theaters. The journalistic, handheld frenzy that has marked combat photography since the Vietnam War, however, has not been conducive to epic narratives of heroism.[31] The transient nature of television imagery and the jarring, incoherent stories that come out of televised combat are not ideal ways to tell the tale of heroes.

Sports began as the metaphor for war, but by the end of the twentieth century, modern combat no longer compared in the popular imagination. Partly this was because representations of war had failed to seem like sport. With television dominating their consciousness, Americans needed slow motion and the instant replay to transform their warriors into secular saints, just as endless slow-mo highlights of Michael Jordan's dunks and Tiger Woods's approach shots on ESPN's *Sportscenter* deified them as athletic gods. Because television was used so often in Vietnam to capture the brutality of war, military censors have seldom since allowed television crews to get close enough to the action to portray the heroism of fighting soldiers. War has failed to be a metaphor for sports.

The cult of celebrity created a wholly new way of practicing mass politics, and a burgeoning global sports and entertainment industry began to transform popular understandings of public morality and social virtue. Character as a TV event had to be quick drama, fit into the spaces between commercial breaks. Best of all were scripted contests such as professional wrestling. Minnesota's election in 1998 of former professional wrestler Jesse Ventura as its governor is perhaps the best example of the value provided by the dramatic consistency of a choreographed sport. Ventura's unimpeachable virtue had been constructed on the weekly story lines that had built him into a wrestling hero. (The uncertain outcomes of real sports pale in comparison—after all, there is always the danger of a boring game.)

In a manner similar to how Reagan signaled the triumph of celebrity, Ventura's election showed how celebrity in sports was even more powerful than celebrity in the movies. The morality displayed in the alternative world of sports is clear-cut. We know who the good guys are, and we can root for them with hands full of popcorn and team jerseys decorating our bodies. In wrestling, Ronald Reagan's 1980 caricature of the Soviet Union as a cartoon evil empire threatening America had a popular life long after the Berlin Wall and the Soviet Union itself had fallen.[32]

Just as the ever-increasing importance of motion pictures and the entertainment industry marked the mid–twentieth century, the late twentieth century saw sports occupy the center of public life. City and state governments granted massive taxpayer subsidies to professional sports teams, just so they would represent their cities in the national media. Nike and other sports equipment companies paid athletes such as Tiger Woods millions of dollars to endorse their products. At the end of the nineteenth century, college athletic programs were the haven for elite gentlemen to test their valor against each other in contests such as football, baseball, and rowing. By the end of the twentieth, these programs had become money-making machines. In the year 2000 the NCAA, representing most of the colleges and universities in the United States, received an astounding $6 billion, seven year contract from a television network to televise college basketball games during the "March Madness" national championship tournament. Ironically, a century after the elite amateurism that originally defined athletics had been steadily whittled away by the professionalization of sports, college athletes are still forbidden to receive a single penny of this money.[33]

The astronomical sums of money involved point to the centrality of the entertainment industry in modern American society, but what is often missed is that most Americans gladly paid huge amounts of money to see their heroes in action, to wear the same clothing they did, and, ultimately, to fantasize that they and their children might turn out to be just as good. "I am Tiger Woods" was the mantra that a congregation of children— white and nonwhite—chanted in Nike's television and print advertisements in 1996. When young children all over the world heard and learned the phrase "I want to be like Mike" as basketball player Michael Jordan conquered the world during the 1992 Olympics, the heroizing of professional athletes eclipsed the celebration of motion picture stars that had helped carry Ronald Reagan to the White House. The morality of actors may have been so well acted that it was convincing, but playacting paled in comparison to the moral drama of sports play.

Conclusion: Branding the Body versus Bodies Wearing a Brand

Soon after signing Tiger Woods to an endorsement contract unprecedented in largesse, Nike ran an initial advertising campaign featuring Woods. The television and print ads emphasized the racial exclusivity that had marked golf in America. In one, Woods stated, "There are still courses in the United States that I am not allowed to play because of the color of my skin." A Tiger burning bright would change all that, of course, with a blend of power, grace, skill, and sheer confidence that could not be denied. "Hello, World," Tiger Woods announced in TV and print ads, asking America and the world if they were ready for the new partnership of Tiger and Nike. The answer to the challenge seemed to be a resounding yes. A year later, in October 1997, a poll published in USA Today reported that Nike's campaign featuring Tiger Woods was by far the most popular advertising campaign of the year.[34]

In 1997, a month after journalist John Feinstein described the previously racist Augusta National Golf Club welcoming a nonwhite Tiger Woods into its ranks, Feinstein continued to report on the racial politics of Woods's existence. After an incident in which golfer Fuzzy Zoeller made some racially inflammatory remarks, Feinstein detailed how Nike chairman Phil Knight was upset at Woods for not attending a tribute to Jackie Robinson. "Nike spent a lot of money on a series of ads paying tribute to Robinson . . . and, given that one of the reasons for Woods's multimillion dollar deal with the company was to reach new African-American customers, Knight apparently felt Woods should have attended."[35] The moral drama of Tiger's racial identity played out on a very expensive stage.

Phil Knight felt that Nike deserved a form of return for its massive investment that went beyond increased sales and revenue. When Nike signed its initial five-year endorsement contract with Woods in 1996, the corporation had a strong stock price, and its future possibilities for increased revenue and expansion of sales globally were spectacular.[36] Standard & Poor's, the stock rating company, reported in the summer before Woods's endorsement deal that Nike was in a good position for growth.[37] Nike's stock price was climbing as its revenues grew, and Woods's signing made the news in business publications.[38] Standard & Poor's also forecast that Nike's "business outside the United States" would be the "engine for future growth." The growth of its international sales was "testament to the emerging power of its brand globally."[39]

The importance of Nike's "brand power" lay behind Knight's insistence that Woods do more than merely endorse Nike products. The power of a corporate brand was as a commodity in itself, so that consumers would pay more for a T-shirt otherwise identical to any other T-shirt merely because of the brand label that distinguished it. Tiger Woods and other celebrity sports stars created the premium value that such brands could command, and a widespread desire for Woods to be a racial savior further contributed to his ability to increase the value of Nike's brand.[40]

The ways in which "branding" as a practice changed from the nineteenth century to the end of the twentieth century reflected a major shift in how race as a property functioned in the United States. For much of the nineteenth century, the legal enslavement of African Americans through their matrilineal inheritance meant that race was also a legal status passed on biologically (an enslaved mother's children were by birth also enslaved). Race was metaphorically a way of branding the human body, so that some bodies had more value than others—blackness became equated to being legal property owned by others and whiteness, on the whole, to the power to treat others as property or potential property and the right to a number of other legal protections denied those branded as black.[41] Race was an indication of property relations, of the body's social, legal, and economic relations within a larger society. Race was a categorization that both reflected and shaped market relations.

Tiger Woods's racial identity, in contrast, reflected a world of where corporate brands themselves were commodities, and the acquisition and display of such brands on the human body gave social value to certain human bodies above others.[42] Mass production and mass consumption had transformed the United States from a society in which the majority labored to produce luxury goods for a few to one in which everyone labored to produce goods (objects, services, bodily performances such as sports and entertainment) in the anticipation of participating in a shared consumption of these same goods. Distinctions in products consumed (some products branded as superior) became more important in many ways than the distinguishing categories of race that had branded bodies a century before. Before, legally enforced racial categories had relegated different bodies to strictly inferior positions in relation to other bodies; now, racial identity was itself increasingly a commodity that might or might not have value in relation to other commodities that marked the body.

It was in this way that Tiger Woods's racial categorization became secondary to the ways in which his body could be branded by corporate affiliations. His relationship to Nike was literally more important than his category of racial belonging. This explains how Michael Jordan and Tiger Woods have approached racial politics, always with an eye to possible effects on the value of Nike's brand name. When Phil Knight signed Tiger Woods, he believed the value of Nike's brand would be increased by the deep desire Americans had for a black hero. His support for Tiger Woods reflected the commercial value of Woods's blackness for Nike.[43]

When Tiger Woods turned professional in 1996, he stood at the coincidence of a number of large-scale trends in twentieth-century U.S. history. Changing racial politics, the spread of celebrity in definitions of morality, the rise of corporations in marketing leisure and entertainment—it was a world unlike that of a hundred years before, and it would have been impossible even to imagine the phenomenon of Tiger Woods in 1896. Just as in the Horatio Alger tales of a century before, the idealization of an individual overcoming the hierarchical social order functioned, in the end, to reinforce another hierarchical social order—that of capitalism. Ideologies of individual merit helped justify a social order in which a select number of individuals own the lion's share of a society's collective property. The escape from hierarchical social structures in the United States has almost invariably been described as the result of almost superhuman individual transcendence, and whether that individual is Tiger Woods or Bill Gates, the concentration of wealth in the hands of the few must seem deserved. The historical context for Tiger Woods's racial transcendence—and of the heroizing of all well-paid individual athletes—must be seen in this light, rather than as some small glimmer of hope that he actually might solve racial and class inequalities that have been systemic in U.S. society.

NOTES

1. Gary Smith, "The Chosen One," *Sports Illustrated* (December 23, 1996) issue commemorating Tiger Woods as their 1996 Sportsman of the Year.

2. For pioneering work on sports in American society, see the following books by Allen Guttmann: *A Whole New Ball Game: An Interpretation of American Sports* (Chapel Hill: University of North Carolina Press, 1988); *Women's Sports: A History* (New York: Columbia University Press, 1991); *Games and Empires: Modern Sports and Cultural Imperialism* (New York: Columbia University Press, 1994); *The Erotic in Sports* (New York: Columbia University Press, 1996); *From Ritual to Record: The Nature of Modern Sports* (New York: Columbia University Press, 1998); and Guttmann et al., eds., *Essays on Sport History and Sport Mythology* (Arlington: Texas A&M University Press, 1990). Thanks to Matthew Lum, my research assistant, for helping gather much of the interesting material on Tiger Woods. I am also grateful for the comments of members of the University of California Humanities Research Institute (UCHRI) group of fall 1996 and the Yale University Race, Culture, and Migration Brown Bag Lunch Seminar, both of whom read an

earlier version of this essay. Thanks especially to Brandy Worrall for a close read and valuable suggestions.

3. For an introduction to the history of the modern Olympic movement, see Allen Guttmann, *The Games Must Go On: Avery Brundage and the Olympic Movement* (New York: Columbia University Press, 1984), and *The Olympics: A History of the Modern Games* (Urbana: University of Illinois Press, 1992). Also see the work of sociologist Douglas Hartmann, whose 1997 University of California–San Diego Ph.D. dissertation "Golden Ghettos: The Cultural Politics of Race, Sport, and Civil Rights in the United States 1968 and Beyond" and upcoming book *Golden Ghettos and Contested Terrain* detail the changing politics of race in the Olympics.

4. Activities that were accessible to all—for example, track events that simply involved running fast—still began as the domain of those privileged elites who could take the time to run in races. Industrial workers and others whose time and daily exertion had been sold as labor might have been able to run like the wind, but working twelve hours a day left no leisure time to play in the Olympics. As another example of a sport that began as the domain of the elite, football began as the exclusive activity of Ivy League gentlemen. John M. Murrin describes how football began as a rite of domination among the "Big Three" of Harvard, Princeton, and Yale, only spreading much later to the Midwestern giants such as Notre Dame, Michigan, and Ohio State and eventually to the universally played and beloved sport of today (unpublished paper, "Rites of Domination: Princeton, the Big Three, and the Rise of Intercollegiate Athletics," delivered at the Princeton 250th Anniversary Lecture, October 10, 1996).

5. Karl Marx, *Capital* and the *Economic Manuscripts of 1844*.

6. Standard & Poor's reports that Nike's total annual revenues since 1997 have been in the $8 or $9 billion range.

7. For a collection of interesting documents about Jackie Robinson's career, see Jules Tygiel, ed., *The Jackie Robinson Reader: Perspectives on an American Hero* (New York: Dutton, 1997).

8. Virginia Domínguez, *White by Definition: Social Classification in Creole Louisiana* (New Brunswick, N.J.: Rutgers University Press, 1986).

9. Somewhat in jest, but further revealing the absurdity of such calculations, this is not even counting as Asian American the one-eighth American Indian coursing through his veins, a legacy of the original immigrants from Asia crossing over the Bering land bridge.

10. Henry Yu, "How Tiger Woods Lost His Stripes: Post-National American Studies as a History of Race, Migration and the Commodification of Culture," in *Post-National American Studies,* ed. by John C. Rowe (Berkeley and Los Angeles: University of California Press, 2000). The phrase "how Tiger lost his stripes" was suggested to me by George Sanchez, who was also a fellow at the University of California Humanities Research Institute group in the fall of 1996 that produced the above volume of essays.

11. There has been a good amount of interesting literature already on transnational movements of labor and how these diasporic movements have been at the heart of ethnic identity in the nation-states that arose at the same time. The United States was like many nations in the nineteenth century that derived part of its sense of national homogeneity from racializing and excluding diasporic labor from definitions of the national body. See for example, Peter Linebaugh and Marcus Rediker, *The Many Headed Hydra: Sailors, Slaves, Commoners and the Hidden History of the Revolutionary Atlantic* (Boston: Beacon Press, 2000).

12. Ashley Montagu, *Man's most Dangerous Myth: The Fallacy of Race*, 5th ed. (New York: Oxford University Press, 1974).

13. During the twentieth century, sports became one of the most prominent ways in which immigrants adopted meaningful practices in an effort to fit in socially. Italian Americans with baseball, for instance, achieved the height of acceptance when New York Yankee players such as Joe DiMaggio and Phil Rizzuto achieved prominence. A recent exhibition curated by Brian Niiya at the Japanese American National Museum in Los Angeles detailed the ways in which Japanese Americans used sports to create a sense of ethnic community at the same time that they claimed a place with American society. See also the recent book by Joel S. Franks, *Crossing Sidelines, Crossing Cultures: Sport and Asian Pacific American Cultural Citizenship* (New York: University Press of America, 2000), for another example.

14. Lest we think that such examples were anomalous or irrelevant for the current day, take the example of Korean-born orphans adopted by "white" Americans in Minneapolis. How are the new parents to treat the "cultural" heritage of their child? Should they deny that the biological link has a cultural expression and thus pretend that the child is like any white child? Such a utopian fantasy would be principled, idealistic, and, most likely, psychologically cruel, for there can be little doubt that the child will receive repeated and stark messages from other people that she or he is not white. To immerse the child in her or his "Korean heritage" might prove a pragmatic shield against a debilitated sense of self-worth, but it would be a child-raising strategy equally propagated on a link between culture and biology. So we remain stuck in a dilemma.

15. If you are a descendant of Asian immigrants to this country, for instance, you are forever being asked where you are originally from, regardless of whether you were born in Los Angeles or Denver or New York. The confusion is not over whether an individual is American-born or not, since the askers are inevitably not satisfied with the answer of Los Angeles or Denver or New York. What they are looking for is national origin, and therefore biological origin, even if the moment of origination is an act of migration undertaken by a grandparent. What they want to know is whether you are Japanese or Korean or Chinese or Vietnamese. (I suppose they believe they can tell if you are from the Philippines or Polynesia or India and therefore do not have to ask.) If a shared Asian American identity is

formed for the most part from the experience of being treated as "Orientals" in a similar manner by other Americans, including being mistaken for one another, perhaps one of the largest reasons for the continued practice of excluding South Asians and most Filipinos and Pacific Islanders from a sense of identity with Asian Americans is that they are not mistaken for migrants from East Asia.

16. One of the other solutions to the problem of multiple boxes for racial, cultural, or ethnic heritage has been to count each box as a whole person for that category. For instance, if someone checks African American, Asian American, and Hispanic on the census, then he or she would be counted once in the category African American, once for Asian American, and once for Hispanic, leading to the problem that the total numbers for all the categories might be greater than the total population of the United States.

17. See Gary Nash, "Mestizo America," in *Sex, Love, Race: Crossing Boundaries in North American History*, ed. by Martha Hodes (New York: New York University Press, 1998).

18. See Stephen Masami Ropp, "Do Multiracial Subjects Really Challenge Race? Mixed–Race Asians in the United States and the Caribbean," *Amerasia Journal* 23,1 (1997), for an accessible explication of this process in Latin America.

19. For how social scientists, missionaries, and liberal theorists in the twentieth century hoped for intermarriage and race mixing as the solution to problems of racial conflict, see Henry Yu, "Mixing Bodies and Cultures: The Meaning of America's Fascination with Sex between 'Orientals' and Whites," in Hodes, ed., *Sex, Love, Race*.

20. Leigh Montville, "On the Job Training," *Sports Illustrated*, September 9, 1996. Quoted also in John Garrity, *Tiger Woods: The Making of a Champion* (New York: Fireside Books, 1997), 74.

21. Quoted from Garrity *Tiger Woods*, 97.

22. John Feinstein, "Master of All He Surveys," *Golf Magazine* (June 1997): 114–118, 118. On Robinson's meaning for desegregation, see Joseph Dorinson and Joram Warmund, ed., *Jackie Robinson: Race, Sports and the American Dream* (New York: M. E. Sharpe, 1998); and Jules Tygiel, *Baseball's Great Experiment: Jackie Robinson and His Legacy* (New York: Oxford University Press, 1997). Also, on Joe Louis, see Richard Bak, *Joe Louis: The Great Black Hope* (New York: Da Capo Press, 1998). On African Americans in sports, see Arthur Ashe Jr., *A Hard Road to Glory: A History of the African-American Athlete, 1619–1918*, 3 vols. (New York: Warner Books, 1998; reprint New York, Amistad Press, 1993). On sports and race in the United States, see the pathbreaking work of sports sociologist Harry Edwards; also Jeffrey Sammons, *Beyond the Ring: The Role of Boxing in American Society* (Urbana: University of Illinois Press, 1988); and, more recently, Kenneth Shropshire, foreword by Kellen Winslow, *In Black and White: Race and Sports in America* (New York: New York University Press, 1998). A recent book has ignited debates about biological race theories and sports: Jon Entine, *Why Black Athletes*

Dominate Sports and Why We Are Afraid to Talk about It (New York: Public Affairs, 2000).

23. Rick Reilly, "Strokes of Genius," *Sports Illustrated*, April 21, 1997. Quoted also from Garrity *Tiger Woods*, 103. On African Americans in golf, see Calvin H. Sinnette, *Forbidden Fairways: African Americans and the Game of Golf* (New York: Sleeping Bear Press, 1998); and Pete McDaniel, foreword by Tiger Woods, *Uneven Lies: The Heroic Story of African-Americans in Golf* (New York: American Golfer, 2000).

24. Feinstein, "Master of All He Surveys," 114.

25. Thanks to Hazel Carby and Michael Denning for suggesting the importance of Tiger Woods's father as military hero and the connections between such "safe" black male bodies and the dangerous criminalized black male in popular culture. See Hazel Carby, *Racemen* (Cambridge: Harvard University Press, 1998).

26. Earl Woods, with Pete McDaniel, *Training a Tiger: A Father's Guide to Raising a Winner in Both Golf and Life* (New York: HarperCollins, 1997); and Earl Woods, with Fred Mitchell, *Playing Through: Straight Talk on Hard Work, Big Dreams and Adventures with Tiger* (New York: HarperCollins, 1998).

27. Smith, "Chosen One," 33.

28. Ibid., 33.

29. For paeans to Muhammad Ali's political impact, see Mike Marqusee's *Redemption Song: Muhammad Ali and the Spirit of the Sixties* (New York: Verso, 1999); and the 1996 Academy Award–winning documentary *When We Were Kings*, directed by Leon Gast. David Owen, "The Chosen One," *New Yorker* August 21 and 28, 2000, 106–119.

30. See Leonard Steinhorn and Barbara Diggs-Brown, *By the Color of Our Skin: The Illusion of Integration and the Reality of Race* (New York: Dutton, 1999).

31. See Neal Gabler's *Life the Movie: How Entertainment Conquered Reality Starring Everyone* (New York: Alfred A. Knopf, 1998), for an interesting view on the phenomenon of entertainment media coming to dominate narrations of experience.

32. Since the U.S. political system has favored men to the extent that every single president has so far been male, chances are that the first nonwhite president will also be male. If this person is an athlete, there is even less chance it will be a woman, given the male-oriented bias of professional sports. Contrast, for instance, the heroizing of male athletes with the very different ways in which female figure skaters are considered. Is there any chance that Kristi Yamaguchi or Michelle Kwan will translate the celebrity and moral character developed in ice rinks into a popular understanding of them as political leaders? It is highly doubtful. Ice skating, the most popular spectator sport in the United States, idealizes a delicate femininity at odds with the vicious, win-at-all-costs conflict of war and of team sports. There was high moral drama surrounding Tonya Harding's famous application of baseball technique to Nancy Kerrigan's knee, but Kerrigan's suffer-

ing inspired little adulation. Perhaps the first woman to control the White House will come from a team sport such as volleyball or soccer. Let us hope. But the hypermasculine world of politics and of sports still needs a great deal of change. Tonya Harding was probably closer in moral outlook to a successful politician than any other female athlete then or since.

33. Recent debates over college sports and amateur status have been documented in books such as Rick Telander, Richard Warch, and Murray Sperber, *The Hundred Yard Lie: The Corruption of College Football and What We Can Do to Stop It* (Urbana: University of Illinois Press, 1996); Allen L. Sack and Ellen J. Staurowsky, *College Athletes for Hire: The Evolution and Legacy of the NCAA's Amateur Myth* (New York: Praeger, 1998); Andrew S. Zimbalist, *Unpaid Professionals* (Princeton: Princeton University Press, 1999); James J. Duderstadt, *Intercollegiate Athletics and the American University: A University President's Perspective* (Ann Arbor: University of Michigan Press, 2000); Murray Sperber, *Onward to Victory: The Crises That Shaped College Sports* (New York: Henry Holt, 1998) and *Beer and Circus: How Big-Time College Sports Is Crippling Undergraduate Education* (New York: Henry Holt, 2000); and the recent study by William G. Bowen and James L. Shulman, *The Game of Life* (Princeton: Princeton University Press, 2001).

34. "Money" section report on popularity of Tiger Woods advertising campaign, *USA Today*, October 20, 1997; James K. Glassman, "A Dishonest Ad Campaign" (on the Nike ad portraying golfer Tiger Woods as a victim of racism), *Washington Post* 119,287, September 17, 1996; Larry Dorman, "We'll Be Right back, after This Hip and Distorted Commercial Break" (on hype surrounding the entrance into professional golfing world of twenty-year-old Tiger Woods), *New York Times* 145, September 1, 1996, sec. 8; Robert Lipsyte, "Woods Suits Golf's Needs Perfectly," *New York Times* 145, September 8, 1996, sec. 1; David Segal, "Golf's $60 Million Question: Can Tiger Woods Bring Riches to Sponsors, Minorities to Game?" *Washington Post* 119, 270, August 31, 1996; Ellen Goodman, "Black (and White, Asian, Indian) like Me" (on golfer Tiger Woods multiracial makeup), *Washington Post* 118, April 15, 1995; Ellen Goodman, "Being More than the Sum of Parts: When Tiger Woods Speaks of His Background as Multiracial, He Speaks for a Generation That Shuns Labels," *Los Angeles Times* 114, April 14, 1995; "Tiger, Tiger, Burning bright" (on Tiger Woods winning the U.S. Amateur Golf Championship), *Los Angeles Times* 113, September 1, 1994. Tiger's color also made news internationally: in a two hundred-word *Agence France Presse* story on December 5, 1996, titled "L'Annee du Tigre" (The year of the Tiger), the focus was on Nike's advertising slogan about Tiger potentially being kept off of golf courses because of his skin. The paper quoted in French Tiger's Nike-sponsored charge of American racism: "il y a encore des golfs aux Etats Unis ou on ne m'autorise pas a jouer a cause de la couleur de ma peau."

35. John Feinstein, *Golf Magazine* (July 1997): 24. Feinstein criticized Woods and his seeming lack of political awareness, attributing this failing to his corporate

sponsorships. See John Feinstein, *The First Coming: Tiger Woods, Master or Martyr* (New York: Ballantyne Books, 1998).

36. In the quarter before Tiger Woods signed his endorsement deal, Nike's quarterly revenues were $1.49 billion; in the quarter in which he signed with Nike, total revenues were $1.9 billion and spiked at $2.76 billion in the spring quarter of 1997, before dropping back to about $2.3 billion a quarter for the next year (Standard & Poor's report for the fiscal years ending May 31, 1996; May 31, 1997; and May 31, 1998.

37. "Through its aggressive worldwide marketing efforts and global infrastructure spending, the company is positioning itself to continue to expand markets and gain market share on a worldwide basis. Outside the U.S., the markets in which the company operates are less mature and offer tremendous potential for growth. The strength of its brand continues with advance and futures orders scheduled for delivery over the next six months up a record 55.0%. The company's financial condition is excellent" (Standard & Poor's report for the fiscal year ending May 31, 1996).

38. "Nike Inc. zipped ahead 1 3/8 to 109 3/4. It signed a multimillion-dollar contract to have golfer Tiger Woods promote its products. Woods won three amateur titles and just turned pro" (Leo Fasciocco, "Nike Climbs 1 3/8 as Shoe Stocks Perform Well," *Investor's Business Daily*, August 19, 1996, A11.

39. Standard & Poor's report for the fiscal year ending May 31, 1997. The perception of so many people that Tiger Woods had the potential for foreign marketing involved their connection of international sales with an American-born mixed race/culture body, and the narrative that allowed that connection was a cultural theory that fixed his ethnic fractions with origins in foreign nations. The potential of developing Asian markets for golf wear and athletic products was tied to the international appeal of Tiger's partial Asian heritage. Lost in the blackness of America's perception of Tiger, his Asian stripes could be earned on the global market, parlayed into increased sales for Nike in Southeast Asia and other growth markets for Nike's leisure products. If Michael Jordan has been the best ambassador for the international growth of basketball as a marketing vehicle, then Tiger Woods can be golf's equivalent, instantiating such global possibilities in his body. The image of Woods also serves to hide the idealization in golf of white male hierarchy by providing a nonwhite, multiracial body as a fantasy pinnacle.

There is the perverse irony of selling products back to the places where capital has gone to find cheap labor. Marketing golf in Thailand, Indonesia, and other Southeast Asian nations such as Vietnam evokes the ultimate capitalist dream: to pour relatively little capital into a location in order to produce products for export to places that will pay a healthy markup on production costs but also to recoup as much as possible from even those sites of production. Of course, it's not the women and children being paid thirteen cents an hour in Indonesia who will be able to play golf and buy Nike shoes. But even if it is local elites who make their portion of the profit from managing the cheap labor and creating the professional services and infrastructure for production, the dream remains of new markets springing up alongside labor sites. The story of capitalism since the eighteenth century has been displacement of people from agricultural forms of subsistence. See *The Golf War: A Story of Land, Golf, and Revolution in the Philippines,* a film by Jen Schradie and Matt DeVries (Anthill Productions, 1999), http://www.golfwar.org.

40. For how Nike marketed celebrity to establish brand identity, see Donald Katz, *Just Do It: The Nike Spirit in the Corporate World* (New York: Random House, 1994). Also see Dan Wetzel and Don Yeager, *Sole Influence: Basketball, Corporate Greed, and the Corruption of America's Youth* (New York: Warner Books, 2000).

41. See Cheryl Harris, "Whiteness as Property," *Harvard Law Review* 106, 8 (June 1993): 1709–1791.

42. Thanks to Walter Johnson for the alluring imagery of branding to explicate this point.

43. On the economics of sports and entertainment industries for African Americans, as well as for a compelling argument about how social science has racialized economic injustice, see Robin Kelley, *Yo' Mama's Disfunktional: Fighting the Culture Wars in Urban America* (Boston: Beacon Press, 1997).

About the Contributors

José M. Alamillo is an assistant professor of Comparative American Cultures at Washington State University. His interests include Chicano/Latino Studies, Racial and Ethnic Studies, U.S. Labor and Working Class History, Race and Sport, and Oral History Methodology. He has written on the politics of identity in Chicano softball and the history of relations between citrus workers and growers in California.

Amy Bass is an assistant professor of history at Plattsburgh State University in Plattsburgh, New York. She teaches courses on popular culture and race and also has worked as a researcher and writer for *NBC Sports* at the 1996 Olympics in Atlanta and the 2000 Olympics in Sydney.

John Bloom has taught in the field of American Studies at a number of institutions, most recently at the University of Maryland at Baltimore County. He is the author of two books on sports and culture: *A House of Cards: Baseball Card Collecting and Popular Culture* and *To Show What an Indian Can Do: Sports at Indian Boarding Schools*, both published by the University of Minnesota Press.

Gena Caponi-Tabery is an associate professor of American Studies at the University of Texas, San Antonio. She has written a biographical scholarship on author Paul Bowles and the book *Signifyin(g), Sanctifyin', and Slam Dunking: A Reader in African American Expressive Culture* (University of Massachusetts Press).

Annie Gilbert Coleman is an assistant professor of history at Indiana University–Purdue University at Indianapolis, specializing in the history of the western United States. Her article that appears in this book won the W. Turrentine Jackson Prize in November 1996.

Montye Fuse is an assistant professor of English at Arizona State University. His interests include Asian American literature, particularly Korean

American and Filipino American; interethnic relations; and comparative ethnic studies.

Randy Hanson is an assistant professor in the School of Justice Studies at Arizona State University in Tempe. He has published and presented work on the environmental movement in indigenous communities.

Michiko Hase is an assistant professor of Women's Studies at the University of Colorado at Boulder. Hase's work addresses the intersections of race, class, and gender in global contexts.

George Lipsitz is a professor of Ethnic Studies at the University of California at San Diego and is the author of numerous books, including *The Possessive Investment in Whiteness: How White People Profit from Identity Politics* (Temple University Press); *Dangerous Crossroads: Popular Music, Postmodernism, and the Poetics of Place* (Verso); *Time Passages: Collective Memory and American Popular Culture* (University of Minnesota Press); and *A Life in the Struggle: Ivory Perry and the Culture of Opposition* (Temple University Press).

Keith Miller is an associate professor of English at Arizona State University and author of *Voice of Deliverance: The Language of Martin Luther King, Jr., and Its Sources* (University of Georgia Press).

Sharon O'Brien is the James Hope Caldwell Professor of American Cultures and Professor of English and American Studies at Dickinson College, Ph.D., Harvard University. Her teaching specialty is American literature of the nineteenth and twentieth centuries. Research interests include women writers, popular culture, feminist theory, and the relationship between literature and society. She is the author and editor of numerous works on Willa Cather, including the book *Willa Cather: The Emerging Voice* (Harvard University Press).

Connie M. Razza is a Ph.D. candidate in the Department of English at the University of California, Los Angeles and a union organizer for the United Auto Workers. Her current project, "Working Out: The Literature of Black Women's Fitness and Community," examines the significance of discourses of community health and individual fitness on the position of contemporary middle-class black women in their communities. She first became a UAW activist during the successful academic student employee organizing campaign at UCLA.

Samuel O. Regalado is a professor of history at California State University, Stanislaus. He is the author of numerous works on gender, race, and sports, including his book *Viva Baseball! Latin Major Leaguers and Their Special Hunger* (University of Illinois Press).

Gregory S. Rodríguez is an assistant professor in the Mexican American Studies and Research Center at the University of Arizona. He has conducted research on the significance of boxing in Mexican American history.

Julio Rodriguez is the Ainsworth Visiting Scholar of American Studies at Randolph Macon Woman's College.

Michael Nevin Willard is an assistant professor of history and the director of American Studies at Oklahoma State University. He is the coeditor with Joe Austin of *Generations of Youth: Youth Cultures and History in Twentieth Century America* (New York University Press).

Henry Yu is an assistant professor of history at the University of California at Los Angeles. He has published work on Asian American intellectual and cultural history in the *Journal of American–East Asian Relations, Amerasia Journal*, and a number of edited volumes.

Index

A. J. Spalding Sporting Goods Corporation, 90
AAU. *See* Amateur Athletic Union
ABC. *See* American Broadcasting Company
African American Cultural Style, 3–4, 6, 7, 10n. 4, 39–64; African origins of, 58–60; Jackie Robinson and, 119–36
African Americans, 1–4, 39–64; Black Athletes and Cold War Politics, 186–88; Black Power, 7, 185–200; Boston, 177–78; image of the Black Male, 192–93, 209; masculinity, 192–93, 209, 334–40; Olympic Games and, 186; skiing and, 156–57. *See also* Ali, Muhammad; Carlos, John; Douglass, Frederick; DuBois, W. E. B.; National Brotherhood of Skiers; Owens, Jesse; Robinson, Jackie; Smith, Tommy; Winfrey, Oprah; Woods, Tiger
AIM. *See* American Indian Movement
Alamillo, José, 6, 355
Ali, Muhammad, 4, 7, 185, 187, 190, 209–21, 281, 320, 339, 350n. 29; identification with Third World, 216; images of blackness/whiteness and, 217–18, 220; multiple media images of, 220; rope-a-dope strategy, 212, 218, 222n. 21; *When We Were Kings* and, 7, 209–21
Amateur Athletic Union (AAU), 22–23
Amateur Athletics, 322
American Broadcasting Company (ABC), 190
American Civil Liberties Union, 198
American Indian Movement (AIM), 246
Andrews, David, 312
Angelou, Maya, 4
Arledge, Roone, 190
Arum, Bob, 281
Ashcroft, John, 228, 242
Ashe, Arthur, 54–55, 320, 334, 339

Asian Americans, 6, 348–49n. 15; ethnic Chinese basketball teams, 45; Issei immigrants, 76–77; Japanese American organizations, 77, 81; Japanese Americans, 6, 75–84; Japanese American women and baseball, 82–83. *See also* Baseball players and managers; Baseball teams; Woods, Kultida; Woods, Tiger
Aspen Skiing Corporation, 143
Athletes and ideal of moral character, 340–343
Athletes as heroes: 120, 130–31, 135, 189, 252, 255, 288–89, 292, 296, 322, 334–40. *See also* Athletes and ideal of moral character; De La Hoya, Oscar; Masculinity; Robinson, Jackie; Sports; Western individualism
Athletes turned politician, 341–42
Athletic shoe companies: Adidas, 308, 311; Fila, 308; Nike, 199, 308, 322–23, 325, 336, 343–46; Reebok, 308

Ballrooms, 41, 44, 45, 49
Barber, Red, 125, 127, 133–34
Barthes, Roland, 129
Baseball, 2, 5, 57; African Americans and, 119–36; industrial recreation as social control and, 89–94; emphasis on statistics and power hitting in white major leagues, 125–26; integration of, 169–83; Japanese Americans and, 6, 75–84; jazz and, 120–21; Mexican Americans and, 6, 86–110; modernization in Mexico and, 88–89; Native Americans and, 82, 246–62; promotion of labor organization and, 105–10; segregation in, 2, 5, 80, 128; stadiums and urban development, 8. *See also* Baseball players and managers; Baseball teams; Mexican Americans; Negro League baseball; Racial formation; Racism; Robinson, Jackie

tion of, 186; boxing and, 279–96; Duke Ka-
hanamoku and, 13–14; media coverage of
1912 U.S. Olympic team, 23; 1912 Games in
Stockholm Sweden, 23–24; 1936 Games in
Berlin Germany, 196; 1968 Games in Mex-
ico City Mexico, 185–200, 215; 1972 Games
in Munich Germany, 195; 1976 Games in
Montreal Canada, 196; 1992 Games in
Barcelona Spain, 199
Olympic Project for Human Rights (OPHR),
185–91, 193–95, 199–200, 203–4n. 18
OPHR. *See* Olympic Project for Human Rights
Oriard, Michael, 296
Outrigger Canoe Club (OCC), 20, 26, 28. *See
also* Hawai'i; Kahanamoku, Duke; Surfing
Owens, Jesse, 188

Parker, Reverend Theodore, 178
Peck, Janice, 276
Perez, Louis, 94
Plimpton, George, 212–14, 218–19
Plotkin, Sidney, and William Scheuerman, 238
Plume, David, 285
Popular culture: Chicano history and study of
sports, 88; race and study of sports, 1
Powell, Colin, 334
Proposition 187, 286

Quinlan, Handsome Dan, 170. *See also* Blackface minstrelsy
Race: anthropological conception of culture
and, 327–34; black athlete in American
imagination, 187–88, 190; blackness, 42–43,
189–90, 193, 201–2n. 9, 345; black/white
paradigm of racial formation, 4, 312; challenges to notions of racial inferiority, 4, 6, 7,
43–44, 61–62, 91, 102–3, 120, 127, 134–35,
185–200; civilization and, 14–21, 220–21;
color blind definition of in sports media, 2,
9, 291–92; development of Hawaiian tourist
industry and, 13–38; fictional nature of
racial categories, 332; masculinity and,
15–21, 35nn. 6, 9–10, 14–16, 19–21, 24, 28,
35nn. 6, 9–10, 69n. 65, 87, 201–2n. 9, 287,
315n. 3; narratives of population migration
and, 326, 329–31; Negro basketball, 53;
racial categories in Latin America, 333;
sports and biological definitions of, 3, 250,
325–34; whiteness, 7, 15–21, 141–63,
169–83, 330, 345. *See also* Ali, Muhammad;

Gender and race; Racial formation; Skiing;
Woods, Tiger
Racial formation, 1–4, 43; African American
intellectuals and vernacular jazz dance,
63–64; Americanization, 89–94; 108–110;
assimilation, 87, 89, 93, 272–75; 289–92,
299; civil rights, 61, 63–64, 185–200, 339;
contested racial meanings of cockfighting,
90–91, 93, 97; corporate racial identity,
339–40; cross- and multi-racial alliances
and interactions, 43–44, 82, 94, 100, 102,
127, 159–60, 283–84, 295–96; integration 6;
invisibility of black basketball players in
basketball history, 53–56; neoliberal explanations of racial inequality, 250–51; nostalgia for non-white cultures, 212, 214,
218–19, 260–61; racial diversity in Boston,
182; rhetorics of cultural deficiency, 247–53,
289; skiing and ethnic history, 143–56, 161;
Social Darwinism, 7, 15–21, 209–10, 212,
220–21; sports, structural inequality and, 3,
8, 225–43; transcending racial status,
264–72, 280, 287
Racism, 9, 43–44; anti-Irish racism, 178; anti-
Japanese xenophobia, 77; ballot initiatives,
286; baseball used for assimilation and social control, 87, 89, 93; Boston, Massachusetts, 176, 178; Boston busing crisis, 178–79,
182; environmental, 230; toward players of
color in European soccer, 305–308, 315n. 8;
segregated schools for Mexican Americans,
96; St. Louis, Missouri, 225–43. *See also*
Blackface minstrelsy; Soccer (European)
Randolph, A. Philip, 60, 186
Razza, Connie, 8, 356
Reagan, Ronald, 204, 236, 341
Reebok, 199
Regalado, Samuel, 6, 86, 356
Reilly, Rick, 334
Remington, Frederick, 163
Rice, Thomas Dartmouth, 58–59, 72n. 119. *See
also* Blackface minstrelsy
Rickey, Branch, 119–20, 130–31, 174–75. *See
also* Robinson, Jackie
Roberts, Clifford, 336
Robeson, Paul, 47, 55, 202n. 10, 203n. 16
Robinson, Jackie, 2, 6, 7, 86, 119–36, 175, 183,
187, 190, 320, 325, 334–36, 339; condemna-
tion of Paul Robeson, 202n. 10; influence of
Negro League baseball on, 132–35; portrayed

Sports Matters